BISON
BOOKS

D0837163

After Lewis and Clark

MOUNTAIN MEN AND
THE PATHS TO THE PACIFIC

Robert M. Utley

Maps by Peter H. Dana

UNIVERSITY OF NEBRASKA PRESS

LINCOLN AND LONDON

∞

First Nebraska paperback printing: 2004

Library of Congress Cataloging-in-Publication Data
Utley, Robert Marshall, 1929–
[Life wild and perilous]
After Lewis and Clark: mountain men and the paths to the Pacific / Robert M. Utley; maps
by Peter H. Dana.
p.   cm.
Originally published: A life wild and perilous. New York: Henry Holt, c1997.
Includes bibliographical references and index.
ISBN 0-8032-9564-2 (pbk.: alk. paper)
1. Frontier and pioneer life—West (U.S.)—Biography.   2. Pioneers—West (U.S.)—
Biography.   3. Trappers—West (U.S.)—Biography.   4. Fur traders—West (U.S.)—
Biography.   5. Fur trade—West (U.S.)—History.   6. Overland journeys to the Pacific.
7. West (U.S.)—History—To 1848.   8. West (U.S.)—Discovery and exploration.   I. Title.
F592.U87   2004
978'.02'0922—dc22   2004016266

For Russ Dickenson,
Mountaineer

Chief Ranger, Grand Teton National Park . . .

Director of the National Park Service . . .

Valued colleague and friend.

I defy the annals of chivalry to furnish the
record of a life more wild and perilous than that
of a Rocky Mountain trapper.

—Francis Parkman

CONTENTS

Maps may be found following page 206.

INTRODUCTION

OR AMERICANS, the history of the Trans-Mississippi West dawned
with the nineteenth century. The Louisiana Purchase opened fresh
vistas beyond a western boundary that traced the course of the
mighty river bisecting most of the North American continent. President
Thomas Jefferson knew not what he had bought from Napoleon, but he
had long been interested in lifting the veil from the western reaches of the
continent. Spaniards, Englishmen, Frenchmen, and Russians knew some
of the geography, but mainly around the fringes. Indian tribes, their cultures reflecting the immense geographical diversity, knew the heartland.
All, in their respective regions, had imprinted human history on the landscape, the Europeans for three centuries, the natives for millennia. For the
first half of the nineteenth century, much of the young American republic's
energies concentrated on discovering and recording the contours of this
immense land.

Not alone on revealing the contours. In the fertile mind of Thomas Jefferson himself stirred nebulous visions of a continental destiny for the
American people if not for the United States itself. In less than two
decades, in the ambitions of an influential segment of national leadership,
such musings had hardened into doctrine. Secretary of State John Quincy
Adams best expressed it in 1819: "The world shall be familiarized with the
idea of considering our proper dominion to be the continent of North
America," he wrote. "Europe shall find it a settled geographic element that
the United States and North America are identical."[1] Even more than

geographical revelation, therefore, the history of the United States in the first half of the nineteenth century is a saga of national expansion—a raucous, relentless, contentious drama, of themes both bright and dark, that deposited the western boundary on the Pacific shore.

In these two great movements of American history, exploration and national expansion, a gathering of colorful and eccentric men numbering less than a thousand at one time played a decisive part. They were the mountain men—the bold adventurers who sought individual freedom and financial reward in the beaver streams of the Rocky Mountains. In their allotted span on the western scene, hardly more than a generation, they came to know the American West as well as the Indians whose trails they followed. What they learned did not remain locked in their minds. It began to seep out in their own time and cascaded forth as their time ran out.

Not only geography but geopolitics benefited from their years of wading in icy mountain streams. Few of the breed would have fully comprehended John Quincy Adams's vaulting declaration, but nearly all were expansionists nonetheless. Some foresaw and actively promoted the continental destiny he declared. Others merely formed part of the tiny vanguard of the westward movement that brought it to fruition. As beaver trappers and fur traders, the mountain men wrote one chapter in the history of the West. As explorers and discoverers, they wrote another. As national expansionists, they wrote still another. This single generation of frontiersmen played a momentous role in the history of the West and in the history of the nation of which it became a part.

The mountain men did not head west for selfless patriotic motives, although forthrightly patriotic nearly all were, nor even for the thrill of unveiling lands unknown to their countrymen, although thrilled some were. They went to make money in a pursuit that promised adventure, excitement, personal freedom, and the nearly total absence of authoritarian restraint. Nonetheless, they were the point men, the advance guard, of a nation unfolding westward, geographically and politically.

This narrative is grounded in the belief that the big themes and their inherent smaller themes are best viewed and understood in the experiences of selected mountain men. Some consciously and personally advanced the process of exploration and expansion. Such were Jedediah Smith, Joseph R. Walker, Ewing Young, Joseph Meek, Thomas Fitzpatrick, and Christopher Carson. Others simply represented a class that collectively and incidentally furthered the process. Such were James Bridger, David Jackson, Old Bill Williams, Pegleg Smith, Black Harris, and Warren Ferris. In the lives of both activist and mere contributor, however, may be glimpsed a significant phase of the process by which the United States became a continental nation. This is their story.

The chapters are not designed as biographies or even minibiographies. Some focus more heavily on a protagonist than others. Some wander far from the man identified in the chapter heading. All aim at showing how a handful of people, acting within a swirl of larger events of which they were mostly unaware, made their contribution to a significant phase of American history—the opening of the West.

Moose, Wyoming, 1992–96
Georgetown, Texas, 1996

A LIFE WILD AND PERILOUS

1

COLTER AND DROUILLARD:

CONTINENTAL CROSSING

O N MARCH 9 AND 10, 1804, Captains Meriwether Lewis and
William Clark, United States Army, witnessed ceremonies that signaled the onset of their nation's expansion beyond the Mississippi
River to the Pacific Ocean. The rites took place in St. Louis, the bustling little riverfront community where the flag of Spain flew from a staff in front
of the seat of government for Upper Louisiana. Most of the town's citizens
were French, still loyal to their heritage forty years after the mother country relinquished her American empire. In a sudden and bewildering sequence of international power plays, however, Spain sold Louisiana back to
France, and Napoleon promptly sold it to the fledgling United States.

While a detachment of United States soldiers presented arms, Captain
Amos Stoddard officiated on behalf of both France and the United States.
On March 9, in front of Government House, the Spanish crown's banner
came down and the French republic's went up. As a concession to the patriotic sensibilities of the townspeople, Stoddard allowed the tricolor to remain aloft overnight. The next day, near noon, it descended the staff, and
the Stars and Stripes was hoisted. Stoddard and the Spanish officials inscribed their signatures on the formal documents of cession. So, as witness, did Captain Lewis. In addition to his commission in the army, he had
recently held the post of private secretary to the president of the United
States.[1]

The command of Lewis and Clark, already called the "Corps of Discovery," lay in winter camp on the east bank of the Mississippi opposite the

mouth of the Missouri River. Since November 1803, at dank Camp Dubois, the two captains had filled out their ranks to more than forty men and labored to equip and train them for a journey across the continent.

At Camp Dubois, two members of the Corps of Discovery had already shown singular potential, one for undisciplined rowdyism, the other for staunch dependability. One was a newly enlisted soldier, John Colter, the other a mixed-blood civilian, George Drouillard.

John Colter joined the army at Maysville, Kentucky, as Lewis piloted a keelboat with a dozen men down the Ohio River in the autumn of 1803. A robust man in his late twenties, Colter claimed the rudiments of literacy and the skills of hunter and woodsman. During the tedious winter at Camp Dubois, he drew deeply enough from the whiskey jug to give his superiors more than his share of disciplinary troubles.[2]

About the same age as Colter, George Drouillard was the offspring of a French Canadian father and a Shawnee Indian mother. Like Colter, he exhibited enough learning to qualify as literate, but to Lewis and Clark his critical value lay in his mastery of the Indian sign language and his awesome performance as a hunter. He was vigorous, decisive, courageous, resourceful, and completely reliable.[3]

When the keelboat and two pirogues (large dugout canoes with flat bottoms) of the expedition shoved off from the Illinois shore on May 14, 1804, Colter and Drouillard were already accomplished outdoorsmen. In the next two years, as the Corps of Discovery crossed the continent to the Pacific and then trekked and boated back to St. Louis, both would learn and grow. Colter matured and quit misbehaving. Drouillard rose to top rank in the esteem of Lewis, who called him "this excellent man" and invariably chose him for special missions.

EARLY IN 1801, even before his inauguration as third president of the United States, Thomas Jefferson had invited Captain Lewis, twenty-seven and thus roughly the age of Colter and Drouillard, to join his household as private secretary. Seven years of military service had equipped Lewis with knowledge in two realms with which the president had to deal. One was the frontier West, already drawing Americans across the Appalachian Mountains and down the great valleys descending to the Mississippi River; Jefferson himself had never traveled far beyond Virginia's Blue Ridge. The other was knowledge of the regular army, an institution for which Jefferson, steeped in the militia tradition, had little sympathy.[4]

In earlier years, Jefferson had shown interest in the remote reaches of North America and had even participated in abortive attempts to have them explored. He did not, however, select Lewis with the intention of sending him to explore the Far West. For nearly two years, neither Lewis nor Jefferson gave much attention to *that* West. For them, West meant the Trans-Appalachian West.[5]

What turned Jefferson's attention once more to the Far West was the publication in London in 1801 of Alexander Mackenzie's *Voyages from Montreal*. In 1789 the North West Company's veteran fur trader, seeking a way across the continent, had descended the river that took his name and found himself at the Arctic Ocean rather than the Pacific. In 1793 he had tried again and this time surmounted the great mountain barrier to the head of a river that flowed toward the Pacific. He did not explore it but struck directly to the coast.

Jefferson read Mackenzie's book at his Monticello mountaintop in the summer of 1802. Mackenzie's geography, lacking a final water link to the Pacific, interested Jefferson less than the challenge Mackenzie posed for his own nation: to discover the continental passage, colonize the Pacific Coast and tap its fur resources, and establish commerce with the Orient. That, Thomas Jefferson believed, ought to be done by the United States, not Great Britain.

Jefferson's vision of the United States as an agrarian republic numbered him among the earliest of the young nation's expansionists. An increasing population of small farmers moving west would ensure agrarian supremacy, he believed, but it depended on a constant supply of arable land. At first, Jefferson foresaw one or more new republics beyond the Mississippi, but they would be American in population, institutions, and affinity for the mother country. Later, his views edged ever closer to the idea of a single continental nation. A major purpose of the Lewis and Clark expedition, therefore, was to beat the British to the Pacific—to match the transcontinental feat of Alexander Mackenzie and counter the design that he urged on his countrymen.[6]

By the end of 1802, the president had sounded out a suspicious Spanish envoy in Washington about a scientific expedition into Spanish Louisiana and had sought congressional authority. By the spring of 1803, Congress having assented, he had commissioned his private secretary to organize such an expedition.

To help lead it, Lewis called on an old army comrade. Younger brother of George Rogers Clark of Revolutionary War fame, redheaded William Clark was a veteran frontiersman and Indian fighter, four years older than Lewis, less learned but more open and jovial. He had left the army to manage the family's Kentucky lands.

Although the venture that Jefferson and Lewis began planning late in

1802 would trespass on Spanish territory, at first it had nothing to do with the Louisiana Purchase, which Jefferson's emissaries were simultaneously negotiating. The diplomatic exchanges with France over Louisiana centered on the traditional friction with Spain over New Orleans. The aim was not the acquisition of a huge western territory but free access to the port of New Orleans and thus the free navigation of the Mississippi River on which the economy of Trans-Appalachian America depended. The sudden and unexpected offer of all Louisiana (whatever that might be) presented an opportunity of momentous potential. To his lasting credit, Jefferson seized it. Thus, he did not buy Louisiana and send Lewis and Clark to explore it. By the time of the purchase, he had already determined on the expedition, secured congressional authorization, and selected the personnel. Fortuitously, they ended up exploring American territory rather than Spanish or French.

The fantasy that represented conceptions of the West in 1803 provided the ethereal foundation on which Jefferson constructed his written instructions to Lewis. The president's image of the western half of the continent, representing the best thought of the time, dramatizes how much had to be learned before the United States could become a continental nation.

By the beginning of the nineteenth century, the Pacific Coast had been defined from Spanish California to Russian Alaska, and the mouth and lower course of the Columbia River had been identified. On the east, the Missouri River had been traced with fair accuracy as far as the earthen towns of the Mandan Indians. To the north, Alexander Mackenzie and other wide-ranging partisans of the North West and Hudson's Bay Companies had given rough form to the lakes, rivers, and plains between Hudson Bay and the Rocky Mountains, but the water connections from the Continental Divide to the Pacific Ocean remained to be worked out. Between the Missouri and the Pacific, literature and maps portrayed a jumbled image drawn from inference, speculation, theoretical geography, wishful thinking, and fancy.

Grounded largely in French travel literature beginning with Father Jacques Marquette in 1673, the image evolved from two basic ideas: "Garden" and "Passage to India." The Garden, applying descriptions of Lower Louisiana to all Louisiana, embraced a fertile, well-watered soil and mild climate ideally suited to agriculture—a prospect highly appealing to Jefferson, who saw the Republic's success bound to a population of yeoman farmers. The Passage to India postulated a height of land in which all the major rivers of western North America sprang from a common source. The Missouri headed there and could be easily navigated all the way to its mouth. A great "River of the West" also headed there, only a half day's easy portage from the source of the Missouri, and offered ready navigation westward to the Pacific. In some formulations, the height of land was mountainous, in others merely an elevated plateau. The mountains assumed varying shapes on the maps, but in most they were shown as a single ridge, either in north and south configurations or in an unbroken range extending from the far north to the Spanish possessions. In most too they appeared but a short distance from the Pacific, which greatly narrowed the continent's true width. Wherever placed, in nearly all calculations the western mountains rose no more than about three thousand feet from their base and could not compare in height or complexity with the Blue Ridge of Virginia.[7]

Jefferson's instructions to Lewis touched on many topics: mapping, relations with the Indian tribes, collection of information and specimens in all the branches of natural science, agricultural suitability, fur and other resources. Their essence, however, contemplated commerce with the Orient and drew on his distorted notion of continental geography. A single sentence etched his dream and revealed a preconception that Father Marquette, 130 years earlier, would have understood: "The object of your mission is to explore the Missouri river, & such principal stream of it, as, by it's course and communication with the waters of the Pacific Ocean, whether the Columbia, Oregon, Colorado or any other river may offer the most direct & practicable water communication across this continent for the purposes of commerce."[8]

Through the vast fantasyland that the Far West formed in the learned mind of 1804, the Lewis and Clark expedition blazed a narrow corridor of geographical reality. The two captains discovered the true character of the Missouri's headwaters, so different from the prevailing notion. They learned the magnitude and complexity of the northern Rockies. They dashed forever the idea of navigation to the Pacific by way of the Missouri (although Clark clung to a vague hope of some alternative). They revealed a continent much wider than anyone supposed. This and much more to revise the conventional understanding they reported to Thomas Jefferson on their return in 1806.

IN THE CONTINENTAL CROSSING of Lewis and Clark, both John Colter and George Drouillard ranged widely as hunters, and both frequently received special assignments. For all Colter's feats, however, it was Drouillard whose talents proved most in demand and in the end most important to the success of the expedition.

The most prolific and dependable of all the hunters, Drouillard performed prodigies of hunting. Grizzly bears seemed to offer a personal challenge. Huge, belligerent, swift, deadly, and exceptionally hard to kill, they roamed the plains and mountains in large numbers and posed a constant danger to the corps. Confronting a grizzly, Drouillard behaved as aggressively as the beast itself, rushing to the attack despite the risk or the state of his weaponry.

One such example occurred late in June 1805. After wintering with the Mandan Indians, the leaders had sent the keelboat back downriver and early in April embarked upstream in two pirogues and six smaller dugout canoes. Two months later, the Great Falls of the Missouri forced a laborious portage of nearly a month's duration through a country teeming with grizzlies.

On the evening of June 27, Drouillard and Joseph Field came in with nine elk and three bears. One of the bears was huge, "as large as a common ox," with hind feet nearly a foot long ("exclusive of the tallons") and seven inches wide. In later years even the most experienced trapper shrank from entering a thicket thought to harbor a grizzly. But Drouillard and Field had followed bear tracks into a brushy river bottom. Climbing a tree (which grizzlies could not do), they edged out on a limb about twenty feet above the ground. Then they gave a "hoop," and the bear, quietly hidden in the foliage, dashed toward the noise, paused immediately beneath the tree to look around, and fell with a bullet in the head from Drouillard's rifle.[9]

Although he brought in literally tons of meat for the sustenance of the corps, Drouillard's pivotal role lay not in hunting but in the duty for which he had been hired—Indian interpreter. As the corps neared the Rocky Mountains in the summer of 1805, his proficiency with the sign language became indispensable.

As the Missouri plunged over the Great Falls and, farther up, snaked ever more narrowly among mountain chasms, the Jeffersonian image of a great river navigable to its source dissolved. At the Three Forks of the Missouri—the Jefferson, Madison, and Gallatin—the corps turned west, up the Jefferson toward looming mountains that hardly resembled Virginia's Blue Ridge. Clearly, canoes could not go much farther. Progress now depended on transferring men and equipage to horseback, and that in turn depended on finding Indians who would part with horses.

Scarcely less important, the captains needed to tap into the geographical knowledge of resident Indians about the lay of the mountains and rivers, especially how to find the westward-flowing stream that would carry them down to the ocean.

The corps had passed the winter of 1804–05 with the Mandan and Hidatsa Indians, who dwelt in earth lodges along the Missouri River. From the Hidatsas they had learned much, for alone of the village tribes they raided westward as far as the Rocky Mountains. The Hidatsas told of the Shoshones, people who harvested salmon from the mountain streams in the summer and in the fall moved east to the plains to hunt buffalo. With the corps traveled Toussaint Charbonneau and his wife and infant son. A resident trader with the Hidatsas, he had bought the young woman, Sacagawea, from these people, who had captured her five years earlier in a raid against her Shoshone band. With summer swiftly waning, Lewis and Clark searched ever more urgently for Shoshones who could furnish horses and geographical guidance.

Drouillard and two others formed the advance party that under Lewis at last made contact. As they searched, they became the first known Americans to cross the Continental Divide—at Lemhi Pass in the Beaverhead Mountains. Beyond, in the Lemhi River valley, they found the Shoshone village of Chief Cameahwait, who turned out, when the entire corps had been reunited, to be the brother of Sacagawea. She helped with communication, but awkwardly at best; she translated her brother's words from Shoshone to Hidatsa, her husband translated Hidatsa to French, and another rendered the French into English. Here and later, therefore, Drouillard's sign language came into play as a supplementary if not a better means of interpretation.

From the Shoshones the corps finally obtained horses. From the Shoshones too, and later from the neighboring Flatheads, Lewis and Clark gained important information about the mountain barrier they confronted. With Drouillard facilitating the exchange, the chiefs constructed relief maps on the ground, piling dirt to represent mountains and gouging troughs with sticks to represent rivers.

A major task assigned Lewis and Clark by Thomas Jefferson was diplomatic. The captains told the Shoshone and Flathead chiefs, as they told the leaders of all the tribes they met, that the Great Father of the whites desired peace with and among all tribes. In return, he would send men among them with goods to trade, including guns and ammunition.

Thus innocently did Lewis and Clark trigger a quake whose tremors would shake and reorder the Indian world and its relationship to the white world. Shoshones and Flatheads, virtually without firearms, suffered grievously from Blackfeet and Hidatsas equipped with muskets by British traders. More than the traditional hospitality of these friendly people motivated their helpful reception of the American explorers. They wanted guns and ammunition to even the odds of war.[10]

The terrain maps of the Indians, copied on paper by the captains, proved discouraging and ominous. A reconnaissance down the Salmon River disclosed impassable gorges and raging cataracts. Instead, with a

Shoshone guide, the corps struck directly north and crossed to the head of the Bitterroot River. Still bearing north, near its mouth the horsemen finally turned west and traced Lolo Creek to Lolo Pass, portal through the lofty Bitterroot Mountains. Lashed by a snowstorm and freezing cold, subsisting on weakened horses, the expedition threaded a tangle of descending ridges and at last, on September 20, emerged on the Weippe Prairie.

Here the exhausted and ragged travelers came to a river on which canoes could be floated, and here they met still another Indian tribe of which the Shoshones and Flatheads had told, the Nez Perces. With Drouillard signing, the chiefs sketched maps on deerskin that laid out the route to the ocean. The river at Weippe Prairie was the Clearwater, whose snowmelt flowed into the Snake and the Columbia and finally into the Pacific.

For the Corps of Discovery, the Clearwater marked the end of the portage between the heads of the Missouri and the River of the West. So beguilingly short in conventional thought, it had drawn the explorers into a harrowing monthlong journey across nearly four hundred miles of some of the most rugged mountains in North America.

To the Nez Perces, Drouillard assisting, Lewis and Clark made the usual speeches about peace and trade. Like their neighbors, the Nez Perces badly needed a source of guns and ammunition, and the captains' words found receptive ears. Like their neighbors too, the Nez Perces were naturally friendly people, to Lewis and Clark the most appealing of all the tribes they dealt with.

Following an awful winter at Fort Clatsop, a log shelter near the mouth of the Columbia River, the spring of 1806 found the Corps of Discovery back among the Nez Perces, eastbound for home. Again Drouillard's talents were called on, as the explorers impatiently waited for melting snow to unclog the Lolo Trail across the Bitterroot Mountains. A Shoshone lad turned up among the Nez Perces, and he made possible another chain of oral communication through Sacagawea and Charbonneau: from Salish (the Nez Perce language) to Shoshone to Hidatsa to French and finally to English. Again, however, Drouillard surely employed the sign language to speed words and meaning through this cumbersome system. Once more the talk was about peace and trade, especially guns and ammunition.

During the winter at Fort Clatsop, Lewis and Clark had settled on a plan for the homeward journey. After crossing the Bitterroot Mountains, the corps would divide. Clark would take part up the Bitterroot River, retracing the outbound trail. From the Three Forks of the Missouri he would cross to the Yellowstone and explore that river to its mouth. With the rest of the men, Lewis would strike directly east, up the Blackfoot River. The previous September, the Shoshone guide had said there was a shorter way across the Continental Divide to the Missouri, and the Nez Perces had confirmed that the Blackfoot, together with the Lolo Trail, was their own yearly route to the buffalo range. If true, it cut six hundred difficult miles from the explorers' westbound route. Lewis also wanted to investigate the Marias River, which he thought reached far enough north to tap the rich beaver country of the South Saskatchewan and possibly influence the fixing of a boundary between British and American territory. Lewis and Clark would reunite at the mouth of the Yellowstone for the final descent of the Missouri to St. Louis.

Confirming the Indian report, in six days of easy travel Lewis and his contingent surmounted the Continental Divide and came down to the Missouri to camp at the Great Falls. Then, with only Drouillard and Joseph and Reuben Field, Lewis set forth on horseback for the Marias. By July 25, the men had ascended high enough to see that the river issued from the mountains far south of where Lewis had thought. Next day they turned back for the Missouri, only to meet a group of eight Piegan Blackfeet warriors.

The meeting occurred with so little warning that both sides had to react with wary civility. That night they camped together and in an improvised hide shelter, with Drouillard interpreting, held a council. From what the Indians said, Lewis glimpsed the extent of Blackfeet trade relations with the British. From what Lewis said, repeating the standard speech to western tribes, the Indians extracted an ominous message: the Americans intended to provide guns and ammunition to the Shoshones, Flatheads, and other enemies of the Blackfeet.

Whether that thought or simply temptation motivated what followed, the whites awoke the next morning to find the warriors stealing their rifles. Before the victims had even roused themselves from sleep, the Blackfeet had three rifles and were sprinting for cover. Reuben Field gave chase, overtook one of the Indians, and plunged a knife into his chest. He staggered some fifteen steps and fell dead.

Drouillard, meantime, had pounced on another Piegan. "Damn you, let go of my gun," he shouted as he wrested the weapon free.

His shout awakened Lewis, who joined the pursuit with a pistol, cornered the Indian who had his rifle, and forced him to lay it on the ground. The Field brothers rushed up and wanted to kill the thief, but Lewis refused. He also turned down Drouillard's plea to dispatch the Indian he had subdued.

Now the Piegans tried to make off with the whites' horses. Drouillard and the Field brothers went after one group. Lewis, alone and on foot, pursued two men running off his own horse. Gasping for breath, he came close enough to shout at the Indians and aim his rifle. One turned and pointed his musket at Lewis, who fired. The ball hit the man in the stomach. He fell to his knees, then turned, partly raised on an elbow, and sent a ball at Lewis, who "felt the wind of his bullet very distinctly." The fatally injured warrior crawled behind a rock to join his companion. With his shot pouch back in camp, Lewis prudently withdrew.

The captain and his comrades had decisively routed their assailants, killed two, and recovered their rifles. They had lost two of their six horses but more than made up for them with thirteen horses the Indians had left behind. Hastily, they saddled and packed seven of the best horses and embarked on a forced march to get out of the area as quickly as possible. Before leaving, they burned most of the Indian possessions. At the first meeting, Lewis had given one Indian an American flag and another a medal. Now he retrieved the flag but "left the medal about the neck of the dead man that they might be informed who we were."[11]

Whether or not they needed to be informed, the event marked the first violent encounter between Blackfeet and Americans. There would be many more. Although foreshadowing thirty years of bitter hostility between these adversaries, the clash did not cause it. Lewis helped set the stage by alerting the Blackfeet that white traders would soon be among their enemies with firearms, and that would ultimately prove to be one of the causes. Despite several opportunities in the next three years, however, the Blackfeet did not seek revenge for the bloodshed on the Marias. That would come after events that still lay in the future—events in which, ironically, two of the major players would be George Drouillard and John Colter.[12]

2

COLTER AND DROUILLARD:

MOUNTAIN MAN PROTOTYPES

Less than a year after the incident on the Marias, in the spring of 1807, John Colter paddled his solitary way down the Missouri River. Alone of the Corps of Discovery, he had not reached St. Louis the previous September. Instead, at the Mandan villages, he had sought early discharge to join two fur trappers bound for the mountains. The captains, willing to accommodate "any one of our party who had performed their duty as well as Colter had done," agreed. The three men probably passed the winter on Clark's Fork of the Yellowstone, which provided Colter with knowledge of the upper Yellowstone and its Indians that he would put to good use within a year. The partnership did not work out, and in the spring Colter took his leave.[1]

At the mouth of the Platte, Colter spied keelboats tied to the bank and fifty to sixty men laboring at their overhaul. Turning his canoe to the shore, he rejoiced to find in the camp a handful of veterans of the Corps of Discovery, including George Drouillard. The expedition was bound for the Rocky Mountains, the first of many seeking to tap the fur resources of which Lewis and Clark had told. The leader, Manuel Lisa, lost no time in persuading John Colter to join the party and return to the country that he now knew better than any white man.

Lisa had been the first to seize the promise held forth by Lewis and Clark. Their contributions to geography and science had yet to be published, but their reports of a vast new land rich in fur resources spread swiftly. St. Louis remained a bastion of conservative French merchants, hesitant to risk scarce capital in speculative ventures. Lisa, a stocky Spaniard whom almost no one liked, had long been at odds with the French aristocracy as well as with Spanish officialdom. But he shrank not from risk. As such, although of Spanish heritage, he represented the vanguard of Americans who would soon convert St. Louis into a rowdy mecca for men eager to capitalize on the opportunities disclosed by Lewis and Clark.[2]

Narrowly averting a fight with Arikaras and Assiniboines and slowed by other misfortunes, the Lisa expedition labored upstream through the summer and autumn of 1807. Colter served as both hunter and guide. Probably at his urging, since he knew the country and its Indians, Lisa abandoned the Missouri and turned up the Yellowstone. Late in October, the keelboats put to shore at the mouth of the Bighorn River, and the men began raising a rude log structure that Lisa named Fort Raymond in honor of his son.

Manuel Lisa had come west for beaver, whose glossy fur made the best felt for men's hats and commanded healthy prices in American and European markets. The British fur men to the north traded European goods for pelts taken by the Indians. Since Indians would not trap enough to supply the demand, however, Lisa intended to harvest furs both by trade and by trapping.

COLTER, DROUILLARD, AND LISA'S OTHER MEN were the earliest of the mountain trappers. In their personal qualities, their professional abilities, their daily lives, even their near anonymity, they typified the mountaineers that a decade and a half later would spread over the Rocky Mountains.

They came to the mountains chiefly to make money. They came in hopes that the swarming beaver reported by Lewis and Clark would make them money, money with which to go home and live out comfortable lives. Mountain life added other motives hard to overcome—adventure, freedom, independence, love of outdoor life, the challenge of hardship and danger. But money remained in the forefront of their minds.[3]

Beaver seemed to promise money. Their pelts commanded high prices from European and American hatters. For many generations and through styles ranging from the tricorn to the broad-brimmed to the high-crowned "Beau Brummell," men had prized headgear fashioned from beaver pelts. Only the wool of a pelt went into the "beaver," the skin and hair finding other uses. Craftsmen patiently worked the wool into felt, which was then shaped into a hat to which a covering of decorative fur was applied. Until the advent of the silk hat in the late 1830s, one hundred thousand beaver pelts a year furnished the prime wool essential to the hatter's craft.[4]

In this drawing, Frederic Remington captured the appearance and spirit of the typical mountain man. He wore gaudy but serviceable clothing, cradled a Hawken rifle, and packed his beaver catch and other possessions on a led horse. COURTESY DENVER PUBLIC LIBRARY, WESTERN HISTORY DEPARTMENT.

The trapper's life was dangerous, arduous, and miserable. Indians killed scores of unwary trappers wading the cold streams and setting their traps. Near beaver sign, such as downed trees and the partly submerged log-and-brush lodges, they took to the water to avoid leaving a scent on the bank. They usually worked in pairs, fixing their powerful steel traps on the streambed about four inches beneath the surface. A bait stick smeared with castoreum from a beaver's sex gland angled from the bank to overhang the submerged trap. A chain ran from the trap to a stake firmly planted in deeper water. Once in the trap, the beaver could swim no farther than the length of the chain and drowned as the heavy trap sank to the bottom. In a day or two the trappers returned to check their traps and set them anew.[5]

Normally, the hunters skinned the animal at once and scraped the pelt free of fat and flesh. In camp they stretched it on a circular hoop fashioned from willow boughs and hung it to dry. When dry, the pelts were folded in half, with the fur side in, and compacted by crude presses into bales of about sixty, each bundled in deerskin, to be loaded on horses or mules for transport.[6]

As early as 1807, when Colter and Drouillard worked out of Lisa's fort, their way of life drew heavily on the Indians. To cope with the wilderness and its human and animal adversaries, they inbibed deeply of Indian technique, tools and weapons, costume, practice, and even thought and belief. Garbed in greasy buckskin, warmed by a mackinaw blanket, waist and shoulder belts securing knife, tomahawk, pistol, powder horn, shot pouch, and "possibles" sack, mounted on a horse with flintlock rifle across the pommel, and leading another packed with traps, pelts, and camp equipment, they anticipated Washington Irving's observation that "You cannot pay a free trapper a greater compliment, than to persuade him you have mistaken him for an Indian brave; and, in truth, the counterfeit is complete."[7]

As Lewis and Clark veterans, Colter and Drouillard possessed the skills vital to wilderness survival. Wilderness skill consisted of two sets of capabilities. First was a set of specialties: beaver trapping, marksmanship with rifle and pistol, horsemanship, swimming, mountain climbing, game hunting, bodily combat with all weapons, survival in extreme weather and terrain, and sign reading, to name only a few.

Especially vital was the reading of nature's signs. The trapper's world abounded with visual, audible, olfactory, and other clues. Failure to perceive them and read their meaning, either when present or absent, could spell the difference between life and death. As a later mountaineer pointed out, "Every man carries here emphatically his life in his hand, and it is only by the most watchful precaution, grounded upon and guided by the observation of every unnatural appearance however slight, that he can hope to preserve it."[8]

Second were personal characteristics—physical, mental, emotional, and even an extrasensory power that is best understood as instinct. Physical strength and endurance were essential, as was fortitude and bravery. Also critical was quick, accurate thinking leading to instant action. But those who lived long enough to develop instinct had a big advantage over the less experienced. Instinct fortified sign reading but also operated in the absence of signs. Instinct gave warning when nothing else did, or communicated important or trivial information when nothing else did.

The trappers subsisted almost entirely on meat, ten or more pounds a day, prepared without salt or other seasoning. Buffalo was the staple. Hump, tongue, and ribs afforded the prime cuts, but all parts went into the kettle in lean times. Antelope, deer, elk, bear, and mountain sheep gave variety, but none pleased the trapper's palate like buffalo, whether roasted, broiled, fried, boiled, or pounded into a sausage and stuffed with herbs into casings made from the intestines. Game migrated widely, creating for Indians and trappers alike periods of feast and famine. Both prepared for want by pounding and drying meat into pemmican, a nutritious, easily transported food that usually, but not always, averted starvation.

Such was the life of Colter and Drouillard. Such, with refinements born of experience, was the life of the generation of trappers that followed.

THE LISA EXPEDITION reached the mouth of the Bighorn River too late in 1807 for a fall hunt, but he quickly took measures to alert the local Indians that he stood ready to trade. They were Crows, as opportunistic and unpredictable as Lisa himself. In 1806 Crow raiders had relieved Captain Clark, descending the Yellowstone, of many of his horses. But like their neighbors and friends the Shoshones and Flatheads, the Crows welcomed traders who might furnish guns and ammunition to fight the Blackfeet and Sioux. Those near Fort Raymond greeted the Americans warmly, and Lisa dispatched emissaries to the distant winter camps to let all know of his presence and to scout good beaver streams. The messengers were John Colter and George Drouillard.

John Colter left no chronicle that has survived, but he told others enough to establish his winter journey of 1807–08 as an incredible feat of persistence and endurance. Alone, with rifle and thirty-pound pack, he trudged through five hundred miles of snow-choked mountain wilderness to carry Lisa's invitation to the Crows and any other tribes he could find. At times he must have rested and recuperated in Indian lodges, and likely one or more Indians accompanied him on portions of his trek. At the least, they pointed to Indian trails that would guide him to his next destination.

Colter's exact route has been endlessly probed and debated. He crossed to the Bighorn Basin and scouted the upper reaches of the Wind River, a favorite Crow wintering ground sheltered by the Wind River Range on the south and the Absaroka Range on the north. He was the first white to lay eyes on Jackson Hole, with the majestic *"trois teton"* of later trapper lore soaring as backdrop. He climbed Teton Pass to Pierre's Hole, at the western base of the Teton Range, then returned to trace the shore of Jackson Lake. He stood on the north edge of Yellowstone Lake and probably marveled at the giant chasms and falls of the Yellowstone River. He thus became the first white man to explore part of what later fell within Yellowstone National Park. He missed the geyser basins to the west but saw the thermal wonders on the rim of Yellowstone Lake. "Colter's Hell," however, as incredulous listeners termed it when he recounted his adventures, lay farther east, on the river the Crows called the Stinking Water but that fastidious mapmakers renamed the Shoshone.[9]

Colter returned to Fort Raymond in the spring of 1808 to learn that two others had gone to the Crows during the winter. One, Edward Rose, simply passed the cold months in a warm Crow lodge and gave away all his goods besides. This did not endear him to Lisa but launched a legendary career among the Crows, to whom he returned after a quarrel with Lisa. The other was George Drouillard, who made two journeys, one in early winter, the other in spring. He covered nearly as much unexplored country as Colter, but it lay to the south and east of Fort Raymond and did not subject him to the high-mountain winter of Colter's route. Drouillard's first trek took him to the Bighorn Basin, where he saw "Colter's Hell" and other areas penetrated by Colter. The second and longer excursion followed the Bighorn and Little Bighorn Rivers (past the hilltop where Custer died sixty-eight years later) and revealed the upper stretches of Rosebud Creek and the Tongue River.[10]

When Lisa returned to St. Louis that summer of 1808, Drouillard went with him. Colter remained, assigned by Lisa to bring in more Indians to trade.

Making his way up the Yellowstone and across Bozeman Pass to the Gallatin, Colter fell in with a party of Flathead Indians, come from the mountains for their yearly buffalo hunt. He was conducting them to Fort Raymond for trade when, some fifteen or twenty miles up the Gallatin from the Three Forks, Blackfeet warriors suddenly sprang to the attack. Outnumbered, the Flatheads fought desperately but forlornly. The odds shifted, however, when a nearby force of Crow warriors plunged into the fray. Colter fought as fearlessly as any warrior, but fell with a ball in his leg. Dragging himself into a small thicket, he methodically loaded and fired his rifle until his friends, now with the superior numbers, drove off the Blackfeet. Colter's conspicuous role as a fighter with the Crows and Flatheads did not escape the notice of the retreating Blackfeet.[11]

After recuperating from his wound at Fort Raymond, Colter returned to the Three Forks country for a fall beaver hunt. John Potts, another veteran of the Lewis and Clark expedition, went along. As Colter and Potts paddled up the Jefferson River, each in his own canoe, Blackfeet suddenly appeared on the east bank and commanded them to come ashore. Supposing the Indians meant robbery only, Colter quickly cast his traps into the water and obeyed. Potts hung back. No sooner had Colter climbed from his canoe than the warriors swarmed over him, seizing his weapons and stripping him naked. As Potts still refused to beach his canoe, one of the Blackfeet raised his musket and shot him in the hip. Potts fell to the bottom of the canoe, then pulled himself up and fired back, killing an Indian. Infuriated, the Blackfeet loosed a fatal volley that riddled Potts. Some waded into the river and pulled the canoe to the bank, where they butchered the corpse and flung the pieces in Colter's face.

Colter expected to be executed at once. After a council, however, the leader pointed east, across a level plain, and in the Crow language declared, "Go, go away." Colter started walking, then quickly saw the purpose—a race for life. Off he bounded, a crowd of whooping Blackfeet in pursuit. A powerful man and swift runner, he gradually left them behind, aiming for the Madison River five miles distant. Halfway across the open space, blood began to spurt from his nose and mouth, but only one of the Indians remained close on his heels. Suddenly stopping and turning, Colter confronted his adversary, who rushed forward with a spear. Colter seized it and threw the man off balance. The spear broke, leaving the head and part of the shaft in Colter's hands. The Indian fell on his back, and Colter rammed the spearhead through his body. Retrieving the weapon and grabbing the dead man's blanket, Colter resumed his dash as the howling throng came into view. Reaching the Madison River, he dove in and swam to a nearby raft of driftwood. Plunging beneath it, he made his way up until he got his head above the surface of the water. There he remained throughout the day, as the Indians searched the riverbanks and even tramped on the top of the woodpile. Finally they gave up and left.

Spared quick death at the hands of Blackfeet, Colter faced slow death by starvation and exposure. Alone in the wilderness, naked except for a blanket, weaponless except for the spear point, his feet shredded by prickly pear, he started the agonizing journey to Fort Raymond, more than two hundred miles distant. He traveled both day and night, pausing only for hasty rests. Roots and tree bark furnished his only food. Eleven days later, more dead than alive, he reached his destination.

Colter's race for life marked the onset of unremitting conflict with the Blackfeet. Not for many years would they give another American the chance they gave Colter. His part in helping the Crows and Flatheads, and his triumph on the Jefferson and Madison, are the point from which to date Blackfeet antagonism.[12]

Recovered from his ordeal and supposing all Indians reposing snugly in their winter camps, Colter set forth to retrieve the valuable traps he had dropped from his canoe into the Jefferson River. Crossing Bozeman Pass again, he camped on the Gallatin River. As he broiled buffalo meat over a campfire, he heard twigs and leaves crackling in the dark behind him, followed by the cocking of guns. Swiftly he threw himself over his fire and rolled into the black night beyond as musket balls laced the campsite and scattered the coals of his fire. Scaling a mountainside, he turned back to Fort Raymond, vowing that "he promised God Almighty that he would never return to this region again if he were only permitted to escape once more with his life."[13]

Other trapping parties out of Fort Raymond also tested the Three Forks country during the fall hunt of 1808, but the growing rancor of the Blackfeet discouraged thorough work. The following spring the chief factor, Benito Vasquez, reorganized his trappers and sent them south to find and trap the "River of the Spaniards." Vasquez himself then closed the fort and headed for the Mandan villages with meager returns of fifteen beaver skins and ten buffalo robes. John Colter went with him.

At the Mandan villages, on September 22, 1809, Vasquez and his party greeted the Lisa entourage bound upriver. Reflecting the optimism Lisa had taken to St. Louis the previous year, it was a formidable expedition, more than 150 men packed with cargos of trade goods into thirteen keelboats and barges. In St. Louis old money and new money had coalesced in the St. Louis Missouri Fur Company. One of the men who stepped ashore at the Mandan villages was George Drouillard, again determined to try his hand in the beaver country.

Despite the dismal prospects described by Vasquez, the expedition continued to its destination. Lisa returned to St. Louis to prepare an outfit for the next season. Andrew Henry led forty men and horses overland to reopen Fort Raymond, while Pierre Menard took the boats and their cargos on up the Missouri and the Yellowstone. Colter went with Henry, apparently forgetting his vow to abandon the country if only God would allow him another escape from the Blackfeet.[14]

The principal aim of the St. Louis Missouri Fur Company was to establish a post at the Three Forks of the Missouri, both to trap this richest of all beaver country and to open trade with the Blackfeet. In the spring of 1810, guided by John Colter, some eighty men, including George Drouillard, made the journey from Fort Raymond to the Three Forks. Pierre Menard led, with Andrew Henry second in charge. Henry, a youthful Missouri lead miner, was widely admired for his handsome appearance, strong personality, intellectual attainment, and honesty. He was destined to become one of the most successful yet least recognized explorers of the northern Rockies.[15]

On April 3, 1810, on a tongue of land at the confluence of the Jefferson and Madison Rivers, some of the men began building a log stockade while others left to trap up the Jefferson and down the Missouri. On April 12, only ten miles up the Jefferson, Blackfeet fell on eighteen trappers. By the time help arrived, two had been slain and mutilated and three others were missing. Gone too were traps, skins, ammunition, and horses.[16]

John Colter had been with the party scattered by Blackfeet. He escaped and found his way into the post. He had once promised his maker to leave this country, he declared, hurling his hat to the ground, and "now if God will only forgive me this time and let me off I *will* leave the country day after to-morrow—and be damned if I ever come into it again." And leave he did, never to return.[17]

Although discouraged, Menard hung on. In May the trappers resolved to endure constraint no longer. In a party of thirty, kept together for self-defense, they worked their way back up the Jefferson. This proved unwieldy and inefficient, so they divided into groups of four, two men to tend camp, two to work the traps. Garnering more pelts and observing no Indian signs, all grew bolder.

George Drouillard, who should have known better, began to venture out alone. Others protested, but he turned them aside. "I am too much of an Indian to be caught by Indians," he answered. Twice his solitary quests met with success. "This is the way to catch beaver," he exulted.

On the third morning he left again, followed by two Shawnee deer hunters. The main party shortly took the trail. Soon they overtook the two hunters, "pierced with arrows, lances and bullets and lying near each other." Beyond some 150 yards they found Drouillard and his horse, Drouillard "mangled in a horrible manner; his head was cut off, his entrails torn out and his body hacked to pieces." From the position of his body and the marks on the ground, he had skillfully maneuvered his horse to serve as a shield, riding in a circle and defending himself with rifle, pistol, knife, and tomahawk.[18]

The death of Drouillard, on top of a long chain of misfortunes, demoralized the men at the Three Forks. As Menard had advised Pierre Chouteau, in a letter carried to St. Louis by John Colter, "the resources of this country in beaver fur are immense." But unless the company could either destroy or make peace with the Blackfeet, "it is idle to think of maintaining an establishment at this point."[19]

By midsummer of 1810, they had given up. Menard returned to St. Louis, leading some of the men and transporting such furs as had been accumulated. Henry and the rest of the men had a final fierce battle with Blackfeet. Abandoning the post, they then trekked up the Madison River and crossed a low pass to the head of another river, which rose in a broad lake at the foot of the pass. Crow raiders ran off with some of their horses, but on this river Henry and his men threw up another log edifice as base for a fall hunt and in which to pass the winter. Henry's Fort, lying on the bank of Henry's Fork of the Snake River south of Henry's Lake, was the first American trading post west of the Continental Divide.[20]

· · ·

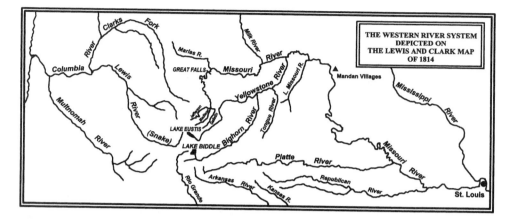

THE WESTERN RIVER SYSTEM
DEPICTED ON
THE LEWIS AND CLARK MAP
OF 1814

Lewis and Clark got the Missouri and Columbia systems essentially correct, with impor-
tant help from John Colter and George Drouillard. The Multnomah was imaginary, a
notion that the Willamette reached far eastward to the Rockies, but it remained on maps
for more than thirty years. The Yellowstone River correctly heads in Lake Eustice, later
named Yellowstone Lake. Lake Biddle is the present Jackson Lake, which lies near the
source of the Snake River, not the Bighorn. In fact, the head of the Bighorn lies hardly
thirty miles east of Jackson Lake. The relationship of the heads of the various river
systems reflects Zebulon Pike's concept of a "grand reservoir of snows and fountains"
where all sources could be visited in a single day.

JOHN COLTER AND GEORGE DROUILLARD had ended their short exposure to history, the one to prevent the Indians from getting him, the other
because the Indians got him. During their six years in the Far West, they
developed into quintessential mountain men, among the earliest of a generation of adventurers who would evolve their own distinctive culture in the
Rocky Mountains. In their reckless courage, their physical stamina and endurance, their enchantment with the spell of the wild, their mastery of
wilderness skills, their attitudes toward Indian friends and Indian enemies,
and their steadfast quest for the furs that promised a modest financial reward if not wealth, they prefigured the generic mountain man who made
his life in the Rockies in the 1820s and 1830s.

While representing a type soon to emerge on the western scene, Colter
and Drouillard also made significant contributions to history. They were
leading players in Manuel Lisa's efforts to open the sources of the Missouri
and Yellowstone Rivers to trapping and the Indian trade. They and their
comrades disclosed this country as harboring fortunes in beaver fur but, in
incurring the enmity of the Blackfeet, denied it to Lisa and his successors.
While kindling more than twenty years of cruel war with the Blackfeet, the
white invaders also helped to forge trading bonds with Shoshones, Flat-

heads, and especially Crows, and thereby helped to lay the groundwork for years of generally amicable relations with these enemies of the Blackfeet.

Most important, Colter and Drouillard were premier explorers. Although lacking the grounding in contemporary literature and cartography of their officers, both had crossed the continent twice with the Corps of Discovery and acquired their own conception of its geography. Both had then scouted great tracts of country unseen by either Lewis or Clark. When they descended the Missouri to St. Louis, Drouillard in 1808 and Colter in 1810, they took with them an enlarged understanding of western geography and the explorer's keen desire to pass on what they had learned.

Drouillard's contribution, in the five-month interval before he returned to the mountains and his death at the hands of Blackfeet, took tangible form. He drew his own map of the Yellowstone and Bighorn region that he and Colter had explored. Clark copied it and transcribed its data onto a master map he was preparing.

Colter drew no map but made his contribution in conversations with Clark. By 1810, when Colter came down from the mountains, the task of preparing the expedition's maps and report had fallen entirely on Clark. A year earlier, en route to Washington, a mentally ill Meriwether Lewis, governor of Missouri Territory, had died by his own hand. The map of the West that Clark began drawing in 1810 incorporated what he had learned from Drouillard in 1808 and what Colter told him in 1810.[21]

In its depiction of the source and southern tributaries of the Yellowstone, Clark's map owed much to Colter and Drouillard. The 1808 maps inspired by Drouillard laid down his route in 1807 and 1808. The 1810 map traced Colter's route, although the misshapen geography fuels continuing debate over where he actually went.

Ironically, Colter and Drouillard helped perpetuate one of the most enduring misconceptions about western geography. Their chief, Manuel Lisa, had for years been obsessed with the idea of opening a trade between Missouri and Spanish Santa Fe. The old idea of a common source for all the great western river systems led him to speculate that the head of the Missouri or Yellowstone might lead to the head of the Rio Grande and thus to Santa Fe. In their travels, Colter and Drouillard queried the Indians about such a connection. They probably misunderstood what the Indians told them. The shortened distance they pictured represented how far the Indians journeyed to meet northward-ranging Spanish traders rather than how far to the Spanish settlements. Clark's map, however, bore notations indicating but a few days' ride from the Bighorn Basin to the Spanish settlements and thus kept alive the dream of a Santa Fe trade based on the upper Missouri.[22]

Reinforcing the dream, Clark's map showed the Missouri and Yellowstone reaching far south of their true sources and the Rio Grande reaching far north to meet them. Clark borrowed his geography in this area from the report and maps of Lieutenant Zebulon M. Pike, whose official expedition of 1806–07 had probed the upper Arkansas and Rio Grande before abruptly ending, thanks to hypersensitive Spanish officials, in the Santa Fe jail. Pike conceived the Yellowstone, Platte, Arkansas, Red, and Colorado Rivers, together with the Rio Grande, all originating in a "grand reservoir of snows and fountains." "I have no hesitation in asserting," he wrote, "that I can visit the source of any of those rivers in one day." And so Clark's map suggested.[23]

Despite its anomalies, William Clark's map represented an immense cartographic leap beyond the maps he and Lewis had consulted on the eve of their departure in 1804. Beautifully engraved by Philadelphia mapmaker Samuel Lewis, it appeared in 1814 as part of Nicholas Biddle's *History of the Expedition under Command of Captains Lewis and Clark.* Now the learned world could read of the two captains' adventures and study a map of elaborate detail that laid out, with only moderate distortion, the Missouri and the Columbia and the great mountain mass dividing them.

The 1814 map claims another, less obvious significance. Its mountains and river courses reflect much of the content of the sketch maps hastily prepared around mountain campfires as Indians conveyed to the two captains their understanding of the geography of their homeland. Like Lewis and Clark, moreover, the mountain men who followed rarely blazed their own trails. They followed Indian trails, and their mental maps owed as great a debt to Indians as did the final Lewis and Clark map.

John Colter never saw the engraved map or the handsome and significant publication it accompanied. He had lived up to his vow never to return to the mountains. Having told his old captain all he knew about the Yellowstone and Bighorn country, this man who Thomas James declared "can only live in a state of excitement and constant action" settled into the quiet life of a yeoman farmer on the Missouri frontier. Marrying a woman remembered only as Sally, siring a son, he cleared a plot of land, built a cabin, and passed his few remaining years as a neighbor of Daniel Boone. Jaundice took his life in 1813, aged not yet forty.[24]

Although neither John Colter nor George Drouillard ever saw the engraved rendering of William Clark's map, it stands as a modest monument to these two great mountain men, prototypes of those to come.

3

ROBINSON, HOBACK, AND
REZNOR: DOOMED TRIO

IN THE EARLY YEARS of beaver-powered mountaineering, Edward Robinson, John Hoback, and Jacob Reznor united inseparably in both life and death. They came out of Kentucky, possibly together; but of the three, only Robinson emerges as more than a faceless name. Incredibly, considering the hardships the trio endured in the mountains, he was sixty-six years of age in 1811, a veteran of wars between white settlers and Indians for possession of Kentucky. In some long-ago fight, he had lost his scalp to a warrior's knife. Always afterward, he wore a large handkerchief tied over the top of his head.[1]

The three Kentuckians launched their trapping careers under the tutelage of Manuel Lisa. With Colter and Drouillard, they followed Lisa up the Missouri in 1807, and with Colter and Drouillard they took part in the St. Louis Missouri Fur Company's venture of 1809–10. In the spring of 1810 they helped erect Henry's Fort at the Three Forks of the Missouri. After Colter had forsaken the mountains and Drouillard had been dismembered by Indians, they went with the sixty men who in the summer of 1810 followed Andrew Henry up the Madison River and across the Continental Divide to the north fork of the Snake River—henceforth Henry's Fork.[2]

From Henry's Fort on Henry's Fork, the trappers conducted a fall hunt that garnered a substantial store of beaver skins. Although Crow warriors had stolen most of their horses, they had put the Blackfeet behind them, and they ranged widely in search of promising beaver streams. They crossed to Jackson Hole and probed its bordering mountains—the Tetons,

Gros Ventres, and Absarokas. They trapped the Snake, and John Hoback gave his name to a canyoned river, rich in beaver, emptying into the Snake.

For the occupants of Henry's Fort, the winter of 1810–11, after the fall hunt, proved uncommonly severe. Several log huts served as rude shelters, and the men ventured out only to "make meat." By the spring of 1811, with fading prospects of resupply from St. Louis, Henry abandoned the post. The trappers divided into groups, some to stay in the mountains, others to make their way home. Henry and one contingent took forty packs of beaver pelts to the Yellowstone and boated down to an eventual meeting with Manuel Lisa, hurrying up the Missouri with a fresh outfit backed by a reorganized firm styled simply the Missouri Fur Company.[3]

For their part, Robinson, Hoback, and Reznor decided to go home to Kentucky. They took with them a store of geographical knowledge about the mountains and headwaters of the Missouri, Snake, and Green Rivers. They also pioneered a travel route safer and easier than the pathway Lewis and Clark had carved out of the Blackfeet-infested mountains to the north. Colter and Drouillard had trod portions of this route in 1807–08, but Robinson, Hoback, and Reznor put it all together to link the upper Snake with the Missouri River at the Arikara towns. Crossing Teton Pass from Pierre's Hole to Jackson Hole, they threaded Togwotee Pass to the source of the Wind River and followed it down to the Bighorn Basin. After clambering over the Bighorn Mountains, they made their way along the High Plains river courses to the Missouri.

On May 26, 1811, in an episode reminiscent of John Colter, two dugout canoes containing the three men nosed into the Missouri shore at the mouth of the Niobrara River. Here they discovered a company of some sixty men taking breakfast before resuming their upriver journey. This was not the Lisa expedition, still laboring up the Missouri in the rear. Instead, the Kentuckians had met a band of adventurers destined not for the mountains but for the Pacific Coast, the first to attempt a continental crossing since Lewis and Clark. They traveled for no less a sponsor than the reigning giant of the American fur trade, John Jacob Astor.

Robinson, Hoback, and Reznor breakfasted with the "Overland Astorians." As naturalist John Bradbury recorded in his journal, these three mountaineers had trapped the Rockies until they "*imagined* they were tired of the hunting life." They had "families and good plantations in Kentucky" and were going home. "But on seeing us, families, plantations, and all vanished; they agreed to join us, and turned their canoes adrift."[4]

As for Colter four years earlier, the mountains cast a spell not easily broken.

BEHIND THIS SECOND AMERICAN CROSSING of the continent lay a grand design of commerce and empire. It had formed in the mind of John Jacob Astor, the astute German immigrant who had established himself in New York shortly after the American Revolution and had since built a powerful commercial domain on the fur resources of the Great Lakes.

Through fur magnates in Montreal, Astor kept abreast of the exploitation of the great mountain-born rivers flowing into Hudson Bay. Since 1670, this vast land east of the Rocky Mountains had been the monopoly of the Hudson's Bay Company, based in London. The collapse of France in North America, however, had not emptied the country of the supremely skilled French Canadian fur men who worked west from Montreal. The North West Company, backed by Astor's Montreal friends, vigorously contested the London company's prerogatives. The savage competition that resulted spread British trading posts up the Saskatchewan River and its tributaries to the base of the Rockies. Competition generated explorations such as Alexander Mackenzie's and spurred the British drive toward the Pacific that so alarmed Thomas Jefferson and induced him to mount the Lewis and Clark expedition.

The tumult in England's North American West stirred Astor as it stirred Jefferson. As the British sought profit for their capitalists and empire for their nation, Astor reasoned, so should the United States. The Louisiana Purchase had expanded the young republic beyond the Mississippi, across the Great Plains, and into the Rocky Mountains. The limits of the purchase remained to be determined, including the boundary between British and American territory in the north and Spanish and American in the south. Beyond the Rockies, the Pacific slope from California to Alaska exhibited a patchwork of overlapping claims by Spain, Russia, Great Britain, and the United States. Astor intended to emulate the British and establish still another American claim while also adding to his own fortune.

By 1808, Astor's dream of a global commercial empire had evolved into the Pacific Fur Company. At the mouth of the Columbia, the company would establish its first outpost. Inland others would follow, eventually connecting Astor's Great Lakes system to the Pacific. From the seminal post on the Columbia, the sea-lanes would bear Astor furs to Asian ports where silks, spices, and other oriental exotics would provide return cargoes, and to England and other European sources of manufactured goods coveted by American consumers and vital to the Indian trade.

By the spring of 1810, Astor had completed arrangements for locating Astoria at the mouth of the Columbia River. While pursuing financial and logistical plans for dispatching one expedition by sea and another by land, the tycoon had not neglected the imperial aspect of his scheme. He had secured from federal authorities a tentative official "approbation" that in his mind took on connotations of full government support. He had early taken pains to keep Thomas Jefferson informed, and in 1810 he enjoyed no more ardent backer than Secretary of the Treasury Albert Gallatin.

The two expeditions got under way in the fall of 1810. On September 6 the *Tonquin* cast off from New York harbor piloted by a captain whose incessant tyranny provoked one crisis after another. The overland contingent assembled in St. Louis three days earlier. By November they had established a winter camp on the Missouri River at the mouth of the Nodaway. From here, in the spring of 1811, they would embark on their continental crossing.

Leading the Overland Astorians was Wilson Price Hunt, who had set himself up as a St. Louis merchant in 1804, at a youthful twenty-one. From his counting room five years later, Astor recruited him to command the overland expedition. Why is a puzzle. Never before or after was this businessman a mountaineer or even an outdoorsman, much less a captain of such men.

Edward Robinson, John Hoback, and Jacob Reznor were such men. When they beached their canoes at the mouth of the Niobrara on May 26, 1811, Hunt welcomed their easy readiness to turn back to the mountains and quickly signed them on.[5]

FOR ROBINSON, HOBACK, AND REZNOR, more than the lure of the mountains influenced the abrupt reversal of their plans. Hunt offered them a full trapping outfit with subsistence and ammunition in return for half their take in beaver pelts. Equally persuasive, talks with Hunt ended in their designation as guides to lead the expedition to Henry's abandoned post on Henry's Fork.

Hunt had originally intended to follow the route of Lewis and Clark. In St. Louis, however, he discovered that the two captains had not been able to make most of the journey by boat, that more than the easy portage of conventional thinking divided the heads of the Missouri and the "River of the West." In St. Louis too he learned that John Colter believed that an easier passage of the continent lay by way of the Yellowstone and Bighorn Rivers. Moreover, on the way up the Missouri to winter camp in the fall of 1810, Hunt talked with Colter himself. The veteran mountaineer almost yielded to the temptation to abandon his new wife and farm and accompany the Astorians. By the time Hunt talked with the three Kentuckians, therefore, he had decided to turn from the Missouri up the Yellowstone.[6]

Robinson, Hoback, and Reznor led Hunt to still another change of plans. The route by which they had just come from the Snake River country required an earlier shift from water to land, but it avoided the Blackfeet menace altogether, was shorter, did not involve difficult mountain crossings, and lay through a country of plentiful game. They knew nothing about the country west of Henry's Fork, but they happily agreed to guide the Astorians as far as that branch of the Columbia.[7]

On June 12 the Astorians reached the Arikara towns near the mouth of the Grand River. Here they abandoned their keelboats to begin their westward journey by land. Not until the middle of July, however, did intense bargaining with the Indians yield enough horses to resume the journey. On July 18, Robinson, Hoback, and Reznor pointed the caravan southwest, up the Grand River. The expedition consisted of sixty-two men, one woman, and two children. The four company partners and their clerk rode horseback, as did interpreter Pierre Dorion and his Indian family. The rest walked, while the balance of the eighty-two horses carried equipment, supplies, and trade merchandise.[8]

A newcomer to the party, taken on at the Arikara towns, was well known to the three guides. Edward Rose had come up the Missouri with Manuel Lisa in 1807, had passed the winter of Colter's great journey in a Crow village, and after a dispute with Lisa had returned to the Crows. Since then, he had spent at least two extended periods with these Indians and had come to know them better than any other white man. Since the expedition would pass through the country of the Crows, inveterate horse thieves of unpredictable disposition, Hunt believed Rose a valuable addition to the company.

A big, powerful man of volatile temper yet undoubted ability, Rose had already gained a sinister reputation among the fur men. No one trusted him, and everyone regarded him as unscrupulously motivated by no interests but his own. By the time the Astorians approached their first mountain barrier, the Bighorns, Hunt had come to regret his decision to hire Rose.[9]

Distrust intensified as the Astorians met a band of Crows. The overlanders had already bought fresh horses from some Cheyennes, but now bartered with the Crows for more. Several days of bargaining yielded enough horses, bringing the number to 121, as well as buffalo robes and beaver pelts. When Hunt attempted to end the session, however, the Crows turned ugly, a development attributed to Rose. Fearful that he would stir more trouble with the Indians and might even desert with some of the men and horses, Hunt offered him half a year's pay, a horse, and three beaver traps to go back to the Crows. Rose eagerly accepted.

The day after Rose's departure, September 3, the expedition penetrated the Bighorn Mountains, only to find themselves surrounded by high peaks and deep gorges, surely on a course unlikely to take them to the western base of the range. Robinson, Hoback, and Reznor had become confused over their eastward passage of these mountains. Hunt backed out and again made camp on the eastern flank. The next day, surprising all, Edward Rose suddenly appeared with an escort of Crow warriors. The chief, he said, had sent him to advise the white men they had taken a wrong turn. Rose pointed out the proper path, then took his leave. What motivated his sudden, uncharacteristic charity, no one ever discovered.[10]

Safely across the Bighorns, Robinson, Hoback, and Reznor had no further difficulty finding their way to the Snake. Near the head of the Wind River, with game suddenly scarce, they diverged from their home-bound route. As they recalled from experience, or as Crow or Shoshone Indians may have advised, game could usually be found on the upper Green River—the "Spanish River," as Americans came increasingly to know it. Instead of following Togwotee Pass to the Snake, therefore, they turned south and, following a distinct Indian trail, crossed the Continental Divide at Union Pass, which separates the Wind River and Gros Ventre Ranges.

From this lofty summit, mountains extended in every direction. One of the three guides, as Washington Irving wrote, "after considering the vast landscape attentively, pointed to three mountain peaks glistening with snow, which rose, he said, above a fork of the Columbia River. They were hailed by the travellers with that joy with which a beacon on a sea-shore is hailed by mariners after a long and dangerous voyage." Hunt called them "Pilot Knobs," but they later came to be known as the Three Tetons—the Grand Tetons—and for a generation of mountain men they served as beacons such as Irving envisioned.[11]

The waters of the Columbia—the Snake River at the eastern foot of the Tetons—could have been reached simply by turning down the Gros Ventre River from Union Pass. Other streams flowing south from this summit, however, brought them to the Green River, where they found plenty of buffalo and paused to lay in a store of meat. From here they descended the Hoback River to the Snake and the southern edge of Jackson Hole.[12]

As the Kentucky guides declared, the Astorians had arrived on the branch of the Columbia toward which they had aimed. For Hunt, this formidable river, which he called the "Mad," meant two things. First, the time had come to begin detaching trapping parties to hunt beaver, whose pelts would ultimately be gathered into Astoria. On October 1, with rain soaking the valley and snow falling on the mountains, two pairs of trappers set forth on this hazardous mission of unknown duration.

Second, still swayed by the old idea of navigable waters draining the mountains all the way to the ocean, Hunt set his men to fashioning dugout canoes. However, a reconnaissance down the canyon by which the Snake exited Jackson Hole, combined with advice from Shoshone Indians, convinced him that the rushing waters of this gorge would smash any vessel. Instead, the Astorians made their way across Teton Pass on the well-beaten Indian trail that a generation of trappers would follow to breach the Teton Range between Jackson Hole and Pierre's Hole. October 8 brought the overlanders, after a journey of nearly three months from the Arikara towns, to the ruins of Henry's Fort on Henry's Fork of the Snake River.[13]

Robinson, Hoback, and Reznor had performed their service as guides. Except for the false start into the Bighorn Mountains, they had piloted the Astorians to Henry's Fort. Now, under the terms by which Hunt had outfitted them, they wanted to remain in their old hunting grounds and seek beaver. Together with Martin Cass, they formed the third party Hunt detached for this purpose. At the last moment a fifth man, Joseph Miller, joined the four trappers.

As the five men made preparations to embark on their expedition, Hunt had the rest of the men chopping down trees and hollowing dugout canoes. Still obsessed with reaching the Pacific by water rather than land, he judged Henry's Fork much more inviting than the canyon cataracts he had probed from east of the Tetons. Robinson, Hoback, and Reznor seem not to have been far enough down this fork of Hunt's "Mad River" to advise of the obstacles that lay before him. The fateful decision to abandon horses and take to canoes would fully confirm Hunt in the name that he applied to the Snake River.

WILSON PRICE HUNT'S WATERBORNE OVERLANDERS soon discovered that the Snake River did not afford an easy descent to the Columbia. Cataracts, falls, and finally deep gorges with sheer walls forced laborious portages and ultimately abandonment of the canoes. Desperate quests for Indians who might furnish horses followed, together with dwindling food supplies, scarce game, and winter snow and cold. In attempts to find a way to the Columbia, the company divided and subdivided, retraced trails that ended in impassable mountains or canyons, and grew weak from hunger, fatigue, and despair. Men drowned, starved, and lost their way in an unforgiving wilderness. Hunt and his immediate following reached their destination in the middle of February 1812, four months after putting their canoes in Henry's Fork. Another party had arrived a month earlier, and a third did not make it in until early May.[14]

"We had endured all the hardships imaginable," Hunt wrote in his journal as he looked on the Columbia River. The ordeal had resulted from poor leadership, geographical ignorance, and above all the decision to trust the expedition's fortunes to a river of unknown character. Blocked by Hell's Canyon of the Snake, he had clambered over the Blue Mountains and descended to the Columbia. One day the wagon wheels of emigrants would mark it as an unforgettable segment of the Oregon Trail.

Down the Columbia Hunt united with the seaborne Astorians. The *Tonquin's* voyage had been a litany of misfortune and crisis, largely the result of the despotism of Captain Jonathan Thorn. By the late spring of 1811, however, nearly a year before Hunt's arrival by land, Astoria had been planted on a hilltop commanding the broad mouth of the Columbia River. That summer, Captain Thorn had piloted the *Tonquin* on a trading voyage north to Vancouver Island, where his insolence so outraged the Indians that they massacred the entire crew—all but one, who ignited the powder magazine and blew up the ship, Indians, and all else aboard.

Precariously, Astoria clung to its hilltop overlooking the Columbia River.

WITH THE TERRORS of the "Mad River" the Kentucky trio did not have to contend. They and their two new companions, however, faced adversity fully as terrifying. In the course of a year, they wandered an erratic course of more than a thousand miles around a land known only to Indians. Although they contributed almost nothing of their new geographical knowledge to a larger audience, they deserve to be remembered as the first white men to traverse a vast country soon to become the heartland of the Rocky Mountain fur trade.

Striking south from Henry's Fort, the trappers followed the Snake River until it began its westward turn, then veered south over low mountains to the Bear River. On its lower course they found streams alive with beaver and halted to garner a rich harvest of pelts. They assumed this southward-flowing river to be an arm of the ocean, but did not follow it far enough to discover Great Salt Lake, into which it emptied.

Instead, they turned directly east and, their horses laden with beaver pelts, trekked more than two hundred miles through mountains and deserts. Their route took them across the Continental Divide but through no discernible pass; in this area, in fact, the Continental Divide separates to encircle a barren red desert later maps would label "Great Divide Basin." It allowed no outlet for watercourses even had many existed. The wanderers thus missed the gateway of South Pass that lay to the north.

Hungry because of scarce game, robbed by Arapaho Indians, the destitute trappers sought a winter camp. It may have been in the northern foothills of the Medicine Bow Mountains, or it may have been to the north-west, along another stream destined for repute among mountain men. If the latter, the southern tributary of the Wind River the Crows called Popo Agie (pronounced *Popósya*), they had again missed South Pass, only a few days' journey to the south.

Game continued scarce, with the few fish that could be taken from the streams furnishing a bare subsistence. Worse, as the spring of 1812 dawned, the same Arapahos again fell on the travelers and took virtually everything. To compound this disaster, Martin Cass stole away in the night with one of two horses not seized by the Indians.

Turning west, the four wayfarers probably ascended the Wind River on their trail of the previous autumn with Hunt's Astorians. Somewhere along the way, Shoshones made off with their single remaining horse. Famished, wasted, destitute, clad in tatters, they toiled through the mountains to the Snake River plain. The middle of August 1812 found them far down the Snake, some seventy miles above the mouth of the Boise River.

On a hot August 20, John Hoback fished in the Snake while his three companions rested in a clump of willows. Alerted by a noise on the bank above him, Hoback turned to see white men scrambling down the slope to drink from the river. His shout of joy greeted the newcomers and roused Miller, Robinson, and Reznor from their slumbers.

A turn of good fortune had united the Kentucky trio with six Astorians. Under Robert Stuart, these men were en route east with dispatches for John Jacob Astor reporting the developments at Astoria. Again, the fortunes of Robinson, Hoback, and Reznor had been joined to the grand design of John Jacob Astor.[15]

ROBERT STUART and his fellow dispatch bearers would stake out an even greater claim than Hunt as pioneers of the Oregon Trail. Already, when they met Joseph Miller and the Kentucky trio on August 20, 1812, the eastbound Astorians had traveled to the Snake on the same route by which Hunt had reached the Columbia. A sequence of circumstance and accident now diverted Stuart from Hunt's westbound track to still another continental passage—one destined for momentous significance in America's westward expansion.

Stuart could count on guides to lead him to the Missouri River by way of the Wind River and the Bighorn Mountains, for the ragged wayfarers once again declared their determination to go home. As Astorian Alexander Ross recalled, "they swore that they had met to part no more till they parted in that land which had given them birth," and they appeared "quite overjoyed and happy at the prospect of once more returning to their native homes."[16]

They changed their minds. Only nine days later, the combined party arrived at the point on the Snake where a canoe disaster at "Caldron Linn" had forced Hunt to abandon the river. He had cached all the equipment and supplies that could not be carried, and now Stuart opened the caches. Six of the nine had been plundered, but the remaining three contained ammunition and beaver traps that set the Kentuckians to thinking. Rather than return home in poverty, they persuaded Stuart to outfit them for a two-year hunt from the contents of the caches. Astorian John Reed was following on Stuart's trail to find the caches and gather any pelts accumulated by the men Hunt had left behind, including the three Kentuckians. Thus they could look forward to further support from Astoria. For his part, Joseph Miller had endured enough; he remained with Stuart.[17]

Misfortune dogged the Astorians. Game grew scarce, and the bleak Snake Plain seemed to offer no more than a thoroughfare into Blackfeet country. Miller talked Stuart into leaving the Snake and striking south into the country he had penetrated with Robinson, Hoback, and Reznor the previous autumn. By September 8 they were on the Bear River, which Miller and his comrades had trapped so successfully. They had reached it, however, on its northward course, before the lava wall that turns it sharply south toward Great Salt Lake. Miller failed to recognize the stream as the Bear, grew confused, and got the travelers lost.

Next Crow warriors fell on their trail. In a first encounter, under the guise of trading, they tried to bluff Stuart into relaxing his guard. That failed but so distracted the whites that they took a course that brought them back to the Snake River at the lower end of its canyon around the Snake River Mountains and the Teton Range. Here on September 19 the Crows acted more directly, suddenly dashing through camp during breakfast and stampeding all the horses.[18]

Cast afoot, the seven men destroyed all they could not carry and set forth on an erratic course that took them down the Snake by raft and around the Snake River Range to Pierre's Hole. Back now on Hunt's westbound route, they spotted the "Pilot Knobs" thrusting above the mountains to the east, and on October 7 they topped the snow-choked Teton Pass to descend into Jackson Hole.

From this mountain-circled valley, the Astorians turned up the Hoback River, the same descended by Hunt's party the year before. The motive was severe hunger. For days the Astorians had traveled through a country almost empty of game and had lived precariously on an occasional antelope and beaver. Miller knew this country from his travels with the Kentuck-ians, and some of Stuart's men had also been there with Hunt. They took to the Hoback because it led to the "Spanish River," where Hunt had found game and where Stuart hoped his famished party could make meat. Fur-thermore, back on the Snake a Shoshone Indian had told of a way through the mountains south of Hunt's and had even offered his services as guide, only to desert within two days. Stuart may also have hoped to find this southern pass.[19]

On the upper Green River the men met with bitter disappointment. No buffalo nor even recent trace of buffalo could be found. A southeasterly course along the western foothills of the Wind River Mountains finally turned up a wasted old buffalo bull, enough to avert the immediate crisis. Further good fortune brought them to a Shoshone camp where the inhabi-tants, though poor themselves, provided meat and a jaded horse.

Revived, the Astorians pressed on, sometimes following well-beaten In-dian trails, sometimes guided only by instinct. Snow and cold tormented them, but an occasional buffalo and even a bighorn sheep warded off hunger. In the last days of October, with winter on the land, they made camp on a small creek. Elated to find water, they did not yet know they had reached a stream (Muddy Creek) that flowed into the Sweetwater River, which in turn ran down to the North Platte.[20]

Thus Robert Stuart led the first known party of white Americans through South Pass (although they probably went somewhat south of the pass itself). This grassy corridor of rolling plains, some twenty miles wide, separated the Wind River Mountains on the north from a range of low mountains on the south, the northern rim of the Great Divide Basin. The summit of South Pass, discernible only to the observant traveler, divided the head streams of the eastward-coursing Sweetwater from the branches of the Sandy River, flowing southwest across a sterile plain to the Green River. Among these gentle hills and ridges, the snowmelt of the Wind River Mountains separated, part to reach the Gulf of Mexico, part to reach the Gulf of California.

Scarcely any geographical feature held more portent for America's westward movement. Lewis and Clark had shown that a continental pas-sage could not be navigated with only an easy portage between rivers rolling to the two oceans. Stuart, however, had discovered the key to a con-tinental passage by land, a broad and easy break in the Rocky Mountains that would enable wagons to reach the Columbia with only one difficult barrier, the Blue Mountains of Oregon.

Stuart's arrival in St. Louis on April 30, 1813, stirred public acclaim, and by now Stuart understood the importance of his feat. As a reporter for the *Missouri Gazette* wrote: "By information received from these gentle-men, it appears that a journey across the continent of N. America, might be performed with a waggon, there being no obstruction in the whole route that any person would dare to call a mountain in addition to its being much the most direct and short one to go from this place to the mouth of the Columbia river."

Newspapers throughout the nation picked up the *Gazette*'s account. Al-though no Oregon emigrant of the 1840s would so minimize the Blue Mountains, no newspaper reader of 1813 could doubt that a way had in-deed been found across the continent.[21]

But people forgot. A series of developments over the next few years caused Stuart and the knowledge he proclaimed to fade in the national consciousness. The idea of an easy pass over the Rockies did not die, but the pass Stuart had discovered had to be rediscovered. Ironically, the fate of John Jacob Astor's Pacific enterprise played no small part in dimming Stu-art's discovery in the national memory.

AT THE OUTSET, Astor's global aspirations gave high promise of success, both commercial and imperial. His men fastened a solid American pres-ence on the mouth of the Columbia River, critically strategic in both com-mercial and imperial terms. The North West Company's David Thompson, striving to sort out the complicated system of passes and rivers that would afford the British an overland passage to the Pacific, reached the mouth of the Columbia in July 1811, four months after the *Tonquin* had dropped an-chor and given birth to Astoria. Although Thompson lost the mouth of the Columbia to Astor, he had traced its course from the source, and his com-pany operated six inland posts that contested the river and its tributaries with the Astorians.[22]

In June 1812 the Nor'westers gained a decisive new weapon as the United States declared war on Great Britain. When the news reached the Columbia in January 1813, Astor's partners lost their nerve. Anticipating the appearance of a British warship, they sold the fort and all its contents to the North West Company. Most Astorians, who were Canadians anyway, hired on with the new owners. On December 12, 1813, Captain William Black of the Royal Navy presided over a ceremony in which the Union Jack ascended a flagstaff and Astoria became Fort George. Astoria and all sur-rounding territory, the captain proclaimed, now belonged to Great Britain by virtue of wartime conquest.[23]

Astoria signaled only one of several setbacks that sent the fur trade into decline. The Missouri Fur Company's encounters with the Blackfeet reverberated in St. Louis counting rooms, and the wartime intrusions of British traders on the upper Missouri and Mississippi raised further obstacles. Manuel Lisa retreated down the Missouri and took station for his remaining few years near the mouth of the Platte. National economic depression shrank capital and blunted initiative even in boisterous St. Louis.

Yet Astoria had not been a total ruin. By a strange twist of fate, Astor had left the United States with a firm imperial claim. The Treaty of Ghent, ending the War of 1812, provided for each nation to return such territory as it had seized from the other. Although Astor's lieutenants had sold Astoria to the North West Company, Captain Black had asserted British dominion over the Columbia Basin as a wartime conquest. Fort George's symbolic reversion to the United States in 1818, bereft of gain for Astor, restored Astoria's standing in the book of American claims to the Pacific Northwest.

Secretary of State John Quincy Adams made the most of Astoria. With Great Britain, he negotiated the Convention of 1818 fixing the northern limit of the Louisiana Purchase at the forty-ninth parallel as far as the crest of the Rocky Mountains. Beyond, the Oregon country remained in dispute, neither side willing to concede the other's idea of a proper boundary. To resolve the impasse, Oregon would be jointly occupied, open to the citizens of both nations, until another effort to be attempted in ten years.

While he dealt with Great Britain, Adams also dealt with Spain. In the Adams-Onís Treaty of 1819, the two nations agreed on the southern and western limits of the Louisiana Purchase and thus on the boundary separating the United States from New Spain. In this negotiation, Adams also persuaded Spain to relinquish her claims to the Pacific Northwest. That drew a line between Spain's western dominions, including California, that followed the forty-second parallel from the Continental Divide in the central Rockies to the Pacific Ocean. Within the next few years, moreover, Russia gave up her claims south of Alaska—south of the 54°40′ later to achieve renown as a political slogan.[24]

Oregon, therefore, extended from Alaska to California between the Continental Divide and the Pacific. Now only the United States and Great Britain contended for this enormous territory. Although neither yielded any concession on the negotiating table, both recognized that the truly disputed area lay between the forty-ninth parallel and the Columbia River. In the negotiations of 1818, the United States had been willing to settle for the former and Great Britain for the latter. In subsequent diplomacy, had either chosen to back down, the boundary could have been fixed on one of these lines. Meantime, "joint occupation" created a battleground in which the prizes, as in Astor's first conception, remained beaver and empire.[25]

"STRANGE INFATUATION!" Alexander Ross had marveled at the powerful spell beaver and mountains cast over Edward Robinson, John Hoback, and Jacob Reznor.[26] Joyously, they had greeted the accidental meeting with Robert Stuart on August 20, 1812. It afforded them the opportunity to put the dangerous wilderness behind them and go back to their Kentucky homes. Yet in only nine days Ross's "strange infatuation" asserted itself, and the three trappers parted with Stuart, again to test their fortunes in the wilderness that had repeatedly brutalized them.

As expected, in less than a month John Reed arrived at Caldron Linn to carry out what remained in the caches. The three trappers, busily engaged in taking beaver from the Snake, welcomed the Astorian leader and completed their outfit.

Reed's party included seven men whose adventures contributed more than their share of red ink to Astoria's ledgers. Reed had found them in a Shoshone village farther down the Snake. Four were refugees from Wilson Price Hunt's Overland Astorians who had got lost in the mountains the previous winter and had never reached Astoria. Three had fallen in with a band of Shoshones, worn out their welcome, and to restore it had led their Indian friends to the caches at Caldron Linn. Armed, equipped, and decorated from the riches uncovered, Shoshones and trappers crossed the mountains for a summer hunt on the buffalo plains. Here a Blackfeet war party burst into their camp, killed several, and sent the rest fleeing into the mountains. Indians and whites alike, deprived of horses, meat, and all their new possessions, straggled back to their Snake River homeland. There a fourth wasted overlander, lost in the mountains all winter, found the Shoshone camp.

The other three white men were also veterans of Hunt's expedition. With a fourth, they had been detached in Jackson Hole as the first of the trapping parties to remain inland. They completed a successful fall hunt, wintered in the mountains, and in the spring struck for the Missouri River, their packhorses laden with beaver pelts. Crow marauders blocked the way, killed one of the four, and left the other three afoot and impoverished. As ragged and destitute as their former comrades, they too took refuge with the Shoshones.[27]

The remaining contents of the caches retrieved, Reed and his party, with the survivors of Hunt's company, turned back down the Snake. Robinson, Hoback, and Reznor stayed behind, well equipped for a fall hunt and by now well acquainted with the best beaver streams of the Snake River country.

For nearly a year, from the autumn of 1812 to the autumn of 1813, the three Kentuckians successfully trapped the country they had come to know so well. Late in September 1813, near the mouth of the Boise River, they found a log house erected a month earlier by John Reed. He had been sent with eight men back to the Snake country to make his own hunt and to look for Robinson, Hoback, and Reznor. Instead, they found him. But again luck had deserted them. Two weeks earlier, Indians had robbed them of their beaver catch, horses, equipment, and nearly everything else.

The three trappers drew another outfit from Reed and joined his fall hunt. In addition, Reed's party consisted of the four trappers he had rescued the previous year and two hunters. One of the latter was the same Pierre Dorion who had served Hunt as interpreter in the overland crossing, and now as then he had with him his Iowa Indian wife and two children (one an infant, replacing one of the two who had journeyed with Hunt and later died). Two men dropped out during the autumn, one dead by syphilis, the other in a "moody fit" that sent him into the wilderness to vanish forever.[28]

Reed used his house at the confluence of the Snake and Boise Rivers as base for a fall and winter hunt. Robinson and Hoback worked out of here while Reznor accompanied Giles LeClerc and Pierre Dorion to a location several days' journey up the Boise River. Here they threw up a rude shelter. The two small parties trapped well into the winter.[29]

The Shoshone Indians in the vicinity proved friendly, but a militant band of "bad Snakes," the "Dog Ribs," bullied the Astorians. Early in January 1814, after Reed had erected another cabin across the river to avoid them, the Dog Ribs burned the first. Alerted by a friendly Indian, Dorion's wife (whose name unfortunately is lost to history) bundled her children and set out on horseback to find her husband.

Three days later, on a wintry morning, she approached the hut of her husband and his companions. "I observed a man coming from the opposite side," she recounted, "and staggering as if unwell: I stopped where I was till he came to me." The man was Giles LeClerc, wounded and bloody. That very morning, he said, Indians had fallen on the whites while working their traps. Her husband and Jacob Reznor had been slain; only LeClerc had escaped.

The Indian woman boosted LeClerc onto the horse with the infant and turned back toward Reed's base. Twice LeClerc fell off, and after being nursed for a full day he died in the night. Placing both children on the horse, she followed the path down the river to her destination.

There "sad was the sight! Mr. Reed and the men were all murdered, scalped, and cut to pieces. Desolation and horror stared me in the face."[30] There, dismembered, lay old Edward Robinson, veteran of Kentucky wars, and his inseparable companion John Hoback. Up the Boise River, in like condition, lay Jacob Reznor. The doomed trio had reached the end of the trail that would never take them to their Kentucky homes.

Packing on the horse such food as remained in the gutted cabin, Dorion's widow strapped her two children on top and plunged into the wilderness. With incredible perseverance, fortitude, endurance, and wilderness skill, she braved adversities that would have killed almost any Astorian. In three months she made her way across the snow-mantled Blue Mountains and down to the Columbia to find refuge among the Walla Walla Indians. There, in April 1814, Astorians listened in awe to the tale she recounted.

Edward Robinson, John Hoback, and Jacob Reznor left only a faint mark on history. Even before he succumbed to tomahawk and knife, however, Hoback's name identified a river that would assume importance as a link between the Green and Snake Rivers. Beyond that, they amassed a store of geographical knowledge surpassing that of every contemporary fur man. Through Wilson Price Hunt, they shared a little of it with the world. Through Robert Stuart, directly or indirectly by way of Joseph Miller, they may have communicated a little more. Like Colter and Drouillard, they developed the skills, instincts, habits, and daring mind-set of the mountain men soon to follow. Like Colter and Drouillard, their exploits rank them as precursors of the mountain man generation.

4

JEDEDIAH SMITH:
ATYPICAL MOUNTAIN MAN

N O MOUNTAIN MAN in his time held more potential for enriching the world's understanding of the North American West than Jedediah Strong Smith. What he did contribute formed only a tiny fraction of what his experience, purpose, intellect, and influential connections would have unveiled but for the untimely intervention of Comanche lances. In his eight years of mountaineering, he traveled across more unknown western wilderness than any contemporary. Driven by a resolve to make known his findings, moreover, he kept records and drew maps that clarified geography and related it to the history unfolding across its vast and varied expanse.

When Jedediah Smith appeared in St. Louis in 1822, the maps of the West still exhibited more fantasy than reality. They drew primarily on the Lewis and Clark map of 1814, Lieutenant Zebulon Pike's map of 1810, and an influential map published by Baron Alexander von Humboldt in 1808. In visits to New Spain, the great German scientist had tapped into the records of the Spanish explorers Francisco Domínguez and Silvestre Escalante, who in 1776 had journeyed northwest from Santa Fe seeking a route to California. Exhausting themselves in the canyon country of the Colorado River and the Wasatch rampart beyond, they turned back. Their journals and maps furnished Humboldt with both fact and error.

The cartographic West of 1822 still pictured the great rivers rising in close proximity to one another, although no longer in Pike's "grand reservoir of snows and fountains." West of a still-monolithic Rocky Mountain

For Jedediah Strong Smith, trapping was the means to fulfill his main interest, exploration. No man knew more of the American West than he. His travels throughout the Rockies and to California and Oregon gave him a "mental map" of the continent unmatched by anyone. He kept meticulous records and intended to share his findings with the world. His untimely death on the Sante Fe Trail in 1831, at the age of thirty-two, delayed for more than a decade what he would have revealed. COURTESY DENVER PUBLIC LIBRARY, WESTERN HISTORY DEPARTMENT.

range, the most recent maps, reflecting Humboldt and thus Escalante, showed a large lake named Timpanogos and several rivers draining to the Pacific Ocean. One was the Colorado of the West. Another (an inference of Lewis and Clark) was the Multnomah, a long watercourse paralleling the Snake and emptying into the Columbia near its mouth. Most intriguing, however, was the "Rio San Buenaventura," a great river that headed in the Rockies themselves and flowed all the way to San Francisco Bay. Here, far south of the trace of Lewis and Clark, was the old idea that had beguiled Thomas Jefferson and that refused to die: a "River of the West" that could float travelers from the crest of the Rockies to the Pacific Ocean.[1]

These and other distortions Jedediah Smith was to correct on the map that took shape in his mind over the next eight years. Some of his findings found their way into the public realm, but most of what he stood ready to reveal in 1831 his countrymen would not begin to learn for more than a decade.

Beaver made possible Jedediah Smith's exploratory achievements. His trapping ventures sustained his compilation of geographic and scientific data. He mastered the art of catching beaver as well as any mountain man, yet exploration remained his central interest. Indeed, his greatest feats of discovery taxed his business associates with unsurpassed cost in lives and dollars. Shortly before his death, he revealed his true priorities to a friend:

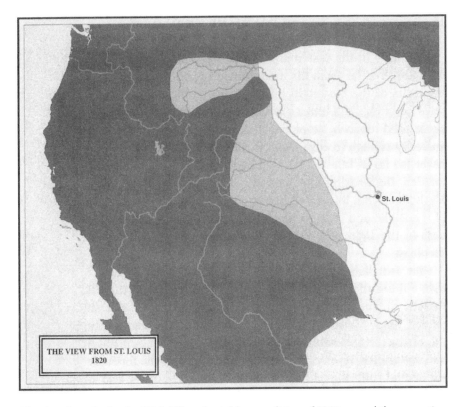

THE VIEW FROM ST. LOUIS
1820

The view from St. Louis, 1820. When the Ashley expedition of 1822 opened the generation of the Rocky Mountain trapper, St. Louis fur entrepreneurs held a reasonably accurate conception of the upper Missouri and the Great Plains as far as the base of the Rocky Mountains. Their ideas of the southern Plains derived from Zebulon Pike's expedition of 1806–07 and the efforts of traders such as Chouteau and de Mun to open trade with Spanish Santa Fe. Above the Mandan villages, St. Louisans knew in hazy outline the upper Missouri and the Yellowstone. Manuel Lisa's far-ranging men of 1807–11, notably John Colter, George Drouillard, and Andrew Henry, had brought back firsthand information, much of which had been laid down in distorted fashion on the Lewis and Clark map published in 1814. Men of the Northwest Company, soon to merge with and take the name of the Hudson's Bay Company, had traded and trapped the Columbia and Snake basins long enough to become familiar with them, but only the vaguest notion of this country had reached St. Louis as a result of the Astorian venture of 1811–14, and most of this had been forgotten. A sparse population of Spaniards occupied the Pacific Coast of California and Rio Grande Valley, but only a handful had even a sketchy knowledge of what lay between. Americans had none.

"I started into the mountains, with the determination of becoming a first-rate hunter, of making myself thoroughly acquainted with the character and habits of the Indians, of tracing out the sources of the Columbia river, and following it to its mouth; and of making the whole profitable to me, and I have perfectly succeeded."[2]

Not only in the systematic recording of his western travels did Jedediah Smith differ from his mountaineering comrades. Some of the defining traits of the mountain man culture he did not share. Drunken high jinks never counted him a participant. He almost never drank intoxicants, never used tobacco, never boasted, rarely indulged humor or relaxed his austerity enough to edge into the hilarious antics of his companions, and never (so far as known) crawled beneath the robes of a compliant Indian maiden. Dominating the character of this serious young man was a stern Methodism that immersed him in meditation, prayer, and constant study of the Bible, and that tormented him with an abiding sense of unworthiness in the sight of God. Few mountain men troubled themselves with theology.

Yet Jedediah Smith excelled in those essential aspects of mountain man culture that enabled him to survive and thrive in the wilderness and thereby to command the respect of his comrades. He not only, as he intended, made himself "a first-rate hunter" and "thoroughly acquainted with the character and habits of the Indians." He possessed physical strength and endurance, reservoirs of energy and courage, the fortitude to bear privation and suffering with good cheer, coolness in crisis, and all the wilderness skills of his craft, fortified by native intelligence and more than the usual formal education. Valuing these qualities, together with a demonstrated capacity for leadership, mountain men could tolerate his piety and other eccentricities.

Jedediah Smith's modesty left his youth only vaguely recoverable. After the American Revolution, his New England parents, seeking better lives, moved to the Susquehanna Valley of southern New York, where Jedediah was born on January 6, 1799. Like so many frontier families, the Smiths numbered a large progeny and endured a threadbare existence; and like so many, they succumbed to the lure of the West. From New York the Smiths skirted Lake Erie to a new home in Pennsylvania, then later pushed on to Ohio's Western Reserve. By 1821, Jedediah had left home and made his way to Illinois. By early 1822, he had landed in St. Louis—"a lean young fellow," in his biographer's words, "brown of hair and blue of eye, perhaps six feet tall, who talked with a self-possession that belied his twenty-three years."[3]

JEDEDIAH SMITH APPEARED in St. Louis at a propitious moment for westering ambitions. In the East and in Europe, rising fur prices registered rising demand. The effects of the Panic of 1819 had begun to wear off, unlocking capital to underwrite new fur enterprises in the West. Missouri had achieved statehood in 1820, and one of her new senators, Thomas Hart Benton, championed the cause of the fur companies.

The British figured importantly in the revival of the fur trade. Americans accused them of trading ventures and even trading posts in United States territory, and a determination to check such foreign affronts fired company and government officers alike. Protection of the fur trade and control of the Indians underlay Secretary of War John C. Calhoun's ambitious defense plan of 1818, which called for military posts extending from the Great Lakes to the upper Missouri. No one ever discovered a British trading post on American soil, or proved that the British incited Indians to attack Americans after the War of 1812 ended, but British influence could easily be observed. In 1821 the North West Company and Hudson's Bay Company had ended years of destructive rivalry by merging under the latter name. Reenergized, traders at posts on the Saskatchewan River regularly dealt with the Blackfeet.

To counter the British, in 1819 Secretary Calhoun sought to establish army garrisons on the upper Mississippi and the upper Missouri. On the Missouri, Colonel Henry Atkinson's drive for the mouth of the Yellowstone proved too ambitious, blunted by the breakdown of steamboats and other logistical failings. He settled for a post, Fort Atkinson, far down the Missouri at Council Bluffs, forty miles above the mouth of the Platte. Even so, the presence of troops facing the British from the edge of the Indian country gave heart to St. Louis entrepreneurs.[4]

On another front, a British challenge also arose. The Convention of 1818, fixing the boundary on the forty-ninth parallel as far as the Continental Divide, opened Oregon to joint occupation. Since the collapse of Astoria in 1814, however, the British had roamed unopposed throughout Oregon. Hudson's Bay trading posts commanded the Columbia Basin. St. Louis magnates, forgetting their rout by the Blackfeet a decade earlier, resolved to push up the Missouri to the Three Forks and across the Rockies into Oregon. Financial as well as imperial motives urged that the British not be allowed to take Oregon's beaver without competition.

Another development, sudden and unexpected, energized St. Louis financial circles. In 1821 Mexico threw off the rule of Spain, and wide-ranging Missourians discovered a warm welcome in Santa Fe. Previous initiatives had dashed against belligerent isolationism, as Spanish officials threw American intruders into jail and confiscated their possessions. Now Mexican authorities opened the New Mexican capital to commerce, and Missourians pioneered the Santa Fe Trail. Although Missouri mules and Mexican specie dominated the exchange, many who made their way across the plains sought instead the furs of the Mexican mountains.

Against this backdrop, St. Louis hummed with what newspaper editors delighted in labeling "enterprise." Four well-financed and well-organized companies prepared to exploit the upper Missouri. In 1821 Manuel Lisa's Missouri Fur Company, reorganized after his death a year earlier and led by the dynamic Joshua Pilcher, planted Cedar Fort (or Fort Recovery) on the Missouri above the mouth of the White River, and another, Fort Vanderburgh, at the Mandan villages. From these bases, a party under Robert Jones and Michael Immell headed for the Yellowstone and built Fort Benton in Crow country near the site of Lisa's old fort at the mouth of the Bighorn. The "French Fur Company"—Berthold, Pratte and Chouteau—managed to get their base, Fort Kiowa (or Lookout), established near Cedar Fort in the autumn of 1822. A third firm, the Columbia Fur Company, reached for the Mandan villages overland from the Mississippi. The driving forces of this outfit were Kenneth McKenzie and other former Nor'westers who had cut their British moorings and associated themselves with men of less vigor and vision but possessed of the requisite United States citizenship.[5]

The fourth firm united the names of William H. Ashley and Andrew Henry. Ashley, lieutenant governor of Missouri and brigadier general of the state militia, teamed up with the veteran Andrew Henry to exploit the Three Forks country from which Henry had been driven by Blackfeet a decade earlier. Their advertisement published in St. Louis newspapers in March 1822 invited one hundred "enterprising young men" to apply for employment in an expedition to the sources of the Missouri River.[6]

Reaching St. Louis in the early spring of 1822, Jedediah Smith heard of the Ashley-Henry venture. "I called on Genl Ashley to make an engagement to go with him as a hunter," Smith recalled. "I found no difficulty in making a bargain on as good terms as I had reason to expect."[7]

JEDEDIAH SMITH HAD CAST his lot with a remarkable band of adventurers. Eastern newspapers described them as "the yeomanry of Missouri," "of vigorous and masculine appearance, well armed and prepared for a three years' tour" expected to lead across the Rockies and down the Columbia to the ocean.[8] Among his companions were at least three names that would resonate in western history: Mike Fink, David E. Jackson, and James Bridger.

Legendary riverman on the Ohio and Mississippi, Mike Fink belonged to an earlier time and place and would not live to become a mountain man. Jackson and Bridger, however, would reach the top.

At thirty-four, David Jackson was older than most of the Ashley men, twice the age of Bridger. A Virginian, veteran of the War of 1812, Jackson had migrated to Missouri and failed to prosper in any of the trades he attempted. He was a quiet man, stubborn in his convictions, and by 1822 he was ready to gamble on the opportunities Ashley held forth.[9]

Hardly out of adolescence, Jim Bridger got a fast start with Ashley. Years later a friend described him as "a very companionable man. In person he was over six feet tall, spare, straight as an arrow, agile, rawboned and of powerful frame, eyes gray, hair brown and abundant even in old age, expression mild and manners agreeable. He was hospitable and generous, and was always trusted and respected." At seventeen, his wilderness skills remained to be honed, but he rose swiftly and took rank with the most accomplished of trappers and explorers.[10]

These "Ashley men" had enlisted in an undertaking founded on two unusual precepts. First, while not averse to trading with the Indians for furs, they went primarily to hunt and trap themselves. As early as 1807–10, Manuel Lisa and Andrew Henry himself had recognized that Indians could not be depended on for a steady flow of furs in paying quantities. Already, Joshua Pilcher's Missouri Fur Company had Immell and Jones on the Yellowstone trapping rather than trading. From a base at the mouth of the Yellowstone, Ashley and Henry intended to reach up the Missouri to the Three Forks in a like operation.

The distinction between trading and trapping presented legal difficulties. Like their competitors, Ashley and Henry obtained the federal trading license required by law, even though they intended to trap rather than trade. The Superintendent of Indian Affairs in St. Louis undoubtedly understood the difference but chose to overlook it; he was William Clark of Lewis and Clark renown. The western military commander, General Henry Atkinson, and the Indian agent for the upper Missouri, Benjamin O'Fallon, also knew the difference. They resolved the conflict by perceiving no "impropriety" in trapping the territory of Indians not yet brought under federal jurisdiction, especially when considered pawns of the British. All Indians above the Mandans fit this definition. O'Fallon cautioned, however, that once formal relations had been established with those tribes, hunting and trapping of animals properly belonging to them should be banned. Ever the legalist, Secretary of War Calhoun lectured Clark on the law. Ever the pragmatist and sympathetic with the fur men, Clark deftly sidestepped the issue. The Blackfeet understood the distinction perfectly, and they did not sidestep the issue.[11]

The second precept of the Ashley-Henry operation centered on the terms of engagement that Smith found a good bargain. The only *engagés*, fully salaried men, were clerks and boatmen. Smith and his companions bound themselves, in exchange for arms, equipment, and other supplies, to turn over to the company half the yield from their rifles and traps and part with the other half at prevailing prices. Their only other obligation was to help build and defend their fort. Although Ashley and Henry had to deal with the problem of discipline and subordination, their innovation swiftly evolved into the free trapper of mountain man fame.[12]

Under Andrew Henry, the first contingent of the expedition, a keelboat and 150 men, part traveling by land, got under way from St. Louis on April 3, 1822. Schooled on the Three Forks and the Snake in 1810–11, Henry would serve as field captain. Bankrolling the venture, Ashley meant to remain in St. Louis and handle the company's business affairs. The second boat, laden with supplies and with Smith ranging inland as hunter, sailed on May 8. Below the frontier station of Fort Osage, its mast tangled in an overhanging tree branch and spun the vessel broadside to the current. With ten thousand dollars' worth of cargo, it capsized and plunged to the bottom. Undaunted, by late June Ashley had another boat loaded and started up the river under his personal command. Smith went along.[13]

Engagé boatmen inched the keelboat against the Missouri's swift current with large oars fixed to the cargo box, or with poles seated in their shoulder sockets as they walked running boards the length of both sides, or with long cables run from mast to shore and towed along a muddy bank overgrown with trees and brush and swarming with insects. Sometimes, when the wind blew favorably, the sail afforded respite though not speed. Past Council Bluffs and Fort Atkinson, past the Missouri Fur Company's Cedar Fort, through the rolling plains country of the Sioux, the vessel made its way up the Missouri. On September 8 it reached the earthen, palisaded Arikara towns above the mouth of the Grand River. Here Hunt's Astorians had obtained horses in 1811, and here Ashley bargained for horses with the Indian leaders. He knew Henry would need more horses, and he wanted to cut loose from the slow-moving boat and hasten by land to the mouth of the Yellowstone.

When the Ashley party, including Smith, reached their destination on October 1, Henry and his men had already thrown up a crude log fort, four structures connected by pickets to enclose an interior corral. It stood on a tongue of land on the south bank of the Missouri, with the mouth of the Yellowstone a quarter of a mile to the east. And Henry did indeed want horses. On the journey up the Missouri, Assiniboines had run off twenty-four of his own.[14]

Ashley and Henry plotted strategy. By the time the keelboat arrived two weeks later, they had mapped a winter movement toward the fur country and arranged for Ashley to return with more men and supplies in the spring of 1823. With the boatmen and the few furs Henry's men had accumulated, Ashley headed his keelboat back down the Missouri and reached St. Louis a month later.[15]

As soon as Ashley had left, Henry sent out two advance parties to conduct a fall hunt and prepare for a spring thrust deeper into the fur country. One, under John H. Weber (pronounced *Weeber*), ascended the Yellowstone and turned up the Powder. The other Henry himself stationed higher on the Missouri, at the mouth of the Musselshell, then returned to his base for the winter. Smith passed the winter of 1822–23 at the Musselshell base.[16]

On April 4, 1823, the ice broke up in the Missouri River, freeing the men at the Musselshell to push on up the river for the spring hunt. Not all went; as free trappers they could do as they pleased, and some embarked downstream instead. Smith may have gone down with these men, or he may have traveled with the trappers for a week until an accidental discharge of a rifle sent a ramrod through both of Daniel Potts's knees. He had to be taken down to Henry's Fort, and Smith may have taken him.[17]

Among those who had returned to Henry's Fort after wintering on the Musselshell were Mike Fink and his inseparable companions, Carpenter and Talbot. They had boated and caroused together before enlisting with Ashley and had added another madcap antic to their vast store. In turn, at seventy paces, they shot tin cups of whiskey from the heads of one another. During the winter, however, Fink and Carpenter fell to quarreling over a woman in their past. At Henry's Fort, it erupted again. Fink challenged Carpenter to their favorite sport. Carpenter sensed what Fink intended but stepped forward anyway, cup of whiskey on his head. Fink paced off the distance, raised his rifle, and fired. The ball smashed Carpenter in the center of his forehead. "Carpenter," Fink chided, "you have spilled the whiskey." Enraged, Talbot drew his pistol and shot Fink in the heart. The "half horse half alligator" would never leave his fabulous footprint on the Rocky Mountains.[18]

Meantime, eleven men composed the trapping party working its way from the Musselshell up the Missouri in dugout canoes. The farther they went, the deeper they penetrated dangerous country. In the decade since the Blackfeet had driven Henry from the Three Forks, nothing had lessened their malice toward Americans. On May 4, near the mouth of Smith's River above the Great Falls, they struck, slaying four men. The rest, burying 172 steel traps and abandoning 30 more set in the river, fled the country as precipitately as had Henry in 1810.[19]

Henry's trappers were not the only ones to discover anew the intensity of Blackfeet animosity. The Missouri Fur Company's Immell and Jones, trapping up the Jefferson River, encountered Blackfeet and made a dash for the safety of Crow country. On May 31, in a narrow gorge of the Yellowstone River near the mouth of Pryor's Fork, they rode into a Blackfeet ambush. Advancing single file and much strung out, the twenty-nine trappers fell easy prey to warriors pouring down the steep slopes. Immell, Jones, and five others died at once, and four men were wounded. The survivors abandoned everything and dove into the Yellowstone to make their escape. Horses, beaver, traps, and all else, valued at more than twelve thousand dollars, fell to the Blackfeet.[20]

These twin disasters near the sources of the Missouri held grave implications for the plans of both fur companies. Blackfeet hostility raised an enormous obstacle to any attempt at exploiting the prime beaver country of the Three Forks. Secure in his fort at the mouth of the Yellowstone, however, Henry had yet to recognize what his own experience should have forecast.

Instead, he worried about horses. To mount the expeditions for which Ashley was even then bringing men and supplies up the Missouri, Henry had to have more horses. The Crows declined to sell, and that left the Arikaras as the best source. Henry selected Jedediah Smith to carry word to Ashley. Sometime in early spring, shortly after he returned from upriver, Smith launched himself in a dugout to boat down the Missouri.[21]

AGAIN, in St. Louis newspaper advertisements during the first three months of 1823, William H. Ashley sought one hundred men to go up the Missouri to the Rockies as hunters. This year, however, his hunters would sign on as engagés, their salary fixed at two hundred dollars a year. Even so, Ashley had laid the groundwork for the free trapper, and before he withdrew from the mountains the institution would reach full flower.[22]

In competence, these new Ashley men fell short of last year's company. Abandoning the incentive of free trapping, Ashley found it hard to compete in a St. Louis labor market limited by the demands of three other fur companies and the growing Santa Fe trade. Even so, the list included more names destined for fame: William Sublette, Thomas Fitzpatrick, James Clyman, Hugh Glass, and Moses Harris, among others. The ubiquitous Edward Rose joined at the Arikara villages. These Ashley men, whose names would recur through history, were all young, in their early twenties, slender, lithe, physically strong, accomplished outdoorsmen, intelligent, courageous, and with marked potential for leadership.

Men to power the two keelboats, *Yellow Stone Packet* and *Rocky Mountains*, posed a difficult problem. Ashley commissioned James Clyman to recruit them. Tall, rawboned Clyman was reticent and withdrawn but as brave, sagacious, and decisive as any of Ashley's men. Of literary bent, he read Shakespeare, Byron, and the Bible, and he wrote copiously—diary, observations, recollections—in a crude but expressive orthography. To carry out his assignment, Clyman scoured the "grog Shops and other sinks of degredation" and came up with a crew of French Canadian voyageurs and "some St. Louis gumboes." Of the expedition that shoved off from St. Louis on March 10, 1823, Clyman recalled: "A discription of our crew I cannt give but Fallstafs Battallion was genteel in comparison."[23]

Taking on Jedediah Smith on the way up the Missouri, on May 30 the keelboats dropped anchor in midstream opposite the Arikara towns. Unlike the usually complaisant Mandans, the Arikaras had a record of capriciousness, friendly and cooperative on some occasions, ugly and lethal on others. Their earth lodges, palisaded against attacks by the enemy Sioux, clustered in two towns, separated by a ravine, on the west bank of the Missouri above the mouth of the Grand River. They cultivated nearby fields of corn, melons, and other crops and ranged the plains as horse-mounted buffalo hunters. Ashley approached them cautiously because a recent altercation with the Missouri Fur Company at Cedar Fort had cost them two young men and left their hearts black toward Americans.

On a sand beach at the foot of the lower town, Ashley parleyed with two chiefs, Edward Rose interpreting. They said they felt bad over the killing of their two warriors but did not blame Ashley. They stood ready to open trade for the horses Ashley needed. On May 31, ferrying trade goods to the beach by skiff, Ashley's men began the exchange. Interrupted by a severe storm, the bargaining finally concluded on the evening of June 1 with the acquisition of nineteen horses. With forty men, Ashley intended to take these animals overland to Henry's Fort, and the men set up camp on the beach to guard the stock and prepare for the journey. Because of his experience, Smith may have been given charge of the beach party.[24]

After midnight, Rose brought Ashley word that several of the beach party had entered the village—Arikara women had always aroused the masculinity of white visitors. One, Aaron Stephens, had been killed, "and war was declared in earnest." For the rest of the night, the forty men ashore lay on their arms while, in Clyman's words, "their was a continual Hubbub in the village."[25]

At first light, from behind the pickets shielding the town, the Indians opened fire with "London fuzils." The whites fired back with rifles, but could see almost nothing at which to take aim. As the balls flew, Ashley ordered the keelboats to weigh anchor and take off his men. "The boatsmen could not be made to touch an oar," recalled one who watched their panic, even though the distance was only thirty yards. Ashley got the two skiffs under way, but the fire cut down the oarsmen before they could reach the shore. Seven men, three of them wounded, swam to the skiffs before they drifted downstream. Outgunned and with no protection but rearing or downed horses, men and animals dropped swiftly. Within fifteen minutes, the dead sprawled among the carcasses of the horses, and the living were swimming to the safety of the boats.[26]

The disaster cost Ashley fifteen killed and another nine wounded, besides a crippling blow to his plans. Ridiculing the boatmen for their cowardice, he pointed with pride to the behavior of the shore party. "Never in my opinion did men act with more coolness and bravery than the most of those exposed on the sand beach," he declared. Apparently none rivaled Jedediah Smith in this, his first test of combat. "When his party was in danger, Mr. Smith was always among the foremost to meet it, and the last to fly," recalled a survivor of the bloodbath; "those who saw him on shore, at the Riccaree fight, in 1823, can attest to the truth of this assertion."[27]

Putting ashore at the first timber downstream, Ashley made plans to regroup, run the gauntlet, and push on to Henry's Fort. His demoralized boatmen would have none of it. Faced with mass desertion, he called for volunteers to stick by him until help could be summoned from Henry. Thirty, including only a few boatmen, stepped forward. Ashley selected Jedediah Smith and a French Canadian to bear the message.[28]

Before departing, Smith performed a final function, as related in a letter written by Hugh Glass to the parents of one of the slain, John Gardner: "We brought him to the ship where he soon died. Mr Smith a young man of our company made a powerful prayr wh[ich] moved us all greatly and I am persuaded John died in peace."[29]

WHILE JEDEDIAH SMITH and his companion made their way by foot northwest across the eastward-flowing tributaries of the Missouri River, Ashley floated down the river. By June 7 he had set up a new base on an island near the mouth of the Cheyenne River, seventy-five miles below the Arikara villages, and vowed to retreat no farther. Counting only twenty-three loyal stalwarts, however, he decided to send the larger of the two keelboats, *Yellow Stone Packet*, down to Fort Atkinson with forty-three deserters and five wounded.[30]

Ashley's keelboat tied up at Council Bluffs on June 18, bearing among its papers his letter of June 4 to Indian Agent Benjamin O'Fallon and Fort

Atkinson's commander, Colonel Henry Leavenworth. It outraged those officials and moved them to hasten to Ashley's aid. The letter also angered the Missouri Fur Company's Joshua Pilcher, who looked on Ashley's appeal as a welcome pretext for punishing the Arikaras and sending an unmistakable message to all the tribes up the river, especially the Blackfeet. Within two days, one of Pilcher's men was on his way with a reply from O'Fallon. Already, wrote the emotionally verbose agent, Leavenworth was readying his command to hurry up the river, determined to avenge "your brave men, who fell victims to the Sculping knife of the inhuman A'rickarars." This would be no "mere exhibition of soldiers." "The blood of the *A'rickarars* must run from many vital veins or the laudable enterprise of American Citizens is at once arrested, and the fur trade of the upper Missouri is suspended for a long time."[31]

Meanwhile, far to the north, Jedediah Smith completed his mission and delivered Ashley's message to Andrew Henry. Leaving twenty men to defend the fort, Henry loaded fifty in dugouts and launched them on the Missouri. As the little flotilla approached the Arikara villages, Indians swarmed on the shore and signaled the whites to land. Henry ignored them and passed without drawing fire. He joined his partner at the mouth of the Cheyenne sometime during the first week in July.[32]

Despairing of timely relief, Ashley and Henry decided to move farther down the Missouri to discover whether horses could be obtained from the Sioux. Under Henry, the main force camped at the mouth of the Teton (or Bad) River while Ashley continued to the French Fur Company's post of Fort Kiowa. Here he learned of the approach of the Leavenworth expedition and happily turned back to rejoin Henry.[33]

When finally assembled on July 30 at Ashley's camp at the mouth of the Teton River, Colonel Leavenworth's "Missouri Legion" presented an imposing force, more than capable of dealing a deadly blow to the Arikaras. In addition to his 230 infantrymen, bolstered by artillery, Leavenworth counted 40 of Pilcher's fur men and 80 of Ashley's. The Ashley men were divided into two companies, one captained by Jedediah Smith, the other by Hiram Scott (whose name would one day be immortalized in a Platte River landmark, Scotts Bluff). Edward Rose received a designation as ensign, Thomas Fitzpatrick as quartermaster, and William Sublette as sergeant major. More than trebling the size of the legion, 750 mounted Sioux warriors joined.[34]

Jedediah Smith's selection to command one of the companies testified to the confidence he had won from Ashley and Henry. As captain, however, he found little opportunity to demonstrate his leadership, for the Leavenworth expedition turned into a fiasco. Advancing by both land and water, on August 9 the Missouri Legion closed on the Arikara towns. Galloping far to the front, the Sioux clashed with mounted Arikaras in the open valley below the lower town, felled about fifteen, and drove the rest back to their stockade. Jim Clyman thought the spectacle resembled a swarm of bees more than a battle.

Thereafter, Leavenworth proved incapable of making a decision and carrying it out. Artillery bombardment inflicted little damage on the earthen town. For two days, regulars and fur men moved here and there preparing to execute orders that the colonel invariably canceled. Disgusted, the Sioux went off to plunder the Arikara cornfields and soon withdrew altogether, taking with them six army mules and seven of Ashley's horses. Disgusted themselves, both army officers and fur men watched with rising fury as Leavenworth met with the Arikara chiefs, smoked the peace pipe, and opened negotiations. He himself wrote out a treaty restoring peace on condition that the Indians behave in the future and return the property Ashley's men left on the sandbar after the fight of June 2. The chiefs promised good behavior but could not find Ashley's property. Finally, ingloriously ending Leavenworth's two days of indecision, on the night of August 13 the Indians quietly abandoned both towns and fled. As the Missouri Legion began its withdrawal on August 15, smoke roiled skyward in the rear. Correctly suspecting some of Pilcher's men of firing the Arikara towns, Leavenworth reacted with his own fury, setting off a war of words between the two men that reverberated for months in Missouri and eastern newspapers.[35]

Colonel Leavenworth pronounced the operation a huge success: "The blood of our countrymen has been honorably avenged, the Aurickarees humbled, and in such manner as will teach them and the [other] Indian tribes to respect the American name and character." Hardly anyone who was there agreed, including the Sioux, who thirty years later still voiced contempt for white soldiers.[36]

BACK AT FORT KIOWA in late August, Ashley and Henry faced financial ruin. During the march upriver, they had learned of the disaster to their party above the Great Falls and the even greater disaster to the Missouri Fur Company's Immell and Jones on the Yellowstone. Plainly, the Blackfeet intended to deny their beaver streams to white trappers. Now, equally plainly, the Arikaras could be counted on to obstruct the Missouri River gateway to the Blackfeet country. The Three Forks area, the prime objective of Ashley and Henry as well as Pilcher's Missouri Fur Company, suddenly lost much of its appeal.

Before the advent of steamboats in 1832, beaver pelts and buffalo robes gathered at Fort Union and other upper Missouri posts were floated down to St. Louis in Mackinaw boats. Beginning with Ashley's clash with the Arikaras in 1823, the fur vessels risked attack from Arikaras or Sioux. W. M. Cary sketched this scene. COURTESY DENVER PUBLIC LIBRARY, WESTERN HISTORY DEPARTMENT.

Before learning of the Leavenworth expedition, Ashley had reflected on alternatives. Beyond the Continental Divide, the Columbia still beckoned. In a land filled with unnavigable or unpredictable watercourses, moreover, horses seemed a better mode of transportation than boats. Finally, nearly ten years later, St. Louis citizens still had vague memories of Robert Stuart's "southern pass." Such thoughts had prompted Ashley's trip down the river to Fort Kiowa in July to see if horses could be obtained from the Sioux. There word of Leavenworth's approach with a punitive force had diverted Ashley from this purpose and hastened him back upriver.[37]

In the wake of Leavenworth's blunders, Ashley and Henry had to rethink strategy. If they could get enough horses, they decided, they would abandon the river and seek new beaver tracts south of the Blackfeet country. As soon as horses could be obtained from the Sioux, Henry would return to the mouth of the Yellowstone, traveling overland and bypassing the Arikaras, who were correctly assumed to have moved in with the Mandans. From Henry's Fort, he would push up the Yellowstone and exploit its southern tributaries in the less dangerous country of the Crows. Meantime, Ashley would launch another party directly west from Fort Kiowa, eventually to link up with Henry's men in the Crow country beyond the Bighorn Mountains.

To captain this trek across a land still imperfectly known, Ashley chose Jedediah Smith.

5

JEDEDIAH SMITH: SOUTH PASS
AND THE SISKADEE

J EDEDIAH SMITH STRUCK WEST from Fort Kiowa late in September 1823. His little company numbered sixteen, most with bonds forged on the sand beach.[1] Among them were Bill Sublette, Tom Fitzpatrick, Jim Clyman, and Thomas Eddie. With their objective the heart of Crow country, Smith also included Edward Rose. Even though "a designing vagabond" (in Washington Irving's words), Rose enjoyed high stature among the Crows, with whom he had lived off and on since 1807.[2]

Since Ashley had failed to buy enough horses from the Sioux, the French Fur Company lent some, together with a guide to get the expedition started. The horses served as pack animals. The men walked.[3]

The first days were hard—the land dry and dusty and carpeted with prickly pear, the White River a source of chalky water drinkable only with severe next-day consequences. Nearing the eastern foot of the Black Hills, however, the men found good water and, better yet, a band of Sioux that provided a few horses to replace those borrowed from the French Fur Company. With the borrowed horses, the guide turned back to Fort Kiowa.

Buffalo Gap opened the way to the Black Hills, and Smith and his men were the first known whites to penetrate these dark highlands. After threading the ridges and canyons along the southern edge of the hills, the trappers descended to the furrowed grasslands of the Powder River basin. Approaching the Crow homeland, horses giving out, Smith sent Rose ahead to bargain for fresh horses.

Five days later the expedition nearly lost its captain. Leading the exhausted horses single file through a brushy bottom, the men spotted a big grizzly bear charging down a slope toward the center of the line. The beast turned and raced to the head of the column just as Smith emerged from a thicket. Instantly the bear pounced, seizing him and throwing him to the ground, smashing several ribs, and clawing his head.

None of the trappers claimed medical skills. But Smith directed one or two men to go for water and said, as Clyman wrote, "If you have a needle and thread git it out and sew up my wounds around my head." It bled copiously, for the scalp had been torn nearly off and hung only by an ear. Clyman found a needle and thread, "got a pair of scissors and cut off his hair and then began my first Job of dressing wounds." He got the scalp sewed back on, but said there was nothing to be done for the ear. Smith insisted that Clyman try. He did. "I put my needle stiching it through and through and over and over laying the lacerated parts together as nice as I could with my hands." Within two weeks, Smith had recovered sufficiently to resume his captaincy, although he bore scars for the rest of his life. "This gave us a lisson on the charcter of the grissly Baare which we did not forget," observed Clyman.[4]

The party obtained fresh horses from a band of Cheyennes, and almost immediately Rose appeared with some Crows and more horses. Striking northwest across the branches of the Powder, the horsemen cut the Tongue River and ascended one of its feeders into the Bighorn Mountains. They reached the other side by a route north of that followed by Hunt's Astorians in 1811, and after angling southwest across the Bighorn Basin they worked their way over the Owl Creek Range and dropped to the Wind River. Here, where mountains converged from north and south to narrow the upper valley, lay country explored by John Colter in 1807–08 and twice trod by Robinson, Hoback, and Reznor in 1811.[5]

A winter village of Crow Indians welcomed Smith and his men with a cordiality reflecting the exalted status of Edward Rose. Such was his influence that they found themselves entirely at his mercy. Only through him could they communicate, and only on his word, dosed with liberal gifts from the meager stock of trade goods, would the Indians cooperate. As snows fell on the Wind River and Absaroka Ranges in November 1823, Smith and Fitzpatrick pondered a means of breaking free.

BOUND OVERLAND from Fort Kiowa to Henry's Fort at the mouth of the Yellowstone, Andrew Henry encountered mishaps rivaling Smith's. Mandans, usually the friendliest of Indians toward whites, mistook Henry's party for enemy tribesmen and fired into his camp in the dark of night, killing two men and wounding two more. They also made off with two horses. Later the chagrined Mandan chiefs apologized profusely. Arriving at his fort, moreover, Henry discovered that Assiniboines or Blackfeet had stolen more than twenty of his horses, and shortly afterward he lost another seven.[6]

But the worst setback of Henry's September march occurred on the Grand River, after the company had turned west from the Missouri to give wide berth to the Arikaras. Hugh Glass encountered a grizzly sow even more ferocious than the bear that mauled Jedediah Smith.

With a background possibly nautical and even piratical, Hugh Glass had come to the frontier by way of a Pawnee village where he learned wilderness skills. His exploits justified the appraisal of one who trapped with him: "In point of adventures dangers & narrow escapes & capacity for endurance, & the sufferings which befel him, this man was preeminent— He was bold, daring, reckless & eccentric to a high degree; but was nevertheless a man of great talents & intellectual as well as bodily power—But his bravery was conspicuous beyond all his other qualities for the perilous life he led."[7]

Proceeding apart from the column as his defiant independence usually dictated, Glass and another man, Moses "Black" Harris, entered a thicket and surprised a grizzly sow and her cubs. The bear reared on her hind feet to attack as Glass sent a rifle ball into her chest. The wound proved fatal, but not quickly enough. As Glass clambered up a tree, she seized him and threw him to the ground, lacerating him from head to foot with two swipes of the razorlike talons of her paws. Pursued by one of the yearling cubs, Harris ran from the thicket, then turned and brought down the smaller animal. Henry's men raced to the scene. The sow sprawled dead atop Glass. They pulled off the carcass. He lay on his back, bleeding from gashes in his scalp, face, chest, back, shoulder, arm, hand, and thigh. With each gasp, blood bubbled from a puncture in his throat. As Daniel Potts remarked, Hugh Glass had been "tore nearly to peases."

He should have been dead by now. The men bandaged his wounds but could do little else. By the next morning he still had not died. Henry could tarry no longer. At any moment he could encounter Arikaras. Fashioning a crude litter, the men hoisted Glass on their shoulders and resumed the march. They made agonizingly slow progress. Finally, after several days, Henry resolved that he could no longer risk the entire party for a man certain to die. He offered an enticing sum to anyone who would volunteer to stay behind and care for Glass until he died. John S. Fitzgerald and nineteen-year-old Jim Bridger stepped forward.[8]

Shortly after Henry reached his fort, Fitzgerald and Bridger came in with Glass's rifle and other possessions and reported him dead and buried. He was not. Though feverish and prostrated, he burned with a will to live and seek vengeance on the men who had abandoned him. He could not walk, but he could crawl. Berries and a torpid rattlesnake smashed with a stone provided his first nourishment. The Grand River supplied water. He dug edible roots with a sharp rock. Chance turned up a dead buffalo with marrow still rich in the bones. Later wolves brought down a buffalo calf that he succeeded in seizing. In a six-week demonstration of incredible strength, fortitude, luck, and determination, Glass crawled back to Fort Kiowa, nearly two hundred miles. He then set forth to track down those who had deserted him.

While Glass labored up the Missouri, Henry abandoned his post at the mouth of the Yellowstone, the scene of unrelieved misfortune, and moved his company up the Yellowstone to the mouth of the Powder. Here, barred by rapids from further progress by boat, he took to land. Acquiring forty-seven horses from Crow Indians, he dispatched a party under John H. Weber, one of his captains of 1822, to trap up the Powder and across to the Bighorn. With the balance of the company, he continued up the Yellowstone and began building a post at the mouth of the Bighorn, near Manuel Lisa's establishment of 1807–08.

Even in Crow and Assiniboine country, the Blackfeet kept watch on Americans. No sooner had Henry vacated his fort at the mouth of the Yellowstone than a Blackfeet war party dropped by to investigate. Nearby they found the graves of Mike Fink and his erstwhile pal Carpenter. "According to their usual barbarity," recorded a British trader to whom the Blackfeet told the story, "they commenced to open the graves in order to strip the bodies of whatever clothes might be wrapped around them, but finding that they were in putrid state, they left them without offering further molestation."[9]

As the new Henry's Fort took shape, Hugh Glass showed up, stunning his former comrades and intent on revenge. Fitzgerald had left, in fact had passed Glass on the Missouri as he ascended. Jim Bridger was there, though, and Glass confronted him, only to forswear vengeance on one so young and inexperienced. The older Fitzgerald enjoyed no such exemption. Glass would bide his time.

Meanwhile, the momentum behind the overland thrust of the fur business flowed not from Andrew Henry's new fort but from the winter camp of the Crow Indians in the mountain-sheltered upper valley of the Wind River. Here were Smith, Fitzpatrick, and their companions. Here was a Missouri Fur Company group under Charles Keemle and William Gordon that had followed on Smith's trail. Here finally were John H. Weber's party detached by Henry at the mouth of the Powder. They had trapped over the Bighorn Mountains and up the Wind River to join the growing assembly of whites enjoying the hospitality of the Crows.

Winter cold and Crow warmth encouraged a long stay, but all had come in search of new beaver grounds, and besides all felt themselves captive to the devious purposes of Edward Rose. As Keemle recalled, "he alone understood their language, and, of course, could tell them any and every thing he pleased. . . . His word was law, and he well knew how to give it an elevated tone. Nothing could be done without 'Chee-ho-carte.'" For the restless Smith, his uncompleted mission combined with the power of Rose to urge a move even as winter gripped the land.[10]

JEDEDIAH SMITH'S TRAPPING AMBITIONS were not bounded by the Crow country. Ashley wanted to investigate the headwaters of the Columbia. They lay less than fifty miles west of the Crow village, where creeks rose that fed the Snake and ultimately the Columbia. But the Crows told of a still richer beaver ground west of the mountains, not on any part of the Columbia system but on a south-trending river they called the Siskadee Agie, the Prairie-Chicken River. This was the "Spanish River" of the Astorians, the Rio Verde or Green of the Spaniards—a river that emptied into the Gulf of California. On the Siskadee, the Crows averred, the whites would find so many beaver they need not set traps. The animals could simply be clubbed.[11]

As Robinson, Hoback, and Reznor had shown the Astorians in 1811, the upper Green could be reached from the upper Wind by an Indian trail across Union Pass, the high meadow separating the Wind River and Gros Ventre Ranges. In February 1824, Smith and his party attempted to break through the snows that buried Union Pass. They failed, and had to turn back to the Crow village.

Next the Ashley men plumbed the geographical knowledge of the Crows with the same technique Lewis and Clark had found effective. "I spread out a buffalo robe and covered it with sand," recalled Clyman, "and made it in heaps to represent the different mountains." Tracing in the sand, the Crows communicated that the southeastern end of the Wind River Mountains could be rounded by way of a tributary of the Wind River they called Popo Agie. The upper course of this stream gave access to a larger river, the Sweetwater, whose head in turn would point the trappers down to the Siskadee. Leaving the Weber and Keemle-Gordon parties to deal with the Crows as best they could through Edward Rose, Smith and his followers began skirting the tip of the Wind River Range.[12]

Swiss artist Karl Bodmer accompanied the German prince Maximilian on a tour of the upper Missouri in 1833–34. The voyage up the Missouri from Fort Union took them from the rolling plains to the base of the mountains. Bodmer painted this View of the Rocky Mountains *as well as other alpine landscapes.* COURTESY JOSLYN ART MUSEUM, OMAHA, NEBRASKA.

In midwinter the Popo Agie and Sweetwater offered a dismaying field of exploration. Temperatures plunged, and snow-laden north winds blew like a "hericane," so hard that even when fires could be kindled they swept away. Buffalo and mountain sheep provided meat, but it could seldom be cooked for want of fire. The men could do little but shiver in their robes and wait for better days. As the wind moderated, snow piled huge drifts on the Sweetwater. Finally the sojourners found a sheltered cove among rocky crags abounding in mountain sheep and lay in camp for two or three weeks.

By the middle of March 1824, Smith decided the time had come to seek the Siskadee and get on with the spring hunt. Besides, the hunters had nearly cleaned out the mountain sheep. The "hericane" still roared, driving stinging blizzards of snow from the slopes, and scarcity of game added to the ordeal. On the sixth day, Clyman and Sublette brought down an antelope, and when the rest of the party came up "we butchered our meat in short order many of the men eating large slices raw." The next morning, "we found we had crossed the main ridge of the Rocky mountain." Unknowingly, Smith and his companions had celebrated a historic moment by gorging on raw antelope.

The gentle summit of South Pass, so unlike the high snow-blocked Union Pass at the northern end of the Wind River Range, opened to the Big Sandy, which ran down to the Siskadee. There, Jedediah Smith and his little corps unveiled the rich beaver grounds of the Green River and took the first halting steps toward building this spacious valley, with its abundance of grass, water, timber, and game, into the heartland of the fur trade.

Dividing the small party, Smith sent Fitzpatrick with Clyman and two others to trap the upper Green. Smith took the remaining six and headed downstream. They had already agreed to gather no later than June at the campsite on the Sweetwater, where powder, lead, and other surplus supplies had been cached.

For Fitzpatrick, pelts accumulated quickly. But hungry Shoshones the trappers had befriended, and with whom they had shared food and shelter, stole all their horses. They finished the hunt on foot, cached all they could not carry, and early in June turned downriver. On this same day, they met a party of the guilty Indians, escorted them at rifle point to their camp, and recovered all their horses save one.

Smith and his followers also gathered a fine harvest of beaver, probably on Black's Fork of the Green, and rejoined Fitzpatrick on the Sweetwater, as planned.[13] Smith did not regard his mission completed with the opening of the Green. He intended to explore even farther west and conduct a fall hunt. The fruits of the spring hunt, however, had to be taken down to St. Louis. None knew where the Sweetwater flowed, whether into the Platte or the Arkansas. But it brimmed with the spring runoff, and Smith hoped the pelts could be boated to market.

Fitzpatrick and two men drew the assignment. They constructed a bullboat, that versatile vessel of Indian design consisting of a skeleton of saplings covered with buffalo hide, and started with their cargo down the river.

With seven men, Smith prepared to face west once again. But Jim Clyman was missing and had to be found. He had scouted alone as far as the canyons of the North Platte. Barely avoiding an Arikara war party, he had despaired of reuniting with his comrades and struck out eastward. Smith discovered Clyman's signs near Indian signs, which led to the obvious conclusion. Sadly, Smith and his little party turned back toward South Pass and the Green River.

Clyman hiked down the Platte in midsummer heat. Pawnees robbed him and nearly took his scalp. He reached the Missouri starving, wasted, and disoriented. Stumbling forward one day with head bowed, he lifted his eyes and "with great surprise I saw the stars and stripe. . . . I swoned emmediately." He had found his way to Fort Atkinson, where Colonel Leavenworth made him a temporary soldier and issued him clothing and "rashions."

Clyman had been at Fort Atkinson only ten days when Fitzpatrick and his two companions arrived, "in a more pitible state if possible than myself." In a canyon of the North Platte below the mouth of the Sweetwater, rapids had swamped their bullboat and scattered its cargo into the waters. They retrieved and dried most of the beaver but lost two rifles and all their ammunition. Caching the furs, they toiled eastward in a trek as rife with hardship as Clyman's and reached Fort Atkinson near the end of August.[14]

At the Missouri Fur Company's outpost at Bellevue, below Council Bluffs, Lucien Fontenelle staked Fitzpatrick with mules and equipment in return for the cached furs. Fitzpatrick turned west at once and was back at Bellevue with the furs by late October 1824.[15]

Before leaving, Fitzpatrick had written Ashley in St. Louis of the plentiful fur country the Smith party had opened and the easy passage of the Rockies by which it could be reached. Never one to squander time in indecision, Ashley had at once organized another expedition to the mountains. By the time Fitzpatrick got back to Bellevue, Ashley was there, ready to take charge of a company of twenty-five men and a string of pack mules even then pushing west from the Missouri.[16]

JEDEDIAH SMITH'S DISCOVERY of an easy crossing of the Rocky Mountains made news. Robert Stuart's same discovery thirteen years earlier had also made news, but it had faded in the public memory. Smith rediscovered the "southern pass" of Stuart, but his achievement did not fade. Henceforth, for more than twenty years, South Pass was *the* way to the Far West.

Oddly, the source of the news was Andrew Henry, who descended the Missouri to reach St. Louis on August 30, 1824. Newspapers noted his arrival but reported only that he had brought a cargo of furs and had observed that the Arikaras had reoccupied their towns near the mouth of the Grand River. Not until November did the press publicize his most important news: "By the arrival of Major Henry from the Rocky Mountains, we learn that his party have discovered a passage by which loaded waggons can at this time reach the navigable waters of the Columbia River. This route lies South of the one explored by Lewis and Clarke, and is inhabited by Indians friendly to us."[17]

What Henry reported had been learned indirectly from Jedediah Smith, through Weber's trappers on the Bighorn and Wind Rivers. Some of them had returned to Henry's post as early as February 1824. Smith had not yet crossed to the Green, but they knew what the Crows had advised and what he intended. Based on their report, Henry decided to send a winter express through to Ashley informing him of affairs in the mountains and prospects for the future.

Five men made the journey, including Hugh Glass, who had unfinished business somewhere on the Missouri. To avoid the Arikaras, they traveled southwest to the Powder and across to the North Platte, where they constructed a bullboat and began their descent. Near the mouth of the Laramie River, they put ashore to receive the hospitality of a camp of Indians who represented themselves as Pawnees. Too late the whites discovered their hosts to be Arikaras. Pursued by warriors, they ran for life. Two died, two made good their flight down the Platte, and Glass hid in a rocky cove as the Indians searched.

The lucky pair of escapees made their way safely to Council Bluffs. They reported Glass and their two other companions dead at the hands of the Arikaras and added, as tersely printed in the St. Louis press: "Captain Smith, with some of the party, had crossed the Mountains."[18] This announcement, in fact true although the messengers knew only what Smith intended, made little impression. Not until five months later, when Henry declared the crossing of the Rocky Mountains convenient for loaded wagons, did the nation take note.

Hugh Glass had not been killed. His rifle gone, a knife his only tool, he set out for the Missouri. Subsisting on berries, roots, and newborn buffalo calves, he found his way to Fort Kiowa in early June. From there he descended the Missouri. At Fort Atkinson he finally caught up with John Fitzgerald, only to discover him armored against vengeance in the uniform of the United States Army. Colonel Leavenworth could not allow one of his soldiers to be murdered, but he ordered Glass's rifle returned and equipped him to take the field again.[19]

Henry's announcement of an easy pass through the Rocky Mountains marked his retirement from the fur trade. In July 1824, now fully informed of Smith's findings, he had dispatched Weber to follow Smith through South Pass and begin harvesting the beaver said to be crowding the streams beyond the Continental Divide. With the rest of his men, he closed down the fort at the mouth of the Bighorn and embarked for St. Louis with the furs Weber had gathered during the winter.[20]

Ashley expected Henry to continue to serve as field captain, but the veteran fur man wanted to return to a quieter, less dangerous life. When he died in 1833, not yet sixty, a St. Louis newspaper lauded him as "a man much respected for his honesty, intelligence, and enterprise. . . . One of those enterprising traders who first explored the wild and inhospitable regions of the Rocky Mountains."[21]

The rediscovery of South Pass opened a new chapter in the history of the fur business, one that featured the mountain man as a key figure. Not only Andrew Henry had withdrawn from the Bighorn country but Keemle and Gordon also. Like Ashley, Joshua Pilcher wanted his partisans to probe beyond the Continental Divide. But the Missouri Fur Company limped toward collapse, and in July 1824 Keemle and Gordon withdrew. As a final indignity, as they floated down the Yellowstone, Crows with whom they had lived in friendship all winter robbed them of most of their possessions.[22]

The new stage for the unfolding drama lay west of the Continental Divide, and the players included not only Jedediah Smith, John Weber, and William H. Ashley, but also men from the Rio Grande and men from the Columbia.

THE SHIFT of the fur business from water to land and from the upper Missouri to the Rockies did not quiet the anger of westerners over the outrages of the Arikaras and Blackfeet. For most St. Louis capitalists, the Indian trade remained paramount. No trading establishments survived above Forts Kiowa and Recovery, and the northern limit of dependable security rested at Council Bluffs and Fort Atkinson. If the Arikaras got away with decimating Ashley's men on the sand beach, emboldened Indians of all tribes would bar the upper river to Americans and give their trade and allegiance to the British. As early as September 1823, as Smith and Henry embarked on their overland expeditions, Indian Superintendent William Clark urged Secretary of War Calhoun to dispatch a military force upriver in the spring of 1824, both to awe the Arikaras and all other tribes with a display of power and to bring them into treaty relations with the United States.[23]

The confusion between trapping and trading complicated the War Department's design. "It appears to us," editorialized the influential *Niles's Weekly Register* in siding with Indians, "that the lands yet unceded must be regarded as their own, and if so, we suppose that a party of white persons cannot have any more right to enter upon it for the purpose of catching and killing the wild beasts of the forest, than the Indians would have to enter our settlements and carry off whatever they pleased."[24]

Colonel Leavenworth, stung by the attacks of Pilcher and other fur men on his conduct of the Arikara expedition, agreed. "This *trapping* business is carried on under a license to *trade*," he wrote, and therefore "this *trapping* business should be fully and completely suppressed." He favored the proposed military expedition, but for the purpose of ousting white hunters and quieting the Indians.[25]

This issue tangled congressional consideration of the War Department's proposal. Missouri's Senator Thomas Hart Benton sponsored a bill to station a large force on the upper Missouri for the protection of the fur trade, but he had to relent as other senators worried about illegal hunting on Indian lands. The compromise, enacted in May 1824, was for treaty commissioners backed by a military escort to ascend the Missouri and make peace with all the tribes.[26]

The law reached the president's desk too late for an upriver movement in 1824. Not until May 1825 did the expedition set forth from Fort Atkinson. The treaty commissioners were General Henry Atkinson and Indian Agent Benjamin O'Fallon. Their "escort" consisted of nearly five hundred soldiers. Up the Missouri the emissaries negotiated their way from tribe to tribe, impressing each with colorful military displays, lavishing on each an array of presents, and concluding with each a treaty of peace and friendship. All, even the lately belligerent Arikaras, touched the pen and partook of the presents.

The treaties were all the same. The Indians acknowledged the supremacy of the American Great Father and his power to regulate all trade and intercourse. They promised to protect American traders and turn over all foreign traders to American officials. Provisions dealt with regulation of trade and redress of grievances. None addressed hunting or trapping on Indian land.

Having concluded treaties with Poncas, Sioux, Cheyennes, Arikaras, Hidatsas, and Mandans, the expedition proceeded to the mouth of the Yellowstone and even beyond in hopes of bringing Blackfeet, Assiniboines, and Crows to the table. Only the Crows could be coaxed in, and the council with their chiefs almost ended in battle. What role the interpreter played in the altercation is not clear, but that he was Edward Rose raises a suspicion of some mischievous scheme. When the Crows tried to appropriate their presents before permitted, O'Fallon bashed four chiefs over the head with his pistol butt, and the troops turned out under arms. Rose waded in swinging a musket and knocked down several warriors. The next morning, after a mollifying late-night feast, the Crow leaders appeared "& recd. additional presents, said their wounds were covered & they would throw all that had passed behind them."[27]

In its most serious failing, the Atkinson-O'Fallon expedition did not even talk with Blackfeet, much less dampen their hostility toward Americans. Nor did it resolve the confusion between trading and trapping. All fur men, whether intending to trade, trap, or both, continued to obtain trading licenses from Superintendent Clark in St. Louis. The expedition and its treaties did, however, lay the groundwork for Americans to return to the upper Missouri. As trappers overspread the Rockies, trading posts sprang up on the Missouri, to pursue the Indian trade and finally to serve as bases for projecting more trapping ventures into the mountains.

In these undertakings, however, the fur men no longer looked to the army for help. In 1827 Colonel Leavenworth abandoned Fort Atkinson and withdrew his garrison far down the Missouri to a new site, where he established Fort Leavenworth. The new post could be more easily supplied, and it supposedly gave protection to both Santa Fe traders and the fur traffic on the river. For the fur men, the fort in time proved mainly an obstruction, its officers more concerned with barring whiskey from the Indian trade than in facilitating the fur trade.[28]

IN THE EARLY AUTUMN of 1824, Jedediah Smith and his six trappers (including Bill Sublette) found themselves on the Snake River—Lewis's Fork of the Columbia as it was more generally known. After parting with Fitzpatrick in June, they had crossed South Pass, trapped the Green, and pushed on westward, probably by way of the Bear and Blackfoot Rivers. Both Hunt's and Stuart's Astorians had trod this country, and it was etched in detail on the minds of Robinson, Hoback, and Reznor before their demise. For Smith, it was promising new territory; his small band had taken nine hundred beaver.

Here on the Snake River the commerce and empire of two nations collided, as it had when John Jacob Astor sent his men to the Columbia in 1810. A more unlikely advance guard of British power Smith could hardly have conceived—a ragtag crew of Iroquois free trappers attached to a Hudson's Bay Company brigade. Their leader was "Old Pierre" Tevanitagon, granted immortality in the name of Pierre's Hole at the western base of the Tetons. Independent, strong-willed, often careless and lazy, the Iroquois had been plundered by Shoshones, and they greeted Smith with relief. In return for escort through dangerous country, Old Pierre turned over 105 skins to Smith.

On October 14, 1824, where the Lemhi River flows into the Salmon, Smith met a more responsible agent of British imperialism: Alexander Ross of the Hudson's Bay Company (ironically, a former Astorian). For the Iroquois Ross felt contempt, for their escort suspicion. "With these vagabonds," he wrote in his journal, "arrived seven American trappers from the Big Horn River but whom I rather take to be spies than trappers." Predicting an influx of Americans in the coming season, he worried over their effect on the Iroquois. Feeding the fear, Smith turned aside all attempts to buy his pelts, cached for later retrieval, for less than three dollars a pound. Such a sum could easily lure the Iroquois away from the British.[29]

More discomfiting, Smith meant to stay with Ross's brigade. On the fringes of Blackfeet country at the onset of winter, he and his six men would stand a better chance of survival. Ross judged Smith "a very intelligent person" and his followers "shrewd men," but he had orders from London to do everything he could to hold Americans at bay. Now they insisted on accompanying him back to his base, Flathead Post, on Clark's Fork of the Columbia.

Following the usual British route between the Snake River Plain and Flathead Post, Smith observed country explored nineteen years earlier by Lewis and Clark: east across Lemhi Pass to the Beaverhead (and thus into plainly U.S. territory), back over the Continental Divide to the head of the Bitterroot, down that stream to Clark's Fork, and down Clark's Fork to Flathead Post.

Jedediah Smith was the point man in the contest for Oregon. The upper Green River lay in Oregon. The Snake River Plain lay in Oregon. And Flathead Post, base for his reluctant hosts, lay on Clark's Fork in Oregon. Smith had visited them all. Under the Convention of 1818, Great Britain and the United States jointly occupied Oregon. Since Astor's rout in 1814, however, the British had had Oregon all to themselves. Only along the coast had Americans—sea captains out of Boston—competed for furs, and by Smith's time that trade had begun to decline. If Americans were to have any presence in Oregon, they had to come over the mountains. Smith's appearance in Alexander Ross's camp on the Salmon River served notice, as Ross himself foresaw, of a host of Americans crossing the Continental Divide to challenge British dominion in Oregon.

6

ÉTIENNE PROVOST:

L'HOMME DES MONTAGNES

L'HOMME DES MONTAGNES, the "Man of the Mountains," the French scientist Joseph N. Nicollet labeled Étienne Provost in 1839. Not until the 1830s, when Provost was in his fifties, did observers give face and form to the name. "Monsieur Proveau," noted one, "with a corpus as round as a porpoise." "A burly Bacchus," added another, "a large heavy man, with a ruddy face, bearing more the appearance of a mate of a French merchantman than the scourer of dusty plains." The Étienne Provost who first appeared in the West more than two decades earlier doubtless prefigured the rotund, muscular, hard-drinking, canny mountaineer who moved entrepreneur Bartholomew Berthold to pronounce him "the soul of the hunters of the mountains."[1]

Born in Quebec in 1785, Provost first came to the mountains in 1815. Over the next decade, he epitomized the American trappers who based themselves in New Mexico and probed both north and west. Under Spanish rule, New Mexican officials turned back all American efforts to trade or trap anywhere near the undefined international boundary. Imprisonment and confiscation of property awaited those caught in the toils of Spanish officialdom. Under Mexico, following the expulsion of Spain in 1821, traders found a warm welcome, but trappers had to pursue their calling covertly or under a dubious official guise acquired through subterfuge or bribery.

Even the unforgiving wrath of Spain failed to slow the approach of daring Americans. Manuel Lisa never gave up his dream of a New Mexican connection, and after driven from the upper Missouri he sent parties south along the Front Range of the Rockies to trap the South Platte and the Arkansas. Others made their way overland from St. Louis.

One such expedition, led by Auguste P. Chouteau and Jules de Mun, ascended the Arkansas in the autumn of 1815. They bore a license to trade with the Arapaho Indians, but they went to trap also. One of their engagés was Étienne Provost, already thirty years of age.[2]

Numbering nearly fifty engagés, the Chouteau–de Mun company established a base on the Arkansas River at the mouth of the Huerfano. Trappers of another company were to have joined at the base site, but destitute of supplies they had sought relief across the mountains in Taos, anchor of New Mexico's northern frontier. This brought de Mun to Taos and subsequently to Santa Fe, where the governor treated him well and even issued a license to trap New Mexican streams. A subsequent governor, however, proved less hospitable. Seemingly ignorant of the Louisiana Purchase and regarding any Americans west of the Mississippi River as intruders on Spanish soil, he subjected Chouteau, de Mun, and twenty-four of their men to a litany of abuses extending over a two-year period. Before gaining release in September 1817, they passed forty-eight days in the "dungeons of Santa Fe" and had property valued at more than thirty thousand dollars confiscated.

The entanglement with Spanish officials and the outrage it stirred in the United States overshadowed the wide-ranging trapping activities of the Chouteau–de Mun expedition. Étienne Provost shared the indignities of the Santa Fe dungeons, but he and his comrades also trapped the beaver streams west of the Front Range of the Rockies. They penetrated a Rocky Mountain heartland destined to rival the northern Rockies in plenitude of beaver. They were the first known Americans to explore South Park—the "Bayou Salado" surrounding the upper waters of the South Platte—and North Park, the source of the North Platte. The rugged ranges edging these two parks on the west discouraged a crossing of the Continental Divide to the Middle Park.

A hint of what these trappers learned of the central Rockies reached the outside world. The official exploring expedition of Major Stephen H. Long in 1820 left the commander's name on one of the highest peaks, but he kept well to the east and traced an easy route southward along the base of the mountains. Even so, his guide described some of what lay amid the summits to the west. The guide was Joseph Bissonet, one of Provost's comrades of the Chouteau–de Mun venture, and Long's report and map evidence how thoroughly these early pioneers had worked the Rockies. The map even showed the North Park, labeled "Bull Pen."[3]

After Mexico had overthrown Spain in 1821, New Mexicans eagerly greeted Missouri traders. Captives of extortionist Chihuahua merchants, the citizens hailed a new source of manufactured goods. In its first years, however, the Santa Fe trade was a stepchild of the fur business. The Americans who forged the commercial link between Missouri and Santa Fe were trader-trappers of the same stamp that ranged the lands of Crows and Blackfeet at the same time. Instead of with Indians, they exchanged their trade goods with New Mexicans, thus laying the foundation for a commerce destined to flourish for more than half a century.

In the early 1820s, these traders were also trappers, and increasingly the caravans that blazed the Santa Fe Trail returned to Missouri with loads of fur taken from Mexican streams. The natives themselves had never tapped their fur resources, partly because of feeble markets and partly because they had never mastered the skills of trapping or preparing the skins. Trapping, therefore, fell to American newcomers. Étienne Provost was one of the earliest of a growing corps of Americans who discovered in Taos a base for supplying their expeditions and disposing of their furs.

New Mexicans resented Americans profiting from their resources. In 1824 the government prohibited foreign trapping. The ban, however, could be evaded in several ways. Americans could become Mexican citizens, or employ Mexican surrogates to obtain a license, or engage enough Mexicans to rationalize a license on the grounds of teaching natives how to take the furs themselves, or bribe officials, or simply risk getting caught and having their catch confiscated. All these ploys Americans tried. All, even the most ostensibly legal, carried a heavy burden of uncertainty. Licenses proved no guarantee against official caprice, greed, or changing policies and personnel.[4]

As beaver grew scarce on the Rio Grande and the headwaters of the Pecos River in the Sangre de Cristo Mountains, the Taos trappers looked to the northwest, to the Rio Verde that, farther upriver, Ashley's men called the Siskadee. The men of Taos pioneered no new trails. Domínguez and Escalante had been followed by Spanish trading expeditions that opened a commerce with the Utes, who sold captives seized from other tribes as slaves for New Mexican households. By Provost's time, Taoseños held a crude knowledge of the San Juan, Colorado, and Green Rivers and their surrounding mountains. The eastern half of what would become the Old Spanish Trail, the road the priests of 1776 sought to link New Mexico and California, had taken on rough form. Provost and his comrades, therefore, explored little unknown country, but they were the first to harvest its beaver wealth.[5]

ÉTIENNE PROVOST WAS ONE of the earliest Americans to seize the opportunities opened by New Mexico's changed attitude toward foreigners. In partnership with François Leclerc, he established himself in Taos in 1822. In the autumn of 1823 the partners took a company to the Green River and returned with such success that the following autumn, 1824, the number of Taos trappers headed for the Green trebled, to as many as eighty men.[6]

In September 1824 the Provost-Leclerc trappers established a base camp on the Green River near the mouth of the White, flowing from the east. This was the heart of the Uinta Basin, a broad flatland sheltered on the north by the Uinta Mountains and on the west by the Wasatch Mountains. To the south lay a maze of rocky red cliffs and plateaus gashed by one of the plunging canyons of the Green River.

As the men scattered to scour likely streams, Provost himself led a party of ten westward, over the Wasatch Range and down to Utah Lake. On a nearby riverbank, disaster struck. They came across a group of Shoshone Indians whose friendly invitation to have a smoke masked a mood turned foul by a recent encounter with Hudson's Bay Company trappers. The chief explained that for sacred reasons the pipe ceremony could not be held in the presence of metal objects. Obligingly, the trappers stacked their arms and gathered for the smoke. At a signal from the chief, the warriors drew knives from beneath their blankets and fell on the whites. Eight men died. Only Provost and one companion broke loose and escaped.[7]

Domínguez and Escalante had seen this same country in 1776, but Provost and his doomed men were the first known Americans to find their way to Utah Lake. Spelled Provo, Provost left his name there on a river and a city. The massacre may have occurred on the Provo River, which drains from the Wasatch into Utah Lake; but the Jordan River, flowing north from Utah Lake into Great Salt Lake, is an even better possibility. Whichever, Provost probably looked on Great Salt Lake in September 1824. Escalante and Domínguez had not reached Great Salt Lake, leaving Provost as possibly the first white to lay eyes on this central geographical feature of the Great Basin.[8]

Unknown to Provost, however, other trappers converged on this area at this same time. One of them also saw Great Salt Lake.

As ÉTIENNE PROVOST fixed his base for trapping in the Uinta Basin, to the north William H. Ashley's men sustained their westward drive. In the van, Jedediah Smith fell in with Alexander Ross's Snake Country Expedition in late October 1824 and, much against the Scotsman's wishes, accompanied him back to Flathead Post.

As Andrew Henry had intended, John H. Weber and more than twenty-five men followed Smith's trail through South Pass and down to the Green.

Crossing a low divide farther west, they completed a successful fall hunt on the Bear River and marveled at the beauty of Bear Lake. "When the wind blows," observed Daniel Potts, it "has a splendid appearance."[9]

The Bear River rises in the Uinta Mountains and flows north until, blocked by a lava flow, it turns abruptly south. Within this great curve lies Bear Lake. On the lower reaches of the Bear River, Cache Valley offered a covelike retreat from mountain storms. Weber's men considered it ideal for their winter camp of 1824–25. The rivers and creeks running off the Wasatch, moreover, teemed with beaver. One of the rivers quickly took Weber's name.

One of Weber's trappers was James Bridger, whose youth had softened the wrath of Hugh Glass the year before. Around a winter campfire in Cache Valley, the men speculated on the further course of the Bear River, which disappeared through a mountain spur rimming the valley on the west. To settle a wager, they chose Bridger to follow the river and report where it went. He returned to say that it emptied into a large lake that tasted of salt. All agreed that Bridger had found an arm of the Pacific Ocean.[10]

The issue of which of the two fur men "discovered" Great Salt Lake depends on whether Provost saw it at all. If he did, he saw it in September 1824. If he did not, Jim Bridger assuredly saw it later in the winter.

WHILE ÉTIENNE PROVOST counted his losses in the Uinta Basin, and John Weber's Ashley men settled into winter camp in Cache Valley, Jedediah Smith, William L. Sublette, and their five companions cast inquisitive eyes around Flathead Post. They imposed themselves on Alexander Ross's hospitality for nearly a month, from November 26 to December 20, 1824. They observed a trading fair with Flatheads, Pend d'Oreilles, and Kutenais, and little else about the Hudson's Bay Company operation escaped their notice.

The Ashley trappers could not know that the ways of the "Honourable Company" verged on portentous change, with effects certain to heighten tensions between Americans and British in disputed Oregon. While Smith and his men prowled Flathead Post, the authors of change arrived on the Columbia River after an overland journey from York Factory, on Hudson Bay. They were George Simpson and John McLoughlin.

Only thirty-two in 1824, George Simpson had been appointed governor of the company's territories in America. Tireless, driven, peremptory, full of certitude, keen of judgment, and decisive in imposing reform, he had come to inspect the remote Columbia Department, creation of the defunct North West Company, and discover the reasons for its dismal balance sheet.[11]

With Simpson was the new Chief Factor of the Columbia Department. Eight years Simpson's elder, huge of frame, intellect, and personality, John McLoughlin would dominate the Columbia Basin for the next two decades. As American trappers and American settlers would discover, McLoughlin's fierce aspect masked generosity and compassion, and despite repeated conflicts with Simpson he made the Columbia Department a paying enterprise.[12]

Simpson's destination was Fort George—formerly Astoria, symbolically repossessed by the United States in 1818 but still headquarters of the Columbia Department. He had not even reached the fort before he decided what was wrong with the department: "shamefully mismanaged and a scene of the most unfortunate dissention." He would spend the winter at Fort George instituting correctives.[13]

Simpson bestowed special attention on the Snake Country Expedition. Begun by the Nor'westers, this annual hunt in the Snake drainage struck Simpson as poorly conducted. Although he thought it could be converted from a "forlorn hope" into a profitable enterprise, he had more compelling reasons for reform, as much imperial as commercial. He recognized that the only truly disputed part of Oregon lay between the forty-ninth parallel and the Columbia River, and this he wished to guard against American intrusion. The best defense, he believed, was a beaver-free buffer zone south and east of the Columbia. This made political sense, by stripping the Snake country of beaver and thus of incentive for Americans to venture west of the Continental Divide. It made commercial sense, by profiting from every beaver that could be harvested in a land sure to fall to the Americans anyway. In assigning Peter Skene Ogden to replace Ross as head of the Snake Country Expedition, Simpson explained that "the more we impoverish the country the less likelyhood is there of our being assailed by opposition."[14]

A man of boundless energy and endurance, a scrappy veteran of the bitter wars between the North West and Hudson's Bay Companies, Ogden had already reached Flathead Post when Alexander Ross arrived with his Snake Country Expedition late in November 1824. At once Ogden took command and turned it around. On December 20 the procession headed south, bound for the Snake country. It consisted of about sixty trappers—twenty-five "servants" and thirty-five freemen, many of the latter Iroquois with their families. For protection through Blackfeet country, Jedediah Smith and his comrades followed.

As Simpson knew, Americans were already west of the Continental Divide. They came from Taos. They came from the Bighorn and Wind Rivers, and from the Missouri up the Platte, to funnel through South Pass to the Green, the Bear, and the Snake. Now, with the driving force of George

Simpson propelling them, the British swept south with a mandate to exterminate the beaver population of the Snake country. In the spring of 1825 these converging forces collided.

ON THE MORNING of May 23, 1825, Étienne Provost and some fifteen trappers descended the western Wasatch slope to the valley of a river that may already have taken the name of John H. Weber. Provost headed a polyglot company—French Canadians, Spaniards, Iroquois deserters from the Hudson's Bay Company, and even a Russian. From his winter camp in the Uinta Basin, he and his men had pushed their spring hunt, without much success, northwest across the Wasatch Mountains and down to the rivers draining into Great Salt Lake. Provost worked the beaver waters unaware of the proximity of the Ashley men under Weber, who had broken camp in Cache Valley and carried their spring hunt south to the Weber River and down it to the big sheet of salty water Jim Bridger had told them of several months earlier. On this spring morning of 1825, however, Provost chanced on other whites, the camp of Peter Skene Ogden and the Snake Country Expedition.[15]

No Hudson's Bay Company brigade had ever penetrated so far south, although Ogden had taken all winter to get here. With Jedediah Smith and his six Ashley men nearby, Ogden's following of engagés and unruly Iroquois freemen had contended with cold and snow as well as Blackfeet who struck periodically. Impassable snowdrifts, weak horses, and watchful war parties trapped the brigade in the Lemhi Valley for three weeks, until Smith—"a sly cunning Yankey," according to Ogden's clerk—forced a passage across the Lemhi Mountains and down to the Snake River Plain. For both Smith and Ogden, the spring hunt got under way in April on the Snake and its southern tributaries, the Blackfoot and Portneuf. May found Ogden trapping south up Cache Valley and across to the Ogden and Weber Rivers and Smith uniting with Weber on the Weber River near its mouth.[16]

In Weber's camp, Smith and Sublette recounted their observations at Flathead Post and their travels with the Hudson's Bay Company brigade. They noted that each night, as the British pitched camp, they hoisted the Union Jack. Indignant at this insult to the United States—Weber's men were as ignorant of diplomatic accords as they were well versed in mountain geography—the Americans resolved to apply their own frontier remedy by simply tearing down the offending foreign flag. Commercial motives fortified the patriotic, for Hudson's Bay deserters had told of the company's tyranny and prompted visions of still more deserters coming over with their beaver catch.[17]

Although Étienne Provost had known nothing of Weber's men, he learned of them the very day he fell in with the British. Ogden had already discovered that he was trailing American trappers, for the streams below the winter snow line had been swept clear of beaver, and Ute Indians had told him about his competitors. "The whole Country overrun with Americans & Canadians," he noted in his journal on May 22, "all in pursuit of the Same object."

For Ogden, the unease occasioned by the appearance of Provost turned to chagrin only hours later. During the afternoon of May 23, 1825, twenty-five trappers, flying an American flag, paraded to within a hundred yards of Ogden's camp and laid out their own camp. Here on the banks of a river well within the bounds of the Mexican republic, in a "Country overrun with Americans & Canadians," the commercial and imperial ambitions of the United States and Great Britain clashed.[18]

The agent of American ambitions was Johnson Gardner, a blustering mountaineer who had gone up the Missouri with Ashley and had crossed South Pass with Weber. Although he saw no British flag, as night came on Gardner paid a brief visit to Ogden and his clerk, William Kittson. The British, Gardner declared, were trespassing on United States territory and must leave at once. Moreover, the Americans stood ready to offer Ogden's men $3.50 a pound for their beaver, supplies at lower than company prices, and haven for those who wished to desert. Ogden dared not oppose such defections. "Free or engaged men were the same in this land of liberty." The Americans would fight to defend any who wanted to change sides.

Gardner returned the next morning. "Do you know in whose country you are?" he demanded. Ogden replied that he did not, for that had not been determined. Wrong, averred Gardner; it belonged to the United States and Ogden must get out at once. Ogden stood firm: not until he received instructions from his superiors would he get out.

On the other issue, however, Ogden lost. The Iroquois and Canadian freemen nurtured resentments of the Hudson's Bay Company reaching back to their service with the North West Company. The perpetual debt the London firm imposed by selling supplies high and buying beaver low added festering grievance to a tradition of fierce independence. Gardner offered the exchange of British bondage and debt for American freedom and profit. After a barrage of angry threats, some minor scuffling, and a near resort to arms, part of Ogden's freemen collected their furs and went over to the Americans. In a scene repeated the next morning, when Gardner and Kittson almost came to blows, still more deserted. Twenty-three men, including two engagés, abandoned the Snake Country Expedition.

Deprived of almost half his freemen, Ogden retreated from the field of

This engraving, executed for Joe Meek's memoirs, depicted the fate of scores of trappers working the northern Rockies—death by arrow or ball fired by Blackfeet, who for nearly three decades, until decimated by smallpox, waged unrelenting war on the mountain men who took Blackfeet beaver from Blackfeet streams. COURTESY DENVER PUBLIC LIBRARY.

conflict, hastening back over the usual route to Flathead Post. The withdrawal left the spring hunt a shambles and the volatile Governor Simpson acutely displeased.

Of the country they traversed, Ogden and Kittson formed an accurate conception. Kittson drew a map, primitive but encompassing the geography from Flathead Post down the Continental Divide to Great Salt Lake. The lake itself, labeled "Large Bear Lake," was depicted for the first time on a map. Buried in Hudson's Bay Company archives until 1950, it made only a modest contribution to contemporary knowledge. Cartographers continued to fantasize a geography that Kittson's map, for all its crudity, snapped into clear focus.[19]

AFTER THE ROUT of the British, Provost met Jedediah Smith and an accomplished mountaineer named Zachariah Ham. From Ham Provost learned of more Ashley men just east of the mountains, including William

H. Ashley himself. A month earlier, on April 22, 1825, Ashley had dispatched Ham and six men to trap westward from the Green River into the Wasatch Range. On the way the leader left his name on Ham's Fork of the Green River. By late May, when Gardner and Ogden confronted each other on the Weber River, Ham had probably found his way into Weber's camp.[20]

As Ham related, Ashley had reacted instantly to word brought down by Tom Fitzpatrick in October 1824 of an easy pass across the Continental Divide to beaver riches on the Green. Andrew Henry had withdrawn from the mountains, leaving Ashley little choice but to head the supply caravan himself. He got off from Council Bluffs in late November, but a winter full of hardship and delay kept him from the mountains until the spring of 1825.

With twenty-five men and a string of horses and pack mules, Ashley had ascended the Loup Fork of the Platte, dropped to the South Platte, and followed it until he could veer directly west through the northern spurs of the Front Range of the Rockies and reach the Laramie Plain. Feeling his way around the northern tip of the Medicine Bow Range, he crossed the Continental Divide along the southern edges of the Great Divide Basin rather than through South Pass.

Early in April, while yet within this bleak basin, Ashley had his first introduction to the Crow Indians. They had treated Smith and Weber well, but Ashley's stock proved too enticing. On April 4 Crow raiders ran off seventeen of his best animals and all but dismounted the caravan. As he remarked, whites "learned not to put temptation in the way of these extraordinarily adept thieves."[21]

Plagued by April snows, Ashley and his men descended the Big Sandy to the Green. Here, on April 20, he divided the company into four parties. Three would trap while the fourth, under Ashley, would load the merchandise into bullboats and drift down the Green River in an effort to sort out the murky geography. Zachariah Ham would take seven men directly west into the Wasatch Mountains. Tom Fitzpatrick would lead another six southwest, along the base of the Uinta Mountains. Jim Clyman would head north with the third group of six to the upper Green, where he had trapped a year earlier.

With Clyman went a fledgling mountaineer, a young mulatto named James Beckwourth. He was an able hand and would later become an even greater power among the Crow Indians than Edward Rose. He lived a long life and with the help of a ghostwriter published a widely read book. Like all mountain men, Beckwourth was a master of the tall tale. None, however, surpassed him. In all his tales, some invented, some gilded seeds of truth, he is the peerless hero. He played a genuine role in the fur trade, and his name recurs in both history and legend.[22]

Before casting off on the Green, Ashley almost incidentally set the foundation for the most dazzling institution of the fur trade. To reunite his scattered contingents, he told the leaders, he would find a suitable site downstream to cache part of the merchandise. There he would "make such Marks as would designate it as a place of General Rendezvous for the men in my service in that Country." Here all would assemble before July 10.[23]

All this Étienne Provost heard from Zachariah Ham in Weber's camp. In Ashley's "General Rendezvous," Provost saw a chance both to resupply his men and to dispose of his furs without transporting them back to Taos. He would find Ashley and attend his rendezvous. From Ham he knew that Ashley was headed down the Green River into the Uinta Basin, site of Provost's base camp. He would turn back up the Weber River and cross the Wasatch in search of the St. Louis entrepreneur.

ON JUNE 7, 1825, descending the Strawberry River from the Wasatch summit, Étienne Provost met Ashley and his seven men plodding on horseback up the valley. Provost brought Ashley up to date on the movements of Weber and Smith and told of Johnson Gardner's bombast that had brought twenty-three Hudson's Bay freemen and their catch under Ashley's banner. All of Ashley's men were now, said Provost, moving east to the "General Rendezvous."

Ashley surely recounted for Provost his exploits since taking to the Green River in bullboats. Even Provost had not been far enough up the Green to know how it cut its way through the Uinta Mountains—the only major range in North America, excepting Alaska, that lies on an east-west axis. Ashley was the first known white man to find out, forty-four years before John Wesley Powell embarked on a like voyage.

The "gap" by which the river entered the Uinta Mountains, Ashley noted in his diary on May 3, "appears hardly large Enough to contain the Water." With this understatement, the two frail craft bearing eight men plunged into Flaming Gorge. Buffeted by wind and snow, bobbing on rushing waters, oppressed by gloomy slopes rising ever more steeply on either side, they shot through Flaming Gorge and Red Canyon and emerged into the open space of Brown's Hole. On May 9 they plummeted into Ladore Canyon and on into Split Mountain Canyon. Sheer rock walls, falls, and cataracts forced numerous portages and halts to repair the battered boats.

On May 14 Ashley discerned too late "a verry great & dangerous fall." The swift current took command and shot the boat over the boiling precipice. At the bottom it crashed broadside into a boulder and swung into an eddy. Two men jumped out and pulled the boat to the shore. (As Jim Beckwourth told it, Ashley had been thrown into the "Green River Suck," and Beckwourth had plunged in to save him. Towing his chief to the bank, he seized a pole extended by Tom Fitzpatrick and hoisted himself and Ashley out of the water. "That Beckwourth is surely one of the most singular men I ever met," Ashley remarked to Fitzpatrick. At this time, of course, Beckwourth was with Clyman on the upper Green and Fitzpatrick was trapping the northern slopes of the Uintas.[24])

Two days later Ashley's boats floated out of the canyons into the Uinta Basin. From two of Provost's hunters, Ashley learned the barren character of the country downriver. Caching most of the surviving cargo of the boats, he acquired two horses from Ute Indians and six from more of Provost's men.

Ashley still tried to make sense of the geography. "Set out for the river Columbia," he scrawled in his diary on June 3 as he led his horsemen up the Duchesne River toward the Wasatch Mountains. On June 7, high on the Strawberry River, he sought a trail that he understood "goes direct to the lake on the head waters of the Columbia." His mind doubtless pictured the Multnomah of Lewis and Clark and contemporary maps. On this same day, moreover, he met Étienne Provost, who confirmed that a big lake lay just over the mountains.[25]

Ashley and Provost needed to raise Ashley's cache on the Green and then work their way through the mountains to the site appointed for the "General Rendezvous." Provost had the horses to transport Ashley's goods. With one of Ashley's men, he descended to the Green and on June 14 reappeared with the goods. Together the two parties headed back up the Strawberry River in search of other Ashley parties and finally to stage the first of the sixteen yearly rendezvous that would order the Rocky Mountain fur trade.

BEFORE THE END of June 1825, all of Ashley's parties had gathered at the site appointed for the fur trade's first rendezvous, including twenty-nine deserters from the Hudson's Bay Company, most with families.

Only Jim Clyman had met with any misfortune. On the upper Green River he had admitted seventeen Indians to his camp (probably Atsinas, or Gros Ventres of the Prairie). They repaid his hospitality by burying a tomahawk in the skull of the night guard, one LaBarge, and trying to make off with the trappers' rifles. After an exchange of gunfire, Clyman decided to break off the hunt and head for rendezvous.[26]

Ashley had marked as the rendezvous site the mouth of the last stream entering the Green River from the west before it disappeared into the canyons of the Uinta Mountains. He had named it "Randavouze Creek," but for obscure reasons it later took the less fitting name Henry's Fork. Ashley and Provost were the last to arrive. In descending "Randavouze Creek," they had discovered a superior site twenty miles upstream. Everyone, about 120 not counting women and children, moved up the creek and camped at the new location. Here, in a broad valley lush with grass, cottonwood groves, and sparkling water, the Uinta Mountains rising abruptly on the south, Ashley presided over the first rendezvous.[27]

The 1825 rendezvous lasted only one day, July 1. Except for the camaraderie of scattered friends reunited, it was a day strictly of business. Ashley bought the trappers' beaver and sold them the goods he had brought up from St. Louis. For most of the skins he paid three dollars a pound, although some drew only two and some as much as five. Ashley packed out 8,829 pounds of beaver, worth in St. Louis between forty and fifty thousand dollars.

If the 1825 rendezvous seemed sedate compared with the carnivals of later years, it nonetheless laid the groundwork. Ashley discovered that trappers were willing to remain in the mountains year-round. That meant they had to be supplied in the mountains and their catch hauled out of the mountains. That in turn meant that the true profits of the fur business fell to the supplier-buyer rather than the trapper. From these discoveries sprang the annual supply caravan from St. Louis and the annual summer rendezvous.

At this first rendezvous too, Ashley formed a better idea of what should be packed on the mules of the caravan. Besides the essentials—traps, powder, lead, flint, knives, coffee, sugar, tobacco, blankets—an obvious commodity of huge potential profit was liquor. On Henry's Fork, conviviality drew no inspiration from alcohol, but this would be the last time. The Hudson's Bay freemen and their families suggested other merchandise, as Old Pierre Tevanitagon informed Ashley: the ribbons, bells, beads, and other trinkets increasingly important as mountain men began to take Indian wives.[28]

Provost disposed of 153 pounds of beaver skin to Ashley, but for only $2.50 per pound. They may have been less than prime beaver. From Ashley he purchased a variety of goods, including cloth, sugar, coffee, and tobacco.

At the 1825 rendezvous Provost glimpsed the beginnings of a new order. Taos would not relinquish its role as a base for trapping the southern Rockies, but it would be increasingly overshadowed by a system organized around the St. Louis–based supply caravan and the mountain rendezvous.

Provost ceased to count himself a Taos trapper. For the next two decades, he based himself on the Missouri River. His funeral, twenty-five years almost to the day after the Henry's Fork rendezvous, took place in the cathedral on the St. Louis waterfront.[29]

7

JEDEDIAH SMITH: CALIFORNIA, OREGON, AND THE CIMARRON

A T THE HENRY'S FORK RENDEZVOUS on July 1, 1825, William H. Ashley acquired a new partner. Ashley preferred the amenities of St. Louis to the outdoor life of the mountaineer. Thrice since cementing the partnership of Ashley and Henry, he had been called from his St. Louis office, and now his field captain, Andrew Henry, had withdrawn altogether. Ashley needed a master of men and mountains who could free him to deal with the business of fur in the comforts of St. Louis. The choice fell on humorless, grimly conscientious Jedediah Smith, who had conspicuously demonstrated his mastery of men and mountains.

After the rendezvous, the new partners headed for St. Louis, both to take out the furs and to equip a new caravan to provision the trappers wintering in the mountains. Shrewdly, Ashley fixed on a roundabout route. Aware that the Atkinson-O'Fallon expedition was making peace with the tribes of the upper Missouri, he aimed for the mouth of the Yellowstone. At the mouth of the Bighorn River, he packed his cargo into bullboats and floated down the Yellowstone to an almost perfectly timed union with the government expedition. Obligingly, General Atkinson loaded all the furs onto his army keelboats and provided free transportation down the Missouri as far as Council Bluffs. The new partners reached St. Louis on October 4, 1825.[1]

Less than a month later, Smith led out a caravan of seventy men and 160 animals loaded with provisions for the men in the mountains. Winter virtually wiped out the herd and stalled the expedition on the Platte River.

Ashley had to be informed. The messenger, accompanied by Jim Beckwourth, was Moses Harris, renowned for his powers of walking.

"Black" Harris, so called because of his dark skin, was one of the stars of the cast of trappers. He came up the Missouri with Ashley in 1823 and had figured in Hugh Glass's encounter with the murderous grizzly. He had experienced "as many perilous adventures as any man probably in the mountains," observed a friend. "He was of wiry form, made up of bone and muscle, with a face apparently composed of tan leather and whip cord, finished off with a peculiar blue-black tint, as if gunpowder had been burnt into his face." So accomplished a raconteur did Harris become that another who knew him exclaimed that "the darndest liar was Black Harris— for lies tumbled out of his mouth like boudins out of a buffler's stomach."[2]

Because of the report carried across the frozen plains by Harris and Beckwourth, for a fourth time Ashley had to head a field expedition. Early in April 1826 he joined Smith, and together they proceeded to the mountains. By late May they had reached the site appointed for the second rendezvous, in Cache Valley.[3]

Ashley's men had endured a terrible winter, aggravated by the long delay in the arrival of the supply train. They had camped first in Cache Valley and then, when snow piled too deeply, on the shores of Great Salt Lake near the mouth of the Weber River. Shoshones had camped with them, as had Hudson's Bay freemen with their families. Women and children, whether Indian or mixed blood, would henceforth be a fixture of trapper life and provide the enlarged market for goods Ashley had anticipated after talking with Old Pierre Tevanitagon the previous summer.

The spring hunt had been productive, not only of beaver but of geographical understanding. Ashley had seen much new country in 1825, but he had returned home still a prisoner of the myths engraved on contemporary maps. He had correctly divined the Green to be the "Rio Colorado of the West," but Indian reports had led him to think the Bear and other rivers emptying into Great Salt Lake to be the headwaters of the "Rio Buenaventura." This river, in turn, took its rise in "Grand Lake" and flowed all the way to the Pacific. The Platte and the Buenaventura, Ashley told St. Louis newsmen before heading west in 1826, afforded an easy wagon road from Missouri to California, designed by "the Great Author of nature, in His wisdom," for thousands to travel in safety "without meeting with any obstruction deserving the name of a MOUNTAIN."[4]

Discoveries during the spring hunt should have disposed of this conception. Possibly seeking the Buenaventura, a party led by William L. Sublette and David E. Jackson struck into the desert northwest of Great Salt Lake. Before turning north to the more congenial southern tributaries of the

Snake, they sent four men in a bullboat to circumnavigate the lake. It was a difficult and thirsty twenty-four days, for mudflats form the western shore and yield no fresh water.

That the four men failed to find an outlet for the Buenaventura did not trouble Ashley. Back in St. Louis in the autumn of 1826, he said they "did not exactly ascertain its outlet, but passed a place where they suppose that it must have been." Fed by Ashley's assurance that wagons and carriages could "go with ease" up the Platte and down the Buenaventura, this most enduring of all cartographic fantasies continued to link Great Salt Lake and the Pacific Ocean.[5]

The 1826 rendezvous in Cache Valley lasted for several days, perhaps even weeks, and began to take on the attributes of the glittering annual fair it became. Not only free and engaged trappers of Ashley's following, but Indians, French Canadians, and Iroquois freemen participated. Tents mingled with tepees, and women and children abounded. This year Ashley had not neglected the libation essential to a true rendezvous. For once, Jim Beckwourth's description probably did not embellish the reality: "Mirth, songs, dancing, shouting, trading, running, jumping, singing, racing, target-shooting, yarns, frolic, with all sorts of extravagances that white men or Indians could invent, were freely indulged in. The unpacking of the *medicine water* contributed not a little to the heightening of our festivities."[6]

For Ashley, the 1826 rendezvous marked a final trip to the mountains. The year's returns, amounting to some sixty thousand dollars in St. Louis, liberated him from debt and awarded him a modest fortune. He had seen enough to know that the largest profit and least risk lay in supplying the trappers and buying their beaver, not in committing capital to the trapping operation itself. Immediately after the rendezvous, in a complicated transaction involving beaver, credit, and arrangements for future supply, Ashley sold his share of the partnership to a new firm composed of Jedediah Smith, David E. Jackson, and William L. Sublette.[7]

THE ROCKY COURSE of Smith, Jackson & Sublette confirmed Ashley's appraisal of how to make money in the fur trade. The supplier made the money. The trapper never got out of debt, never earned enough money to leave the mountains for the comforts of home. Those few who did often discovered that the mountains retained such power over them that they never found the happiness the money was intended to buy. During the late 1820s, as the yearly supply caravan and rendezvous evolved, the trappers refined their own unique culture and adjusted their own yearly rhythm to the new business cycle.[8]

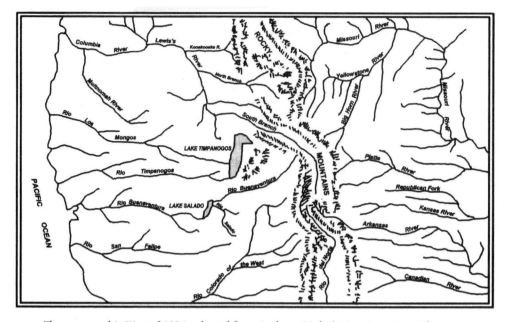

The cartographic West of 1826, adapted from Anthony Finley's New American Atlas, *published in that year. As William H. Ashley imagined standing at the Wasatch summit in 1825, the Buenaventura rose in the Rockies, flowed to Great Salt Lake, and then continued to San Francisco Bay. Lewis and Clark's durable Multnomah still reaches from the Columbia to the Rockies. Both rivers, many believed, would provide emigrants an easy waterborne path to the Pacific. Already, as this map came off the press, Jedediah Smith had discovered that no Buenaventura breached the Sierra Nevada and that the short Willamette, confined by mountains, underlay the concept of the Multnomah. Though badly distorted, the Columbia, Colorado, Rio Grande, and Missouri are recognizable, but the Great Basin, with its mythical lakes and rivers, remained cartographic fancy until the Frémont-Preuss map of 1845.*

What the trappers did between rendezvous differed from the popular understanding. They did not wander in lonely solitude through the mountains trapping beaver. That would have been suicidal, an invitation to watching Blackfeet. Instead, they traveled in brigades of forty to sixty men, including camp tenders and meat hunters. From brigade base camps, they fanned out, usually in pairs, to set their traps. Then they were most vulnerable, and then Indian ambushes took their heaviest toll.

Nor did the mountaineers hunt constantly. (They called a trapping expedition a hunt, a term also applied to seeking game for food.) There was a spring hunt and a fall hunt. The spring hunt garnered the winter fur and thus the best pelts, the fall hunt pelts of lesser quality. Summer of course was rendezvous. Winter was simply winter camp, waiting for the spring hunt.[9]

Contrary to conventional views, of the thousand or so mountain men who roamed the Rockies in the 1820s and 1830s, only a minority were Americans. Typically they had emigrated with their families from Kentucky or Tennessee to Missouri or Arkansas before heading for the mountains. Some reached their destination by way of New Mexico, but most went up the Missouri, the Yellowstone, or the Platte.

A large majority, three-fourths or more, claimed French, French Canadian, or Creole blood. Many traced their origins to the Montreal-based fur ventures that for a century and a half competed with the London-based Hudson's Bay Company. The last and most aggressive of the Montreal firms was the North West Company. After it merged with and took the name of the Hudson's Bay Company in 1821, French Canadians continued to play a prominent part in both the Canadian and American fur trade. The French predominance prevailed at every level, from common laborer to top management.

A third group also owed its identity to the North West Company. Eastern Indians, full-blood or mixed-blood, mostly Iroquois and Delaware, had been recruited for service in the westward thrust of the Canadian fur trade. They had not shed their Indian character, but they had absorbed enough of the alien ways to function as mountain men. Like the French Canadians, they easily shifted allegiance between English and American firms.[10]

Reflecting most societies, that of the mountain men was stratified, although upwardly mobile. Basically there were two strata, hired and free, with further stratification of the former.

Engagés, "engaged" men, worked for the company, first Smith, Jackson & Sublette, later the competing companies that began to challenge the domination of Ashley's heirs. To whichever firm engaged, engagés occupied one of three social levels. The lowest form was the *mangeur de lard,* or pork eater. Veterans applied this derisive term to greenhorns new to the mountains. They tended camp, stoked the fire, butchered and cooked the meat, packed and unpacked the animals, and did all the other drudge labor that the better sort disdained. Next in the hierarchy stood the "engaged" hunters and trappers. Equipped by the company and paid an annual salary, they either hunted meat for the brigade or trapped beaver for the company. The highest class consisted of what may be termed "sharecroppers." The company equipped and supplied them in return for a stipulated share of their catch or for the entire catch at a price agreed in advance.

The free trapper, unbeholden to any company, looked with condescension from the pinnacle of the social pyramid. He equipped and supplied himself, traveled with a company brigade or not as he wished, and sold his catch to whoever offered the highest price. He was the aristocrat, the "cock of the walk" as Washington Irving termed him, and in his attire and outfit he flaunted the crest and plumage of the cock of the walk.[11]

Joe Meek's amanuensis, putting the old trapper's words into proper English, described the free trappers thus:

> They prided themselves on their hardihood and courage; even on their recklessness and profligacy. Each claimed to own the best horse; to have had the wildest adventures; to have made the most narrow escapes; to have killed the greatest number of bears and Indians; to be the greatest favorite with the Indian belles, the greatest consumer of alcohol, and to have the most money to spend, i.e. the largest credit on the books of the company. If his hearers did not believe him, he was ready to run a race with him, to beat him at "old sledge," or to fight, if fighting was preferred. . . . The only authority which the free trapper acknowledged was that of his Indian spouse, who generally ruled in the lodge, however her lord blustered outside.[12]

Meek did not exaggerate the influence of Indian women, as he had reason to know from personal experience. The Flathead or Shoshone woman who could gain a free trapper as a husband enjoyed high stature in her tribe and truly, as Meek declared, "ruled in the lodge." That was her role with a man or her own tribe, and she asserted it equally with a white spouse. The role combined authority in domestic matters with responsibility for housekeeping—moving and setting up camp, cooking, preparing skins, making and mending garments and footwear, and other household chores. The pleasures of the nighttime robes followed the daytime drudge. Indian wives expected and received lavish gifts, for husbands strove to exhibit them as the most brilliantly clothed and ornamented of the women at rendezvous. Such unions might last for weeks, months, years, or a lifetime. Some trappers reared mixed-blood families, acquired political influence in the tribe, and acted as mediators between two cultures, interpreting each to the other. Women and children traveled with trapping brigades, or returned to their tribal origins when it was inconvenient to accompany their husbands, or simply camped near a trading post until their husbands returned from a hunt.

Trappers intent on sex without the encumbrance of marriage found that when Flathead, Shoshone, or Nez Perce bands congregated at rendezvous to trade and share in the fun. Indian standards of sexual propriety were high, but not so high that compliant women could not be found to gratify the lust of men long deprived.[13]

Both Washington Irving and Joe Meek sometimes succumbed to an ex-

The Piegan Blackfeet, Kenneth McKenzie's new trading clients, were still of volatile temper and difficult to deal with when Maximilian visited them on the upper Missouri in 1833. Karl Bodmer seized the opportunity to capture them for his patron and posterity. This is his view of an Encampment of the Piekann Indians. COURTESY JOSLYN ART MUSEUM, OMAHA, NEBRASKA.

cess of romanticism. For his social preeminence, the free trapper often paid a high economic price. The very freedom that fed his social pretensions made him especially vulnerable to market fluctuations. Still, despite repeated failure to take from the Rockies what Ashley had taken, the free trappers came close to Irving's portrait: "We find them, accordingly, hardy, lithe, vigorous, and active; extravagant in word, and thought, and deed; heedless of hardship; daring of danger; prodigal of the present, and thoughtless of the future."[14]

AFTER ORGANIZING their partnership on the Bear River in July 1826, the firm of Smith, Jackson & Sublette laid plans for a fall hunt. To Smith fell the undertaking most appealing to his inquiring mind. While Sublette and Jackson led a company into the dangerous but well-known Blackfeet country, Smith would lead another into altogether unknown country. Trappers had learned of Great Salt Lake itself less than a year earlier. Of the lands beyond they remained in ignorance, although they presumed that somewhere to the west ran the Buenaventura River. Smith would combine his obsession with exploration with the fall quest for beaver. He and about fifteen men would work down the Wasatch Range and probe the country to the west, south of Great Salt Lake, for untapped beaver streams. If possible, they would return to Cache Valley after the fall hunt. If not, they would be back in time for rendezvous in July 1827.[15]

"I wanted to be the first to view a country on which the eyes of a white man had never gazed and to follow the course of rivers that run through a new land," Smith recorded as he set forth.[16] Half a century earlier, Fathers Domínguez and Escalante had gazed on this land, but only from the edge, at the western base of the Wasatch Mountains. Even so, they could have speculated for Smith that this expanse of rock, sand, and salt supported no beaver.

The fall hunt turned up precious little to hunt, even to eat. Smith's company fell on the Sevier River, which rises among the multihued cliffs and plateaus of Bryce Canyon and strikes north before abruptly turning west to disappear in the salt bed of Sevier Lake. Surmounting a divide to the head of the Virgin River, the trappers now sought food more than beaver. Paiute Indians, less prosperous than the mountain tribes, furnished enough pumpkins and squash to avert starvation.

Early in October, nearly dismounted, hungry, with few beaver skins, Smith thought of turning back. But among the Paiutes he talked with some Mojaves, who lived farther south and told enough of their homeland to draw him forward. Rather than abandon this "unpromising country," he would winter among the Mojaves, attempt to remount his party, and look for the beaver streams that had so far eluded him.

The Mojaves lived on the Colorado River. When Smith reached the mouth of the Virgin, his keen geographical sense instantly identified the big river into which it empties below the Grand Canyon. "It could be no other but the Colorado of the west," he wrote, "which in the Mountains we call seetes-kee-der."[17]

The Mojaves lived better than the Paiutes. They had horses, and the fertile valley of the Colorado River nourished fields of pumpkins, squash, wheat, beans, and corn. Deserts and barren mountains, however, etched the horizon to the east and the west, and the Indians described the country downstream in bleak terms. Moreover, although they would trade for food, they would part with none of their horses. With men and animals exhausted, provisions dangerously low, and winter descending on the Rockies, Smith judged it too risky to return to the mountains.

The Mojaves said that the Mexican settlements lay ten days' journey to the west. There Smith determined to go. From the Mexicans he hoped to obtain fresh supplies, then trap northward. "In that direction I expected to find beaver and in all probability some considerable river heading up in the vicinity of the Great Salt Lake. By this route I could return to the deposite."[18]

Long before Jedediah Smith failed to find a Rio Buenaventura to lead him easily back to the "deposite," his plan encountered formidable obstacles, both geographical and human. The first was the Mojave Desert, that sweep of rock and sand drained by a river that yields virtually no water and that Smith called the Inconstant. It was a thirsty, fatiguing crossing, as it had been for the Spanish friar Francisco Garcés in 1776. Fifteen days, each an ordeal, at last brought the travelers, on November 26, 1826, across the San Bernardino Mountains and down to the green valley of the same name, lush with fields and orchards tended by mission Indians.

Smith approached this valley of Catholic missions and pueblos with trepidation, fearful of "bigotry and disregard of the rights of a Protestant." Instead, he found the Franciscan padre at San Gabriel Mission, Father José Sánchez, an amiable, hospitable, helpful friend. Smith's troubles, it turned out, arose from a secular rather than ecclesiastical source in the person of Governor José María Echeandía. This tall, gaunt, and deeply suspicious autocrat, resident in San Diego, could not grasp the concept of beaver hunter. Indeed, he persisted in calling Smith and his men *pescadores,* fishermen, the closest his mind could come to picturing what Smith said he did.

Yankees had come by sea from Boston and pursued a lively trade with Mexican California. But none had ever entered by land from the east. Echeandía probably saw this ragged little band of mountaineers as the beginnings of a threat to the somnolent pastoral world hugging the Pacific coast, as in truth they were. Like those earlier Americans foolish enough to venture to Santa Fe during Spanish times, the Smith company became enmeshed in a web of bureaucracy and irresolution from which escape seemed impossible. The governor, profoundly skeptical of any such occupation as beaver hunting, could not decide whether to imprison his unwanted guests, expel them, hold them pending instructions from Mexico City, send Smith himself to Mexico City, or even to decide to decide. After enduring a month of maddening vacillation, Smith enlisted the aid of a ship captain in the harbor, and Echeandía relented. The Americans could leave—by the route they had entered.[19]

In mid-January 1827, reprovisioned and with fresh horses, Smith and his men recrossed the San Bernardino Mountains. The governor had ordered them to leave the way they had come. Smith professed to believe that they had complied; after all, no Californians lived east of the coastal mountain ranges. (Disingenuous, to say the least; Smith knew that Mexico extended eastward through Texas and northward to the forty-second parallel.) Now the trappers turned north, to the streams Smith predicted would yield beaver and to the "considerable river" that he expected to follow back to the "deposite."

The rivers tumbling from the Sierra Nevada to feed the San Joaquin yielded beaver in sufficient quantity for the trappers to accumulate a substantial catch as they worked their way northward along the Sierra foothills. But as late as May, far down the valley where the San Joaquin turns west toward the ocean, Smith had yet to find his "considerable river." The snow-mantled bulwark of the Sierra Nevada (he called the entire range "Mt. Joseph" in honor of Father Sánchez) disclosed no gap through which such a river might flow.

With rendezvous less than two months in the future, Smith knew he had to get his furs over the mountains. The first week in May the caravan turned up the rough canyon of the American River and climbed sixty miles into heights still buried in snow. With six horses fallen, the rest could not break through this "freezing desolation." Back in the valley, he reached a painful decision. He would leave most of the men with the furs in camp on the Stanislaus River while he and two companions attempted another assault on the mountains. After rendezvous, he would return and take up a fall hunt.

On May 20 Jedediah Smith set forth up the Stanislaus River. He took with him Robert Evans and Silas Goble, six horses, two mules, sixty pounds of dried meat, and hay for forage. Slowed by drifts and assaulted by storms, they struggled upward to reach the Sierra summit at Ebbits Pass on the seventh day. A branch of the Walker River brought them down to the valley floor at Walker Lake.

Had Smith succeeded in breaking through the mountains at the head of the American River, he would have descended to the Humboldt Sink and discovered the river that faintly suggested the Buenaventura. The Humboldt Valley would have opened a pathway to the Salt Lake Valley.

Instead, Smith and his companions aimed directly east across a desert serrated by one narrow mountain range after another. "High Rocky hills afford the only relief to the desolate waste," he observed, for at their base an uncertain water hole could often be found. "The intervals between are sand barren Plains."[20] Tormented by thirst and heat, stock giving out, subsisting at length on horse meat, exhausted by struggling through loose sand, even the usually confident Smith despaired of surviving. At times they buried themselves in sand to cool their bodies. On the twenty-fifth day, Robert Evans gave out. Smith pushed ahead and stumbled on a water hole that enabled him to go back and save his comrade. Finally, on June 27, "I saw an expanse of water Extending far to the North and East. The Salt Lake a joyful sight was spread before us."[21]

On July 3, 1827, Smith and his two worn companions emerged from the eastern foothills of the Wasatch Mountains to the south shore of Bear Lake. They led one mule and one horse that were, "like ourselves, mere skeletons." Rendezvous was in full swing. "My arrival caused a considerable bustle in camp for myself and party had been given up as lost. A small Cannon brought up from St Louis was loaded and fired for a salute."[22]

Smith had again played the pioneer. He and his comrades were the first known whites to surmount the Sierra Nevada and the first to cross the Great Basin. The character of both these defining features of the Far West remained to be elaborated. But thanks to Jedediah Smith, the mountaineers at the rendezvous on Bear Lake now knew some important truths about what lay between them and the Pacific Ocean.

One fable, however, Smith had failed to extinguish: for more than a decade to come, men would search for the Rio Buenaventura.

RENDEZVOUS 1827 put the fledgling firm of Smith, Jackson & Sublette on the path to solvency. Jedediah Smith contributed nothing; such furs as he had gathered remained in the Central Valley west of the Sierra Nevada. Rather the credit fell to Sublette and Jackson, with the able young Robert Campbell serving as clerk. With a big enough brigade to fend off the Blackfeet, they aimed their fall hunt of 1826 at the Three Forks of the Missouri.

En route, though not on the vast scale of Jedediah Smith, Sublette and Jackson also trod new country. After trapping around the north end of the Tetons into Jackson Hole, they turned north to the head of the Snake and dropped into a fantastic land of geysers, bubbling pots of hot mud, and gurgling cauldrons covered by thin colored crusts. They viewed the great blue sheet of Yellowstone Lake, which they named for Bill Sublette, and almost certainly marveled at the thermal wonders of the geyser basin drained by the Firehole River. They were the first certain explorers of Yellowstone National Park.[23]

The Three Forks territory yielded plentiful beaver as well as occasional clashes with Blackfeet, one of which took the life of Old Pierre Tevanitagon. Back in Cache Valley by November, the trappers went into winter camp while Sublette, accompanied by that champion walker Black Harris, footed down to St. Louis to organize the 1827 caravan. (Snow prevented travel on horseback.) Jackson conducted a spring hunt on the Green River. By rendezvous, when Smith rejoined his partners, the firm had amassed 7,400 pounds of beaver, discharged all debt, ordered the next year's supplies, and counted a modest profit.[24]

Ten days after his arrival at the Bear Lake rendezvous, Jedediah Smith hit the return trail. He had told his men in California to wait for him no longer than September 20. That gave him nine weeks to get back. With eighteen men he set forth on July 13, 1827.

AFTER REJOINING his waiting company in California, Jedediah Smith intended to head north, up the Central Valley and the seacoast toward the heart of the Hudson's Bay Company domain. Again he betrayed his mixed motives: "I of course expected to find Beaver, which with us hunters is a primary object, but I was also led on by the love of novelty common to all, which is much increased by the pursuit of its gratification."[25]

Certain that men and animals could not negotiate the "Sand Plain" across which he had groped his way from the Sierras to Great Salt Lake, Smith saw no alternative to taking the longer path by which he had reached California a year earlier. Again the Sevier and Virgin Rivers guided the party to the Colorado and the valley where the Mojave Indians lived. Here in mid-August the trappers paused to rest their horses and trade for corn and beans.

On August 18 Smith began the river crossing, horses swimming and provisions and gear loaded on a cane raft. With Smith and eight men in midstream, the Mojaves suddenly sprang to the attack. Ten men remaining on the shore fell victim to arrows and clubs, while the others fended off waterborne assaults. They reached the opposite bank in safety, although one man had taken a severe blow to the head from a war club.

Confronted by several hundred warriors, Smith scattered most of his goods along the shore in hopes of diverting his assailants with the lure of plunder. When that ploy failed, he gathered the survivors in a small cotton-wood grove and prepared to fight to the last. The Mojaves closed in slowly, taking advantage of the scanty cover. When some drew within range, Smith had two of his best marksmen fire. Their balls killed two and wounded a third. "Upon this the indians ran off like frightened sheep and we were released from the apprehension of immediate death."[26]

Death less immediate loomed. They were nine men, one badly hurt, adrift in a desolate land with fifteen pounds of dried meat but no horses or even containers for water. "After weighing all the circumstances of my situation as calmly as possible, I concluded to again try the hospitality of the Californians."[27] Once more Smith confronted the Mojave Desert, but his talent for finding water in an apparently waterless land got them through. Chancing on Indians from whom to purchase four horses and some demi-johns for water helped, and ten days from the Colorado the jaded travelers dropped into the San Bernardino Valley.

Reluctant to test the Californian hospitality too openly, Smith clung to the eastern fringes of the valley. He wrote to Father Sánchez at San Gabriel Mission but did not go there. Instead, he butchered some of the mission cattle and added enough horses to mount all his men. Then he withdrew east of the San Bernardino Mountains and turned north. On September 18, only two days before his promised return, Smith reached the Stanislaus River and rode into the camp he had left four months earlier.

Jedediah Smith had merely postponed his test of Californian hospitality, for he needed more horses and supplies to move his company to the north. At Mission San José, he discovered Father Narciso Durán much less friendly than Father Sánchez. Worse, Smith fell once more under the power of Governor Echeandía, now headquartered in Monterey. For three months he subjected the American intruders to bureaucratic and legal torture. "It seemed that this man was placed in power to perplex me and those over whom he was called to govern," Smith lamented.[28]

For a second time, Americans had made a landward appearance in California, and still they told implausible stories about hunting beaver. The governor looked on them as spies or worse: they had not left California as ordered, and they were suspected of tampering with the mission Indians. But again he could not decide what to do about them; and again help came from the harbor in the persons of an English trader and a Boston seaman, who provided a legal rationale for releasing the Americans and a pledge to see them out of the country. Not until the end of December, however, did Smith free himself from the toils of Mexican officialdom and turn back to the Central Valley, safely distant from the coastal settlements.[29]

For all the agony, Smith's three months in San José and Monterey had not been entirely wasted. He discovered that in California horses were plentiful and cheap. In the mountains they would be a commodity as profitable as beaver pelts. Furthermore, he sold his accumulated beaver, 1,568 pounds, to the master of a ship in San Francisco Bay for $2.50 per pound. This brought nearly $4,000, with which Smith bought 250 horses and mules to add to the 65 he already had. The procession that splashed up the boggy bottoms of the Sacramento River early in January 1828 made an impressive sight—twenty men driving 365 horses and mules.

For three months the men trapped their way north, probing the streams that fell from the Sierras into the Sacramento, which Smith called the Buenaventura. Clearly this Buenaventura did not breach "Mt. Joseph," which rose in an unbroken wall to the head of the valley and then merged with other ranges curving around its northern edges. There the snowy cone of Mount Shasta served notice of difficult traveling ahead. The mountain streams supported beaver, but a scarcity of traps limited the catch.

Through April and May the company climbed from the valley and turned toward the ocean. The jagged mountains and sheer cliffs scoured by the Trinity and Klamath Rivers proved nearly impassable for men herding more than three hundred animals. Game all but disappeared. Indians hovered on the flanks, loosing arrows when chance offered. Fog slowed and often halted progress. Horses and mules crowded narrow trails and plunged to their death on rocky precipices. At times, a mile or less was counted a good day's travel. At other times, a route barred by a mountainside or canyon forced a long trek on the back trail.

Even the ocean afforded scant relief, for forested slopes fell to the water's edge. Through June, putting Mexican California behind them, the trappers worked up the Oregon coast, taking a few beaver and occasionally trading with Indians of uncertain temper. By mid-July, they had reached the Umpqua River a short distance above its mouth and camped on the west bank of a tributary that subsequently took Smith's name.

Kuitsh (or Lower Umpqua) Indians came to trade. They seemed friendly and, as shown by their possessions, were customers of the Hudson's Bay Company. Smith remained wary. In earlier skirmishes, his men had killed two Indians, and now, to retrieve a stolen axe, he tied up a chief until it was returned. He instructed his men to keep on their guard.

On July 14, Smith took two men and an Indian guide up the river by canoe to find a crossing. In camp, about a hundred Indians mingled with the trappers in a trading session. Drifting back downstream late in the morning, Smith could see no activity in his camp. Suddenly the guide grabbed Smith's rifle and dove into the water as Indians concealed along the shore opened fire. Frantically, the three whites paddled to the opposite bank, scrambled ashore, and took to the woods.

Scanning the campsite from hills across the river, Smith drew an accurate conclusion. His men, lulled by the evidence of a Hudson's Bay Company relationship, had dropped their guard, and the Indians had struck. Unknown to Smith, one man had escaped. The rest, fifteen in all, had been axed to death, and all the contents of the camp, including 728 beaver pelts and 228 horses and mules, fell into the hands of the Kuitshes.

Alone and all but destitute in a dangerous wilderness, Smith and his two companions had but one chance—to seek relief from the Hudson's Bay Company.[30]

IN THE FOUR YEARS since George Simpson and John McLoughlin had taken hold of the Hudson's Bay Company's Columbia Department, they had transformed it into a strong and profitable enterprise. Even before Simpson returned east in 1825, Fort George had been abandoned. The governor wanted a headquarters located where crops could be grown and domestic animals kept and also, reflecting his assumption that all Oregon south of the Columbia would fall to the Americans, a site that solidified the British hold on the territory north of the Columbia. Fort Vancouver, erected on a fertile bench north of the river just above the mouth of the Willamette, met both aims.

Despite Peter Skene Ogden's rough treatment at the hands of Johnson Gardner in May 1825, neither Simpson nor his superiors in London had changed their thinking about the Snake country. It ought to be swept clean of beaver, both for profit and to deter the Americans. Aided by more generous treatment of the freemen and greater reliance on engagés, Ogden's subsequent Snake Country Expeditions turned profits and held their own against the Americans when their paths crossed.

The company's Snake country policy found renewed strength in 1827. British and American diplomats failed to break the impasse acknowledged in the Convention of 1818, due to expire in 1828, and agreed to an indefinite extension of joint occupation of Oregon. Passing on London's instructions, Simpson advised McLoughlin in July 1827 to hunt south of the Columbia "with our utmost strength and activity." "If the country becomes exhausted in Fur bearing animals," he added, Americans "can have no inducement to proceed thither."[31]

Proceed thither they did, however, as the "commissioned gentlemen" periodically discovered on the Snake and around Flathead Post, and as the bearlike McLoughlin himself had personal reason to know. On August 8, 1828, Arthur Black, sole survivor of the Umpqua Massacre, presented himself at the gates of Fort Vancouver, and two days later Jedediah Smith and his two companions appeared. Although in dire straits, Americans had returned to the Columbia.[32]

John McLoughlin treated his unwanted guests with generosity and compassion. The trapping brigade of Alexander McLeod, even then in the field, went to the Umpqua to investigate. Smith and his three men went along. They recovered twenty-six horses and mules, most of the fur catch, and assorted other equipage, including the journals of Smith and his clerk, Harrison Rogers. At the site of the massacre, they buried the mangled remains of eleven of the fifteen victims. The other four were never found.[33]

When Smith returned to Fort Vancouver in mid-December, he found Governor Simpson, here for a winterlong inspection, his first since 1825. Smith dealt directly with Simpson, who responded with a formal courtesy that reproached the American for the trouble and expense he had caused but that acknowledged the obligation of one gentleman toward another in distress. In the end, Simpson bought Smith's horses and furs and extended the hospitality of Fort Vancouver through the winter months.[34]

Simpson took advantage of those months to learn all he could from Smith about American activities and intentions, which he passed on to his superiors in London. In particular, he noted, Smith had given the lie to the charts that showed a "Multnomah" River flowing from a height of land to the Columbia. Americans thought they could get all their stock and implements to this divide and then "embark on large Rafts & Batteaux and glide down current about 800 or 1000 Miles at their ease to this 'Land of Promise.'" Now it appeared that this river, the Willamette, rose only 150 miles directly south of Fort Vancouver.

The other route, by way of the Snake, "Settlers could never think of attempting." Therefore, the governor concluded, "we have little to apprehend from Settlers in this quarter."[35]

For all his managerial talent and personal force, as a prophet George Simpson failed.

ON OCTOBER 11, 1830, the Smith, Jackson & Sublette caravan arrived in St. Louis from the Rocky Mountains. Townspeople took note because it included, besides pack animals and about fifty men, ten wagons. For the first time, wagons had gone to the mountains. "The ease with which they did it and could have gone on to the mouth of the Columbia," commented an editorialist, "shows the folly and nonsense of those 'scientific' characters who talk of the Rocky Mountains as the barrier which is to stop the westward march of the American people."[36]

"These hardy and sun-burnt *Mountaineers*," as a reporter called them, included all three partners, Smith, Jackson, and Sublette. Jedediah Smith had come down from the mountains homesick, guilt-ridden over neglecting his parents, and hungry for the ministrations of the clergy. "Oh when Shall I be under the care of a Christian Church?" he had written his brother the previous Christmas. Even as the caravan turned from the Platte toward the Missouri in September 1830, he received word of his mother's death.[37]

Other motives drew Jedediah Smith from the mountains. His saddlebags contained the maps and journals that recorded his experiences and geographical observations in the Far West, from the Continental Divide to the Pacific. He wanted to lay his vast store of knowledge before the public.

Financial considerations allowed him to withdraw with honor. His California and Oregon adventures had not cast his firm's books into the red, but they had severely thinned the black ink. After parting with his Hudson's Bay friends in the spring of 1829, Smith had found his way to a union with

David Jackson at Flathead Lake, and they in turn had joined Sublette in Pierre's Hole.

Smith himself organized a strong brigade to invade the Blackfeet country in the autumn of 1829. Jackson went along, and Jim Bridger, by now one of the ablest mountaineers, served as pilot. They interrupted the fall and spring hunts with a winter camp on the Powder River. Blackfeet harassment finally drove them back, but not before they amassed a rich store of beaver to take to the 1830 rendezvous. In St. Louis, the catch brought more than eighty-four thousand dollars.[38]

So Jedediah Smith had made up to his partners for his failings and had emerged with a profit of his own. He could turn his back on the mountains if he wanted, and probably on his initiative the three partners decided to end their association.

Other increasingly apparent developments favored such a move. Beaver had grown scarce everywhere but the Blackfeet country, and to hunt there required a large brigade such as Smith had led in 1829–30, which traded efficiency for strong defense. In addition, both from St. Louis and the upper Missouri, the two western arms of the American Fur Company had begun to field competing caravans and trapping companies.

With a comfortable profit to show for their four-year operation, the partners agreed to withdraw. At the 1830 rendezvous on the Wind River just below the mouth of the Popo Agie, they sold out to a combination consisting of Tom Fitzpatrick, Milton Sublette, Jim Bridger, Henry Fraeb, and Jean Baptiste Gervais. The five partners, all accomplished mountain men, styled themselves the Rocky Mountain Fur Company.[39]

Smith, Jackson, and Sublette turned their interest to the "commerce of the prairies" that linked Missouri and New Mexico over the Santa Fe Trail. But they had also agreed to provide the 1831 supply caravan for the new Rocky Mountain Fur Company. Tom Fitzpatrick, however, did not get down from the mountains in time to complete the arrangements. When he finally caught up with them in May, two months late, they had their train on the road to New Mexico. If he would accompany them to Santa Fe, the three promised, they would outfit him there, and he could assemble his own caravan for a journey up the Front Range of the Rockies.

The train faltered on the drought-stricken Cimarron Cutoff of the Santa Fe Trail. Together, Smith and Fitzpatrick set forth in an attempt to find water. At a dry hole, Fitzpatrick stopped to dig while Smith headed for another promising spot. Suddenly fifteen or twenty Comanche warriors burst from hiding and surrounded Smith. He made peace signs, which they ignored. After wary maneuvering, a warrior fired a ball into Smith's back. He reeled in the saddle, raised his rifle, and sent a fatal ball into the Comanche chief. The others swarmed over him with lances and ended the life of Jedediah Smith. He was thirty-two.[40]

JEDEDIAH SMITH INTENDED to publish a book and a master map of the American West. No individual, American or British, knew more about the geography of the entire region from the Missouri to the Pacific. From personal experience, he understood the Great Plains, the northern Rockies, the Great Basin, the lower Colorado, and the Pacific Coast from southern California to the Columbia; and equally important, he understood how they fitted together. At rendezvous he quizzed others about territory he had not seen, and on his map drafts he identified these sources. In St. Louis during the winter of 1830–31, he worked on his maps and journals, and when he left for Santa Fe in May 1831 others continued the work.

After Smith's death, his papers disappeared, probably in a fire. Fragments of copies of his journals turned up a century later, but no map was ever found. William H. Ashley had one or more Smith maps, and he took them with him to Washington when elected to the U.S. House of Representatives in 1831, a seat he held until 1837.

Ashley thus became the conduit by which a tiny fraction of the knowledge Smith had set to paper reached the public. In 1836 Albert Gallatin published a map of North America that owed a debt to Smith. Three years later David H. Burr, geographer for the House of Representatives, published a map of the United States that drew directly from a Smith map, almost certainly obtained from Congressman Ashley. As scholar Carl I. Wheat has written, Burr used Smith's map intelligently and effectively, "and the West is that of Jedediah Smith, from the Rockies to California and from the Columbia River to the present Mexican line."[41]

Burr's map, however, had little influence, and cartographers continued to lay down such fantasies as the Multnomah and the Buenaventura. One exception was London cartographer Aaron Arrowsmith, whose access to the archives of the Hudson's Bay Company opened to him the world of Peter Skene Ogden and other field leaders. In particular, Arrowsmith's 1834 map showed the Humboldt River and Sink, which Ogden had discovered and sketched in 1828–29. Smith had missed this crucial link between Great Salt Lake and the Sierras, destined to provide the thoroughfare for the wagon trains of California-bound emigrants and ultimately the first transcontinental railroad.[42]

Thanks to Comanche lances, therefore, only a few particles of Jedediah Smith's rich knowledge of the American West reached the world. Had he

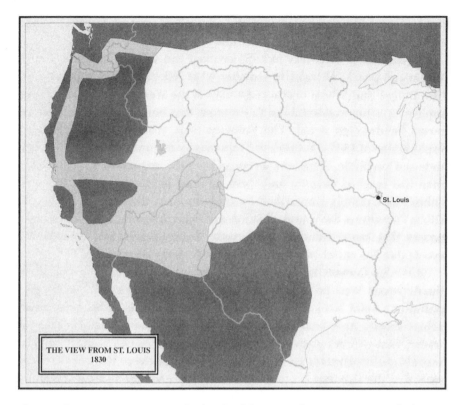

THE VIEW FROM ST. LOUIS
1830

St. Louis

The view from St. Louis, 1830. In the decade of the 1820s, fur men in St. Louis had added greatly to their knowledge of the Rocky Mountain West. The trappers fielded by William H. Ashley and his successor firm, Smith, Jackson & Sublette, had formed an accurate conception of the Missouri, the Yellowstone, and their tributaries; the upper Snake; and Great Salt Lake. Jedediah Smith had completed his monumental four crossings of the continent, which had shown him an edge and then the heart of the Great Basin, as well as the heart of the Hudson's Bay Company domain. What St. Louisans knew, however, drew on reports of the fur men, often publicized by Missouri newspapers. What they lacked was a map to give it visual expression. Smith compiled such a map, but his death on the Santa Fe Trail in 1831 severely limited its contemporary influence. Taos-based Americans had probed northwest to the Uinta Basin and north to the three parks of the Rockies. They had also linked New Mexico with California by way of the Gila River and its tributaries. Not much of their geographical understanding, however, trickled over the Santa Fe Trail to St. Louis. By 1830, therefore, the view west from St. Louis had expanded considerably since 1820, but it fell far short of the specificity by now carried in the collective mind of the mountain men working the northern Rockies and those ranging north and west out of Taos.

lived to carry forward his project, the advance of western mapping would have been hastened by at least a decade.

A remarkable discovery in 1953 enabled two diligent scholars, Carl I. Wheat and Dale L. Morgan, to visualize what Jedediah Smith's map looked like. In that year Wheat uncovered a map of the West drawn by the cartographer for army explorer John C. Frémont that bore a wealth of superimposed handwritten detail. The Frémont map, fruit of his wide-ranging explorations of 1842–45, displayed topography astronomically fixed by latitude and longitude. Somehow, a copy or even the original of Smith's master map had reached Oregon; and there, around 1850, cartographer George Gibbs had carefully transcribed its contents onto the Frémont map. The Gibbs map shows the routes of Smith and other trappers, a wealth of place names that have endured, and cryptic commentary about people and events that has enriched a history often only thinly documented.[43]

Although Comanches deprived Smith's contemporaries of the picture of the American West he would have laid before them, Burr and Gibbs gave posterity a solid basis for appreciating the magnitude of his exploratory achievements. As Wheat has written: "Jedediah Smith was no mere fur trader. That without instruments and beset by difficulties of every sort, he was able to construct a great map of the West discloses the caliber of the man, and the fact that his map remained unknown for so long . . . cannot take away from him the credit for having drawn the first reasonably accurate map of the West."[44]

8

EWING YOUNG:
GILA TRAILS TO CALIFORNIA

AS ÉTIENNE PROVOST WITHDREW from Taos to cast his fortunes on the upper Missouri and in the Rocky Mountains, Ewing Young inherited his mantle as premier trapper of the Mexican republic's northern provinces. He had come to New Mexico in 1822 with William Becknell's pioneering second expedition, the first to draw wagons over the embryonic Santa Fe Trail. A Tennessean, twenty-eight in 1822, Young was a strapping six feet two, a man of rudimentary learning, ordinarily quiet but harboring a hot temper, a scrappy and fearless antagonist with Mexican officialdom and bothersome Indians, shrewd and sometimes devious, ambitious to prosper whether from trapping, trading, farming, milling, or droving, and endowed with a capacity to lead other men in any of these pursuits.[1]

Adobe Indian pueblo and Mexican frontier outpost, Taos dotted a broad plain bounded by the Sangre de Cristo Mountains on the east and the Rio Grande Canyon on the west. Even though the Uinta Basin lost its appeal as Ashley men and their successful rendezvous system came to dominate the northern Rockies, Taos continued to draw men like Ewing Young. The southern Rockies, with forested peaks emptying beaver-rich streams into North Park and South Park, could easily be reached from Taos, which in effect constituted a year-round rendezvous for the exchange of fur for supplies—and the liquid stimulant judged essential to the process. Supplying the trappers and hauling their catch back to Missouri accounted for a large share of the "commerce of the prairies" over the Santa Fe Trail.

After 1825, fresh beaver grounds attracted the Taos trappers. They lay to the south and west, in the mountains and deserts drained by the Gila River and its tributaries. The northern affluents, falling from the White Mountains and the Mogollon Rim, resembled the high-country streams of the Rockies. The southern affluents, snaking across a land studded with cactus, agave, prickly pear, ocotillo, and other fruits of the Sonoran Desert, nonetheless spawned beaver. Most of these streams, in a time before irrigation, ran a continuous head of water, and a green thread of cottonwood and willow traced their course. Wherever deciduous trees grew, beaver flourished.

Spaniards had trod the Gila country in earlier centuries, but Mexicans rarely ventured where such inveterate enemies as Navajos and Apaches held sway. These accomplished marauders constantly terrorized settlers in their own homes, and anyway the humble farmers and herdsmen of the Rio Grande valley lacked both skill and interest in trapping. That remained an exclusive possession of the American newcomers.

The Gila offered another inducement. It lay beyond the view of government officials. Increasingly in the late 1820s, provincial governors in Santa Fe came under pressure from Mexico City to enforce the law of 1824 banning Americans from taking Mexican beaver. Occasionally, on various pretexts, governors issued licenses to Americans, but such documents usually proved as useful as no license at all. Americans could hunt Gila beaver confident of no Mexican official nearer than several hundred miles.

But the beaver still had to be got to market, in Taos or Santa Fe. Like their compatriots to the north, the Taos trappers respected Mexican sovereignty no more than Indian. Where beaver swam and built, there went the trappers. Mexicans resented the loss of so much national wealth to foreigners and made strenuous efforts to block it. But the governors lacked the military strength to cope with the canny Americans, who became adept at smuggling most of their furs to traders bound for Missouri.

Ewing Young exemplified the Taos trappers of the late 1820s. He emerged as the most prominent, the best leader, the greatest aggravation to Mexican officials, and the preeminent pioneer of the Gila. Although Mexican territory, the Gila would one day fall to the American nation as part of its continental destiny. As explorers, Young and his comrades deserve as much credit as their better-known northern counterparts, for they opened the geographically complex and imperfectly understood land sliced by the Gila River and its tributaries.

ARRIVING IN NEW MEXICO in 1822, Ewing Young established himself in Taos, where he pursued his craft of carpentry. His home became a social center for trappers as well as a sometime trading post. The latter he operated in partnership with William Wolfskill, a Missourian well versed in frontier skills. Together the two men trapped the upper Pecos in the fall of 1822, and each made trading trips back to Missouri. But as Young declared, "I want to get *outside* of where trappers have ever been."[2]

Truly outside meant the Gila. In 1826, recruiting eighteen men, Young and Wolfskill planned a fall hunt to the Gila. So did others, four groups in all. The "French Company" had resolved to test New Mexico and had fielded a party under the son of old Bernard Pratte, senior partner of the firm. Sylvester Pratte fell ill and did not take the field himself, but two of the four parties operated with Pratte backing—one of twenty led by Ceran St. Vrain and William S. Williams, the other of thirty led by Miguel Robidoux. Under the guidance of Joseph Robidoux of Council Bluffs, a bevy of Robidoux brothers had descended on New Mexico. In the bizarre business convolutions of the fur trade, Joseph Robidoux both worked for and competed with B. Pratte & Company, a relationship reflected in the Gila expedition of Miguel Robidoux. A fourth group, of eighteen, was headed by John Rowland. Curiously, despite clear indications that these companies intended to trap, Governor Antonio Narbona issued official *trading* passports to all, an act that he almost at once repented and sought desperately to rescind. Too late: suddenly the Gila country teemed with American trappers.[3]

St. Vrain's partner, William S. Williams, had already lived a lifetime of adventure and earned the cognomen "Old Bill." By age forty, he had trapped, hunted, and traded, married into the Osage tribe and acquired a family, ridden as an itinerant parson, traded Baptist theology for Indian mysticism, and served as guide and interpreter for the army. Tall and lanky, with red hair and beard, he had gained renown for his strength and courage, marksmanship, trapping prodigies, and finely honed wilderness skills. For another two decades, Old Bill Williams commanded the respect if not the affection of the mountain men. He constantly surpassed them in eccentricity of speech and behavior and ability to drink up the proceeds of a season's catch in a few days, and he left no one in doubt of his high sense of self-worth. "William S. Williams, M.T.," he tagged his pelts, the "M.T." standing for "Master Trapper."[4]

Jump-off point for Gila trapping was "Santa Rita del Cobre," the old Spanish Copper Mines in the Pinos Altos Range near the head of the Gila. Now operated under lease by an American, Robert McKnight, the Copper Mines provided Gila trappers with the kind of fixed rendezvous Taos offered on the northern frontier. Distant from Mexican officialdom, moreover, the mines also helped trappers evade confiscation, customs, or other governmental interference.

The Young-Wolfskill party included two men destined for a notoriety only slightly less than Old Bill Williams's. Milton Sublette, an immense, powerful youth of twenty-five, had apprenticed on the frontier with his older brother William in the service of Ashley and Henry, but the Gila formed the stage for his debut as a mountain man. "Reckless of life and money," an acquaintance recalled, a widely held view that followed him northward as he made his reputation as the "Thunderbolt of the Rocky Mountains."[5]

The same age as Milton Sublette, Thomas L. Smith had trapped and traded since 1820. He had been on the Green and the San Juan in 1824, during Provost's venture to the Uinta Basin, and had fought Utes and traded with Navajos. A big man like Sublette, rowdy, of fearless courage and unflinching fortitude, with a nearly bottomless capacity for "Taos Lightning," he would trap until droving appeared more profitable, and finally make himself the nemesis of the horse herds of California. His sobriquet of "Pegleg" lay in the near future.[6]

The Young-Wolfskill expedition left the Copper Mines under Wolfskill's leadership. Young had taken sick and remained in Santa Fe. The men hunted successfully down the Gila as far as the mouth of the Salt River, a distance of some 250 miles. Here they ran afoul of Apaches and, barred from taking up their traps, had to withdraw altogether. A shower of arrows hastened their departure. One hit Milton Sublette in the leg. Tom Smith hauled him to safety, but the injury would plague Sublette for the rest of his life.

Now Young took command while Wolfskill stayed behind. With thirty men, he pushed off from the Copper Mines in January 1827. Although intent on taking beaver, Young had a secondary objective: to punish the Indians for daring to interfere with his trappers. An occasion offered near the mouth of the Salt River, for here he picked up three men, the only survivors of a massacre of Miguel Robidoux's hunters. One was Robidoux himself, and a second was James Ohio Pattie, whose narrative of his western adventures has intrigued and confounded historians ever since its publication in 1831. Pattie identified the offending Indians as "Papawars"—Papagos—but they were probably Apaches or Yavapais. Young cared little for tribal distinctions: any Indians merited a mauling, for others would then take heed and avoid white men.[7]

Pattie called Young (whom he never names) "a genuine American leader." And lead he did, deploying his men by night near the Indian village and next morning decoying the warriors into a trap. Tom Smith fired the first shot, killed his man, and sprang forward to get his scalp. (George Yount declared years later that Smith boasted of never killing an Indian whose scalp he failed to take.) A volley from the trappers' rifles felled many others and sent the balance into headlong retreat. A delegation from the village appeared the following day to sue for peace, and Young departed down the Gila confident that a lesson had been imparted.[8]

Through the deserts of the lower Gila and the lower Colorado itself, Young's men trapped during February 1827. Turning up the Colorado, in early March they reached the Mojave Valley and opened an uneasy relationship with the Mojave Indians. Six months earlier, these people had treated Jedediah Smith hospitably, but now they greeted Young with surly demeanor, possibly because Young himself made little effort to conceal his contempt for all Indians.

The inevitable incident provoked a confrontation. The trappers barricaded their camp and easily shattered a dawn attack. A volley of rifle balls dropped sixteen warriors and sent the rest fleeing in panic. Less than six months later, pausing at the Mojave villages a second time en route to California, Jedediah Smith and his party would lose ten men to Mojave revenge.

Farther up the Colorado Valley, around the mouth of the Virgin River, Young's party divided, the result of growing friction between the leader and tempestuous Tom Smith, who balked at taking orders from anyone. How they all eventually got back to Santa Fe in May 1827 is lost in the confusion of dimming memories or fevered imaginations. Pattie told of moving with his group across the Rockies to the Platte, then to the Bighorn and Yellowstone, and finally as far north as Clark's Fork of the Columbia, all within a few weeks. The Little Colorado or the San Juan are more plausible alternatives.

Young had described a huge and pioneering arc through geography poorly known. The mountains and deserts of the Gila and the vast plateau country to the north had been penetrated by American trappers and a fortune in beaver skins harvested from virgin streams. The hunters may even have looked into the Grand Canyon from its north rim. The exploratory achievement had been immense, but the commercial results had been a failure. Despite Young's sly stratagem of concealing his furs in a village west of Santa Fe, the government moved against him. The impetuous Milton Sublette fled with his share of the furs, but Young lost all his to confiscation and found himself under arrest in addition.

Even so, Ewing Young had not finished with the Gila.

THE FRENCH FUR COMPANY—B. Pratte & Company of St. Louis—did not do well on the Gila. Ceran St. Vrain and Old Bill Williams were back in Santa Fe by January 1827, but with what result eluded the record. Miguel

Robidoux got his trapping party obliterated by Indians. But in New Mexico Sylvester Pratte represented big money, especially with the merger that transformed B. Pratte & Company into the Western Department of the American Fur Company. Sylvester backed numerous trapping ventures based in Taos, few of which returned a profit. Finally, in the fall of 1827, he resolved to lead one himself. Aimed at the southern Rockies and the Green River, this endeavor would provide final confirmation of the judgment already pronounced on Pratte by one of the firm's partners: "How can a young man who seems to be guided by a sense of good have so little success in what he undertakes?"[9]

Pratte led twenty-five or so trappers northward, including Old Bill Williams, Milton Sublette, and Tom Smith. Present too was Joseph Bissonet, who had trapped North and South Parks with Chouteau and de Mun in 1815–17 and who had guided the Long exploring expedition of 1820. Ceran St. Vrain, offspring of French nobility and beginning a distinguished career on the frontier, went along as clerk. He wrote clumsily and phonetically, but he could keep the books.

South Park and North Park gave up handsome beaver catches, but in North Park, source of the North Platte River, the expedition met two severe setbacks. There on October 1, 1827, Sylvester Pratte suddenly sickened and died. For a time the group verged on disintegration, but at length all united under the leadership of the able Ceran St. Vrain.[10]

In North Park, calamity struck again. Recklessly exposing himself as usual, Tom Smith fell victim to an Indian sniper hidden in a clump of brush. The bullet struck his left leg above the ankle and shattered the bones. When the men shrank in confused hesitation, Smith called for a butcher knife and began to amputate his own foot. Finally, Milton Sublette steeled himself to finish the operation. No one expected Smith to live, for he refused to submit to cauterization. But he lived. Before the expedition found its way back to New Mexico, he had applied Indian remedies that proved effective and had even whittled himself a wooden leg. Henceforth, Tom Smith would be Pegleg Smith.[11]

St. Vrain's expedition of 1827–28 quashed B. Pratte & Company's interest in New Mexico. From North Park, the trappers had worked the Little Snake and then wintered on the Green. They had tried to take their furs down to Missouri by way of the Platte but had turned back to New Mexico when Indians threatened. Arriving in May 1828, St. Vrain sold the catch for more than five thousand dollars, but that did not cover salaries and expenses. Bernard Pratte, Pierre Chouteau, Jr., and other St. Louis partners had soured altogether on New Mexico. That a now-dead but incompetent son of the senior partner had bungled his mission cast an even heavier pall over the decision. Henceforth the Western Department of the American Fur Company would concentrate on the upper Missouri and the northern Rockies.[12]

BY 1829, Ewing Young's troubles with New Mexican officials had led him to a conclusion already reached by other Taos trappers. Sea captains regularly called at California ports and would buy furs to add to their cargo. The Gila could be trapped and the catch carried on to California and sold to the masters of American or foreign vessels. The time and effort of transport, Apache aggression on the Gila, and official harassment in Santa Fe could be lessened. And for those seeking a still larger catch, the beaver country of the San Joaquin Valley could be swept before heading for the coast. Jedediah Smith had already tested the possibilities of California. Incidentally, he had found Mexican authorities there no less difficult than their counterparts in Santa Fe.

Ewing Young's expedition of 1829–31 was not the first to embrace this pattern. As early as 1827, his friend Richard Campbell, who had probably been with Young in his circuit of 1826–27, led a party of thirty-five trappers west from Taos. They may have retraced Young's inbound route of a few months earlier, jumping off from the pueblo of Zuñi, following the Zuñi and Little Colorado Rivers, swinging north of the Grand Canyon, fording the Colorado where Escalante had crossed in 1776, and descending the Virgin to pick up the trail of Jedediah Smith. In California Campbell encountered none of the obstacles that plagued Smith. Other distractions, including Smith himself, occupied Governor Echeandía. In San Francisco Bay, Campbell sold five hundred skins to a Russian sea captain and by February 1828 had returned to Taos.[13]

Only a few months behind Campbell came another party, of twenty-four men, led by Sylvester Pattie and including his ubiquitous son James O. Pattie. Trapping the usual route down the Gila from the Copper Mines, this group fell apart when it reached the Colorado. Six men stayed with the Patties to float by dugout all the way to the desolate mouth of the Colorado. From there, where they had to cache their furs, they struggled on foot across the terrible deserts of Baja California only to fall captive to unsympathetic Mexican authorities. By the spring of 1828, the Americans had been forwarded to San Diego and given over to the custody of Governor Echeandía, fresh from his exasperating proceedings with Jedediah Smith. Later Pattie wrote luridly of his father's death in a Mexican cell and his own mistreatment by the governor and ultimate vindication, after which he embarked by ship to put the West behind him forever. A thread of truth runs through young Pattie's tortured prose, but most of what he wrote was either invented or exaggerated.[14]

Ewing Young, meantime, tried to recoup his losses after the governor of New Mexico seized the yield of his expedition of 1826–27. In 1828 Young dispatched another party to the Gila, but he sustained even more losses when Apaches drove it back to Taos. Then his friend Richard Campbell came home to tell of California. That decided Young. Perhaps the Campbell model would turn a profit. In August 1829, Young placed himself at the head of forty men and set forth from Taos—north fifty miles to deceive suspicious officials before circling back southwest to Zuñi Pueblo.

Among Young's men was an unprepossessing youth of nineteen, short and stoop-shouldered with freckled face and reddish brown hair. He spoke quietly, sparingly, and modestly, but in the three years since arriving in New Mexico he had sharpened his outdoor skills and revealed courage, strength, endurance, and intellect. Christopher Houston Carson had grown up on the Missouri frontier and had listened eagerly to the stories of the West recounted by his brothers, especially his half brother, veteran trapper Moses Carson. At sixteen, "Kit" had run away from home and joined a caravan on the Santa Fe Trail. Since 1826, he had cooked for Young and Wolfskill in Taos, freighted to El Paso and Chihuahua, and worked for Robert McKnight at the Copper Mines. Impressed by his cool behavior in an expedition to lift a Comanche siege of a wagon train from Missouri, Young had taken on Kit Carson as an apprentice trapper.[15]

Zuñi Pueblo opened an easy way southwest to the Salt River, whose headstreams rose in the White Mountains to the east. The Salt snaked through deep canyons with precipitous yellow walls. Even though trapped in the three preceding years, it still crawled with beaver.

It also gashed the forested uplands of the Apaches, the same who had driven Young's party back to Taos the previous year. As warriors gathered menacingly on the canyon slopes, Young proved still adept at laying ambushes. Concealing most of his men, he enticed a large number of Indians into his camp, then signaled his men to rise and open fire—"which was done," as Carson laconically recorded, "the Indians losing in killed fifteen or twenty warriors and great number in wounded."[16]

The bloodletting avoided further open conflict but ensured constant harassment as the party trapped down the Salt, then turned north up the Verde River. Twisting southward between towering mountain ranges, this river finally debouches into the Salt amid desert hills studded with saguaro cactus. It proved as well stocked with beaver as the Salt, but at night the Apaches stole traps and mules and inflicted other mischief. Near the head of the Verde, Young decided to send part of his men back to Taos, both to take in the accumulated skins and to procure more traps.

Rather than return 150 miles down the Verde to pick up the Gila path to California, Young decided to seek a new route. With eighteen men, he faced directly west, to find himself swallowed by a land of mountain and desert bereft of either game or water. As Carson recalled, it was "a country sandy, burned up, and not a drop of water." In an eight-day trek, they found one spring. "We suffered extremely," Carson remarked; but the ordeal ended at the Colorado River, where men and animals drank their fill, and the Mojave Indians provided food. As Young readily conceded, he had not discovered a new trail to California.[17]

From the Colorado River, the Young party followed a route already twice traveled by Jedediah Smith and once by Richard Campbell—the Mojave Desert and River to Cajon Pass through the San Bernardino Mountains, and thence to the hospitality of Father José Sánchez at San Gabriel Mission. With spring 1830 well advanced, after only one day to reprovision Young turned north for a spring hunt in the San Joaquin Valley.

Not only Americans exploited the beaver resources of Mexico. As Jedediah Smith had discovered, the San Joaquin River and the tributaries feeding it from the Sierra Nevada supported plentiful beaver. Young found beaver scarce, however, and soon learned why when he overhauled a trapping brigade of the Hudson's Bay Company—sixty men, many with their families. Heading it was an old adversary of American trappers, Peter Skene Ogden, who had accumulated one thousand beaver skins. The two groups worked together down the San Joaquin and up the Sacramento nearly to the mountains. Ogden continued north to Fort Vancouver, while Young turned back down the Sacramento Valley.[18]

In July 1830 Young seized an opportunity to make himself useful to Mexican authorities and thus smooth the way for the sale of his furs in San Francisco Bay. Some of the mission Indians at San José had revolted and taken refuge with tribesmen in the Sierra foothills. A weak contingent of soldiers had failed to dislodge them, and officials asked for American help. Young sent twelve men, including Kit Carson, to oblige the Mexicans. "We turned to the village," recounted Carson, "and made an attack, fought for one entire day. The Indians were routed; [they] lost a great number of men. We entered the village in triumph, set fire to it, and burned it to the ground." The next day the "gentiles," threatened with extermination, surrendered the runaways, whom Young's company promptly escorted back to mission custody.[19]

Not surprisingly, Young encountered no official interference with sale of furs to the master of a schooner in San Francisco Bay. With the proceeds

he bought horses and mules, both for his own needs and to sell on his return to New Mexico. But Indians, perhaps the same he had trounced a
month earlier, made off with sixty. Young took characteristically direct action. "We surprised the Indians when feasting of[f] some of our animals
they had killed," Carson remembered. "We charged their camp, killed eight
Indians, took three children prisoners and recovered all our animals, with
the exception of six that were eaten."[20]

Young led his men back to the San Bernardino Valley to reprovision before heading for home. He made the mistake, however, of paying them part
of their wages. In the little pueblo of Los Angeles, they got drunk and mu-
tinied. Young quelled the uprising and herded his following out of town,
but not before, in a drunken quarrel, one shot and killed another. After
trapping the Colorado to its mouth, the men worked their way up the Gila,
taking beaver as they went and incidentally, in a chance encounter with
Apaches, seizing two hundred horses recently stolen from Mexican hacien-
das to the south. Young paused at the Santa Rita Copper Mines long enough
to store two thousand pounds of beaver pelts in a mine shaft. Later, covered
by an official license to trade with Indians, he came back, "traded" for the
furs, and brought them to Santa Fe to dispose of openly and legally. By
April 1831, everyone was back in Taos, the enterprise highly profitable in
both beaver and horses.

The Young expedition of 1829–31 had several important results. It further spotlighted the country of the Salt, Gila, and Verde as prime beaver
grounds. It added to the rising awareness that ships in California ports afforded a ready market for furs. Perhaps most important, it dramatized for
Taos trappers and traders the economic opportunities of California. Many,
including Ewing Young himself, began to think of moving their base from
Taos to Mexico's province on the Pacific.

Not so apparent in 1831, another result was the maturing of Kit Carson.
Only twenty-two when the expedition returned to Taos, he had nonetheless
ended his apprenticeship with high marks. Under Ewing Young, the self-
effacing youth had not only ripened into an exceptional trapper but had excelled as marksman, hunter, and wilderness traveler. He had impressed
Young with his courage and endurance, his unfailing dependability, and his
growing leadership qualities. Like Young himself, he had also shown himself
a fearless, no-nonsense Indian fighter, untroubled by sentiment or sympathy.

Carson thus made an ideal recruit for a caravan forming that late summer of 1831 in Taos. Arriving too late in Missouri to organize the annual
supply train for the newly formed Rocky Mountain Fur Company, Tom
Fitzpatrick had been compelled to accompany Jedediah Smith, David Jackson, and William Sublette to New Mexico. With Smith dead on the Santa

Fe Trail, the remaining partners decided to go separate ways, Jackson to try his hand at bringing mules from California to New Mexico, Sublette to return to the States. Before parting, however, they honored their commitment to Fitzpatrick. When the caravan finally got under way from Taos in the fall, far too late for the 1831 rendezvous, Kit Carson rode as one of Fitzpatrick's company. Thus, schooled by Ewing Young, Kit Carson embarked on the career as mountain man, guide, Indian fighter and Indian friend, and finally general in the Union army that would make his name renowned throughout the nation.

THE MEN DETACHED by Ewing Young near the head of the Verde River reached Taos in the spring of 1830. They told William Wolfskill that his partner had gone on to California and intended to trap the San Joaquin Valley. At once Wolfskill laid plans to join Young in this enterprise. First, seeking to avoid the official troubles that plagued his partner, Wolfskill went through the tedious process of converting to Catholicism and becoming a Mexican citizen. Then "José Guillermo Wolfskill" applied for a trapping license, which Governor Manuel Armijo promptly granted.

In September 1830, while Ewing Young socialized with his newfound Mexican friends in California, Wolfskill organized still another California-bound expedition. Assisting him was the veteran George Yount, who knew the land to the west as well as any man. Some twenty men composed the party, including Zachariah Ham, who had captained an Ashley party on the Green and Bear Rivers in 1825.

Wolfskill and Yount resolved to find a better way to California. The Gila was difficult and plagued by Apaches. The route probably followed by Ewing Young, Richard Campbell, and Yount himself, linking the Virgin River with Zuñi Pueblo, involved deserts, canyons, and high rocky plateaus. Probably at Yount's urging, Wolfskill aimed still farther north. Although they had not likely heard of Fathers Domínguez and Escalante, they unknowingly embarked on a course that would complete what the padres had begun.[21]

Wolfskill and Yount led their men northwest to the Uinta Basin along essentially the same course followed by Domínguez and Escalante, Spanish slave traders, and Étienne Provost and the other early Taos trappers—the Chama, San Juan, and Dolores Rivers, across the Grand, and finally to the Green. Surmounting the Wasatch Range, they fell on the Sevier River. Here the friars had turned back in 1776, but here Jedediah Smith had pushed on in 1826 and 1827. With variations, the Wolfskill party trailed Smith to California by the Virgin, the Colorado, and the Mojave to the San Bernardino Valley.

Wolfskill and Yount blazed no new trails. Their significance lay in joining several old trails into a single new trail that connected Santa Fe with Los Angeles. It was a long trail, longer than the ones it replaced. Nor was it much easier than others. But for the next two decades, thanks to the publicity resulting from the Wolfskill journey, the "Old Spanish Trail" formed a commercial thoroughfare between New Mexico and California. Horses, mules, sheep, and pack trains laden with trade goods made their way back and forth between Santa Fe and Los Angeles.

Wolfskill and his men reached Los Angeles in February 1831, too late for a fall beaver hunt, too early for a spring hunt. They failed to connect with Ewing Young, who had already left for home. The trappers scattered to go their separate ways. Wolfskill and Yount decided to try their hand at hunting sea otter, a venture that turned out badly. Even so, California appealed to both, and for both the future held important contributions to California history.

BACK IN TAOS in the spring of 1831, Ewing Young still saw his future bound to California. Opportunity offered with the arrival of the caravan from Missouri of Sublette and Jackson, the firm recently deprived by Comanches of its third partner, Jedediah Smith. Young sold to these men the furs gathered on the Colorado and Gila during his return from California. Then, after they dissolved their partnership, Young entered into a partnership with Jackson and David Waldo, an old friend of Jackson's who had recently set himself up as a merchant in Santa Fe. Their plan was for Jackson to go to California and purchase horses and mules while Young followed with a trapping party. Young's furs could be sold in California and part of the proceeds used to hire drovers to herd Jackson's animals back to New Mexico.[22]

With Mexican specie loaded on mules, Jackson and ten men left Santa Fe early in September 1831. Descending the Rio Grande, they turned west to the Copper Mines but then veered southwest to the presidio and pueblo of Tucson before turning north and west to the Gila and continuing to California. In later years this route would become part of a major thoroughfare to California. Jackson reached the coast early in November 1831.

With thirty-six trappers, Ewing Young followed Jackson in October 1831. As in 1829, they jumped off from Zuñi Pueblo and picked up the Salt River, trapped its canyons, and then turned up the Verde. Unlike 1829, they sought no new and shorter way to California. Returning to the mouth of the Verde, they swung down the Gila Valley to reach their destination by the more reliable route.

Arriving in the San Bernardino Valley early in February 1832, Young waited nearly two months for David Jackson to show up, passing the time pleasantly with the amiable Father Sánchez at San Gabriel Mission. When Jackson did appear late in March, he drove a much smaller herd than had been planned—six hundred mules and one hundred horses. Young's trapping results had proved equally disappointing, thanks to Apaches and faulty traps.

The partners laid new plans. Young would accompany Jackson to the Colorado and help get the animals across the river. Jackson's party would then be sufficient to drive the herd on to New Mexico. Young would remain in California to trap the San Joaquin and Sacramento Valleys as originally intended. In the summer of 1832 he tried his hand at hunting sea otter, but like Wolfskill he promptly abandoned that excessively maritime enterprise. For the next two years, Young captained a company of trappers that swept the Central Valley of California all the way to the head of the Sacramento, penetrated the mountains that had discouraged Jedediah Smith, and even returned to the lower Gila. At times he competed or cooperated with trapping brigades of the Hudson's Bay Company working south from Fort Vancouver.

By the spring of 1834, Ewing Young despaired of trapping his way to wealth. The partnership with Jackson had not returned a profit and had fallen apart. The intense competition of the Hudson's Bay Company for the beaver of the great interior valley of California limited the catch there. The Gila and Colorado had proved equally discouraging. As Young wrote to a friend from the Colorado in March 1834, "I am not ketching much Beaver but doing the best I can."[23]

After he returned to Los Angeles, Ewing Young's beaver days had ended. Nor would he ever return to New Mexico. Like William Wolfskill and George Yount, he found California congenial and replete with ways of making a living that did not depend on beaver. He would stay.

THROUGHOUT THE 1830s, Taos continued to serve as the New Mexican trapper base. Learning from the Americans, more and more Mexicans sought beaver. Also, encouraged by liberalized laws, more and more Americans became Mexican citizens. Once naturalized and embraced by the Catholic Church, they encountered fewer difficulties with Mexican officialdom. The establishment of Bent's Fort on the Arkansas River in 1833 somewhat diminished the power of Taos, but firm commercial and human relations cemented the two trading centers.

Though safely legitimized by Mexican citizenship, American trappers retained their American character. Many took Mexican wives and gave allegiance to their new nationality. But no one took them for Mexicans, least of all the Mexicans themselves. Even so, they attained an economic, political, and cultural influence disproportionate to their numbers. As the years passed, moreover, they grew increasingly dissatisfied with Mexican rule. As historian David Weber has observed, their part in bringing about the bloodless American conquest of New Mexico in 1846 cannot be determined. "Their contribution, however, as a cultural advance guard for American manifest destiny should not be overlooked."[24]

And so with those like Ewing Young who blazed the Gila trails to California and decided to stay there. Many Taos trappers followed this course. Like their erstwhile comrades in New Mexico, they formed an influential minority. When the test came in 1846, they too remained faithful to their American heritage.

9

JOE WALKER:

THE GREAT BASIN AND

THE SIERRAS

IN MASTERY of the mountain man's craft, none surpassed Joseph R. Walker. In exploratory achievement, only Jedediah Smith surpassed Joseph R. Walker. Unlike Smith, however, Walker lived to expand his record year after year. And after the era of the mountain man closed, he continued to make important contributions to geographical knowledge and national expansion. Joe Walker lays strong claim to the distinction of the greatest mountain man of them all.[1]

A Tennessean, Walker had early learned the arts of the frontiersman. At fifteen, in 1814, he and his older brother fought under Andrew Jackson against the Creek Red Sticks in the Battle of Horseshoe Bend. Afterward, like so many of their restless creed, the Walkers moved to Missouri, where they tried their hand at farming. And like so many of their neighbors, Joe Walker gravitated still farther west to make a life beyond the frontier.

In some ways Walker typified the mountain man. For one, he looked the part—a heavily bearded giant weighing more than two hundred pounds and towering four inches above six feet. In the fullest splendor, moreover, he affected the attire and trappings of his comrades, for his horses and Indian wives as well as for himself. To physical strength, endurance, and fortitude, he added the mountain man's restlessness, rootlessness, individualism, and aversion to authoritarian restraint. His wilderness skills sharpened to perfection, he also knew that mountain men could be led but not commanded.

Yet in other ways, like Jedediah Smith, Walker did not typify the mountain man. Although none of Smith's stiff piety or inner turmoil diluted Walker's good humor, moderation characterized his behavior, speech, and thought. He hardly ever boasted, got drunk, indulged in raucous high jinks, relaxed his self-control, or wavered in whatever serious purpose he had set for himself. Even so, he commanded the respect and shared the easy camaraderie of the vain, exuberant, fun-loving mountaineers who gathered for the yearly rendezvous.[2]

Perhaps most atypical, for Walker beaver were not the West's main attraction. To be sure, he excelled at trapping. Among the earliest Americans to hunt the streams of New Mexico, he had worked off and on with a fellow Tennessean, Ewing Young, in the early 1820s. Other ventures, however, proved more appealing, as guide, hunter, drover, and trader—specialties in demand during the formative years of the Santa Fe Trail. As an able county sheriff on the Missouri frontier, Walker displayed still another side of his multifaceted character.

Finally, in the tradition of Jedediah Smith, trapping furnished the means for Walker to find his true calling. As his biographer concludes: "What Walker wanted was to be a free-lance explorer, a private Meriwether Lewis or William Clark, with sufficient men, resources and freedom of action to travel and live for extended periods in the unsettled and, better, unexplored regions of the west."[3]

Walker found his chance late in 1830. At Fort Gibson, in the Indian Territory, he met Captain Benjamin L. E. Bonneville of the United States Army. Of French birth, brought to the United States by his parents while still a child, Bonneville had served in the regular army for fifteen years. He was now thirty-six and supremely bored by garrison duty at a remote post.

Within a few years, Washington Irving would give flesh and blood to this faceless name on the army roster. A short, stocky fellow, "the moment his head was uncovered, a bald crown gave him credit for a few more years than he was really entitled to." The journal the "genial captain" kept in the West, Irving observed, revealed "his *bonhomie*, his kindness of spirit, and his susceptibility to the grand and beautiful."[4]

The contrast between the "grand and beautiful" of his imagination and the grim reality of Fort Gibson doubtless inspired the improbable scheme Bonneville broached to Walker late in 1830. He intended to seek a leave of absence from the army to lead a privately financed trapping expedition to the Rocky Mountains. He needed an experienced mountaineer to recruit, organize, and lead the trappers and to coach him in the ways of life in the wilderness. He could have found no more qualified man than Joseph R. Walker.

Historians still argue the true purpose behind Bonneville's seemingly wild idea. Undisputed, however, is that the army's commanding general, backed by the War Department, not only granted the leave but instructed the captain, in terms reminiscent of Lewis and Clark, to explore the Rockies and beyond and report on nearly everything of commercial, military, and diplomatic interest—at no cost to the government. Undisputed is that a friend of John Jacob Astor's, who in turn had close ties to the highest levels of the federal government, bankrolled a trapping operation led by an army officer lacking either military distinction or trapping experience. Undisputed is that Bonneville devoted less effort to gathering beaver than to gathering data about the military capabilities of the Indians and, especially, the strength and disposition of the British in Oregon and the Mexicans in California.

"Spy" is too strong a term, but clearly Captain Bonneville had objectives beyond mere trapping. Instead of beaver, he pursued both grand adventure for himself and all the information about the West that he judged useful to his government. Whether Joe Walker knew it or not—and he must have suspected it—he had enlisted in an enterprise as much imperial as commercial.[5]

EARLY IN AUGUST 1832, the Bonneville entourage reached the upper Green River near the mouth of Horse Creek. It made an impressive spectacle: 150 men, packhorses and mules, and a train of twenty white-topped wagons drawn by oxen. Wheeled vehicles had come to the mountains before, but never had a wagon train of this size surmounted South Pass. It foreshadowed the great migration to wend through this gateway little more than a decade later.

The leadership consisted of a loose triumvirate. Bonneville captained. But Walker and Michael Cerré functioned virtually as copartners. Cerré, a young man with experience on the Santa Fe Trail, had been taken on for his business acumen. Walker was the mountaineer and leader of men. Curiously, the three sometimes acted together and sometimes independently. Walker in particular, when Bonneville's designs made no sense, simply set his own course.

One such scheme was Bonneville's determination to build a fort on the Green River near the mouth of Horse Creek. Walker argued that the location, while excellent for rendezvous, provided a terrible setting for either a trapping or a trading base. The open valley afforded no shelter from winter storms, and anyway, trapping brigades wintered at varying sites depending on game and forage. But the captain insisted.

"Fort Bonneville" turned out to be an impressive structure: a formidable stockade of logs set firmly in the ground, fifteen feet in height, and with protruding blockhouses at two opposite corners designed, recorded an observer, "to hinder the approach of an enemy from any quarter." With ample grass for stock on the surrounding plain, "the whole together seems well calculated for the security both of men and horses."[6]

Trappers laughed at Fort Bonneville. They called it "Fort Nonsense" and "Bonneville's Folly." The ridicule gathered force as Bonneville promptly decided to move his base to a new location for the winter. The upper Salmon River, near the mouth of the Lemhi, proved an even worse place to winter than the upper Green.

Bonneville and the men with him on the Salmon simply sat out the winter, trapping hardly at all. Two field parties hunted beaver. David Adams led twenty men to the Crow country, where he lost half to desertion and had a clash with Arikaras that scattered the rest. With another twenty men, Walker conducted a fall hunt on the Madison River (and had the predictable skirmish with Blackfeet), wintered on the Snake near the mouth of the Blackfoot, and headed south for a spring hunt on the Bear River and Bear Lake.

The rendezvous of 1833 brought together Bonneville's forces. Some 350 whites and 500 Shoshone, Flathead, and Nez Perce Indians gathered in July on the upper Green, where all could inspect and make fun of Fort Nonsense. All the big names of the mountains turned up for the festivities: Walker and Cerré with Bonneville; Andrew Drips and Lucien Fontenelle for the American Fur Company; Fitzpatrick, Bridger, Campbell, Vasquez, and Milton Sublette for the Rocky Mountain Fur Company. And for his first rendezvous, Captain William Drummond Stewart, the genial and generous Scottish tourist, laid the basis for a remarkable rapport with the mountain men destined to last for a decade.[7]

Compared with the take of the fur giants, Bonneville counted dismal returns on a year's labor. His poor showing failed to cover expenses, but at rendezvous his mind addressed larger issues. While the trappers cavorted in alcoholic frolics, he sat in his tent penning a long report to General Alexander Macomb, head of the army. He furnished much of the information about the country and the Indians that Macomb had asked for, but his principal concern was Oregon. He had been on the upper Salmon and Snake, technically part of Oregon, but had yet to visit the stronghold of the Hudson's Bay Company on the lower Columbia. Even so, "The information I have already obtained authorizes me to say this much; that if our Government ever intend taking possession of Origon the sooner it shall be done the better, and at present I deem a subalterns command equal to enforce all the views of our Government."

Even though a subaltern's command for all Oregon—a company or less—made a mockery of Bonneville's military judgment, against such forceful convictions Fort Nonsense seems not entirely nonsensical. Perhaps he never visualized his fort as primarily a base for trapping or trading. His mind's eye may have pictured it garrisoned by United States soldiers rather than rough mountaineers. If so, the site made strategic sense, especially if, as he fervently anticipated, the United States moved aggressively to assert its claim to Oregon and open the way for a procession of westward-moving settlers.[8]

In his letter to the commanding general, Bonneville almost incidentally disclosed that he would have to overstay his two-year leave, which he felt justified by the need to examine Oregon personally. He intended, therefore, to head for the lower Columbia, then turn south and come back by way of California.

With the rendezvous of 1833, the time had come for Joe Walker to organize an expedition to California. While Bonneville labored on his report to General Macomb, Walker circulated among the free trappers signing up men. His reputation as a mountaineer and leader, combined with the lure of California, attracted plenty of recruits. When finally assembled, the company numbered about forty-five.

As clerk, Walker engaged Zenas Leonard, a veteran after only two years in the mountains. Leonard doubtless expressed what all felt when he wrote: "Mr. Walker was a man well calculated to undertake a business of this kind. He was well hardened to the hardships of the wilderness—understood the character of the Indians very well—was kind and affable to his men, but at the same time at liberty to command without giving offense,—and to explore unknown regions was his chief delight."[9]

What beyond beaver Bonneville expected of Walker in California can only be guessed. Perhaps, as he intimated to General Macomb, he meant to meet Walker there after visiting the lower Columbia. Reflecting his instructions from Macomb, Bonneville must have intended Walker to gather information about the geography, resources, economy, and government of California as well as, in the wake of Jedediah Smith's experiences, how best to get there. Certainly, Walker's sole purpose was not to find new beaver grounds and trap old ones.

Yet within four years this is what Washington Irving related to his many readers. Indeed, Irving portrayed Walker's assigned mission not as a journey to California but merely as a search for beaver country west and south of Great Salt Lake. Instead, Walker embarked on an unsanctioned jaunt to the Pacific shores. This produced so little beaver as to doom Bonneville's enterprise altogether. Shaped by Irving's facile pen, Joe Walker emerged as the villain of the story, the faithless rebel whose betrayal forced his chief to abandon the mountains.

Irving had to know better. He worked from Bonneville's journal and papers and talked with him personally. At rendezvous Walker openly solicited men for an expedition to California, and he fitted it out for a year's absence, not the few weeks a survey of Great Salt Lake would entail. Moreover, while in Washington on the eve of his western adventure, Bonneville secured a passport from the State Department and a visa from the Mexican consul, in the name of Joseph R. Walker, authorizing entry into Mexican territory. Clearly, Walker's California expedition had been planned from the beginning, and the chance to lead it was probably the prime reason he teamed up with Bonneville.

Throughout, Irving presents Bonneville's enterprise as aimed entirely at making money from beaver while enjoying a splendid western adventure in the process. That the hero of the story failed so abysmally apparently had to be explained. In Joe Walker Washington Irving found his villain.[10]

THE MIDDLE OF AUGUST 1833 found Joe Walker's trappers north of Great Salt Lake. They now numbered about sixty, for while making meat on the Bear River a dozen or more free trappers had joined. With this infusion, the brigade included such stalwarts as Old Bill Williams, Pauline Weaver, Bill Craig, George Nidever, and the brothers Joe and Stephen Meek. Walker now made his first significant contribution to geographical understanding. In 1826 William Sublette and David Jackson had sent four men to navigate the western reaches of the lake. They had found no Rio Buenaventura but had reported to William H. Ashley a place where an outlet might have been.

Unlike his predecessors, Walker conducted a search by land. West of the lake, he discovered, lay not even a solitary dry creek bed, nothing but a shimmering white sea of salt stretching to a hazy horizon. No Rio Buenaventura flowed west from Great Salt Lake, to provide the easy water route to the Pacific of which Ashley and others dreamed.[11]

Walker did, however, pick up the westward-trending river that underlay the myth of the Rio Buenaventura. This was the Humboldt, which rises in mountains beyond the western edge of the Great Salt Lake Desert and flows west and then south to disappear in the bitter gray lakes and marshes of the Humboldt Sink. Walker had stumbled onto the only reliable passage

In the employ of the Scottish tourist, Sir William Drummond Stewart, artist Alfred Jacob Miller went to the rendezvous of 1837 on Green River. His scenes are the only contemporary record of the mountaineer's life in the Rockies. At rendezvous he painted one of the few portraits of a mountain man during the peak of his career. Joseph R. Walker had gained distinction in his exploratory expedition across the Great Basin and the Sierra Nevada in 1833. Miller also portrayed Walker in the full regalia of the mountain man, followed by his dazzlingly ornamented Indian wife. BOTH PICTURES COURTESY JOSLYN ART MUSEUM, OMAHA, NEBRASKA.

through a land of sterile deserts and mountains. Jedediah Smith had missed the Humboldt on his return trek from California in 1827 and had almost perished as a result.

Instead of to Walker, however, credit for discovering the Humboldt belongs to Peter Skene Ogden. At the head of a Hudson's Bay Company brigade, the fifth Snake Country Expedition, he had dropped into the Humboldt Valley from the north in the autumn of 1828 and found the river rich in beaver. He had trapped upstream to the sources and then, in the spring of 1829, trapped downstream almost to the sink. He named it the Unknown River, but it quickly came to be called the Ogden or (for his Indian wife) Mary's River.

Peter Skene Ogden's discovery of the Humboldt enlarged a record of exploratory achievement matching that of his American counterparts, Jedediah Smith and Joseph Walker. In his sixth and final Snake Country Expedition, 1829–30, Ogden ranged south from Fort Vancouver along the western rim of the Great Basin all the way to the Gulf of California, then returned to the Columbia by way of California's Central Valley. His later career took him north into the Hudson's Bay Company's New Caledonia Department as far as Russian Alaska and rewarded his success with promotion to chief factor. After the Whitman Massacre of 1847, he earned the gratitude of American settlers by gaining the release of captives held by the Indians. He died in 1854 at his retirement home in Oregon City, by now American territory. Ogden's extraordinary explorations enriched his company's London archives and bore lightly on English cartography. They had almost no effect on the mental map of the American mountaineers with whom he contested dominion of the beaver grounds of the West.[12]

Joseph R. Walker knew nothing of Ogden's exploration of the Humboldt or of the nomenclature that his visit three years earlier had conferred on it. Walker called it the Barren River. Not until John C. Frémont arrived with more grandiose notions in 1843 and 1845 would maps label it the Humboldt. Ogden River would have been far more fitting.[13]

Walker's men took some beaver on the Humboldt, but not many; Ogden's sweep had thinned the population. What Walker found in greater profusion was Indians—Paiutes curious about the strangers and adept at pilfering traps and other possessions. Rather than court trouble, the captain inclined to patience. A few of his men did not. Twice, defying his instructions, they shot and killed several Indians. When Walker found out, he put a stop to the killing, but it was too late.

By early September, at the Humboldt Sink, the Paiutes had converged in menacing numbers and with threatening behavior. The trappers forted up. Demonstrations of the power of rifles, which the Indians apparently had never witnessed, frightened but did not deter them. Clearly bent on a fight, several hundred warriors approached from different directions. Walker gave orders for a counterattack against one of the bolder groups. Thirty-two trappers mounted and charged. "We closed in on them and fired," related Leonard, "leaving thirty-nine dead on the field—which was nearly the half—the remainder were overwhelmed with dismay—running into the high grass in every direction, howling in the most lamentable manner." Walker then gave orders to use the bows and arrows of the fallen to finish off any still living.[14]

Washington Irving made effective use of this affair in his effort to cast Walker as a scoundrel. Portraying the Paiutes as a "timid and inoffensive race," Irving wrote: "We feel perfectly convinced that the poor savages had no hostile intention, but had merely gathered together through motives of curiosity."[15] In truth, they had gathered through motives of revenge, and their intentions were incontestably hostile. Walker and his men overreacted, as Leonard admitted, but they found themselves in a perilous predicament that, even though brought on by the atrocities of several of their own number, called for decisive action. Many of the trappers had no compunctions against killing any Indians, and none against killing Indians as plainly intent on bloodletting as these Paiutes.[16]

The Humboldt Sink gave way to still another huge sink, one day to be named the Carson Sink. These marshy bottoms received waters from the west, from scattered ranges forming the foothills of the Sierra Nevada. Beyond, the great eastern wall of the Sierras rose defiantly. Ascending by a river that later took Walker's name, the men could spot nothing that looked like a mountain pass. Finally, they simply started probing upward in hopes that fortune would reward them with a passage if not a pass.

Fields of boulders, snow-choked gulches, and sheer-walled canyons exhausted men and animals and on one occasion brought on a near mutiny, quelled only by Walker's firm leadership. Since the Bear River, they had seen no game larger than a jackrabbit, and now their buffalo jerky gave out. Horse meat—ultimately from seventeen horses—provided a poor substitute.

The summit proved more readily attained than the western descent. Faced by the plunging gorges of the Tuolumne River on the north and the Merced on the south, the travelers maneuvered precariously along the rocky spine dividing the two. They were the first known white people to look down on the Yosemite Valley. They marveled, but exhaustion, cold, hunger, and despair dimmed the splendor. At length, a sinuous Indian trail pointed the way down. Snow receded, scrub oak began to appear, and, best of all, deer and bear provided fare for the cook fire. By the end of October

1833, the revitalized sojourners had descended to the balmy floor of the San Joaquin Valley.

In a month of intensely demanding mountaineering, Walker and his men had forced a passage of the Sierra Nevada. Jedediah Smith had surmounted this massive barrier from west to east in 1827. The Walker party was the first to achieve the feat from east to west. The route hardly invited others to follow. Better passages to the north remained to be opened. But Walker had scored a notable first—reaching California from the Green River by way of the Humboldt River and the Sierra Nevada. Except for the Sierra crossing, in the years to come cavalcades of white-topped wagons would follow basically the trail he had pieced together.

In contrast to Jedediah Smith, still sourly remembered in California, Walker met with a cordial reception. He carried a passport and a Mexican visa, and he benefited from the mediation of an American ship captain. His courtesy, respect for foreign sensibilities, and firm control of his men promoted harmony with Governor José Figueroa and his officers. Walker and his followers could remain all winter, the governor decreed, move freely about the country, and take all the game they wanted. They could not, however, trap for beaver or trade with Indians—ostensibly what they had come to do.

The ban on trapping did not seem to bother Walker, for he probably had come to do other things as well. While his men camped at the mission and village of San Juan Bautista, Walker and Leonard toured the province, recording exactly the information about the country and its people that General Macomb had instructed Captain Bonneville to report.

Possibly shedding some light on Walker's primary mission, and probably symptomatic of the feelings of most of the American party, were sentiments recorded by Zenas Leonard. He foresaw all the "vast waste of territory" extending to the Pacific shore as belonging to the United States. "What a theme to contemplate its settlement and civilization." And "yes, here, even in this remote part of the great west [California] before many years, will these hills and valleys be greeted with the enlivening sound, of the workman's hammer, and the merry whistle of the plough-boy." Leonard believed that his government should move quickly and aggressively, "should assert claim by taking possession of the whole territory as soon as possible—for we have good reason to suppose that the territory *west* of the mountain will some day be equally as important to a nation as that on the *east*." Thus brushing aside Mexican rule and British claims, and thus anticipating an American "manifest destiny," Leonard envisioned a future that in fact came to pass—in no small part because of mountain men like him and his comrades.[17]

Walker had no wish to attempt another harrowing crossing of the Sierras. Instead, like Jedediah Smith, in the spring of 1834 Walker led his trappers up the San Joaquin Valley to seek a way around the southern end of the range. Indians showed the way up the Kern River, and the portal that later became Walker Pass led the company down to the Owens Valley. Here about a dozen of the free trappers, some of whom had probably trapped the Gila out of Taos, went their own way. After plundering and terrorizing the inoffensive Hopis in their mesa-top mud towns, these men ended in Santa Fe. The rest of Walker's party struck northeast, seeking to reach the Humboldt and the way back to rendezvous. The route proved waterless and the men restive, so they fell back and followed the well-watered Sierra foothills until intersecting their westbound trail. Once more in the Humboldt Sink they had a deadly encounter with Paiutes that took fourteen Indian lives. By July 1834, they had reunited with Bonneville on the Bear River.

IN WALKER'S ABSENCE, Bonneville had not succeeded in his plan to visit the lower Columbia and return by way of California. He tried, but not very hard. With three men, he had made a winter journey down the Snake River to appear, in March 1834, at the Hudson's Bay Company outpost of Fort Walla Walla (also known as Fort Nez Perces), at the mouth of the eastern tributary of the Columbia River of the same name. The factor extended a cordial welcome but would provide no supplies. Bonneville remained for two days, then turned back to rejoin his company on the Bear River and equip himself for another foray to the Columbia.

On the Bear River, in July 1834, Bonneville and Walker reunited, and Cerré came up from St. Louis with the supply caravan. Walker reported on his expedition to California. Cerré told of journeying to Washington and laying Bonneville's report before General Macomb himself, who read it in Cerré's presence and expressed satisfaction. Left vague, however, was the status of Bonneville's leave from the army.

Still tarring Walker, Washington Irving contrived a scene in which Bonneville expressed anger and dismay with Walker for having exceeded his instructions and gone to California. The one-sided fights with the Paiutes also came in for denunciation. According to Irving, the captain "was so deeply grieved by the failure of his plans, and so indignant at the atrocities related to him, that he turned, with disgust and horror, from the narrators." Irving then has Walker dispatched to St. Louis with Cerré and the year's meager catch of furs, to disappear thereafter from the narrative.[18]

No one else recorded a scene of "disgust and horror." Nor did Walker vanish from Bonneville's life. On the contrary, he captained a fur brigade of fifty-five men that headed for the Crow country for a fall and spring hunt. He would rejoin Bonneville at the 1835 rendezvous at the mouth of the Popo Agie.

Bonneville, meantime, would pass the year in another attempt to scout the Hudson's Bay Company stronghold. With twenty-three men, he would establish himself for the winter on the lower Columbia in the vicinity of the "Multnomah," trade with the local Indians, and return across the mountains in time for rendezvous in July 1835.

As in the previous summer, these ambitious plans encountered the smiling obstinacy of the Hudson's Bay Company. Again the factor at Fort Walla Walla refused to reprovision the Americans. Short of rations, they proceeded down the Columbia, only to find none of the natives willing to trade. Faced with the prospect of a bleak winter in the heartland of the powerful British monopoly, Bonneville turned back and by the end of October 1834 was back on the Snake River. He wintered in the familiar, game-rich haunts of the Bear River.[19]

By contrast, Joe Walker showed up at rendezvous in June 1835 with substantial returns from his fall and spring hunts in the Crow country of the Wind, Bighorn, and Yellowstone Rivers. When Bonneville arrived, the two laid plans for the coming year. The captain would take Walker's catch down to St. Louis and return with a supply caravan in the summer of 1836. Walker and fifty-nine men would trap the Crow country again and meet Bonneville at the rendezvous of 1836.[20]

In Washington, however, Bonneville discovered to his chagrin that he had been dropped from the army rolls for overstaying his leave. Protesting mightily and demanding reinstatement, he stirred a bureaucratic storm in the War Department but ultimately won the support of the commanding general, the Secretary of War, and President Jackson himself. A fortuitous resignation in his regiment averted the need to disturb the seniority list, and by the spring of 1836 he found himself once again a captain in the Seventh Infantry, with duty station at Fort Gibson.[21]

As an explorer, Captain Bonneville had been scarcely more successful than as a fur man. Those laurels, both exploration and trapping, belonged to his lieutenant, Joseph R. Walker. He had not only shown the way from Great Salt Lake to California, fitting the Humboldt Valley into the route as its crucial link. He had crossed the Sierra Nevada at one of its most difficult places and later found a new pass through the southern Sierras. All this and more he related to Bonneville on the Bear River in July 1834. Almost certainly, Bonneville incorporated what Walker had learned in a report he prepared for General Macomb before departing from the Bear River for the

Columbia. This report and other papers he entrusted to Michael Cerré, who mailed them at Council Bluffs. They never reached their destination.

More than a hint of what the report contained is disclosed by one of two maps Bonneville drew, both of which appeared in Washington Irving's book in 1837. Most significantly, the map depicting the area of Walker's exploration does not show a Buenaventura River flowing west from Great Salt Lake to the Pacific—the first map to contain this omission. Rather, Buenaventura is the label attached to the Sacramento River, west of the Sierras in the northern half of California's Central Valley. Through Bonneville and Irving, Walker had dealt a devastating (though not a mortal) blow to one of the most persistent myths of western geography.

Of scarcely less importance, Bonneville's map clearly shows the "Mary or Ogden's River" connecting the Salt Lake Desert with the Sierra Nevada. This river, the Humboldt, was no Buenaventura, floating emigrants and their stock down a broad waterway to the Pacific. But it was the vital corridor that steered emigrants across the Nevada wasteland to the Sierras, beyond which, once the passes were discovered, lay the California Eden.[22]

Although Bonneville explored no new country—he never even saw Great Salt Lake, much less the surrounding terraces of ancient Lake Bonneville—his contributions to geographical knowledge and national expansion are not to be discounted. The reports that did reach the War Department told much about the West and its people and enriched the geopolitical thinking of military and possibly diplomatic leaders. Probably thereafter the papers lay forgotten in some obscure file, and ultimately they disappeared.

These reports, however, do not constitute Bonneville's true legacy. His fortunate—or arranged—meeting with Washington Irving and the subsequent collaboration that led to Irving's book more than fulfilled any ulterior design that underlay Bonneville's western exploits. One of the most gifted and successful authors of his time, Irving set down the captain's adventures in engrossing prose. Widely read, it linked graphic portrayals of the western lands and peoples with the impulse to spread the dominion of the American republic over the Oregon country if not California as well. Published in 1837, Washington Irving's book, for all its unmerited calumny of Joe Walker, must be counted an important factor in the rising public sentiment for continental expansion.[23]

And in that epic yet to come, Joe Walker would play his own important part. Neither the Humboldt nor the Sierras had seen the last of Joe Walker.

10

BILL SUBLETTE: STRUGGLE

OF THE FUR GIANTS

ILLIAM L. SUBLETTE dominated the partnership of Smith, Jackson & Sublette, organized at the rendezvous of 1826 when William H. Ashley resolved to leave the mountains for good. Roaming to California and Oregon, Jedediah Smith was absent most of the time. David Jackson, for all his maturity and business experience, played out his role in the shadow of Sublette.

"Billy," Sublette's men called him after he had become a field captain, a "booshway," in tribute to his "energy, courage and kindness." More than six feet tall, with a lean face and Roman nose, sandy hair, and light complexion, he was twenty-three when he signed on with Ashley for the upper Missouri in 1823. Fighting the Arikaras on the sand beach, freezing in the snows of South Pass, trapping the Green and the Bear with Jedediah Smith, discomfiting the Hudson's Bay Company at Flathead Post, Sublette had developed into a first-rate mountain man, trapper, and leader. As one of the partners who bought out Ashley, Sublette rose to a position of power in the fur trade, becoming an able field captain and astute businessman.[1]

Without relinquishing trapping altogether, Sublette increasingly handled the business affairs of the partnership, taking on the responsibility for organizing and conducting the annual supply caravan. He came to understand the St. Louis business world as well as the Rocky Mountain trapping system. This background made him a key player in the bitter competition that began to assail the fur trade even as Ashley withdrew. Without ever hardening his engaging ways, Sublette emerged as one of the most wily and ruthless of the competitors.

SINCE THE COLLAPSE of his Astorian venture, John Jacob Astor had maneuvered to control the fur trade of the mountain West. Through the shrewd strategies of his lieutenant, Ramsay Crooks, Astor had made his first move in 1822 by establishing the Western Department of the American Fur Company in St. Louis. It remained little more than a shell, however, until 1827, when Crooks finally persuaded Pratte and Chouteau to take over management of the Western Department. Under this arrangement, B. Pratte & Company would buy all their mountain merchandise from, and dispose of all their mountain returns through, Astor's American Fur Company.

Also in 1827, Crooks acquired the Columbia Fur Company, which had been contesting Astor's supremacy on the Mississippi. As the Upper Missouri Outfit of the American Fur Company, this firm seized control of the Missouri River trade from the Big Sioux to the Yellowstone. Below the Big Sioux, the Missouri remained the province of the Western Department in St. Louis, which also exercised an oversight of its neighbor that was more theoretical than real.[2]

The virtual independence of the Upper Missouri Outfit sprang from the powerful personality of Kenneth McKenzie, the veteran Nor'wester who had ruled the Columbia Fur Company since its formation in 1821. At Fort Union, established at the mouth of the Yellowstone in the fall of 1828, McKenzie presided in baronial splendor and fully lived up to the sobriquet by which he was known to friend and enemy alike: the "King of the Missouri."[3]

From the first, McKenzie's ambitions transcended a regal dominion over the Missouri River Indian trade. He could hardly wait to leap from the Missouri into the Rockies, a boldness the more cautious Pierre Chouteau, Jr., had yet to bring to the leadership of the Western Department. In 1828, even before building Fort Union, McKenzie had sent Étienne Provost to stir up the Crow trade; and fortuitously, that same autumn, he received an invitation from the mountains.[4]

The messenger was "Old Glass," the same who had been torn up by a grizzly in 1823 and had since experienced incredible exploits as a Taos-based trapper. Hugh Glass had been sent by the free trappers of the Rockies to say that they wanted a competitor to challenge the soaring prices of Smith, Jackson & Sublette.[5]

McKenzie did not need Glass's encouragement to send his own caravan of merchandise to rendezvous. Nor did his mountain design end there. He

This view of Fort Union, executed by Karl Bodmer in 1833, looks south, to the Missouri River running in front of the fort and the mouth of the Yellowstone beyond. The powerful and capable Kenneth McKenzie, "King of the Missouri," founded Fort Union in 1828. It served as headquarters for other Indian trading posts on the Missouri and as a base for provisioning the American Fur Company's trappers in the Rocky Mountains. The local Indians, seen in the foreground, were Assiniboines. COURTESY JOSLYN ART MUSEUM, OMAHA, NEBRASKA.

also intended to field his own trapping brigades and, in the wake of Provost, to push the Indian trade up the Yellowstone to the Crow country. Most daring of all, he meant to extend trading tentacles up the Missouri to the heart of the Blackfeet country.

By 1830, prodded by Crooks and Astor, Pierre Chouteau, Jr., had suppressed his doubts about confronting the mountains. Lucien Fontenelle and Andrew Drips led the Western Department's caravan to search out the rendezvous. At the same time, Kenneth McKenzie launched his caravan from Fort Union under the leadership of William H. Vanderburgh. Sublette took his supply train, the first to use wagons, to service his own partnership.

Thus 1830 marked the year that the battle for control of the mountain fur trade commenced in earnest. It would pit the American Fur Company against the Rocky Mountain Fur Company, organized at the rendezvous that summer when Smith, Jackson & Sublette dissolved their partnership. Sublette dominated the rendezvous of 1830, held at the confluence of the Popo Agie and the Wind River. The challengers had much to learn about the mountains. They failed even to find the site.

PRATTE AND CHOUTEAU'S FIELD PARTISANS, Lucien Fontenelle and Andrew Drips, had learned their trade on the Missouri River. They had been to the mountains once, with Joshua Pilcher's failed challenge to Smith, Jackson & Sublette in 1827. Fontenelle, thirty in 1830, was the temperamental, hard-drinking offspring of a New Orleans French plantation owner. Andrew Drips, eleven years older, had been brought from Ireland as a child and had matured into a plainspoken man of decisive action combined with stability and good judgment. Both Fontenelle and Drips had been veterans of the upper Missouri trade for more than a decade, having served the old Missouri Fur Company of Lisa and Pilcher.[6]

After wandering vainly in search of the 1830 rendezvous, Fontenelle and Drips cached their merchandise on Ham's Fork of the Green River and divided into parties for a fall hunt that netted few beaver. They passed the winter of 1830–31 in Cache Valley.

Kenneth McKenzie's field party out of Fort Union met with no better fortune. William Henry Vanderburgh had also been to the mountains with Pilcher in 1827, but he too was a product of the Missouri River trade. Educated (but not graduated) at West Point Military Academy, he marched with Colonel Leavenworth against the Arikaras in 1823 and commanded wide respect as an accomplished trader and leader of men.

Like Fontenelle and Drips, however, Vanderburgh failed to reach the 1830 rendezvous, and he turned his fifty followers into trappers for a fall hunt toward the Three Forks. On the Madison River Blackfeet attacked. In a daylong battle, the rifles of the whites dropped forty to fifty warriors and at nightfall drove off the rest. The trappers lost one killed and two wounded but, more crippling, ten horses killed and another fifty injured. By the spring of 1831, with Vanderburgh desperate for replacements, McKenzie was rounding up another fifty horses for Étienne Provost to herd from Fort Tecumseh across to Vanderburgh's winter camp on the Powder River.[7]

For all their business and trading savvy on the Missouri River, the American Fur Company's partisans found the mountains a hard place to compete. Fitzpatrick, Bridger, Milton Sublette, Fraeb, and Gervais knew the Rockies, knew where the beaver were, and knew how to take them. They lacked the opposition's business skills and reservoirs of capital, but they easily outclassed their rivals. Fontenelle, Drips, and Vanderburgh would have to learn, and learning was costly in men, horses, and capital.

For McKenzie, at heart a trader, Vanderburgh's rout pointed up the dangers of acquiring skins by trapping rather than trading. For two decades, the Blackfeet had warred on white trappers, whether British or American. Yet even while tearing up the Snake Country Expeditions of the Hudson's Bay Company, they traded with the same firm at posts on the Saskatchewan River. Lately even the Crows had been talking resentfully about whites stealing beaver from their streams.[8]

If the Indians could be induced to trap, McKenzie much preferred to get his pelts through trade rather than exposing men and animals to the ferocity of a people who looked on all wildlife as theirs, to exploit or not as they wished. In 1831 McKenzie achieved the incredible feat of opening negotiations with the Blackfeet and securing their sanction of a trading post high on the Missouri, near the mouth of the Marias. Fort Piegan (later moved and renamed Fort McKenzie) launched the Blackfeet trade on a rocky course. In 1832 McKenzie extended his reach up the Yellowstone when Samuel Tulloch erected Fort Cass at the mouth of the Bighorn and took firm control of the Crow trade.[9]

Meantime, another McKenzie innovation bore fruit. After a failed attempt in 1831, in the summer of 1832 the American Fur Company's steamboat *Yellow Stone*, with Pierre Chouteau aboard, tied up at the riverbank in front of Fort Union. Henceforth, although often thwarted by the vagaries of the Missouri River, cargos of merchandise could be borne upriver and cargos of pelts and robes borne downriver much more cheaply and swiftly. By 1833, the *Assiniboine* had joined the *Yellow Stone* to make the keelboat seem like a relic of antiquity.[10]

Although McKenzie shifted his emphasis to trading, the American Fur Company did not abandon trapping. By the spring of 1832, Vanderburgh had united with Drips and Fontenelle in the Bear River country. Henceforth, while McKenzie's Upper Missouri Outfit concentrated on the Indian trade, Chouteau's Western Department would oversee the battle with the Rocky Mountain Fur Company—in supplying the mountain men at rendezvous, in transporting returns to St. Louis, and in fielding competing trapping parties.[11]

The conflict escalated at the rendezvous of 1832.

THE ROCKY MOUNTAIN FUR COMPANY had fixed the site of the 1832 rendezvous in Pierre's Hole, the grassy, well-watered basin at the western foot of the Grand Tetons. It took its name from "Old Pierre" Tevanitagon, the Iroquois killed in 1827 in a fight with Blackfeet.

Free and company trappers had already begun to gather when Vanderburgh and Drips with ninety American Fur trappers arrived early in July. Ultimately, as Flatheads and Nez Perces pitched their tepees, there may have been a thousand or more people, with their stock, assembled in Pierre's Hole. It was the largest as well as the most significant rendezvous held in the Rocky Mountains.[12]

Competition made the significance. This was Rocky Mountain's rendezvous, but anyone could attend. The train that arrived first got most of the free trappers' business—in sale of merchandise and purchase of skins. Sublette and Fitzpatrick hurried west for Rocky Mountain. Lucien Fontenelle and Étienne Provost herded American Fur's caravan. They had taken their goods up the Missouri on the maiden voyage of the steamer *Yellow Stone* and packed them overland from Fort Union.

Others showed up. A newcomer of importance was Nathaniel Wyeth. A hardheaded businessman, successful as a Boston ice merchant, Wyeth concocted a scheme much like John Jacob Astor's Astorian venture. By sea and land he would descend on the Columbia, where he planned a three-pronged enterprise. He would tap the fur resources of the Rocky Mountains, supplying his trappers from the Columbia and shipping the furs to market by sea. He would also fill the holds of his vessels with barrels of salmon, harvested from the Columbia and salted for preservation. Finally, he would plant an agricultural colony in the Willamette Valley. Bound for Oregon with eighteen men, Wyeth traveled as far as Pierre's Hole under the protection of Sublette's caravan.[13]

In the race of the suppliers, Sublette won handily, reaching Pierre's Hole on July 8. The steamer's slow pace up the Missouri so delayed Fontenelle and Provost that they did not get off from Fort Union until June 19. Rendezvous was over before they even reached the Green River.

"When the pie was opened then the birds began to sing," recalled Joe Meek of the Sublette caravan's arrival, as "the 'fast young men' of the mountains outvied each other in all manner of mad pranks." Wyeth's "sober and inexperienced New Englanders" looked on in wonder, which only spurred the mountaineers to more spectacular theatrics. But as the kettles of alcohol passed freely, "the horse-racing, fine riding, wrestling, and all the manlier sports, soon degenerated into the baser exhibitions of a 'crazy drunk' condition."[14]

Heightening the festivities was the lifting of a gloom that had settled over the camps when the Sublette train arrived without Tom Fitzpatrick. From the Platte he had ridden ahead to alert the trappers of the caravan's

Mexkemahuastan, Chief of the Gros-Ventres of the Prairies. *These Plains "big bellies" were not the village Indians of the same name who resided near the Mandans but Atsinas, an Arapaho offshoot that trappers usually considered Blackfeet in all but name. Atsinas fought a celebrated battle with trappers in 1832 in Pierre's Hole. Karl Bodmer painted this picture the following year, as he ascended the Missouri with the German prince Maximilian.* COURTESY JOSLYN ART MUSEUM, OMAHA, NEBRASKA.

approach, and he had not been seen since. That same evening, however, he turned up near the rendezvous camps. "The poor man was reduced to a skeleton," observed Zenas Leonard, "and was almost senseless." Without horses or weapons, his feet bare and his clothing in shreds, he could not have lived many more days. "A general rejoicing ensued," added Leonard, "for his appearance among us again, was like that of one risen from the dead."[15]

Fitzpatrick's ordeal reputedly turned his hair white almost overnight. After an encounter with a grizzly bear, he had suffered an even more deadly encounter with Indians. The Gros Ventres, kin of the Araphaos but Blackfeet in all but name, were returning to the mountains in several groups after a three-year visit with their Arapaho cousins on the Arkansas River. The trains of Sublette, Fontenelle, and Bonneville, as well as riders sent to find these trains, had scrapes with Gros Ventre warriors.

Fitzpatrick had the misfortune to run into Gros Ventres. Shortly after crossing South Pass, he chanced on a party blocking the trail. Quickly turning into the foothills of the Wind River Mountains, he galloped up steep slopes with the Indians in close pursuit. His spare horse fell behind, and the one he rode began to give out. The warriors, on foot, gained. Abandoning his mount, Fitzpatrick crawled under a rocky ledge and arranged brush and leaves to cover the entry. The Indians searched in vain, some nearby. At dusk they gave up and, with his two horses, returned to their village. In the darkness Fitzpatrick crept from his refuge and descended, only to blunder into the Gros Ventre camp. Hastily backing out, he returned to his hiding place. The next day the warriors resumed the search, without success. When they left, he emerged to a crag overlooking their camp and saw men running races with his two horses.

With nightfall, Fitzpatrick again set forth on foot, this time circuiting the village and putting enough distance behind to feel safe. His tribulations had just begun. Day after day he pushed forward, living off roots and berries, fearful that a rifle shot aimed at game would alert the enemy. Crossing one of the streams rushing down from the mountains, he saw his rifle and shot pouch swept away. One night a wolf pack assailed him, and he escaped only by climbing a tree and remaining until daylight. Shreds of meat carved from a rotting buffalo carcass helped sustain him. He grew weaker and more haggard until he expected each day to collapse and die. But physical hardihood and surpassing skill as a mountaineer brought him through to a joyous welcome in Pierre's Hole. Revived by meat and corn, he told his story to an astounded audience.

The trappers had not seen the last of their foe (they rarely distinguished between Blackfeet and Gros Ventres). On July 17, a Rocky Mountain brigade of twenty-two under Fraeb and Milton Sublette broke camp and pointed south, intending to cross the Snake River Mountains and work their way southwest to the Humboldt for a fall hunt. About sixteen freemen went along, together with Nathaniel Wyeth and eleven followers. Wyeth had faced a rebellion in his company and lost seven men by desertion. He had placed himself under Sublette to get through the worst Indian country on his journey to Oregon.[16]

Camping at the southern end of Pierre's Hole, these men awoke on July 18 to spot a procession of about two hundred Indians emerging from the foot of Teton Pass. They were Gros Ventres, whose recent behavior toward whites had not been notably friendly. But on this morning the Indians had their families with them and were not looking for trouble. A chief, his rank marked by a scarlet robe across his shoulder, advanced with a peace pipe held high.

Antoine Godin and a Flathead warrior rode out to meet the chief. Antoine's father had been killed by Blackfeet, and here was a chance for revenge. Be ready to shoot him, he instructed his companion. As the three came together, Godin reached to shake hands and at the same time shouted "Fire!" The Flathead fired, and the chief fell dead. Godin snatched the scarlet robe, and the two, flaunting the colorful trophy, galloped back to camp amid a scattering fire from the startled Gros Ventres.

While the trappers sent messengers to summon help from the rendezvous camp, the Indians hurried into a thicket of willows and cottonwoods shading a swampy area created by a beaver dam. The women hastily gathered downed trees and threw up a rude fortress. By the time the army of trappers and Nez Perce and Flathead warriors stormed onto the ground, the Gros Ventres held strong defenses.

"In Indian warfare, we do not marshall our forces, nor approach the scene of conflict in any regular order," explained Robert Campbell. "Each person goes 'on his own hook.'" Even so, William Sublette made a rousing speech. "Then raising the *war whoop*, Mr. S. and myself, with about twenty others, dashed off at full speed towards the willows."[17]

Not many went into the willows with Sublette and Campbell. Wyeth's New Englanders watched from a comfortable distance, and most of the trappers hesitated to get very close to the Indian fort. Sublette, Campbell, and several others crawled close enough to exchange fire but could do no damage without disclosing their position. Bullets from the breastwork hit several men, killing one and mortally wounding another. When a ball tore up Sublette's shoulder, the attackers backed out.

Meantime, Milton Sublette led another force against the Indian rear, while the Flatheads and Nez Perces closed on the flanks. The whites then resolved to burn the Gros Ventres out, but the friendly tribesmen objected so strenuously to such waste of plunder that the plan was discarded.

Near nightfall someone in the fort shouted that, while the defenders might all be killed, so too would all their assailants, as reinforcements were on the way. Whoever interpreted that defiant threat gave the impression that the reinforcements had already arrived and even then were rampaging through the camps back at rendezvous. Swiftly the mountaineers and their Indian allies mounted and dashed back to base camp. No foes threatened it, but nightfall afforded a convenient excuse not to return to the battle.

The Gros Ventres slipped away in the night. The next morning the whites found the fort abandoned, except for the bodies of ten warriors and bloodstains that showed others had been hit. Thirty horses nearby included some stolen from Sublette's supply train and the two that had been seized from Fitzpatrick in his hairbreadth escape.

The trappers felt they had dealt a well-merited blow to a treacherous enemy, and they took special pleasure in having punished the very Indians who had raided Sublette and nearly killed Fitzpatrick. One of Wyeth's New Englanders saw the clash in a different light. "The whole appeared to me a needless and rash affray; for the Black Feet wished to avoid the engagement."[18]

True enough: they had their families along and were not prepared for a fight. True too that Godin and the Flathead acted treacherously in shooting an Indian brandishing a peace pipe. Yet the combatants were mortal foes who asked no quarter and gave no quarter. Given similar advantage, the Gros Ventres would have shown no more forbearance than the whites and their Indian allies. The Battle of Pierre's Hole reflected the standards of both sides in their time and place.

Rendezvous 1832 involved matters more serious than drunken frolics or even Indian fighting. Although American Fur lost the race of the suppliers, the firm's opposition worried the Rocky Mountain partners. Vanderburgh and Drips had hung tenaciously to Bridger and Milton Sublette in their spring hunt, learning mountain trapping from the experts but spoiling the operation for both companies. After regaining his strength, Fitzpatrick conferred with his partners and proposed a compromise. American and Rocky Mountain would divide the fur country and no longer devil each other on the same ground. No, answered Vanderburgh and Drips emphatically, thus reflecting the determination of McKenzie and Chouteau to drive all rivals out of the mountains.[19]

Before launching the fall hunt, the Rocky Mountain partners dealt with another issue, one with ultimately ruinous consequences. On July 25 Fitzpatrick, on behalf of the Rocky Mountain Fur Company, signed an agreement with William Sublette to take the firm's beaver down to St. Louis, dispose of it, and handle all outstanding debts. The document brimmed with financial complexities doubtless bewildering to Fitzpatrick, a great mountaineer but a novice businessman. In effect, he had mortgaged the Rocky Mountain Fur Company to Sublette, who could now manipulate those complexities so as to place the company's future solely under his control.[20]

VANDERBURGH AND DRIPS finally found American Fur's supply caravan on the Green River at Captain Bonneville's camp. After equipping themselves and turning over their catch to Fontenelle, the pair revived their spring strategy and headed north to dog Fitzpatrick and Bridger in the Three Forks. Within a month, on the Jefferson River, they had succeeded. By no tactic could the Rocky Mountain partisans throw off their unwanted companions. "They tried in every way to blind and baffle them," wrote Washington Irving; "to steal a march upon them, or lead them on a wrong scent; but all in vain."[21]

Exasperated, Fitzpatrick and Bridger resolved to sacrifice their own hunt to thwart the opposition. Swiftly, without setting traps, they worked north to Clark's Fork, up the Big Blackfoot, across the Continental Divide to the Great Falls of the Missouri, then south to the Three Forks. With superior numbers, American Fur divided, Vanderburgh to seek beaver on the Madison, Drips to continue to dog Rocky Mountain. At the Three Forks, however, Drips gave up and trapped the Jefferson, while Fitzpatrick and Bridger headed up the Gallatin. Soon, however, they crossed to the Madison and once again fell in with Vanderburgh.

Probably by agreement, so exhausting and profitless had the contest become, Vanderburgh turned down the Madison and then west to seek Drips on the Jefferson. Fitzpatrick and Bridger hunted toward the head of the Madison. Both ran into Blackfeet.

The Rocky Mountain brigade had worked into the heights west of the upper Madison when on October 25 about one hundred Blackfeet barred the way but raised a white flag. Several from each side sat down for a smoke. Bridger, suspicious, rode forward, his rifle across the saddle pommel, and was greeted by a chief with a peace pipe. Alerted by some movement, Bridger cocked his rifle as he leaned to shake hands with the Indian. The sound rightly alarmed the chief, who seized the rifle barrel and thrust it down to discharge into the ground, then threw Bridger to the ground, mounted his horse, and galloped off with both horse and rifle. Racing back to his own lines, Bridger caught two arrows in his back. The two sides exchanged fire until nightfall, when the Indians withdrew.[22]

Bridger survived his double wound, but Vanderburgh had no such good fortune. Earlier, while crossing the mountains west of the Madison on October 14, his company camped on one of the headstreams of the Ruby River, which joins with the Beaverhead to form the Jefferson. Fresh Indian signs prompted Vanderburgh to scout the vicinity. He took seven men with him, including Warren Ferris. Approaching a gully, they rode into a Blackfeet ambush. "Suddenly the lightning and thunder of at least twenty fusils burst upon our astonished senses from the gully," recalled Ferris. Vanderburgh's horse went down on him, but he pulled himself to his feet, yelled "Don't run, boys," and brought down the nearest warrior with his rifle. "The Indians immediately fired a volley upon him—he fell—they uttered a loud and shrill yell of exultation, and the noble spirit of a good and a brave man had passed away forever."

One other of the trappers died in the affray, as the rest spurred their mounts in retreat. Two took wounds. One was Ferris, hit in the shoulder. A friend probed it with a rifle ramrod and dressed it with a salve of his own concoction. Ferris recovered quickly. As for Vanderburgh, the Blackfeet stripped the flesh from his body and threw his bones in the stream. Flatheads later recovered and buried them.[23]

Many blamed Fitzpatrick for deliberately enticing Vanderburgh into Blackfeet country and thus to his death. The charge lacks merit. Vanderburgh chose to cling to Fitzpatrick and Bridger even as they tried every way to shake him off. Moreover, Vanderburgh ignored elementary maxims of any trapper in Blackfeet country and rode recklessly into an ambush. Finally, he and Rocky Mountain were now going their own way, probably as the result of an agreement a few days earlier that neither side had anything to gain by continuing the battle. Vanderburgh died because of tactics his company had adopted to achieve monopoly and because of his own carelessness.[24]

THE ARIKARAS REMAINED no more reconciled to Americans than the Blackfeet. After the Leavenworth fiasco of 1823, they ranged widely in war parties that took the lives of many trappers. In 1824 they had nearly done away with Hugh Glass, but the same mix of determination and skill that had defied death after his grizzly mauling saved him again.

In the autumn of 1828, after conveying to Kenneth McKenzie the appeal of the free trappers for competition in the mountains, Hugh Glass had remained at Fort Union. McKenzie put him on American Fur's payroll as a hunter. He worked out of both Fort Union and the new Crow post, Fort Cass, at the mouth of the Bighorn. Early in 1833, Samuel Tulloch, in charge of Fort Cass, dispatched Glass as a courier to Fort Union. With him went Edward Rose, the mulatto who had achieved such renown among the Crows and distrust among his fellow trappers. A third man joined to travel as far as a nearby hunting camp. As they crossed the frozen Yellowstone River below the fort, thirty Arikara warriors charged down on them. On the ice Old Glass's luck ran out. He, Rose, and their companion were shot, scalped, and stripped of all their possessions.

Shortly afterward, on the Powder River, these Arikaras attempted to run off the horses of another party of trappers. The leader, the same Johnson Gardner who had tormented Peter Skene Ogden in 1825, failed to prevent the loss of his herd. He seized three hostages, however, one of whom had a knife recognized as Glass's. A delegation came to parley, one carrying Glass's rifle. Gardner demanded the return of his horses. The Indians refused and departed. The hostages began to sing their death songs and made a sudden break for freedom. One succeeded. The other two went down riddled with rifle balls and slashed with knives.

In the spring of 1833, at Fort Union, Gardner presented one of the two Arikara scalps to the touring German nobleman Maximilian.[25]

Wahk-Tä-Ge-Li, a Sioux Warrior. *Bands of Sioux from various tribes ranged both sides of the Missouri River from the Niobrara to the Yellowstone. They traded with the American Fur Company at Fort Pierre and at seasonal posts established closer to their migratory paths. Painting by Karl Bodmer,* COURTESY JOSLYN ART MUSEUM, OMAHA, NEBRASKA.

WHILE AMERICAN AND ROCKY MOUNTAIN inflicted costly damage on each other in the mountains, a new and ultimately decisive scheme took shape in the mind of William L. Sublette. After the 1832 rendezvous, he and his close friend Robert Campbell decided to form a partnership. The document organizing the firm of Sublette and Campbell recorded a vague purpose of fitting an expedition "for trading and trapping in the Rocky Mountains." In fact, they had much more explicit, ambitious, and daring plans.[26]

The first move could scarcely have been more hazardous. They resolved to take on the "King of the Missouri" in his own realm, establishing a string of trading posts on the upper Missouri to compete directly with McKenzie's. They could not hope to drive him from the river, but they may have aimed to force either a buyout such as had transformed Columbia Fur into the Upper Missouri Outfit or a division of the fur country such as Fitzpatrick had proposed at rendezvous.

The partners launched their scheme in the spring of 1833. Sublette took two keelboats loaded with trade goods and engagés up the Missouri while Campbell herded the annual supply train for Rocky Mountain to the rendezvous on the Green River, then brought out the year's catch. Accompanied by Nathaniel Wyeth, returning east from Oregon, he went by way of the Bighorn and Yellowstone. At the mouth of the Yellowstone, on September 3, 1833, Campbell and Sublette reunited. Sublette took the furs on down to St. Louis, while Campbell remained to build Fort William, a mere three miles down the Missouri from McKenzie's bastion of Fort Union.[27]

At each McKenzie post paired with a Sublette and Campbell post, fierce competition erupted. McKenzie brought to the fray a cadre of experienced and dedicated traders, superior merchandise, a reserve of customer loyalty, and the resolve to pay any price, whatever the loss, to garner all the Indians' furs and crush the upstart newcomers. What he lacked, and his challengers possessed in abundance, was alcohol.

The government had long sought to prevent liquor from falling into the hands of Indians, but it had always been a staple of the fur trade. Routinely liquor went up the Missouri and out to the Rockies under official permits for the exclusive use of "boatmen." Finally, Congress faced the issue squarely and, despite intense lobbying by the fur men, in July 1832 enacted legislation imposing an absolute ban on liquor in the Indian country.

After military officers at Fort Leavenworth seized a large consignment of American Fur liquor, public and government scrutiny fell heavily on the company. While smaller operators such as Sublette and Campbell easily evaded the law, American Fur could not. On the upper Missouri its store of the potent kegs dwindled to extinction.[28]

Despite that handicap, McKenzie and his lieutenants gradually brought to bear the pressures that, in time, would have destroyed Sublette and Campbell. The King grew confident that, even without liquor, he could rout the opposition.[29]

One coup in which McKenzie took quiet satisfaction occurred in September 1833 in the Crow country. Even here, where Samuel Tulloch presided over Fort Cass and sent paid emissaries to the Crow winter camps, Sublette and Campbell competed. But one of Tulloch's engagés was Jim Beckwourth, the mulatto prevaricator who had forsaken the trapper's life to live with the Crows. What befell Tom Fitzpatrick's Rocky Mountain brigade surely owed inspiration to Beckwourth if not to Tulloch. In Fitzpatrick's absence, a large party of Crow warriors simply swarmed into his camp on the Tongue River and, without firing a shot, relieved his trappers of virtually everything. Meeting Fitzpatrick himself on the way back to camp, moreover, they stripped him of horse, rifle, and clothing. Through the chief, Fitzpatrick succeeded in recovering much of what was stolen. The Indians, however, sold the purloined furs at Fort Cass, a further indignity unrelieved by McKenzie's straight-faced offer to sell them back for what Tulloch had paid. "My goods are brought into this country to trade," he wrote, "& I would as willingly dispose of them to Mr. F. as any one else." But he could not resist boasting that "this has been a severe blow on Sublett & Co."[30]

McKenzie's superiors in St. Louis and New York had a better sense than he of the company's vulnerabilities. He himself had created one of the most glaring. Barred from importing liquor, he had erected a still at Fort Union and, with corn obtained from the Mandans, begun to manufacture his own. Sublette and Wyeth observed this operation in September 1833 and casually mentioned it to officers at Fort Leavenworth. American Fur averted a crisis only by the most adroit maneuvers, including withdrawing McKenzie from the Indian country.[31]

But the largest vulnerability lay in the approaching retirement of John Jacob Astor, now more and more taking his ease in Europe while his son William ran the company from New York. In February 1834, as tortuous negotiations sputtered toward a corporate structure to follow the old man's departure, William Sublette arrived in New York. He had a firm grasp of the uncertainties afflicting American Fur and the political liabilities McKenzie and others on the Missouri had incurred by their handling of the liquor problem. Moreover, Sublette enjoyed the political and financial backing of Congressman William H. Ashley, as his competitors well knew. He could have picked no better time to sit down with his opponents at their own table.

Sublette came away with an agreement that echoed the old Fitzpatrick proposal to divide the fur country. American Fur would withdraw entirely from the mountains for at least one year, and Sublette and Campbell would sell out to American Fur and abandon the Missouri. The treaty commanded the cordial support of Pierre Chouteau, Jr., as he made clear when he forwarded it to a furious Kenneth McKenzie, who in a few more months could have driven Sublette and Campbell from his domain.[32]

The organization finally worked out in the summer of 1834 spawned much confusion in the West. Ramsay Crooks took over the American Fur Company, but it now consisted only of the old Northern Department centered on the Great Lakes. The Western Department and its stepchild the Upper Missouri Outfit ceased to exist as an arm of American Fur. Henceforth, Pratte, Chouteau & Company (later Pierre Chouteau, Jr., & Company) would operate west of St. Louis. The old nomenclature, however, resisted extinction, and the Chouteau firm continued to be popularly known as the American Fur Company.[33]

William Sublette expected the Rocky Mountain Fur Company to collapse within the year, and at the Astor table in February 1834 he may even have promised that it would. By virtue of the agreement made with Fitz-patrick after the 1832 rendezvous, he held all the company's debts, which he believed the 1834 returns could not possibly discharge. Holding Rocky Mountain's debt, he also held the power to destroy the company whenever he chose.[34]

Sublette intended to go up the Missouri in the spring of 1834 and help Campbell close out the partnership's operation. In St. Louis, however, he accidentally picked up surprising news. The previous autumn, on the Yel-lowstone, his brother Milton and Fitzpatrick had arranged with Nathaniel Wyeth to supply Rocky Mountain in 1834 for half the cost charged by Sub-lette and Campbell. Wyeth could do this because he planned to take the furs on to Oregon and ship them to market by water. The contract with Rocky Mountain allowed either party to default on penalty of five hundred dollars.

Suddenly confronted with the unwelcome prospect that Rocky Moun-tain might not go under after all, Sublette abruptly changed plans. Sending his younger brother Solomon to work with Campbell, he hurriedly made up a caravan in St. Louis and headed for the 1834 rendezvous himself. An old hand at plains travel, he easily overtook and passed the neophyte Wyeth and reached the rendezvous site on Ham's Fork of the Green a day or two in advance. It was time enough to confront Fitzpatrick with Rocky Moun-tain's debt and force the exchange of Sublette's supplies for Rocky Moun-tain's beaver. Even before Wyeth arrived to collect his five hundred dollars for default, the Rocky Mountain Fur Company had disintegrated.

A furious Wyeth accused Fitzpatrick of bad faith founded on bribery, but in truth he had no choice. Neither he nor any of his partners had in-tended to dissolve their relationship, and they fully meant to deal with Wyeth. But Sublette held a legal contract that superseded Wyeth's. The year's returns did not liquidate the debts, and Sublette would wait no longer.[35]

Left with a caravan of merchandise and no beaver to take on to Oregon, Wyeth, according to Joe Meek, made a portentous vow: "Gentlemen, I will roll a stone into your garden that you will never be able to get out." Whether he said it or not, he did. That autumn, on the Snake River near the mouth of the Portneuf, he built Fort Hall to house his merchandise. Later he sold the fort to the Hudson's Bay Company, which indeed made it a heavy stone in the garden of American trappers.[36]

As Sublette had promised in New York, Campbell closed out all the posts competing with the American Fur Company on the Missouri. In May he abandoned Fort William and sent a party with the winter's store of furs cross-country to a new Fort William. On the way to rendezvous, Bill Sublette had paused on the Laramie River to lay the foundation for the new post and had left a party to begin construction. One day the new Fort William would take the name Fort Laramie.[37]

Like Ashley before him, Sublette increasingly prized the comforts of St. Louis, where he and Campbell continued a thriving business. From master trapper, Bill Sublette had evolved into master manipulator of men and of the arcane documents that ordered men's affairs.

11

WARREN FERRIS:

TRAPPER AS CARTOGRAPHER

Westward! Ho! It is the sixteenth of the second month, A.D. 1830, and I have joined a trapping, trading, hunting expedition to the Rocky Mountains. *Why,* I scarcely know, for the motives that induced me to this step were of a mixed complexion. . . . Curiosity, a love of wild adventure, and perhaps also a hope of profit.[1]

THUS WARREN ANGUS FERRIS began the story of his five-year odyssey in the West. And thus he displayed learning and literacy uncharacteristic of the mountain men with whom he cast his lot. Most of his education, including wide reading in history and literature and the rudiments of civil engineering gained from his stepfather, he acquired before he turned eighteen. At that age, in 1828, he left his home in Buffalo, New York, and headed west. Pittsburgh, Cincinnati, Louisville, and St. Louis afforded little or no employment. Finally, early in 1830, he found a position with B. Pratte & Company, the old "French Fur Company" that now functioned as the Western Department of the American Fur Company.

Aside from uncommon learning, this adventure-loving youth of twenty possessed the vigor, temperament, adaptability, and talent to assimilate knowledge and skills quickly that earned him status as a mountain man. The hot temper, tenderness, and affection that he betrayed in his letters home, if openly displayed in the mountain man fraternity, seem not to have caused him either grief or ridicule.

This portion of Warren A. Ferris's map of the northern Rockies represents what most trappers carried in their minds. Ferris drew the map to accompany his memoirs, which he hoped to publish. Had the map been made public in 1836, as he intended, it would have significantly influenced western cartography. Instead, it lay undiscovered until 1940. COURTESY HAROLD B. LEE LIBRARY, BRIGHAM YOUNG UNIVERSITY, PROVO, UTAH.

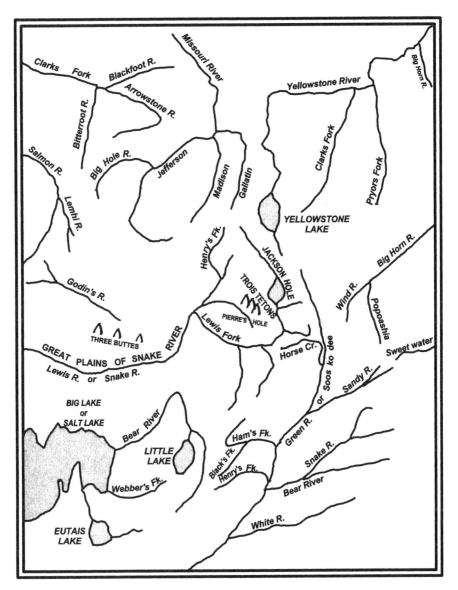

Guide to Warren Ferris Map

Ferris's true significance, however, lay not in his feats as a mountaineer but in his perceptive eye for the telling detail and his perseverance in recording what he saw and did. He was one of the handful of genuine mountain men endowed with the literacy to record the essence of a unique way of life before it disappeared.[2]

Of signal importance too, Ferris's five years as a trapper coincided with the struggle of the American and Rocky Mountain fur companies for mastery of the mountain fur business. Strangely, his narrative never acknowledges the stakes or even the existence of this mortal combat. But his experiences traced its course and denouement.

Warren Ferris went to the mountains in the spring of 1830 as an engagé in the caravan of Fontenelle and Drips, American Fur's initial bid for control of the Rocky Mountains. Among the fifty men who made up the train, Ferris endured the miseries faced by novices in a brutal business pursued in a demanding environment. They never found the rendezvous on the Wind River, they conducted a disappointing fall hunt, and they passed the winter of 1830–31 in the snows of Cache Valley, where they fraternized with the enemy—Henry Fraeb, Jean Baptiste Gervais, and their contingent of the Rocky Mountain Fur Company.

By the spring of 1831, Warren Ferris could set down in graphic terms his baptism in the ways of the wilderness:

> Our horses were in the most miserable condition, and we reduced to mere skeletons. Our gums became so sore from eating tough bull meat, that we were forced to swallow it without chewing; and to complete our misery, many of us were nearly deprived of sight from inflammation of the eyes, brought on by the reflection of the sunbeams on the snow.[3]

By the summer of 1832, Warren Ferris had developed into a seasoned trapper. He had trapped the heartland of the northern Rockies—the tributaries of the Green falling from the Uinta Mountains, the Bear River and Bear Lake, the Snake and its southern affluents, and the jumbled mountains of the Salmon River north of the volcanic Snake Plain. He had fought Blackfeet and made friends with Utes, Flatheads, Shoshones, and Nez Perces, whom he found fascinating and described in detail. And he had socialized with the brigades of the Rocky Mountain Fur Company and even the Hudson's Bay Company, whose John Work now headed the Snake Country Expeditions. Ferris attended his first rendezvous in July 1832—the pivotal gathering in Pierre's Hole that featured the rousing battle with the Gros Ventres and the escalation of the battle between the fur giants. He was with Vanderburgh three months later when the Blackfeet ambush took the captain's life and left Ferris with a hole in his shoulder.

Ferris found less interest in the maneuvers of the battling companies than in the sweep of geography to which trapping life introduced him. He turned an appreciative eye on the land and, driven by his youthful exposure to surveying, noted its distinguishing characteristics. For example, he took approving notice of Pierre's Hole, a "pleasant retreat" webbed with small streams uniting to form Pierre's Fork (now the Teton River). Most impressive, however:

> On the east side of the valley, three majestic peaks of naked rock, rise far above the rest, and are well known to mountain rovers by the name of "The Trois Tetons." The mountains are very abrupt, as far as the pines extend, and the huge pyramids above are absolutely inaccessible.[4]

Ferris not only marveled at such alpine spectacles but took keen notice of the dangers they posed for mountaineers. One example in particular dramatized perils wholly unrelated to Blackfeet warriors. In the summer of 1833, four trappers headed for the annual rendezvous on the upper Green River. They descended Teton Pass and had to cross the Snake River before turning up the Hoback to reach their destination. The Snake ran a full head of water and could not be forded on horseback. They stripped their horses of all accouterments and themselves of all clothing and equipment and lashed them to a raft. As the horses swam ahead to reach the far bank, the naked men pushed the raft into the current and also swam. The current took over, seized the raft, and carried it beneath a huge pile of driftwood, beyond recovery. Lost were clothes, saddles, blankets, rifles, traps, beaver pelts, and everything else. On the opposite shore they retrieved their horses, but had nothing else.

Warren Ferris described the ordeal:

> With scarcely a ray of hope to cheer them on their dreary task, they mounted their bare backed horses, and started in quest of us. The burning heat of the sun parched their skins, and they had nothing to shield them from his powerful rays; the freezing air of the night chilled and benumbed their unprotected bodies, and they had no covering to keep off the cold; the chill storms of rain and hail pelted mercilessly on them, and they could not escape the torture; the friction produced by riding without a saddle or anything for a substitute, chaffed off the skin, and even flesh, and without any means of remedying the misfortune, or alleviating pain, for they were prevented from walking by the stones and sharp thorns of the prickly pear, which lacerated their feet. They were compelled, though the agony occasioned by it was intense, to continue their equestrian march, till amidst this accumulation of ills, they reached our camp.[5]

Five years in the Rockies gave Warren Ferris a firm grasp of a large piece of North American geography. It stemmed from his own experiences and what others told him. It represented the mountain man's state of geographical knowledge in his own time, 1830–35. For the most part, it remained locked in the mountain man's mind. In what he knew, Ferris typified the mountain man. Unlike them, he possessed the literary and cartographic ability to communicate what he knew. In his own time he failed to do so, but posterity can look into his mind and know what he and his comrades knew.

WHAT MOUNTAIN MEN like Ferris knew in 1835 owed an immense debt to Jedediah Smith and Joseph R. Walker. Both had expanded the geographical horizons of the mountain men all the way from the Green River to the Pacific. Both had crossed the Great Basin and the Sierra Nevada. Both knew California—the harbors, the Central Valley bounded on the west by the coastal ranges and the east by the Sierra Nevada. Smith had reached the Columbia River by way of the Willamette—the Multnomah of Lewis and Clark—examined the grassy basin east of the Cascade Range, and journeyed up Clark's Fork to Flathead Post and the Continental Divide.

Trappers more concerned with beaver than geography still had to pay close attention to geography. On a lesser scale than Smith and Walker, they learned the lay of the land they trapped, the creeks and rivers, the mountains and passes, the favored Indian trails—an understanding at least sufficient to guide the beaver quest.

By Warren Ferris's time, every trapper could train his mind's eye on an imaginary map of varying detail and exactitude. By Ferris's time, the composite of these "mental maps" spanned half a continent, from the Missouri River to the Pacific and from the upper Columbia to the lower Colorado. Some portions stood forth in bolder relief than others, and some remained blank. The northern and central Rocky Mountains spread out in greatest detail. The Colorado River below the Grand Canyon, the Green above the southern edge of the Uinta Basin, and the Grand and other rivers draining the Western Slope appeared with reasonable accuracy. The Gila and its tributaries, thanks to Ewing Young and his associates, traced a course from the Copper Mines to the Colorado River. Great Salt Lake etched itself prominently, but the Great Basin west to the Sierras remained a land chiefly of painful impressions related by Smith and Walker. Peter Skene Ogden could have filled in some details, but he did not sit around American campfires.

Smith, Walker, and all the other trappers did sit around those campfires. At rendezvous, the men of wide-ranging brigades described geography as well as recounted adventure. In the flickering firelight, each man's mental map expanded and took on more detail as he listened to what others had discovered.

By Ferris's time, most trappers could visualize a map of the American West more accurate and comprehensive than existed anywhere on paper. Some of what they saw, and knew, leaked out through St. Louis newspapers or spread by word of mouth. Most, however, remained locked in their minds, awaiting the intermediary equipped by training and skill to lay it before the literate world.

Warren Ferris could have been that intermediary. He was not.

OBLIVIOUS OF THE TORTURED BUSINESS MACHINATIONS of his employer and its rivals, Warren Ferris trapped the Rockies with American Fur's brigades. Much of the time he spent in the Clark's Fork country, enticing the Flatheads to trade with his company and recording a growing affection for these friendly people. Year after year he set to paper his adventures, his observations of Indians and trappers, and his travels in a land of intricate geography. Finally, summoned by family problems at home, he ended his trapper's life in the autumn of 1835 and left the mountains forever.

Unemployed, Ferris spent 1836 transforming his journal into a book, *Life in the Rocky Mountains*, and in preparing a map to illustrate it. Late in the year he submitted the manuscript to a prestigious Philadelphia publishing house. This firm, however, had just issued Washington Irving's *Rocky Mountains*, the vibrant story drawn from the journals of Captain Bonneville. Early in 1837 Ferris's manuscript came back with a rejection slip.[6]

Losing interest in the project, Ferris and his brother went to Texas, newly independent of Mexico. There he carved out a successful career as a land surveyor and land speculator, later as a farmer and local public official. He died near Dallas in 1872.

Warren's brother Charles returned to their home in Buffalo, New York, and in 1842 became an editor of the *Western Literary Messenger*. This badly edited magazine, commanding an unimpressive subscription list, led an erratic existence and in 1857 sank into oblivion. Charles, however, apparently without even informing Warren, ran the rejected manuscript serially in the magazine. And there it lay unnoticed until the late 1930s, when Paul C. Phillips and others assembled it from the scattered copies of the magazine that had survived.[7]

Phillips also found the Ferris map. Long in the family, it had come into a private collection in Buffalo, New York. Ferris had drawn it in 1836 to illustrate his book, and he had laid down in great detail all the mountains and rivers he described in his manuscript. Despite numerous distortions, the geography was set in a framework of latitude and longitude. The maps published at the time Ferris worked—those of Washington Irving, Albert Gallatin, and H. L. Tanner—would have benefited immensely from exposure to Ferris's. "Had this map been available to those mapmakers," Carl Wheat has written, "the entire course of western cartography might have been different. . . . Had his map been published (as he hoped it might be) in 1836 instead of in 1940 it would doubtless have exerted a strong influence in contemporary western cartography."[8]

Despite its failure to realize its cartographic potential in its own time, the Ferris map is of prime significance. It reveals the mastery of geographical detail that one mountain man achieved during his five years in the Rockies, and it suggests the scope and content of the map that most mountain men carried in their mind's eye. The time would soon come when they too, like Ferris, could transpose their mental maps to paper—but only, in near anonymity, through the medium of the professional cartographer.

12

TOM FITZPATRICK:

MISSIONARIES TO OREGON

Thomas Fitzpatrick, mountain man and fur trader; Marcus Whitman, medical doctor and Presbyterian divine. They met in the last days of July 1835, as the annual supply caravan plodding toward rendezvous paused at Fort William, the log trading post erected by William Sublette a year earlier on the Laramie River, just above its confluence with the North Platte. The meeting of these two men of such disparate backgrounds and personalities exemplified an uneasy union of mountain men and missionaries that would bear heavily on the future of the Oregon country.

Dr. Marcus Whitman and the Reverend Samuel Parker were headed for Oregon, supposedly called by tribesmen eager to learn of the white people's religion. A traveler could reach Oregon by ship, as had one contingent of the Astorians, but that entailed a voyage of six months or more, around the Horn to the Sandwich Islands (Hawaii) and thence to the Hudson's Bay Company headquarters at Fort Vancouver on the Columbia. The only other course was an overland crossing. For neophyte overlanders, only the mountain man claimed the knowledge, skill, and experience to get them safely across the continent.

Less than three months before meeting Whitman and Parker in July 1835, Tom Fitzpatrick had taken possession of Fort William. The collapse of the Rocky Mountain Fur Company the previous summer had left a void in the mountains. The fledgling firm of Fontenelle, Fitzpatrick & Company sought to fill it. With William Sublette increasingly confining his activities to St. Louis, he persuaded the new firm to buy his strategically sited post.

Erected in 1834 by William Sublette on the Laramie River near its confluence with the North Platte, Fort Laramie played a long and distinguished role in the history of the American West. First named Fort William, by the 1840s almost everyone called it Fort Laramie. Pierre Chouteau & Company, successor to the American Fur Company, operated the fort as a post for trading with Sioux and Cheyenne Indians and supplying trapping parties in the mountains. Emigrants to Oregon and California found it a key way station for reprovisioning and making repairs. In 1849 the army bought it from the Chouteau fur company, and for the next forty years it served as a military base for the protection of overland travelers and campaigns against the Sioux, Cheyenne, and other Indian tribes. Alfred Jacob Miller painted this scene in 1837. COURTESY WALTERS ART GALLERY, BALTIMORE.

For Fitzpatrick, taking over Fort William marked a step in his transition to trader and businessman. As trapper and brigade leader, only Jim Bridger enjoyed equal reputation. With the departure of William Sublette, however, neither Bridger nor any of the other mountain notables possessed Fitzpatrick's knowledge of the commercial side of the fur trade. Although his business sense had limits, as Sublette had demonstrated, Fitzpatrick led the stumbling course by which Pratte, Chouteau & Company finally realized the American Fur Company's Rocky Mountain ambitions.

"A warm hearted, gentlemanly Hibernian," in the words of health seeker William Marshall Anderson, Fitzpatrick bore an enviable stature among his Rocky Mountain peers. Trapper Zenas Leonard thought him coldhearted, ruthless, and selfish, qualities common in the heated crucible of Rocky Mountain competition, but hardly anyone else spoke ill of Fitz-patrick. "White Hair," his Indian name, told of the nearly fatal escape from the Gros Ventres in 1832, which was said to have turned his hair white overnight. Later, "Broken Hand" would describe the results of a rifle acci-dent that shattered his left wrist. In 1839 a German traveler drew this por-trait: "He has a spare, bony figure, a face full of expression, and white hair; his whole demeanor reveals strong passions."[1]

Marcus Whitman differed greatly not only from Fitzpatrick and his fel-low mountaineers but from Parker and most other missionaries. Thirty-three in 1835, a medical doctor, a man of fine mind and appealing character, sincere, honest, he was above all tenacious in pursuing any pur-pose he set for himself. No less godly than others of his profession, no less dedicated to the religious and cultural transformation of races denied the blessings of Christianity, he displayed none of the narrow prejudices that cramped their minds and offended the more worldly.

Congregationalist Samuel Parker adapted less readily to western travel. Twenty-three years Whitman's senior and also well educated, Parker made carping complaint of the lack of comforts and refinements he had left be-hind, and he openly disdained the ungodly. A fellow missionary described Parker as "inclined to self-applause, requiring his full share of ministerial approbation or respect." Joe Meek put it less primly: "pious humbug."[2]

Lucien Fontenelle captained the Chouteau caravan of 1835 as far as Fort William. Both he and his men resented the missionaries Chouteau had inflicted on them. "Very evident tokens gave us to understand that our company was not agreeable," wrote Whitman of the journey from Liberty to Bellevue, "such as throwing rotten eggs at me." At Bellevue, however, cholera struck the train. Although ill himself, Whitman ministered hero-ically to the stricken, including Fontenelle himself. By Fort William, thanks to Whitman if not Parker, the hostility had dissolved. Parker of-fered remuneration for the escort, but Fontenelle declined. "If any one is indebted," he replied, "it is myself, for you have saved my life, and the lives of my men."[3]

At Fort William, Fontenelle turned over the train to his partner and stayed to manage the fort. With the groundwork well laid, Fitzpatrick and Whitman took up where Fontenelle and Whitman had left off. Like most mountain men, Fitzpatrick did not approve of missionaries tampering with Indian lives. As a Methodist cleric wrote in 1841, Fitzpatrick "is a wicked, worldly man, and is much opposed to missionaries going among the Indi-ans."[4] Even so, the doctor's ready willingness to share in camp chores and treat the ills of the men won over Fitzpatrick as it had Fontenelle. By Au-gust 12, when the caravan reached rendezvous on the upper Green River at

Horse Creek, the two had cemented a friendship that would prove important to the work of Marcus Whitman.

THE MISSION FIELD toward which Whitman and Parker journeyed in 1835 remained the realm of the Hudson's Bay Company even though legally, under the Convention of 1828, jointly occupied by the citizens of both Great Britain and the United States. Since 1825, to stem the advance of American trappers, the company's Snake Country Expeditions had sought to transform Oregon west of the Continental Divide into a "fur desert." By the 1830s, company leaders also had cause to fear agricultural settlement. Farmers and stockmen would destroy the fur trade.

Chief Factor John McLoughlin at Fort Vancouver, Sir George Simpson, and even the highest officials in London had long since given up hope of an international boundary running south of the Columbia. They aimed only to hold the country north of the Columbia. Yet the prime agricultural land lay south of the river and almost certainly would one day become United States territory. The Willamette River, Lewis and Clark's Multnomah, headed not in the Rockies, as some Americans still believed, but a scant 150 miles south of the Columbia. It would not bear rafts laden with farmers and their implements from the crest of the Rockies to the Columbia, but it did water a valley of fertile soil, ample rainfall, and temperate climate. Already the company had failed to discourage its own retirees, French Canadians of mixed descent for whom the eastern Canadian provinces held no appeal, from settling on the rich bottoms of the Willamette.[5]

Both McLoughlin and Simpson were slow to shift their worries from American trappers to American colonists, although the early 1830s rang a series of alarms. One sounded loudly with the appearance at Fort Vancouver, in October 1832, of Nathaniel J. Wyeth.

Wyeth embodied the visionary schemes of a Boston schoolmaster, Hall Jackson Kelley, who had devoted nearly a decade to promoting a New England colony on the Columbia River. Wyeth had signed on with Kelley's emigration society, but when Kelley proved increasingly unlikely to turn dream into reality, Wyeth set forth on his own. He would tap the furs of the Rockies, the salmon of the Columbia, and the fertile soils of the Willamette, and he would bind all into a single system with transportation by both land and sea.[6]

Wyeth's little band trapped the Rockies, participated in the historic rendezvous at Pierre's Hole in July 1832, and followed the route down the Snake and over the Blue Mountains opened by the Astorians in 1811–12 and since used by Hudson's Bay Company Snake Country Expeditions.

Wyeth reached Fort Vancouver as the first American party to traverse westward the entire length of what would become the Oregon Trail.

Wyeth posed no immediate threat to the Hudson's Bay Company. His supply ship from Boston had been lost at sea, pushing the entire enterprise to the edge of disaster. Dr. McLoughlin extended the company's usual hospitality and listened as Wyeth explained his designs on the Columbia. Rather than fight off the prospective competition, the canny chief factor perceived more to be gained by aiding, or at least not opposing, Wyeth's aspirations in the fur and salmon business—a strategy later to bring him into conflict with his superiors.

As for American settlers, Wyeth's prospect of getting any to the Columbia seemed remote. Anyway, company policy recognized American colonization of the Willamette Valley as inevitable. Company policy was to delay it as long as possible.

After wintering at Fort Vancouver, Wyeth traveled back to Boston to organize another attempt at realizing his plan. His second overland crossing, in 1834, included no settlers to trouble the operations of the Hudson's Bay Company. But it did include an ominous harbinger—missionaries. Where the clergy went, even to convert Indians, colonists were bound to follow.

ALL THE PROTESTANT MISSIONARIES to Oregon traced their inspiration to the same source. In the autumn of 1831 four Indians—three Nez Perces and one Flathead—descended from the mountains with Lucien Fontenelle's returning caravan. They toured St. Louis and, like numerous other Indian delegations, visited with General William Clark, Superintendent of Indian Affairs. Whether they came simply to see the white people's city or with some further notion of exploring the white people's deity, they exploded before a large public as the heroes of a heartrending saga. As embellished in the religious press, it told of benighted savages trekking across the continent in search of someone who would bring word of the true God to their people. "Hear! Hear!" trumpeted an evangelical editorialist in the spring of 1833. "Who will respond to the call from beyond the Rocky mountains? . . . Who will go? Who?"[7]

The Methodists went first, a year before Whitman and Parker. Jason and Daniel Lee, with two lay aides, traveled under the protection of Nathaniel Wyeth's train of 1834. At the rendezvous on Ham's Fork, they met Nez Perces and Flatheads, who welcomed them with the usual courtesy. The Lees also met Tom Fitzpatrick, at the moment distracted by defaulting on his supply contract with Wyeth and presiding over the collapse of the Rocky Mountain Fur Company.

Jason Lee—"a tall and powerful man, who looks as though he were well calculated to buffet difficulties in a wild country," according to an observer—related to the rough trappers in much the same way as missionaries who came afterward. When he first saw Indians at Fort William, he set down his calling as: "Go forth, thrust in the sickle and reap these red men." At rendezvous, he found that the mountaineers, "some of them, and perhaps all, are opposed to our enterprise. . . . But I must say they have treated me with the greatest politeness."[8]

Wyeth and his trappers escorted the Methodists on to the Columbia, where they discovered a helpful McLoughlin at Fort Vancouver. He persuaded them to forget the Flatheads and Nez Perces of the mountains, where they might complicate trading relations, and instead plant their mission in the Willamette Valley, where he could keep an eye on them. Ironically, their interest in thrusting in the sickle and reaping red men gradually shifted to ministering to whites. Rather than isolating themselves in some mountain recess, they emerged as a positive force in the American colonization of the Willamette Valley.

MARCUS WHITMAN AND SAMUEL PARKER journeyed to Oregon in the service of the American Board of Commissioners for Foreign Missions, representing the Presbyterian, Congregational, and Dutch Reformed Churches. The commissioners had also been animated by the story of the Flathead and Nez Perce delegation, and they dispatched the two clerics to reconnoiter the Columbia and report on the prospects. At the Green River rendezvous in August 1835, the pair found the trappers, like Tom Fitzpatrick, opposed to missionaries; but they also found, like Jason Lee, that trappers could be polite and helpful even while enduring patronizing scolding for their impious behavior.

As the elderly and sanctimonious Parker condescended, Whitman won the hearts of all. He was "another style of man," Joe Meek observed. "Whatever he thought of the wild ways of the mountain-men he discreetly kept to himself." But what endeared him to mountain men and Indians alike was a dramatic feat of surgery. Jim Bridger still carried a Blackfeet arrowhead embedded in his hip, souvenir of the clash on the upper Madison in October 1832. Whitman agreed to take it out. As Parker recorded:

It was a difficult operation, because the arrow was hooked at the point by striking a large bone and a cartilaginous substance had grown around it. The Doctor pursued the operation with great self-possession and perseverance; and his patient manifested equal firmness. The Indians looked on meanwhile, with countenances indicating wonder, and in their own peculiar manner expressed great astonishment when it was extracted.[9]

While Fitzpatrick completed his business and the mountain men caroused, Whitman and Parker held long sessions with Nez Perce and Flathead chiefs. The Indians said they would welcome men who could teach them about the white people's God. "After deliberating prayerfully," according to Parker, and "receiving indications of divine providence," the two clerics agreed that the Nez Perces and Flatheads "present a promising field of labor white for the harvest." That conclusion reached, there seemed no purpose in both proceeding to the Columbia. Parker would go on. Whitman would return with Fitzpatrick's train, report to the American Board, organize a mission party to come out in 1836, and thus "save a year in bringing the gospel to this promising missionary field."[10]

The 1835 rendezvous was also the scene of an event destined to blossom into legendary proportions. A French Canadian bully, Joseph Chouinard, challenged any man of any race or nationality to fight him. Tiring of the bombast, the young, slightly built Kit Carson took him up on it. Mounted, the two charged each other. Both fired their pistols at the same instant. Chouinard's ball went wild, while Carson's smashed his opponent's hand, wrist, and arm. According to a disgusted Parker, the duel characterized a people and a place where "human nature is not oppressed by the tyranny of religion, and pleasure is not awed by the frown of virtue."[11]

Samuel Parker made one final contribution to mountain lore before sailing home from the Columbia, never to glimpse mountains or Indians again.[12] As far as Pierre's Hole, the clergyman traveled with a band of Flatheads and Jim Bridger's brigade of about fifty men. Sabbath of August 23 overtook the procession at the head of the Hoback River, in what had become known as Jackson's Little Hole. To the acute distress of missionaries, trapper bands rarely treated Sunday any differently than other days, but Bridger called a halt for an afternoon's rest. Parker preached a sermon:

The men conducted themselves with great propriety, and listened with attention. I did not feel any disposition to upbraid them for their sins, but endeavoured affectionately to show them, that they are unfit for heaven, and that they could not be happy in the employments of that holy place, unless they should first experience a great moral change of heart by the grace of God, since the only source of happiness in heaven consists in serving and glorifying God forever.

Joe Meek remembered the service differently. "Very little pious reverence marked the countenances of that wild and motley congregation," he recalled. The men listened politely, but in the midst of the sermon buffalo appeared. "The congregation incontinently broke up, without staying for a benediction, and every man made haste after his horse, gun, and rope, leaving Mr. Parker to discourse to vacant ground." That evening, as fat ribs sizzled by the campfires, the preacher "rebuked the sabbath-breakers quite severely." Afterward, to their disgust, he partook heartily of choice cuts of meat.[13]

AGAIN IN 1836 Tom Fitzpatrick led the supply caravan to rendezvous, again held on the upper Green at the mouth of Horse Creek. This rendezvous marked a turning point in Fitzpatrick's career and a momentous turning point in the history of the Rocky Mountain fur trade.[14]

For a year Pratte, Chouteau & Company (the former Western Department of the American Fur Company) had been trying to buy Fort William from Fontenelle, Fitzpatrick & Company (which included Bridger, Drips, and Milton Sublette). Strategically located on the Laramie River near the North Platte, a crossroads of Sioux and Cheyenne migrations, Fort William had been hurting the business of the company's Missouri River post of Fort Pierre. Fitzpatrick inclined toward selling, especially as Fontenelle drifted toward alcoholic ineffectiveness, but could not gain satisfactory terms. In the spring of 1836 Chouteau sent the urbane Joshua Pilcher to make still another try. At rendezvous, nattily turned out in scarlet shirt and white buckskins, he prevailed. The last tottering vestige of the Rocky Mountain Fur Company collapsed, leaving Pratte, Chouteau & Company master of the mountains. Even so, the old nomenclature persisted, and American Fur Company, which operated nowhere west of the Mississippi River, endured as a synonym for the Chouteau company.[15]

However critical to the lives of the "mountain partners," their surrender to the St. Louis fur giant made almost no impression on the hundreds of trappers and Indians gathered at Horse Creek in July 1836. Commanding their astonished attention instead was a unit of Fitzpatrick's caravan that provided greater spectacle and held more profound meaning—Marcus Whitman's Oregon-bound missionary party. While in the East, Whitman and his fellow missionary, Henry H. Spalding, had taken wives. When Fitzpatrick led his train through South Pass, fittingly on Independence Day, he ushered into Oregon the first white women to cross the Rocky Mountains. More even than their husbands, Narcissa Whitman and Eliza Spalding portended the future of Oregon.[16]

The two women differed markedly—Narcissa blue-eyed, of fair skin and complexion, large framed yet attractive, cheerful and outgoing, often imperious; Eliza dark and coarse-featured, frail and sickly, withdrawn, serious, yet of stubborn fortitude and steely resolve. The mountain men paid enthusiastic court to the bubbling Narcissa. The Indians, especially the women, found instant rapport with Eliza, who had begun to learn their language even before leaving rendezvous.[17]

The missionary group consisted of the Whitmans and Spaldings, William H. Gray (a lay aide trained as a cabinetmaker and assigned as a "mechanic"), two Nez Perce boys Whitman had taken east the year before, and two young helpers. The party traveled by horse and mule, with a light wagon and a heavy farm wagon laden with baggage and trailing four milch cows and two calves. Fitzpatrick also transported his goods by wagon as far as Fort William, but there repacked them on mules. Here the missionaries abandoned their heavy wagon but proceeded with the light wagon and the livestock. Both wagon and cows captivated the Indians at rendezvous.

The women received their first jarring introduction to mountain life after crossing South Pass and turning to the Big Sandy, with the setting sun bathing the Wind River Mountains. Over a hilltop galloped a dozen or more shrieking horsemen, who charged full tilt at the caravan and loosed a volley of rifle balls overhead. Fitzpatrick, pointing to a white cloth tied to a rifle barrel, identified them as friends, as indeed they were—Joe Meek and a few companions with a contingent of Nez Perces, come to welcome the supply train in the traditional way.

That night the missionaries spread an oilcloth on the grass and invited two of their Nez Perce friends to dine on venison and buffalo roast, "seasoned with a little salt, with ample sand and dirt." One of the Indians was a noted chief, Rotten Belly. The other was a young man who, under the name of Lawyer, was destined to play a pivotal role in the relations of his tribe with the white people.

At rendezvous, as trapper Osborne Russell recorded, "The two ladies were gazed upon with wonder and astonishment by the rude Savages they being the first white women ever seen by these Indians and the first that had ever penetrated into these wild and rocky regions." "Our females," observed Henry Spalding, "found it quite difficult to get along for the multitudes that pressed around to shake them by the hand, both men and women. Some of their women would not be satisfied till they had saluted our's with a kiss, but they were very orderly."[18]

Narcissa and Eliza also created a sensation among the trappers, who discovered a sudden interest in religion, attended the daily services of the divines, and eagerly accepted the Bibles Narcissa passed out. Of the gregarious

Narcissa, Joe Meek recalled (in the words of his amanuensis), "She shone the bright particular star of that Rocky Mountain encampment, softening the hearts and manners of all who came within her womanly influence."[19]

One who succumbed to her womanly influence was Sir William Drummond Stewart, a British army captain on half pay. Attending his third rendezvous, the Scottish nobleman traveled, dined, and drank in sumptuous splendor, but his generosity and earthy ways made him a favorite with the mountain men.[20]

Joined by Joshua Pilcher, Stewart stood close by to calm the women as the Indians paid homage in a rowdy procession. By the hundreds, Nez Perces, Flatheads, Bannocks, and Shoshones painted their bodies, donned colorful garb, and, brandishing weapons and trophies, paraded by the tents of the white women in noisy disorder. Exhausted and unwell, both remained inside as Stewart and Pilcher explained the proceedings.[21]

The Nez Perces expected the mission party to travel with them to their mountain homeland. As Parker had learned a year earlier, this was a journey longer and more tiring than the usual route down the Snake and across the Blue Mountains. As this question festered, a brigade of the Hudson's Bay Company arrived, captained by John McLeod and Thomas McKay and escorting Nathaniel Wyeth. His western ventures a shambles, Wyeth had sold Fort Hall to the Hudson's Bay Company and was now bound for his New England home to resume his ice business. Wyeth brought a letter from Samuel Parker urging the Whitmans and Spaldings to continue the journey with McLeod and McKay rather than the Nez Perces.[22]

Ironically, therefore, the company itself escorted this portentous little group of Americans to their destination (although not Whitman's light wagon, which had to be left at Fort Hall). "There," Thomas McKay is said to have declared of the white women, "is something that Doct. McLoughlin cannot ship out of the country"—the vanguard of families that would sink roots in the Oregon soil and end the domination of the Hudson's Bay Company.[23] As Wyeth had forecast, however, McLoughlin and his associates, as enchanted by the white women as the trappers, treated the missionaries with the company's accustomed hospitality and even helped them get established. The Spaldings built their mission on the Clearwater River among the Nez Perces, while the Whitmans took station near the company's post of Fort Walla Walla to minister to the Cayuses.

Both Spalding and Whitman acknowledged their debt to Fitzpatrick in seeing them safely to rendezvous. "The Fur Company showed us the greatest kindness throughout the journey," wrote Spalding. "We have wanted nothing which was in their power to furnish us." And on July 14, 1836, before moving to the Hudson's Bay camp, Whitman asked Fitzpatrick for his

At the 1837 rendezvous, Sir William Drummond Stewart presented Jim Bridger with the plumed helmet and steel cuirass of an elite British regiment. Alfred Jacob Miller sketched the scene as Bridger cavorted in front of howling trappers and puzzled Indians. COURTESY JOSLYN ART MUSEUM, OMAHA, NEBRASKA.

bill to cover the services furnished. In reply, Fitzpatrick asked for Whitman's bill for medical services. Whitman said there was no bill. Fitzpatrick answered that likewise he had no bill.[24]

FOR A THIRD YEAR, now in the employ of Pratte, Chouteau & Company, Tom Fitzpatrick captained the supply train to the rendezvous of 1837. Once more it was staged on the upper Green at Horse Creek, where a ramshackle remnant of Bonneville's Fort Nonsense served as the trading store. No Oregon-bound missionaries traveled under Fitzpatrick's protection this year, but he did not lack a significant guest. He was an artist, Alfred Jacob Miller, a member of Captain William Drummond Stewart's luxurious entourage. Miller's paintings of mountain men, Indians, the supply caravan, and rendezvous, accompanied by explanatory text, constitute an invaluable contemporary record of a way of life on the threshold of extinction.[25]

Miller captured with his pen a memorable example of mountain man high jinks. Stewart had shipped from London and hauled across the Rocky Mountains a crate that when opened yielded a burnished steel cuirass and white-plumed steel helmet of the elite British Life Guards regiment. These he ceremoniously presented to Jim Bridger, who buckled the armor on over his fringed buckskins and jammed the helmet over his shaggy head. Astride his horse, Bridger paraded for the assembled multitude as the trappers cavorted and roared with laughter and the Indians looked on in baffled silence.[26]

Although Fitzpatrick escorted no missionaries this year, one appeared at rendezvous. He was William H. Gray, the lay "mechanic" who had accompanied Whitman and Spalding to Oregon in 1836. Of swollen piety and self-esteem, Gray hoped to find a wife in the East and return as a fully anointed missionary. His special charge from Whitman and Spalding was to bring reinforcements for the Oregon missions. He arrived with a Hudson's Bay contingent and, anxious to be on his way, dithered over the delay and the sinful ways of the mountaineers.[27]

After spending most of July 1837 at rendezvous, Gray decided he could not wait for Fitzpatrick to get the train under way for the return journey. Gray had six Indian youths (four Flatheads, a Nez Perce, and an Iroquois), destined for schooling in the East, and he considered them and God sufficient escort. Jim Bridger tried to set him straight. "Sir," he barked, slapping his rifle, "the grace of God won't carry a man through these prairies! It takes powder and ball."[28]

Neither God nor powder and ball prevailed. At Ash Hollow on the North Platte, Sioux jumped the little band of travelers. They dashed across the river, warriors in close pursuit, and forted up atop a hill. After an exchange of rifle fire, a French Canadian trader with the Indians met with Gray and told him the Sioux meant to wipe out the defenders. At this point, according to Gray, warriors burst into the defenses and killed all the young Indians. Although robbed, Gray and two white companions were allowed to depart with their lives.

The divines of the American Board probably believed Gray's version. Mountain men did not. They never forgave William H. Gray for what they believed to be a cowardly trade, brokered by the French Canadian negotiator—Indian lives for white.[29]

WILLIAM H. GRAY persuaded the American Board that Whitman and Spalding needed reinforcements, and so another missionary unit attached itself to the 1838 supply caravan. Gray had also found himself a wife and, envious of Whitman, taken a few medical courses—enough to call himself Dr. Gray until Whitman made him drop the title. Besides William and Mary Gray, the party consisted of Cushing and Myra Eells, Elkanah and Mary Walker, Asa and Sarah Smith, and bachelor Cornelius Rogers. Once more, therefore, mountain men helped plant Americans in Oregon—four white women and their clergyman mates.

Andrew Drips commanded the 1838 caravan. For more than a year, Tom Fitzpatrick disappears from the surviving record, surfaces for a tantalizing moment on the South Platte in 1839, and again vanishes for more than a year. This year he would again have enjoyed the company of the free-spending Scotsman Captain Stewart, indulging his love of the American West in the elegant mode of travel so conspicuous in former years. But Fitzpatrick would have found the missionaries fully as obnoxious and burdensome as did Drips.

Except for introducing more Americans into Oregon, especially women, the reinforcement of 1838 left mainly a sour residue on a page of history. Gray had crossed the continent twice, but the others lacked the adaptability of Lee, Whitman, or even Parker. They complained eternally about the weather, the land, the food, the unceasing labor, the forced desecration of the Sabbath, the sinful mountaineers, and especially the difficulty of rendering proper homage to God. "Often I have no time to read the bible from morning till night," complained Asa Smith. But these faults paled beside an utter incompatibility that produced daily quarrels over matters mostly trivial. "We have a strange company of Missionaries," conceded Mary Walker. "Scarcely one who is not intolerable on some account."[30]

This year the rendezvous site had been moved east, to where the Popo Agie flows into the Wind River to create the Bighorn. Here the missionaries found solace in Sabbaths undisturbed by the demands of travel. "It is ruinous to live without sabbaths as we have," observed Asa Smith. The wicked antics of the mountaineers upset them, however, especially when Jim Bridger's brigade stormed into camp and promptly staged a scalp dance in front of the missionaries' tents. "They looked like the emissaries of the Devil worshiping their own master," clucked Myra Eells.[31]

More than quarrelsome and sanctimonious behavior made these missionaries objectionable. The mountain men knew how Gray, the year before, had defied everyone's advice and led his little party of Indians to their death. That he had sacrificed their lives to save his own none doubted. Now here was Gray again at rendezvous, enjoying the protection and hospitality of the fur company—now reorganized as Pierre Chouteau, Jr., & Company.

About 1:00 A.M. on July 5, with Independence Day celebrations still rocking the trapper bivouacs, the Eellses and Grays awoke to a "rush of drunken men coming directly towards our tent. Mr. Eells got up immediately and went to the door of the tent in a moment. Four men came swearing and blaspheming, inquiring for Mr. Gray. . . . They said they wished to settle accounts with Mr. Gray, then they should be off." Eells stalled while Gray and Myra Eells fumbled frantically to load a rifle and slip under the back tent flap. The interlopers, however, grew mellow and began singing. They asked Cushing Eells to join in, but he answered, surely truthfully, that he did not know their songs. When the cleric declined to assure them of their welcome, they withdrew.[32]

July 8 turned out to be a glorious Sabbath, highlighted not only by divine services but by the arrival of a Hudson's Bay party under Francis Ermatinger. He brought letters from Whitman and Spalding and stood ready to escort the reinforcement on to the Columbia. Also with the newcomers was Jason Lee, headed east to organize a reinforcement for his own Methodist enterprise.

The missionaries moved to the Hudson's Bay camp at once, relieved to be free of the raucous Americans. Even so, Asa Smith could write from this camp to his Boston superiors what may stand as fitting commentary on the union of missionaries and mountain men in the unfolding drama of Oregon:

> We have been very kindly treated by the Fur company & feel ourselves very much indebted to them for the favors they have shown us. . . . We have found no pious men in the company but we have been treated by them in a kind & gentlemanly manner. I have given away several bibles & testaments since we have been here & in every case they have been rec'd very kindly. I think there is no difficulty in travelling with this company, if we treat the men kindly and not feel ourselves above them. They are possessed of a great deal of generous & noble feeling like the sailors, & resemble them very much in this respect.[33]

As early as 1830, the irrepressible Joshua Pilcher had advised the Secretary of War that "The man must know but little of the American people who supposes they can be stopped by any thing in the shape of mountains, deserts, seas, or rivers; and he can know nothing at all of the mountains in question, to suppose that they are impassable."[34] Thanks to Tom Fitzpatrick and his fellow mountaineers, the Oregon missionaries of 1834–38 discovered the mountains, as Pilcher contended, to be entirely passable. Thanks to Fitzpatrick and his fellow mountaineers, the missionaries got to the Columbia and there laid the groundwork for Pilcher's faith in his countrymen's determination to be stopped by nothing.

On the Columbia, the Hudson's Bay Company greeted the missionaries with ambivalence—hospitably and helpfully yet fearfully and suspiciously.

The missions could not have taken root without the company's aid, and they gave promise of fulfilling the company's apprehension. They combined churches and farms. They provided a nucleus for colonization and way stations on the trail. The letters and eastern visits of these servants of the Lord aroused emigration fever in the East and expansionist fever in the Congress. Even while helping them, Hudson's Bay officials recognized the missionaries as the cutting edge of an immigration that would end the company's supremacy in the Columbia Basin.[35]

Unknowingly, Tom Fitzpatrick, mountain man, had acted the part of Tom Fitzpatrick, expansionist.

13

JIM BRIDGER:

END OF AN ERA

H E WAS QUITE FOND of telling yarns," missionary William H. Gray remarked of Jim Bridger at the 1836 rendezvous.[1] In fact, Jim Bridger enjoyed high stature as a purveyor of tall tales—a talent greatly admired by mountain men. He took special delight in regaling greenhorns with the wonders of the West. Recounted so seriously and authoritatively, even the most outrageous duped many listeners.

In one of his favorites, Bridger told of discovering high in the Rockies a creek that flowed down the Continental Divide and parted, sending one branch east and the other west. A trout, he averred, could cross the spine of the continent from Pacific waters to Atlantic waters. Even the most gullible had a hard time swallowing this yarn.[2]

Bridger told other whoppers as well, of glass mountains, of "peetrified" trees with "peetrified" birds singing "peetrified" songs, and of his memory of a time when Pikes Peak was a hole in the ground. Yet in the tangle of mountains on the southern edge of Yellowstone National Park a stream does in fact divide, sending Atlantic Creek to the east and Pacific Creek to the west. At Two Ocean Pass a trout can swim from one watershed to the other.

Bridger knew his geography. His mental map ranked with the best. "Bridger was a wonderful guide and a born topographer," declared one who had traveled with him. "The whole West and all the passes and labyrinths of the Rocky Mountains were mapped out in his mind. He had such a sense of locality and direction that he used to say he could 'smell his way where he could not see it.' "[3]

By the late 1830s Bridger also ranked high as trapper, brigade leader, and Indian fighter. He had ascended the Missouri with Ashley in 1822, at the age of seventeen, and had been in the mountains ever since. Not once had he visited St. Louis. Few mountaineers failed to defer to him as the best of the field partisans. Year after year, despite repeated clashes with the Blackfeet, the fall and spring hunts of his brigade yielded profitable returns.

Bridger personified the mountain man of the 1830s. In later years he turned spare and bony, but in his trapper years he impressed an acquaintance as "a model for a sculptor or painter, by which to express the perfection of graceful strength and easy activity." Tall, heavily muscled, thick necked, lithe, with shaggy brown hair and beard, he had honed all the wilderness skills to perfection. He could neither read nor write, but he understood the land, the animals, and the Indians. "To sum up," continued this observer at the 1837 rendezvous, "his bravery was unquestionable, his horsemanship equally so, and as to his skill with the rifle, it will scarcely be doubted, when we mention the fact that he had been known to kill twenty buffaloes by the same number of consecutive shots."[4]

By the 1837 rendezvous, the life Jim Bridger had known for fifteen years had begun to play out. The Rocky Mountain trapping system launched by William H. Ashley in 1825 neared collapse, as many trappers already recognized. Whether or not Bridger foresaw the end, he continued to probe the beaver streams after most of his peers had given up. The irony of Jim Bridger is that he also erected a trading station that stood as the most vivid symbol of the end of one era and the beginning of another.

WILLIAM H. ASHLEY made a fortune from Rocky Mountain beaver and established the Rocky Mountain trapping system, based on a yearly rendezvous in the mountains at which trappers exchanged beaver pelts for supplies transported by caravan from St. Louis. Yet within five years the system had run into trouble.

Changing fashions furnished one explanation. "It appears that they make hats of silk in place of Beaver," John Jacob Astor wrote Pierre Chouteau, Jr., from Paris in August 1832. Two months later his son, managing the firm in New York, advised Chouteau that nutria fur made an excellent hat that could be sold for less than half the price of a beaver hat. "Beaver must go down," predicted Astor, "and we had better submit to circumstances."[5]

New fashions, however, did not suddenly kill the fur trade. The market softened and would never again offer the rewards Ashley gained. It suffered a heavy blow in the Panic of 1837. But a moderate demand for beaver continued through the 1830s. Despite a widening gap at rendezvous between the prices offered for beaver and the prices demanded for supplies, trappers continued to trap.

As much as changing hat styles, the beaver trade strangled itself. Beyond every man's financial incentive to trap every beaver he could, competition between American companies and with the Hudson's Bay Company took a dreadful toll on the beaver population. As early as 1831, the veteran William Gordon declared that "The furs are diminishing, and this diminution is general & extensive. The beaver may be considered as extirpated on this side of the Rocky Mountains." Allowed to recoup for a few years, he thought, the numbers would rebound. West of the Continental Divide, extermination could also be expected. The Convention of 1828, extending joint occupation of Oregon indefinitely, "lends to the ravaging of the country as both parties do all they can to make the most out of the present time."[6]

Pierre Chouteau himself dealt the fatal blow. He simply quit backing the annual supply caravan. That killed off the rendezvous as an institution. The last, a sorry shadow of former magnificence, was held in 1840 at the favorite site on the upper Green River.

Chouteau's prosperity did not depend on beaver but rather on the Indian trade. As early as 1832, William B. Astor forecast the future of the fur trade. "Every Buffalo Robe you sent us including those per Steamer Louisville, are sold," he wrote Chouteau, "& 300 packs more would sell if we had them."[7] Indians killed the buffalo and brought the robes to a trading post to trade for goods. From the upper Missouri posts such as Forts Union and Pierre, they could be shipped down by steamer—a vast competitive advantage over the British, who lacked suitable rivers for such heavy transport. From Bent's Fort on the Arkansas and Fort William on the Laramie (by 1840 commonly called Fort Laramie), the robes were packed to the Missouri and loaded on steamers. Chouteau rightly saw the future of his firm anchored to the fortunes of his trading posts on the upper Missouri, with buffalo robes the measure of profit.[8]

For the Rocky Mountain trappers, the final years of the decade were not only barren but sad. At the rendezvous of 1839 on the upper Green, their mood created a hushed atmosphere, with little drinking and no gambling. "The days of their glory seem to be past," noted a German traveler. "Only with reluctance does a trapper abandon this dangerous craft," he added; "and a sort of serious home-sickness seizes him when he retires from his mountain life to civilization."[9]

Although phrased by his interviewer, Joe Meek captured the mood more poignantly as he and Doc Newell ruminated at the close of the 1840 rendezvous:

"Come," said Newell to Meek, "we are done with this life in the mountains—done with wading in beaver-dams, and freezing or starving al-
ternately—done with Indian trading and Indian fighting. The fur trade
is dead in the Rocky Mountains, and it is no place for us now, if ever it
was. We are young yet, and have life before us. We cannot waste it
here; we cannot or will not return to the States. Let us go down to the
Willamet and take farms."[10]

They did.

NOT SO JIM BRIDGER. He either failed to understand or refused to accept
that the glory days had passed. Fort Laramie, Fort Pierre, Fort Union—they
could substitute for rendezvous as market for beaver and source of supply.
In the winter of 1839–40, visiting St. Louis for the first time since 1822 (he
quickly fell homesick for the mountains), Bridger formed a partnership
with Henry Fraeb, gained Chouteau's backing, and herded a supply outfit
up the trail to the final rendezvous in July 1840.

This last caravan to rendezvous afforded Bridger a glimpse of two har-
bingers of the future, although he probably did not appreciate their significance. Besides his and Fraeb's outfit, Andrew Drips's Chouteau train hosted
two other parties.

One was still another missionary group bound for Oregon to save Indian souls. The three Protestant couples attracted so little comment as to
suggest that, like many who went before, they held themselves aloof from
the sinful mountaineers. One who did not, who proved a hardy traveler
and splendid companion, was a Jesuit priest, Father Pierre Jean De Smet.
In the next three decades, Father De Smet would travel thousands of miles
through the West ministering to many tribes, winning their affection and
respect as the premier "Black Robe" of them all, and achieving a standing
of near legendary proportions. In this first of his western journeys, assigned to scout the Flatheads as a possible mission field, De Smet and
Bridger became fast friends. Each had something to give to the other, and
to the end of their long lives they gave freely to each other. Bridger, De
Smet wrote years later, "is one of the truest specimens of a real trapper
and Rocky Mountain man."[11]

The other group, in two light wagons, were emigrants, headed for California to make new lives for themselves. As many as forty had promised to
go, but in the end only three adults, with four small children, attached
themselves to the caravan. They were Joel and Mary Walker and Mary's un-
married sister Martha. Joel, brother of the celebrated mountaineer Joe

Walker, had spent youthful energies on the Santa Fe Trail before settling as a Missouri farmer for nearly twenty years. They would end up in California, as intended, but only after traveling to the Columbia and then, a year later, heading south to their destination. And like Marcus Whitman before them, they would not get their wagons to the Columbia.

AFTER THE GREEN RIVER RENDEZVOUS of 1840, Jim Bridger and Henry Fraeb joined Joe Walker for a swing through southern California. By the summer of 1841, the partners were back in the Green River country.[12] On the west bank of the Green a few miles below the mouth of the Big Sandy, Bridger and Fraeb began constructing a rude log post. Apparently they intended it as a base for their trapping expeditions as well as a place to trade with the Shoshone and other local Indians. While Bridger worked on the fort, Fraeb and twenty-three men set forth to "make meat." On July 21, 1841, not far up the Green, they fell in with a large assembly of westering travelers. The chance meeting brought together a diverse collection of people representing significant strands, past and future, in the history of the West.

This was the Bidwell-Bartleson wagon train, the first emigrant train (excepting Joel Walker's family in two wagons the year before) to attempt a crossing to the Pacific. Accompanying the emigrants once again were missionaries, including Father De Smet and a party of Jesuits en route to establish a mission in the Bitterroot Valley among the Flathead Indians. Present too was an elderly and acerbic Methodist clergyman, Joseph Williams. Some Flathead Indians had come down from the mountains to escort the Black Robes to their destination. And serving as guide and counselor on the ways of the wilderness was one who had played the part before: Tom Fitzpatrick.

Finally, relics of the past, there were Fraeb and his ragtag band of mountaineers, just back from California. They found a ready market for what few provisions they could furnish, especially since some of the emigrants had whiskey to lubricate the exchange. Williams was scandalized by the cost of $1.50 per pound for sugar and $1.50 to $2.50 for powder and lead. Besides, the trappers formed "a wicked, swearing company of men," and they defiled the Sabbath by swearing and fishing in the Green River.[13]

The Bidwell-Bartleson emigrants, in many ways uncharacteristic of those to follow, still etched a pattern for the West in the next decade. So did the missionaries, both Protestant and Catholic, who would play an important part in Indian lives, Indian-white relations, and American settlement on the Pacific. So did Tom Fitzpatrick, demonstrating a useful and significant occupation for mountain men whose way of life had vanished. So even did the rudimentary trade between Fraeb's men and the emigrants. Jim Bridger had yet to recognize it, but in addition to the wisdom of a Tom Fitzpatrick, emigrants crossing the continent would have many tangible needs.

Like Fitzpatrick, Bridger still had a large role to play in the history of the West. Not Henry Fraeb. His time had run out. Within two weeks of the trading session on the Green, Fraeb and his hunters had worked south to the Little Snake, a tributary of the Yampa River. There a large force of Sioux and Cheyenne warriors struck.

All day, barricaded behind dead horses, the whites held off their attackers. As evening drew on, the Indians called off the fight and vanished. The defenders lost four men, one of whom was Fraeb. "He was the ugliest looking dead man I ever saw," recalled Jim Baker. "His face was all covered with blood, and he had rotten front teeth and a horrible grin. When he was killed he never fell, but sat braced against the stump, a sight to behold."[14]

THE BIDWELL-BARTLESON ENTERPRISE of 1841 shifted the public spotlight briefly from Oregon to California but called no less insistently on the aid of mountain men. In the winter of 1840–41 a young and bankrupt newcomer to Missouri caught the California fever. Stirred by idyllic portraits of "Upper California" sketched by trapper Antoine Robidoux and "Doctor" John Marsh (an American of dubious medical credentials who had settled in California), John Bidwell organized the Western Emigration Society. Some five hundred people signed up, but in the spring of 1841 only sixty-nine appeared at the rendezvous site, all but five of them men. They elected John Bartleson captain—an unfortunate choice—and Bidwell secretary.

These California emigrants had no idea how to get to California except to head west. None knew anything about plains, mountains, or deserts, and most besides were impoverished. Despite dissension that quickly broke out under Bartleson's arbitrary rule, they had determination. More critical, they had good luck. They fell in with the Jesuit mission party of Father De Smet.

Preparing to return to the Flathead country after a successful reconnaissance in 1840, De Smet had discovered to his consternation that the Chouteau firm would not send a supply caravan to the mountains in 1841. Scouring the St. Louis waterfront, De Smet too had good luck. He met Tom Fitzpatrick and persuaded him to pilot the Jesuits to the Bitterroot Valley. As with Bridger the year before, De Smet formed a lasting friendship with Fitzpatrick. "Every day I learned to appreciate him more and more," the priest later recalled.[15]

When the Bidwell-Bartleson company pulled their thirteen wagons abreast of the De Smet train of five two-wheeled carts, De Smet and his associates, Fathers Nicholas Point and Gregory Mengarini, readily united with the emigrants. The Black Robes gained added manpower for the crossing, while the overlanders received in return something more crucial: Tom Fitzpatrick as guide. "And it was well that we did," recalled Bidwell, "for probably not one of us would ever have reached California."[16]

Before even striking the Platte, Fitzpatrick averted a collision with Indians. A straggling youth, Nicholas Dawson, ran afoul of a band of Cheyenne warriors. They robbed him of mule, rifle, pistol, and even most of his clothes, then beat him with ramrods. When he came running into camp in high dudgeon, the men all made haste to corral the wagons and prepare for battle. Some fifty Cheyennes advanced on the little fortress but then calmly went into camp. Fitzpatrick rode out to parley. The young man, the Indians told him, had grown so terrified at their presence that they had to disarm him. The explanation probably contained only a small grain of truth, but rather than antagonize the Indians Fitzpatrick accepted it. He returned to camp with all Dawson's possessions except his pistol. For the rest of his life, everyone knew the victim as "Cheyenne" Dawson.[17]

Fitzpatrick had contracted to take the missionaries to the Bitterroot Valley, not the emigrants to California. He himself had never been to California, but doubtless he advised them of the deserts and mountains that lay before them. Whether he did or not, at the meeting on the Green River Fraeb and his followers, who had just been to California, drew a grim picture of the journey, especially if the emigrants could find no guide. Seven of the less stouthearted turned back, and the rest began to bicker over whether to change their destination to Oregon.

At Soda Springs, the bubbling "Beer Springs" of the trappers, the travelers divided. About one-third of the emigrants chose to accompany Fitzpatrick and his charges as far as Fort Hall, then continue to Oregon. Thirty-one, including a woman and a baby, stood resolute for California, guide or no guide. At Fort Hall, Fitzpatrick and the Jesuits parted with the Oregon group and followed the old trapper route north to the Bitterroot Valley. Here Father De Smet founded St. Mary's Mission, while Fitzpatrick wintered with the Flatheads.

The ordeal of the Bidwell-Bartleson train as it groped its way toward California underscored the perils of trying to cross the continent without an experienced guide. Almost at once, in the dry and difficult country north of Great Salt Lake, they grew confused. Two men rode to Fort Hall to try to find a guide. They hoped Joseph R. Walker, who had crossed the desert to California and returned in 1833–34, might be there and agree to lead them. Instead, they had to settle for some vague information that failed to save them from near catastrophe.

For more than a month, until late in September, the emigrants blundered among the mountains and mostly dry streams west of Great Salt Lake. Finally they stumbled on "Mary's River"—the Humboldt. By now, however, they had been forced to abandon their wagons and pack their possessions on mules and oxen.

The Humboldt, as Joe Walker and Peter Skene Ogden had discovered, offered the only practicable route across the Nevada desert. The Bidwell-Bartleson party followed the river to its sink, then turned up the west fork of the Walker River. Surmounting the Sierra at Sonora Pass, the emigrants descended through a labyrinth of rough canyons drained by the Stanislaus River. On the Humboldt and across the Sierra, they had lived almost entirely on the tough meat of their increasingly bony mules and oxen. They reached journey's end exhausted, famished, and destitute, but reach it they did.

Nevertheless, none knew better than they how close they had come to disaster and how unfortunate they were not to have found Joe Walker to take them across the Nevada desert and the Sierras. The Bidwell-Bartleson party ranks as the first organized company of American colonists to travel overland to California. With Joe Walker at their head, they probably would have gained added distinction as the first Americans to take wagons to California.

The experience of this group, both before and after the division at Soda Springs, demonstrated that Tom Fitzpatrick had staked out a new profession for old trappers—wagon master for emigrant trains to Oregon and California. As the tide of overlanders swelled in the 1840s, most trains took care to hire a mountain man as captain, guide, pilot, or whatever other title they settled on. Guiding was the least of the responsibilities; by 1840, even though the way to California remained uncertain, the trail to Oregon had been blazed. What proved more important was to teach the greenhorns how to get across the continent—how to kindle a campfire and cook over it, how to pack a mule or a wagon, how to ford a river, how to secure the wagons and stock at night, how to kill and dress a buffalo, and how to get along with the Indians. Fitzpatrick was but one of a score or more mountain men who followed this course in the next twenty years.

AFTER FRAEB'S DEATH, Bridger did not complete his trading post on the Green. In the spring of 1842, he and Tom Fitzpatrick conducted a hunt up the Green, then turned east with their furs. When the Methodist missionary Joseph Williams, returning to the East from Oregon, camped at the fort in July 1842, he "saw nothing there but three little, starved dogs."[18]

Although Jim Bridger continued to regard himself as a beaver trapper, he began to see enough to persuade even him that the future of the West lay not entirely with the beaver. Fraeb's trading session with the Bidwell-Bartleson emigrant train on the Green River in July 1841 may have set him to thinking. Fitzpatrick's new employment as emigrant guide may also have had an effect, especially as he watched his friend undertake another such charge in the summer of 1842.

Arriving at Fort Laramie early in July with the furs garnered in their spring hunt, Bridger and Fitzpatrick discovered still another wagon train, this one bound for Oregon. Although quarreling among themselves as bitterly as had the Bidwell-Bartleson company, these people grudgingly acknowledged the importance, if only sporadically the leadership, of Dr. Elijah White.

Formerly one of Jason Lee's Methodist missionaries, the busily self-important doctor had returned home by ship and joined with others in agitating for the United States to take more aggressive measures to support its citizens in Oregon. He had wangled a commission of doubtful legality as federal subagent for the Indians of Oregon. At Fort Laramie, this second wagon train reaching for the Pacific, 110 emigrants in eighteen wagons, met Jim Bridger and Tom Fitzpatrick.[19]

The White train already had an experienced guide, Stephen Hall Meek, brother of Joe Meek. But reports at the fort pictured the road to the west as infested with Sioux and Cheyennes in ugly temper. In the clash with Henry Fraeb's hunters the previous August, they had lost a dozen or more warriors, and they were said to be looking for a fight. "But our party is large and strong," White wrote to his family on July 2, "and I have been able to obtain the services of Mr. Fitz Patrick, one of the ablest and most suitable men in the country, in conducting us to Fort Hall, beyond the danger of the savages."[20]

In common with the fur caravans of the past and the emigrant trains of the future, the White company paused at Independence Rock while all inscribed their names on this massive register of plains travelers. As the wagons moved out, Asa Lovejoy and Lansford Hastings tarried. Suddenly a large Sioux war party swept down on the pair, stripped them, and made gestures threatening to kill Lovejoy. With their prisoners, the Indians trailed the wagon train and soon caught up. Fitzpatrick sized up the situation at once. He had the train corralled and the men posted in defensive positions. Then, as White described the scene:

Mr. Fitz Patrick went forward to meet them, making demonstrations of peace, and a desire that they should stop. His repeated signs were disregarded, and they rode steadily onward, till nearly within gunshot, when they suddenly halted, apparently intimidated by the array.

After a short pause, Hastings and Lovejoy were liberated, and ran joy-fully to their friends, the tears rolling down their cheeks as they re-counted their escape.[21]

Up the Sweetwater almost to South Pass, the White train chanced across a big village of Sioux and Cheyennes. The chiefs, impressing White as any-thing but friendly, advanced under a British and an American flag for a par-ley. White, with Fitzpatrick and several others, went out to meet them. What transpired remains unrecorded, but after the council the Indians mingled in friendship and trade with the whites in their own camp. Almost certainly Fitzpatrick had marshaled his diplomatic skills to avert bloodshed.[22]

At Fort Hall, Dr. White paid off Fitzpatrick and continued to Oregon, the first sizable wagon train to traverse the entire length of the Oregon Trail. Fitzpatrick turned back for the East, following a circuitous route by way of the Arkansas River to avoid the temperamental Indians along the Sweet-water and the Platte. Even so, Pawnees stripped him of most of his belong-ings before letting him proceed. By November he had reached St. Louis.

JIM BRIDGER had preceded Fitzpatrick to St. Louis and sold their spring fur catch. During the winter of 1842–43, he teamed up with another partner, Louis Vasquez, and again gained Chouteau's financial support. Back in the Green River country in the summer of 1843, Bridger and Vasquez selected a new site for their base, on Black's Fork of the Green southwest of the first post. This broad, well-watered valley offered a much better prospect than the first for intercepting emigrants, and the partners intended to take full advantage of such profit as the growing migration to Oregon might yield.[23]

Jim Bridger still had not given up the trapper's life, which he intended to follow while Vasquez traded at Fort Bridger. That autumn Bridger led a party far to the north, trapping the Milk River and winding up on the Mis-souri at Fort Union. Even so, he had seen enough in the past three years to persuade him that the future of the West included emigrants as well as beaver. In a long letter to Pierre Chouteau, set to paper by Fort Union trader Edwin Denig, Bridger told of his trapping plans but also revealed an understanding of the part he intended Fort Bridger to play in the new era dawning in the West:

I have established a small store, with a Black Smith Shop, and a sup-ply of Iron on the road of the Emigrants on Black's fork Green River, which promises fairly, they in coming out are generally well supplied with money, but by the time they get there are in want of all kinds of supplies. Horses, Provisions, Smith work &c brings ready Cash from them and should I receive the goods hereby ordered will do a considerable business in that way with them. The same establishment trades with the Indians in the neighborhood, who have mostly a good number of Beaver amongst them.[24]

Fort Bridger represented the wave of the future. The day of the beaver hunter had passed. The day of the emigrant had dawned. In the next few years, the people who had cash but needed smithwork and provisions would make Fort Bridger—even as "Old Gabe" himself continued to seek beaver—a valued way station on the roads to Oregon and California.

14

KIT CARSON:

MAPPING THE WAY WEST

C HRISTOPHER HOUSTON CARSON was thirty-one when he attended the last rendezvous in July 1840. In the nine years since he was recruited in Taos by Tom Fitzpatrick to help push the delayed supply train up to rendezvous, Kit Carson had ripened into one of the most accomplished of the mountain man fraternity. Even before signing on with Fitzpatrick, Carson had mastered the techniques of wilderness survival from Ewing Young in his California venture of 1829–31. Though short and slight of build, unprepossessing in appearance and demeanor, and as illiterate as Jim Bridger, he commanded the respect of his peers as a proficient trapper, a courageous Indian fighter, and a dependable teammate.[1]

Only a handful of mountain men knew the West as intimately as Kit Carson. He traveled more widely than most because he remained a truly free trapper. He never captained his own band, he shifted his allegiance among companies as it suited his fancy, and he went where he wanted with makeshift groups that formed and dissolved in a season or two. With Ewing Young, he had worked the Gila and its tributaries and toured California. With Jim Bridger and Tom Fitzpatrick, he had trapped the northern Rockies. He had even for a time thrown in with the Hudson's Bay Company, and so knew the Snake River Plain, the Bear River and Bear Lake, Great Salt Lake, and the Humboldt corridor across the Nevada desert. Kit never gave up his New Mexican base in Taos and so had scoured the North, Middle, and South Parks of the southern Rockies, the tangled Western Slope back of the Front Range, and the Uinta Basin of the Green River.

Mató-Tópe, a Mandan Chief, *another of Karl Bodmer's famous Indian portraits. The Mandans treated Lewis and Clark hospitably during their winter stay in 1803–04 and, with a fixed location in mud towns, were the trader's most reliable customers. The smallpox epidemic of 1837 all but obliterated the tribe.* COURTESY JOSLYN ART MUSEUM, OMAHA, NEBRASKA.

By the fall of 1841, Carson had accepted that the day of the beaver had passed. With a handful of comrades, he came down from the mountains and sought employment at the adobe trading post William Bent had erected on the Arkansas River in 1833. For one dollar a day, he signed on as a hunter.[2]

At Bent's Fort, Kit Carson struggled with domestic troubles. Sometime after the rendezvous of 1835, he had taken an Arapaho wife, Waanibe, "Singing Grass." If his celebrated duel with Chouinard at that rendezvous was rooted in the affections of this woman, Kit won both duel and woman. Waanibe bore him two daughters but died, either of fever or in childbirth. At Bent's Fort, therefore, Carson had two children, one four years old and the other an infant. A brief marriage to a Cheyenne woman, Making-Out-Road, ended abruptly when she cast his belongings from the tepee. Already, however, he had been smitten by a Taos beauty, Josefa Jaramillo, the fourteen-year-old sister of Charles Bent's wife, brother of William Bent of Bent's Fort renown. In Taos in January 1842, anticipating a union with Josefa, Christopher Carson received baptism as a Catholic.[3]

Carson had been in the mountains for sixteen years and longed to visit his family in Missouri. Another motive, however, prompted him to join the

Bent–St. Vrain wagon train to Independence in April 1842: his older daughter Adaline. Leaving the infant with friends in Taos (she died a year later after falling into a kettle of boiling soap[4]), Kit took Adaline back to Missouri, where his sisters assumed responsibility for her care and rudimentary education.

After visiting with his family, Carson went on down the Missouri to St. Louis. Like Bridger, however, he tired quickly of "civilization" and wanted to return to the mountains. He boarded a steamer that would take him up the Missouri to Independence and the road to Santa Fe. Coincidence intervened to change his life decisively and also influence the course of western history for the next quarter century.

On the steamer's deck Kit Carson met Lieutenant John C. Frémont, Corps of Topographical Engineers, United States Army. The handsome young officer explained that he was bound for the frontier to organize a government exploring expedition to the Rocky Mountains. Seizing the opening, the unemployed mountain man "informed him that I had been some time in the mountains and thought I could guide him to any point he would wish to go. He replied that he would make inquiries regarding my capabilities of performing that which I promised. He done so."[5]

Frémont also remembered the moment:

> On the boat I met Kit Carson. . . . I was pleased with him and his manner of address at this first meeting. He was a man of medium height, broad-shouldered and deep-chested, with a clear steady blue eye and frank speech and address; quiet and unassuming. . . . I had expected to engage as guide an old mountaineer, Captain Drips, but I was so much pleased with Carson that when he asked to go with me I was glad to take him.[6]

That chance meeting launched the union of two men of vastly differing backgrounds, personalities, and educations, men destined to share adventure, hardship, and danger, and to give much to each other. It also launched the union of mountain man with government explorer, a fusion of talents that would bear vitally on the opening of the American West.

LIKE EARLIER MILITARY SURVEYS, the expeditions of John Charles Frémont in 1842–45 aimed at the acquisition of geographic and scientific data. But they had other objectives as well, political objectives hidden beneath the ostensible purposes set down in written orders. When Kit Carson took his place behind Frémont, he hitched his mastery of geography

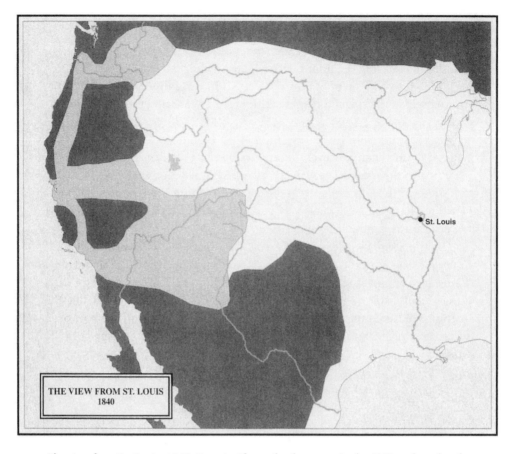

THE VIEW FROM ST. LOUIS
1840

St. Louis

The view from St. Louis, 1840. Two significant developments in the 1830s enlarged and clarified the view of the West from St. Louis. First, in 1833 Joseph R. Walker, in the service of Captain B. L. E. Bonneville, crossed the Great Basin and the Sierra Nevada. Unlike Jedediah Smith six years earlier, Walker found the Humboldt corridor from Great Salt Lake to the Sierras. It appeared on Bonneville's map printed in 1837 in Washington Irving's widely read chronicle of the captain's western adventures. In the Gallatin map of 1836 and the Burr map of 1839, moreover, a small fraction of what Jedediah Smith might have revealed crept into cartography; both cartographers unquestionably had access to Smith's map. Second, Protestant missionaries invaded the realm of the Hudson's Bay Company, the Lees in the Willamette Valley, the Whitmans near the great bend of the Columbia, and the Spaldings on the Clearwater. Their reports gave Americans firsthand glimpses of the Oregon country and helped stir emigration fever. Even so, as the Rocky Mountain fur trade collapsed in 1840, the West remained unmapped by scientific techniques. Beginning in 1842, with crucial help from the former trappers, army engineers set forth to construct a map of the West. The Warren map of 1857 testified to how brilliantly they succeeded.

and mountaineering to two causes: expansion of knowledge and expansion of national boundaries.

For years, congressional expansionists had agitated the Oregon question. To them, the Convention of 1818 was a sellout of American interests, the Convention of 1828 a worse sellout. The United States, they argued, held valid title to Oregon at least as far north as the forty-ninth parallel, if not beyond. If diplomacy could not fix a boundary west of the Continental Divide, they wanted to abrogate the joint occupation and establish a United States territory on the Columbia, even at the risk of war with Great Britain. The issue took on special urgency when, beginning in 1834, Protestant missionaries formed enclaves of American citizens in the heart of Hudson's Bay Company domain. Debates, resolutions, and bills rocked the Congress, directed at forcing resolution of the boundary dispute, supporting Americans living in Oregon, and promoting the emigration of settlers to solidify the nation's hold on that distant realm. Senator Lewis F. Linn led the fight, backed less noisily but no less effectively by his Missouri colleague, Senator Thomas Hart Benton.[7]

Linn and Benton could get no legislation through the Congress. Nor would presidents from Andrew Jackson to John Tyler risk a military confrontation with Great Britain over Oregon. Frustrated by congressional majorities and by the executive branch, expansionists turned for a weapon to a part of the executive branch itself—the army's Corps of Topographical Engineers.[8]

Although the army had fielded topographical officers from the beginning, not until 1838 had they been drawn together in a separate corps answerable, like all the other staff departments, directly to the Secretary of War. No longer subordinate to the Corps of Engineers, led by the highly professional yet politically astute Colonel John J. Abert, reaping the cream of the West Point graduating classes, the Corps of Topographical Engineers developed a proud solidarity and devotion to a mission unconfined by strictly military limits. The officers knew more than how to shoot azimuths and read the stars in the field, more than how to translate their figures to maps that related topography to latitude and longitude. In addition, they integrated into the fledgling scientific community of the United States and partook of the latest intellectual currents wafting across Europe. Clearly they could contribute to national purposes transcending battlefields or campaigns, a potential that congressional expansionists lost no time in exploiting. Picking a precarious path between competing political factions, the officers of the corps charged themselves with exploring and mapping the West and devoting their talents to fulfilling the nation's promise of continental expansion.[9]

Lieutenant John Charles Frémont proved an ideal selection to lead double-barreled western missions. Although not a West Pointer, he had acquired all the necessary technical and scientific abilities. Equally important, he was a romantic, thrilled by western wonders and patriotically roused to share his vision of their grandeur with his fellow citizens. With Colonel Abert and nearly all the topographical officers, Frémont believed in his nation's continental destiny, and he welcomed the opportunity to play his part in promoting it. Finally, not least of his qualifications, in 1841 he married seventeen-year-old Jessie Benton, daughter of "Old Bullion" himself. She provided inspiration for his ambitions of glory, stability to his kinetic temperament, and the vocabulary to phrase his soaring thoughts in compelling prose. Her parents strenuously opposed the marriage but had to bow to her iron will. An ambitious young officer could hardly find a father-in-law more influential than Senator Thomas Hart Benton.[10]

In the inception of Frémont's 1842 expedition, Benton set the pattern for his son-in-law's career as a western explorer. In effect, the powerful senator dictated the orders, Colonel Abert signed them, and Lieutenant Frémont did about as he pleased when he got out on his own. Surely, though, Abert had no uncertainty about the design, of which he heartily approved. In the next four years, Lieutenant Frémont sorely tried the patience of his chief, but his part in publicizing the West and promoting its settlement served not only Benton's purpose but Abert's as well.[11]

KIT CARSON'S ASSIGNMENT was not truly to "guide" Frémont. The lieutenant's orders, a model of brevity, directed him simply to survey the Platte and Sweetwater Rivers as far as South Pass. By 1842, hardly anyone needed a guide on this route. Fur company caravans had followed it for seventeen years, and Oregon and California emigrants had already rutted it with their wagon wheels.

Nor did the expedition lack for seasoned plains travelers. Besides Frémont and the skilled German cartographer Charles Preuss, it consisted of twenty-one men, mostly French Canadian veterans of the fur trade signed up in St. Louis. Lucien B. Maxwell, Taos trapper and trader, went along as hunter. Among the others, Frémont particularly admired Basil Lajeunesse, who would come to rival Carson himself in the esteem of their leader. The composition of this company, in fact, highlighted an anomaly that set Frémont's explorations apart from others conducted by Colonel Abert's corps. All three expeditions consisted of hired mountaineers and voyageurs; he alone held rank in the army.[12]

For both Carson and Frémont, the 1842 excursion up the Oregon Trail was a learning experience. They got to know and appreciate each other as friends and professionals. Frémont learned the "mode of voyaging" beyond the Missouri, as Carson and others taught him about the Great Plains and its rivers, the Rocky Mountains, buffalo and other wildlife, and Indians. At the same time, Carson learned a new employment for former mountain men—helping army surveyors systematically gather data and specimens to amplify scientific knowledge and to arouse public interest.[13]

Frémont proved an apt student. Unlike many self-important officers, he mixed freely with the rough mountaineers, displayed no condescension, admired their powers, and eagerly absorbed all they had to teach and demonstrate. He endured their hardships and privations, exhibited a reckless courage they could applaud, and still exuded an authority that left no doubt who commanded. For all the ridicule that would be heaped on Frémont in the years to come, the mountain men who served him stood firm in their respect and loyalty. For the rest of his life, Kit Carson venerated John Charles Frémont.

For Frémont, the expedition was a grand adventure. Even for the mountaineers, it departed from routine. As the Elijah White train discovered, Sioux and Cheyennes hovered on the road in a foul temper caused by their losses in the fight with Henry Fraeb's hunters. At Fort Laramie, Tom Fitzpatrick agreed to see the emigrants through the Indian country; without his influence and experience, Frémont believed, they would have found themselves in a battle. Below Fort Laramie, Jim Bridger so alarmed the Frémonters with his warnings of the Indian danger that many thought the survey ought to be called off. Frémont would have none of it, and even Carson grew so worried that he made out his will. As it turned out, the tribesmen themselves could not agree on whether to make war or peace, and by the time Frémont reached the upper Platte they had settled the dispute by going off to raid the Crows.

In the Wind River Mountains, Frémont found the experience he sought to excite his romantic imagination. En route, he performed all the mundane tasks of a government explorer—describing terrain, plants, and animals, shooting astronomical readings for the map Preuss would construct, gathering specimens for the scientific community. But amid the rocky peaks reached from the upper Green River, not far from the favorite rendezvous site of the trappers, Frémont felt the ultimate rapture of the visionary and made the appropriate gestures. Twice felled by vomiting and headaches brought on by altitude, cold, and exhaustion, he had a hard time reaching the mountaintop he set as a goal. But from the summit he gazed over a chaos of mountains that swept him with waves of patriotic ardor. He unfurled a specially designed American flag and ruminated on the symbolism of a lowly bumblebee crossing the Continental Divide at that elevation—"a solitary pioneer to foretell the advance of civilization."

The return was anticlimactic, except in the canyon of the North Platte where Tom Fitzpatrick had swamped with his bullboat of furs in 1825. Frémont had packed an inflatable boat of India rubber all the way to the mountains. He and a few of the party tried to run the canyon and met Fitzpatrick's fate. Journals, records of celestial readings, scientific specimens—all went into the boiling waters with everything else in the boat. Only the men escaped.

Charles Preuss, fine mapmaker but grouchy outdoorsman, recorded the arrival at Fort Laramie:

> On the last day of August we returned to the fort in good condition. We were greeted with cannon and rifle fire and replied by shooting our own rifles. Frémont was really at his finest. He donned his dilapidated uniform and looked quite martial when he commanded, "Fire." A young lieutenant is always a strange creature, on the old as well as on the new continent.[14]

Frémont's 1842 expedition yielded disappointing information of scientific value. Records and specimens had been lost in the waters of the North Platte. Preuss's map added little to existing maps and, ending at South Pass, told emigrants nothing of the toughest part of their overland journey. Even the segments it did display failed to identify such critical features as grass, timber, and water.

Yet Frémont's report, printed in an extra thousand copies on motion of Senator Benton, had enormous consequence. Science did not benefit, but the expansionist cause did. Frémont's graphic images and rousing rhetoric, heavily influenced by Jessie's skilled pen, moved Oregon legislation closer to passage in the Congress and heated public fervor for westward expansion. Readers ignorant of the scarcity of scientific results felt a patriotic impulse when they read of the tired little bumblebee high in the Wind River Range and could identify with the young enthusiast as he ruminated: "We had climbed the loftiest peak of the Rocky Mountains, and looked down upon the snow a thousand feet below, and standing where never human foot had stood before, felt the exultation of the first explorers."[15]

The report also introduced Kit Carson to the nation and launched his rise to one of America's brightest icons. His virtues as guide, hunter, plainsman, and mountaineer emerged in anecdotal clarity. "Mounted on a fine horse, without a saddle, and scouring bare-headed over the prairies," wrote Frémont, "Kit was one of the finest pictures of a horseman I have ever seen."[16] Such imagery personalized the young mountaineer in the public mind. Like Frémont himself, in the next few years Kit Carson became a national hero.

Not undeservedly. In style, substance, and achievement, both were genuine heroes. Within the next four years, both, more than any of their peers in either of their professions, advanced the twin purposes of the Corps of Topographical Engineers. In partnership, they served the corps' overt purpose by revealing the essential character of vast areas of the American West. In partnership, they also served the corps' hidden purpose by so dramatizing their exploits as to stoke the fires of national expansion.

IN THE SPRING OF 1843, the Missouri frontier swarmed with overland travelers as never before. Senator Linn's Oregon bill had passed the Senate in February, and although it failed in the House people believed that the federal government would soon move decisively on the Oregon question. "The Oregon fever is raging in almost every part of the union," reported *Niles's National Register* in May. "It would be reasonable to suppose that there will be at least five thousand Americans west of the Rocky Mountains by next autumn."[17]

Later, Oregon settlers remembered 1843 as the year of the "Great Migration." By late May, some nine hundred emigrants and 120 wagons had collected in a sprawling, unorganized mass on the prairies near Westport, Missouri. They had much trouble getting organized, despite the informed counsel of Dr. Marcus Whitman, returning from an eastern visit. John Gantt, a mountain veteran, signed on as guide and imposed enough discipline to herd the disorderly, quarrelsome settlers as far as Fort Hall. Whitman took them on to the Columbia.[18]

California also had its emigrants gathering at the jump-off point. Joseph Chiles, who had gone to California with the Bidwell-Bartleson party of 1841, had collected a dozen or so of his former Missouri neighbors and intended, this time, to get wagons across the Sierras. The Chiles group, which traveled with the Oregon wagons up the Platte Road, had the good fortune to fall in with Joseph R. Walker at Fort Laramie. Of all the former mountain men, he alone knew the way to California, and he agreed to lead the Chiles train there. Augmented by some families that had changed their minds about Oregon, the Walker-Chiles wagons turned southwest from Fort Hall. Scarcity of provisions dictated a division of the group. In the end, Walker took six mule-drawn wagons and twenty-three people south, through Walker Pass, and around the southern tip of the Sierras, while Chiles and thirteen men rode horseback across the mountains. Wagons had yet to achieve the crossing.[19]

Still another train outfitting at Westport in May 1843 brought together an assemblage of some sixty young sports anticipating a "hunting frolic" in the mountains. Accompanied by William Sublette, Captain William Drummond Stewart was making a final pilgrimage to the scenes of his earlier revels with the mountain men. As usual, he traveled in style, ensconced each night in a "very elegant" tent equipped with a suitably distinguished wine cellar. Afterward, Sir William would have to assume the family patrimony in a Scottish castle, there to pass a quiet life with nostalgic memories and trophies of the distant Siskadee.[20]

And finally, not least amid the lively scene near Westport, Lieutenant John C. Frémont poised for a second epochal plunge into the western wilds. The report of his 1842 expedition had just been published, and he and his father-in-law had already mapped out an ambitious program for 1843. Colonel Abert duly ratified Senator Benton's outline, and Frémont was off with an assignment to connect South Pass, the western limit of the 1842 expedition, with a recent survey of the Oregon coast and Columbia Basin by the navy's Lieutenant Charles Wilkes.[21]

Frémont's thirty-nine men resembled the 1842 contingent and even included some of them. Again, Charles Preuss accompanied as cartographer. Again, Frémont was the only soldier. Kit Carson, however, was not here as guide; that post had fallen to Tom Fitzpatrick.

Rather than retrace the well-known Platte Road, this year clogged with emigrant wagons, Frémont and Benton had decided that the expedition should see if an alternate route to the mountains existed farther south. The way lay up the Republican River and then along the heights dividing this stream from the Solomon. Rain and mud slowed progress, exhausted the stock, and diminished provisions. Leaving Fitzpatrick to follow, Frémont and fifteen men pushed forward to the South Platte. They reached Fort St. Vrain, an outpost of Bent's Fort, on July 4, in time to partake of the Independence Day hospitality.

Lucien Maxwell, last year's hunter, had accompanied the explorers of 1843 with the intention of returning to his home in Taos. Frémont charged him with buying provisions and fresh mules in Taos and bringing them back to the Arkansas at the mouth of Fountain Creek. There Frémont would take over and Maxwell could go home. Arriving at the appointed site on July 14, however, Frémont learned of political turmoil in New Mexico and Ute Indians on the warpath. Even if not already slain by Utes, Maxwell probably could not carry out his mission.

As Frémont fretted, prospects suddenly brightened. "I had here the satisfaction to meet our good buffalo hunter of 1842, Christopher Carson, whose services I considered myself fortunate to secure again."[22]

KIT CARSON HAD LED an exciting life since leaving the Frémont expedition at Fort Laramie the previous September. Not least was his marriage to Josefa Jaramillo in Taos on February 6, 1843. In the spring, however, again working for William Bent and Ceran St. Vrain at Bent's Fort, he had become embroiled in the freebooting aggressions of the Republic of Texas against Mexican New Mexico. This endangered commerce on the Santa Fe Trail and prompted the dispatch of a force of U.S. dragoons to hold back the Texans. As a hunter for the Bents' spring train to the States, Carson agreed to turn back with a message imploring New Mexico's governor to send a military escort to meet the dragoons and see the trading caravans through to Santa Fe. In a cauldron seething with violent Texans, violent Mexicans, and violent Indians, Carson counted many a hazardous exploit before July, when he departed Taos for Bent's Fort. En route he met Lucien Maxwell, from whom he learned Frémont's whereabouts and to whom he described the riots in Taos that would prevent any support of Frémont from that quarter.[23]

Happily back on his former chief's payroll—Josefa would not see him for more than a year—Kit Carson proved the solution to Frémont's dilemma. Hurrying back to Bent's Fort, he obtained ten mules and pack-saddles and herded them directly across the plains to Fort St. Vrain. Frémont arrived on July 23 to find his "true and reliable friend" already there. So was the rest of the command, under Fitzpatrick, with whom Carson renewed a friendship dating from 1831.[24]

One goal Frémont had set was to find an emigrant road between the Missouri and Green Rivers that cut out the sweeping arc formed by the Platte and the Sweetwater. Thus he had crossed the Great Plains roughly along the Republican River (which did not offer a road superior to the Platte). Now he would look for easy passes through the Front Range of the Rockies and a direct route beyond to the usual crossing of the Green at the mouth of the Big Sandy. For this mission he selected thirteen men, including Carson, cartographer Preuss, and Basil Lajeunesse and his brothers, of whom Frémont had grown fond. With the main body, meantime, Fitzpatrick would strike north to the emigrant road and follow it to a reunion with Frémont at Fort Hall.

Before leaving Fort St. Vrain, Frémont hired a hunter to keep Fitzpatrick supplied with meat. He was Alexis Godey, a veteran of mountain and plain even though hardly in his middle twenties. "In courage and professional skill," declared Frémont, "he was a formidable rival to Carson, and constantly afterwards was among the best and most efficient of the party, and in difficult situations of incalculable value." Carson did not regard Godey as a rival. They became fast friends and companions in many a tough scrape.[25]

The exploring squad failed in the quest for a direct route to the Green River. The Cache la Poudre involved a strenuous climb through the Front Range but in a gorge Frémont thought could be improved for wagons. Nor did the broad table of the Laramie Plain or the readily circumvented Medicine Bow Mountains beyond present troublesome obstacles. After crossing the North Platte and enduring an Indian scare, however, the party encountered the feature that had given direction to travel since William H. Ashley's time—the Great Divide Basin. In 1825 Ashley crossed this huge sterile saucer, rimmed by a Continental Divide that itself divides and reunites. Frémont did not cross it. Instead, "determining to abandon any further attempt to struggle through this almost impracticable country," he turned directly north to pick up the emigrant road on the Sweetwater.

It was a busy road, crawling with the wagons of settlers bound for Oregon and California, the vacationing hunters of William Drummond Stewart, and now Frémont's expedition, traveling in two divisions, Fitzpatrick's still somewhere in the rear. The road bore the exploring party as far as Soda (or Beer) Springs, on the Bear River. Here Frémont turned from the road to follow the river down to one of his major objectives—Great Salt Lake.

Kit Carson almost missed the examination of the great sheet of salt water, the subject of many a campfire speculation in which some of Frémont's veterans avowed that, despite the absence of visible outlets, it reached the Pacific by an underground river originating in a giant whirlpool somewhere on its surface. On August 19, however, on Ham's Fork of the Green, Frémont dispatched Carson to ride ahead to Fort Hall, obtain what provisions he could, then rejoin the company at the lake. Hospitably received by the Hudson's Bay Company factor, Carson nevertheless discovered that the stream of emigrants had nearly cleaned out the fort. With one mule lightly packed with flour and a few other items, he rode into Frémont's camp at the mouth of the Bear River on September 4—in time to take part in his chief's next daring exploit.

Again Frémont had insisted on packing an inflatable India rubber boat to the mountains. Now he intended to use it to investigate a large island visible from the eastern shore. Carson, Preuss, Basil Lajeunesse, and Baptiste Bernier made up the little group that helped their leader drag the boat through the mudflats to navigable water. A rising gale blew up whitecaps and sprayed the men with water that dried into a salty crust. Two of the boat's air cylinders gave out. Rowing furiously and constantly working the bellows to replace escaping air, the exhausted voyagers at last made landfall.

Camping over the night of September 9 on what one day would be named Frémont Island, the men awoke to discover the lake dark with storm clouds. Although the sun broke through, the boatmen had to face directly into a gale blasting the water into ever more choppy whitecaps. "It required all the efforts of the men to make any head against the wind and sea," but again they reached the mudflats and dragged themselves ashore.

Morale fell as food ran short. Carson provided a supper of seagulls on September 12, and two days later Frémont gave permission to kill a horse. The next day the gloom lifted as the Frémont and Fitzpatrick divisions reunited. Fitzpatrick had carefully husbanded his supplies and had come out from Fort Hall to feed everyone amply. At the fort Frémont bought a few horses and oxen and that night, September 19, slaughtered one of the oxen for a feast. Despite mixed rain and snow, "the usual gayety and good humor were at once restored."

From Fort Hall to Fort Vancouver the route held few uncertainties. The march involved only an occasional hardship, mainly in the Blue Mountains, and Frémont and Preuss devoted themselves to gathering the usual data needed for a scientific survey. Because of the supply problem, at Fort Hall Frémont had discharged eleven volunteers and sent them back to the States. A few days later he again divided the command, Fitzpatrick bringing up the rear.

Early November 1843 found Frémont at The Dalles of the Columbia, where he judged his mission of connecting with the Wilkes survey accomplished. Now, as his orders directed, he would lead his men in a winter trek back to the States, following the Oregon Trail and further examining the Wind River Mountains on the way. He sent word for Fitzpatrick to come forward, placed Carson in charge at The Dalles, and with Preuss and two others floated by Indian canoe down to Fort Vancouver. There, Frémont wrote, Dr. McLoughlin "received me with the courtesy and hospitality for which he has been eminently distinguished," and Frémont quarreled with Preuss for refusing to cut off his beard merely to dine presentably at McLoughlin's table.[26] The chief factor provided all the supplies needed for the return march, together with a barge and three canoes to transport them back to The Dalles.

DESPITE HIS ORDERS, and contrary to what he had told McLoughlin, Frémont did not return by the Oregon Trail. When he changed his mind, if he changed it at all, can only be guessed. As he explained in his report, he intended to make a great sweep south and east to explore the "Great Basin" between the Rockies and the Sierras. In particular, he wanted to find out whether a Rio Buenaventura really flowed from the Rockies down to the Pacific, as some people still believed and some maps still depicted. Next (apparently with no thought of the season), Frémont wanted to investigate the mountain sources of the Arkansas River and follow that stream down to Bent's Fort before heading home on the Santa Fe Trail.

It was a daunting, even reckless, program to launch at the onset of winter. If either Carson or Fitzpatrick expressed reservations, they escaped the written record. Whether or not Frémont really believed the Rio Buenaventura a possibility serious enough to investigate, he probably exposed his true motives when he described the way home as lying through a land "absolutely new to geographical, botanical, and geological science . . . which inflamed desire to know what this *terra incognita* really contained."[27]

What this terra incognita did not contain doomed the plan. It did not contain enough forage for the stock, especially in winter, to enable the expedition to stray very far from the mountains. Ascending the Deschutes River along the eastern foot of the Cascade Range, the twenty-five explorers missed Klamath Lake, crested a summit, and fell on "the first waters of that Great Interior Basin." Fog, rain, and snow made travel miserable, and Indians occasionally ran off stock. Even among the outlying ranges of the Sierras, Frémont, Fitzpatrick, Carson, and the accomplished hunter Alexis Godey scouted widely for suitable campsites. By early January 1844, their condition had turned critical.

After passing and naming Pyramid Lake, the weary band wandered among the rivers and creeks pouring down from the Sierras. "With every stream I now expected to see the great Buenaventura; and Carson hurried eagerly to search, on every one we reached, for beaver cuttings, which he always maintained we should find only on waters that ran to the Pacific; and the absence of such signs was to him a sure indication that the water had no outlet from the great basin."

After an extended reconnaissance with Carson and Fitzpatrick on January 17, Frémont returned to camp and, inspecting the lamed stock, conceded what had long been apparent: "It was evidently impossible that they could cross the country to the Rocky Mountains. . . . I therefore determined to abandon my eastern course, and to cross the Sierra Nevada into the valley of the Sacramento, wherever a practicable pass could be found."[28]

A midwinter crossing of the Sierras not only departed radically from Frémont's orders but risked the annihilation of his command. Even if he made it, he would be leading an official United States exploring expedition uninvited into Mexican territory. He could not turn east until the spring grass greened, but he could have sat out the rest of the winter beside the Truckee or Walker River, the stock feeding on the grassy meadows and the men subsisting on fish and game. The survival of Frémont's command did not require succor in California. If he had not planned the detour weeks or even months earlier, the lure of the mythical Eden just over the mountains excited his fervid imagination.[29]

Rooted in ignorance, rashness, and boundless self-confidence, the assault on the Sierras got under way on January 20. For the rest of the month, the men clambered in confusion among the various branches of the Walker River. Steep ascents, massive snowdrifts, plunging temperatures, and falling snow evidenced the severity of a Sierra winter. Pass after pass disclosed still others ahead, the "great dividing ridge" still farther and still higher. On makeshift snowshoes, equipage loaded on sledges, the exhausted climbers pushed on. An Indian guide deserted. Around nighttime campfires, as snow fell in blinding sheets, Kit Carson recalled his tour of California with Ewing Young, "speaking of its rich pastures and abounding game" not a hundred miles farther.

Finally, on February 6, Frémont led an advance party from an open basin to a nearby peak. Fitzpatrick and Carson went along. From the summit they peered into a distant snowless valley bordered in the western haze by a low range of mountains. "There is the little mountain," exclaimed Carson of Mount Diablo. "It is fifteen years ago since I saw it; but I am just as sure as if I had seen it yesterday."[30]

The way down proved almost as hard as the way up, but now spirits rose as the ordeal neared an end. Famished mules gnawed saddles and bridles and even ate the tail off Fitzpatrick's horse. Famished men led Frémont to slaughter a mule for supper. "Captain," said Carson, "the other messes always use the head, which is just the best part; suppose we use it today." Frémont agreed. "When cooked all night, a mule head is a delicacy," observed Preuss, either in truth or in sarcasm.[31] On March 6, finally leaving the mountains with the American River, the spent but incredibly lucky mountaineers found a hospitable welcome at Sutter's Fort, the adobe capital of Swiss émigré Johann Augustus Sutter's sprawling kingdom of New Helvetia.

Part empire builder, part fraud, Sutter had crossed the continent to Oregon in 1838 and arrived in California by way of the Sandwich Islands a year later. Governor Juan Bautista Alvarado, hoping to create a bulwark against Indian raiders and British and American trappers, had granted him fifty thousand acres in the Sacramento Valley. Both as planter and stockman, Sutter had prospered. As bulwark against foreign intrusion, however, he failed his Mexican patrons.[32]

Frémont considered his California venture not only necessary but fruitful. It allowed him to dispose of the mythical Rio Buenaventura and reveal the Sierras and the Cascades as a massive wall uncut by any river giving access to the Pacific. Only the rivers of the Central Valley, paralleling the coast, emptied into San Francisco Bay. In geopolitical terms, he rightly observed, "this want of interior communication from the San Francisco Bay, now fully ascertained, gives great additional value to the Columbia, which stands alone as the only great river on the Pacific slope of our continent which leads to the ocean from the Rocky mountains, and opens a line of communication from the sea to the valley of the Mississippi."[33]

The Sierras decreed the return route. He would turn them on the south and strike northeast along the edges of the Great Basin to the Salt Lake Valley. This would allow him to ascertain whether any river other than the Colorado drained the Rockies in that region, afford opportunity to examine the southern margins of Great Salt Lake, and allow him to connect with the headstreams of the Arkansas River as originally planned. The journey got under way from Sutter's Fort on March 24, 1844.[34]

Frémont's eastward trek closely followed the route twice pioneered by Jedediah Smith, in 1826 and 1827, and since gaining prominence as the "Old Spanish Trail." The expedition left the head of the San Joaquin near Tehachapi Pass, crossed the Mojave Desert, and reached the Wasatch front by way of the Virgin and Sevier Rivers.

In the Mojave Desert the Frémonters encountered the first of sporadic Indian troubles. On April 24 two Mexicans, a man and a boy, came into camp with a woeful tale. They belonged to a party of six, including two women, who had traveled in advance of a caravan of traders, still in Frémont's rear, headed for Santa Fe on the Old Spanish Trail. Paiute Indians had swept down on the camp and butchered the occupants. The two survivors, mounted and on horse guard, escaped. They asked for help in retaking the horses. Frémont called for volunteers. Carson and Godey stepped forward, expecting others to join them. When none did, they set forth on their own.

The next afternoon, announced by a war whoop, the pair stormed back into camp, driving the horses before them and with two bloody scalps dangling from Godey's rifle barrel. They had trailed the quarry, stealthily taken position near four lodges and the horse herd, and at dawn charged into camp. A volley of arrows greeted them, but the occupants fled—except two struck down by bullets from the attackers' rifles. Frémont considered the feat "among the boldest and most disinterested which the annals of western adventure, so full of daring deeds, can present." As for Preuss, "To me, such butchery is disgusting"—a reaction he had cause to soften when he and the others reached the scene of the massacre. The men had been horribly mangled, and the women had been carried off as captives.[35]

Up the Virgin River through the first part of May, the Paiutes harassed the Frémonters, forcing them to watch carefully over their stock and take extra precautions to avoid ambush. On May 9 warriors caught one of Frémont's best men separated from the command and killed him. After that the Paiutes vanished.

On May 12, Frémont had the good fortune to be overtaken by a party of eight Americans under Joseph R. Walker, who agreed to serve as guide. In conversations over the next two weeks, Walker confirmed what Frémont had already concluded. A huge sink extended from the Wasatch Range to the Sierra Nevada and from the edge of the Columbia Basin to the edge of the Colorado Basin. It contained mountains and deserts and many rivers and lakes, but no waters that found their way to the ocean.

Throughout his report, written after his return, Frémont referred to this "Great Interior Basin," but probably not until Walker joined did its essential character fix itself firmly in his mind. If his wordy prose failed to convey its significance as one of the great distinguishing geographical features of the American West, Charles Preuss remedied the defect. Between the Wasatch and the Sierras, his map left a large empty space across which he printed: "THE GREAT BASIN: diameter 11° of latitude, 10° of longitude: elevation above the sea between 4 and 5000 feet: surrounded by lofty mountains: contents almost unknown, but believed to be filled with rivers and lakes which have no communication with the sea, deserts and oases which have never been explored, and savage tribes, which no traveller has seen or described."[36]

From Utah Lake, late in May 1844, the Frémonters took on the Rocky Mountains. Crossing the Wasatch and descending to the Green along the southern flank of the Uinta Mountains, they crossed the Green River in Brown's Hole and made their way up the Little Snake, passing not far from where Henry Fraeb met his death three years earlier. Turning south, they made careful investigations of the three "parks," so well known to the trappers but still vague in cartography. Each gave rise to a major river—North Park the North Platte, Middle Park the Grand (which united with the Green to form the Colorado), and South Park the South Platte. Down the Arkansas and past the Royal Gorge, the party broke into the open plains and on July 1 arrived at Bent's Fort. "As we emerged into view from the groves on the river, we were saluted with a display of the national flag and repeated discharges from the guns of the fort, where we were received by Mr. George Bent with a cordial welcome and a friendly hospitality."[37]

At Bent's Fort, Joe Walker and Kit Carson took their discharge. Carson hung around for the Independence Day feast Bent staged for Frémont and

Pehriska-Ruhpa, Moenni-tarri Warrior, in the Costume of the Dog Danse. *One of Karl Bodmer's best known Indian paintings portrayed a Hidatsa, village neighbors of the Mandans, who were also known as Minitaris. Hidatsas provided Lewis and Clark with vital information.* COURTESY JOSLYN ART MUSEUM, OMAHA, NEBRASKA.

his men. "The day was celebrated as well, if not better, than in many towns of the States," observed Carson, who rode off at once to Taos and the bride he had left more than a year earlier.[38]

JOHN CHARLES FRÉMONT RANKS with a handful of the premier explorers of the American West. In his two expeditions of 1842 and 1843–44, he explored no country not previously explored by mountain men. Yet he explored it with the eye of a scientist eager to record and lay before the world its rich topography, geology, flora and fauna, and aboriginal inhabitants, and to place the whole firmly within a framework of latitude and longitude. His report and Charles Preuss's map, published in 1845, revealed the West with a depth and comprehensiveness equaled by no one who had gone before.

Here was a West described and pictured from personal observation, not the theories, speculations, and fancies of deskbound mapmakers. The rivers, mountains, and deserts of Preuss's map traced the expedition's route and left white spaces beyond the limits of his vision. They were white

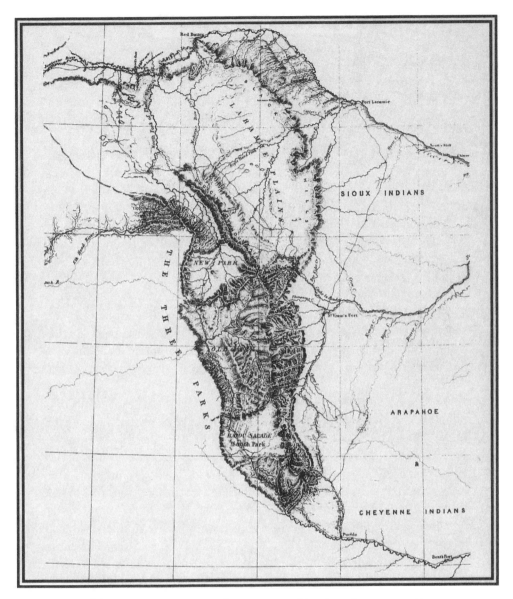

Portion of the Frémont-Preuss map of 1845. As Donald Jackson has written, this carto-graphic landmark, placing the findings of Frémont's first two expeditions in a framework of latitude and longitude, "was the right map at the right time." It was a huge map, encompassing all the West from the Mississippi to the Pacific. Although a "white space" map depicting only what Frémont had personally examined, it showed how to get to Oregon and California and thus proved an invaluable guide for emigrants. Reproduced here as an illustration of the Frémont-Preuss cartography is only one segment: the Front Range of the Rocky Mountains and the three "parks," sources of the North and South Platte and the Yampa, whose beaver population had once drawn the Taos trappers.

spaces, however, enclosed by latitude and longitude and only awaiting the work of others to fill the blanks. The map contained errors, most notably the merging of Utah Lake with Great Salt Lake. But the map showed and the report described (with a literary assist from Jessie Frémont) the road from the Missouri River to the Columbia, the Cascade Mountains, the Sierra Nevada, the Wasatch Range, and the Rockies with their three parks. Gone forever were a Buenaventura and a Multnomah heading in the Rockies and flowing to the ocean. Instead, only the Columbia breached the mountain rampart to connect the continental interior with the Pacific.

Frémont's most significant contribution to an understanding of the West lay in the big empty space encircled by Preuss's carefully hachured mountains and characterized by Frémont as a land of wholly interior drainage. He gave it the name it would bear on all future maps: the Great Basin. As historian Donald Jackson has pointed out, "The Great American Desert of Zebulon Pike and Stephen H. Long was mainly a point of view; Frémont's Great Basin was a geographic reality which only a man who had circumnavigated it, on foot and horseback, could comprehend." This comprehension alone, and its revelation, entitle Frémont to high stature as an explorer.[39]

Ironically, despite the political power of Thomas Hart Benton, Frémont's two exploring expeditions brought little influence to bear on national policy. Both the new president, James K. Polk, and his Secretary of War, William L. Marcy, looked on the young lieutenant as an impractical enthusiast and his cartography as unpersuasive. The Polk administration, moreover, had won office on an ambitious platform of expansion and needed no prodding from a junior lieutenant of engineers.

The role of Frémont's two expeditions lay not in the realm of policy but in their effect on public opinion. They were stories of exotic adventure. They told of the verdant lands on the Pacific, down the Columbia in fertile Oregon and beyond the Sierras in idyllic Mexican California. In countless Americans, they aroused longings for new lands and new economic opportunities. And for the thousands of Americans who acted on the impulse, the maps showed how to get there, especially after the publication in 1846 of a new Preuss map, in seven detailed sections, of the Oregon Trail.

In July 1845, four months after publication of Frémont's report (which combined the reports of both expeditions in one book), a New York newspaper editor coined a phrase that would motivate and explain the thinking of a large segment of the American public. With the annexation of Texas moving toward culmination and relations with Mexico verging on war, John L. O'Sullivan wrote of "our manifest destiny to overspread the continent allotted by Providence for the free development of our yearly multiplying millions." As much as any American of his time, John C. Frémont embodied the spirit of Manifest Destiny and planted it in the hearts of his countrymen.[40]

Both Kit Carson and Tom Fitzpatrick could claim a large share of Frémont's success, both in his geographical revelations and in the popular appeal of his implicit invitation to colonize the far reaches of the continent. They made him an accomplished practitioner of the "mode of voyaging" in the West. Where they knew the way, they showed him, and where they did not, they helped him find the way. Probably neither thought very deeply about the "manifest destiny" of the American people, but both probably foresaw the day when the nation's western boundary would fall on the Pacific shore.

If not, in little more than a year both would play an important part in achieving the nation's destiny, whether providentially manifest or not.

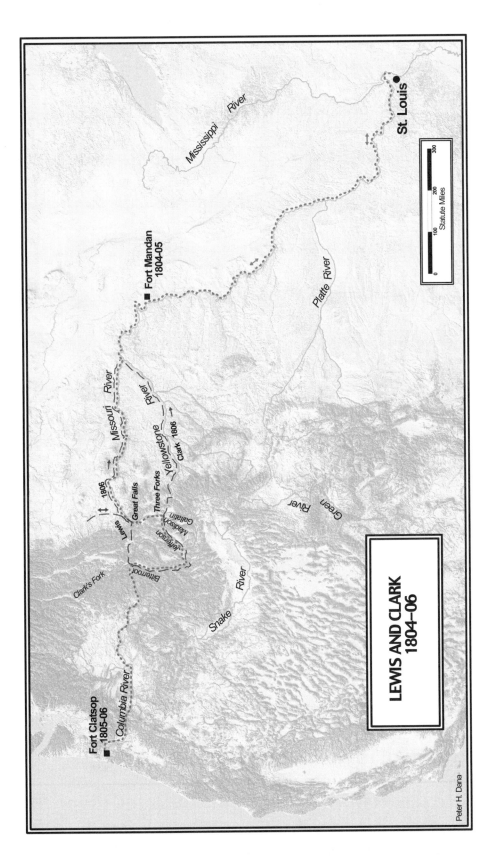

LEWIS AND CLARK
1804–06

St. Louis

Mississippi River

Platte River

Fort Mandan
1804–05

Missouri River

Yellowstone River

Clark 1806

1806

Three Forks

Great Falls

Jefferson

Madison

Gallatin

Lewis

1806

Bitterroot

Clark's Fork

Snake River

Green River

Columbia River

Fort Clatsop
1805–06

Statute Miles

0   100   200   300

Peter H. Dana

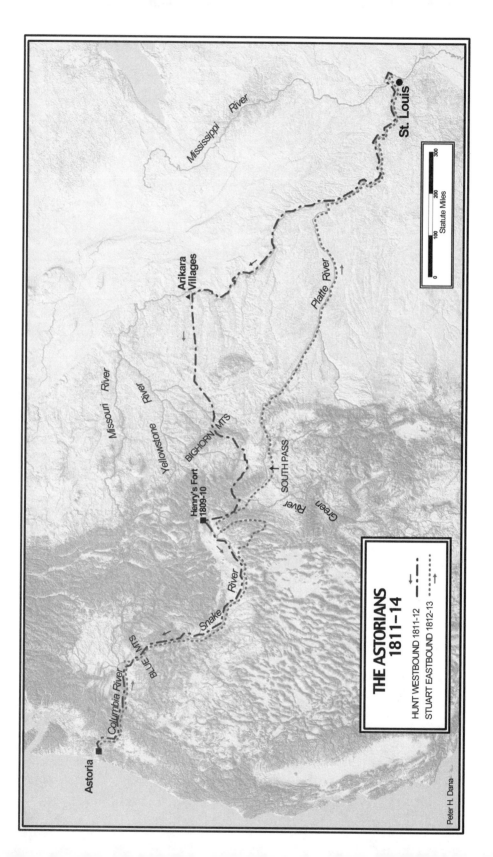

Mississippi *River*

St. Louis

Arikara Villages

Platte *River*

Missouri *River*

Yellowstone River

BIGHORN MTS

SOUTH PASS

Green *River*

Henry's Fort 1809-10

Snake River

BLUE MTS

Columbia River

Astoria

Statute Miles

0 100 200 300

THE ASTORIANS 1811–14

HUNT WESTBOUND 1811-12 —·—·—·

STUART EASTBOUND 1812-13 ············

Peter H. Dana

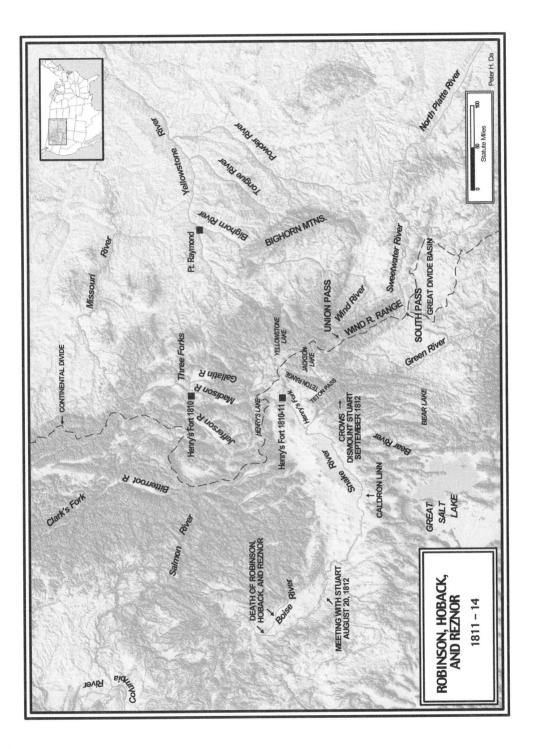

Peter H. Da

Statute Miles
0   50   100

ROBINSON, HOBACK,
AND REZNOR
1811 – 14

North Platte River

Yellowstone River

Tongue River

Powder River

Missouri River

Bighorn River

BIGHORN MTNS.

Ft. Raymond

Sweetwater River

Wind River

UNION PASS

WIND R. RANGE

SOUTH PASS

GREAT DIVIDE BASIN

Green River

CONTINENTAL DIVIDE

Three Forks

Gallatin R.

Madison R.

Jefferson R.

Henry's Fort 1810

HENRY'S LAKE

YELLOWSTONE LAKE

JACKSON LAKE

TETON RANGE

Henry's Fort 1810-11

Henry's Fork

TETON PASS

CROWS →
DISMOUNT STUART
SEPTEMBER 1812

BEAR LAKE

Bear River

Bitterroot R.

Clark's Fork

Salmon River

Snake River

CALDRON LINN

GREAT
SALT
LAKE

DEATH OF ROBINSON,
HOBACK, AND REZNOR

Boise River

MEETING WITH STUART
AUGUST 20, 1812

Columbia River

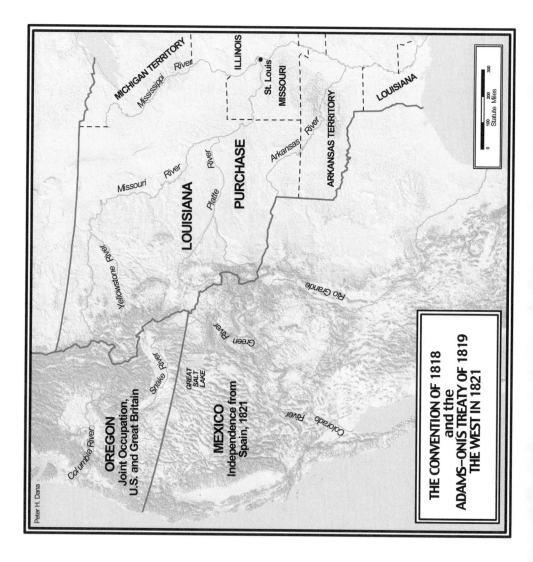

Peter H. Dana

MICHIGAN TERRITORY

Mississippi River

ILLINOIS

St. Louis

MISSOURI

LOUISIANA

Missouri River

Platte River

Arkansas River

ARKANSAS TERRITORY

LOUISIANA PURCHASE

Yellowstone River

Rio Grande

Green River

GREAT SALT LAKE

OREGON
Joint Occupation,
U.S. and Great Britain

Snake River

Columbia River

MEXICO
Independence from
Spain, 1821

Colorado River

0   100   200   300
Statute Miles

THE CONVENTION OF 1818
and the
ADAMS–ONÍS TREATY OF 1819
THE WEST IN 1821

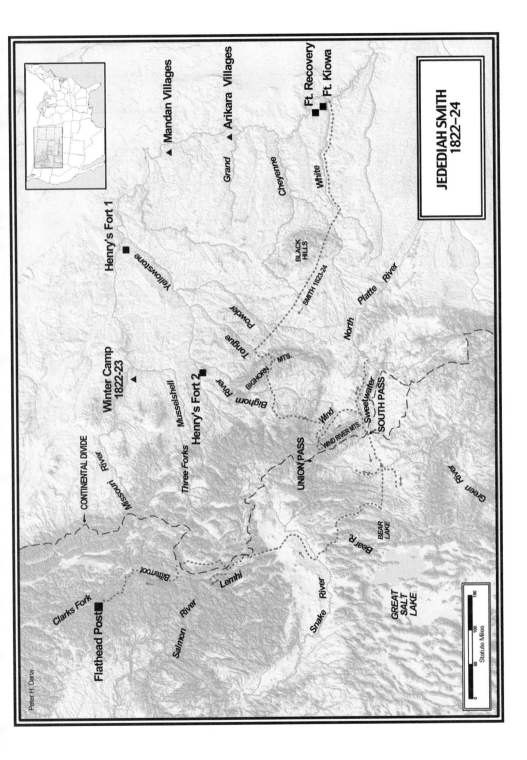

JEDEDIAH SMITH
1822–24

Peter H. Dana

Ft. Recovery
Ft. Kiowa

Mandan Villages

Arikara Villages

Grand

Cheyenne

White

SMITH 1823-24

BLACK
HILLS

North Platte River

Henry's Fort 1

Yellowstone

Powder

Tongue

BIGHORN MTS.

Winter Camp
1822-23

Musselshell

Bighorn River

Henry's Fort 2

Three Forks

Wind

Sweetwater

SOUTH PASS

WIND RIVER MTS.

UNION PASS

CONTINENTAL DIVIDE

Missouri River

Lemhi

Salmon River

Snake River

Bear R.

BEAR
LAKE

Green River

GREAT
SALT
LAKE

Bitterroot

Clarks Fork

Flathead Post

Statute Miles

0   50   100   150

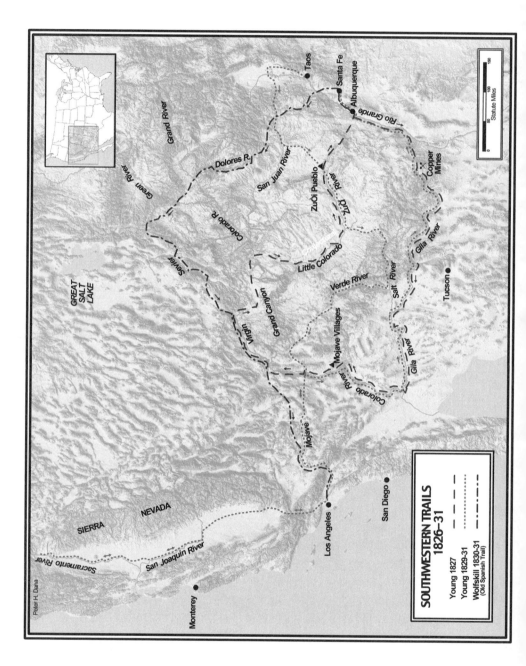

SOUTHWESTERN TRAILS
1826–31

Young 1827 — — —
Young 1829-31 ·············
Wolfskill 1830-31 — ·· — ··
(Old Spanish Trail)

Peter H. Dana

GREAT
SALT
LAKE

SIERRA

NEVADA

Sacramento River

San Joaquin River

Monterey

San Diego

Los Angeles

Mojave

Virgin

Sevier

Green River

Grand River

Dolores R.

Colorado R.

San Juan River

Grand Canyon

Little Colorado

Verde River

Mojave Villages

Colorado River

Gila River

Salt River

Gila River

Zuñi River

Zuñi Pueblo

Copper Mines

Rio Grande

Albuquerque

Santa Fe

Taos

Tucson

0   50   100   150
Statute Miles

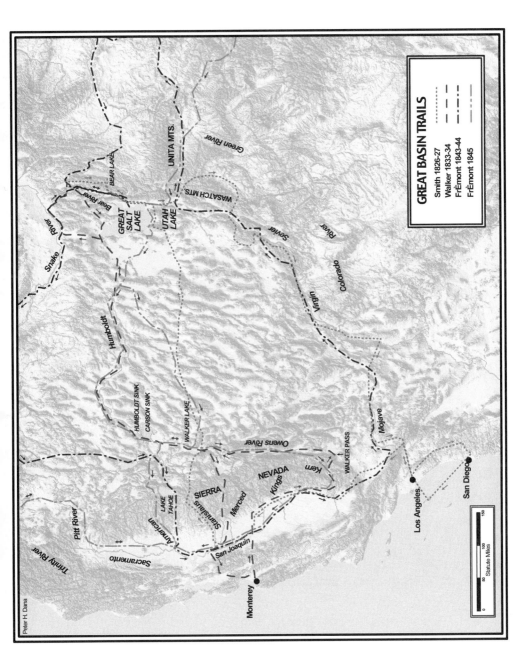

GREAT BASIN TRAILS

Smith 1826-27 ....
Walker 1833-34 — — —
Frémont 1843-44 —·—·—
Frémont 1845 —··—··—

Peter H. Dana

Statute Miles
0   50   100   150

Trinity River
Pitt River
Snake River
Bear River
BEAR LAKE
GREAT SALT LAKE
UNITA MTS.
Green River
WASATCH MTS.
UTAH LAKE
Sevier River
Colorado River
Virgin
Humboldt
HUMBOLDT SINK
CARSON SINK
WALKER LAKE
Sacramento
American
LAKE TAHOE
SIERRA
Stanislaus
Merced
San Joaquin
Monterey
Kings
NEVADA
Owens River
Kern
WALKER PASS
Mojave
Los Angeles
San Diego

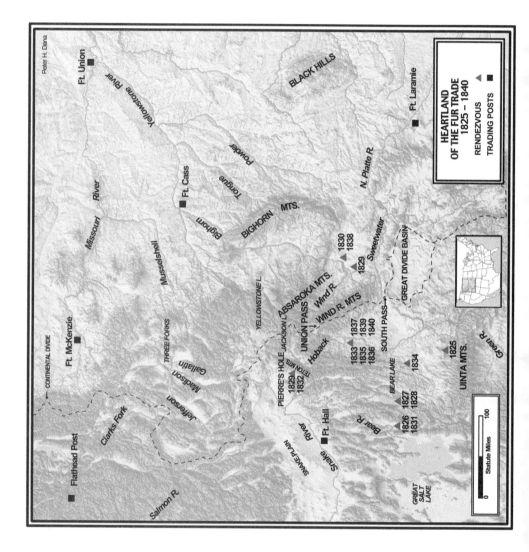

Peter H. Dana

HEARTLAND OF THE FUR TRADE 1825 – 1840

RENDEZVOUS ▲
TRADING POSTS ■

Ft. Union

Yellowstone River

Missouri River

Musselshell

THREE FORKS

Gallatin

Madison

Jefferson

Clarks Fork

Salmon R.

Flathead Post

Ft. McKenzie

CONTINENTAL DIVIDE

BLACK HILLS

Ft. Laramie

N. Platte R.

Powder

Tongue

Bighorn

Ft. Cass

BIGHORN MTS.

Sweetwater

1830
1838
1829

GREAT DIVIDE BASIN

YELLOWSTONE L.

ABSAROKA MTS.

Wind R.

UNION PASS

WIND R. MTS

SOUTH PASS

Hoback

1833 1837
1835 1839
1836 1840

1834

BEAR LAKE

1826 1827
1831 1828

Bear R.

1825

UINTA MTS.

Green R.

GREAT SALT LAKE

Snake R.

Ft. Hall

SNAKE PLAIN

PIERRE'S HOLE

1829
1832

JACKSON L.

TETON MTS.

0   100
Statute Miles

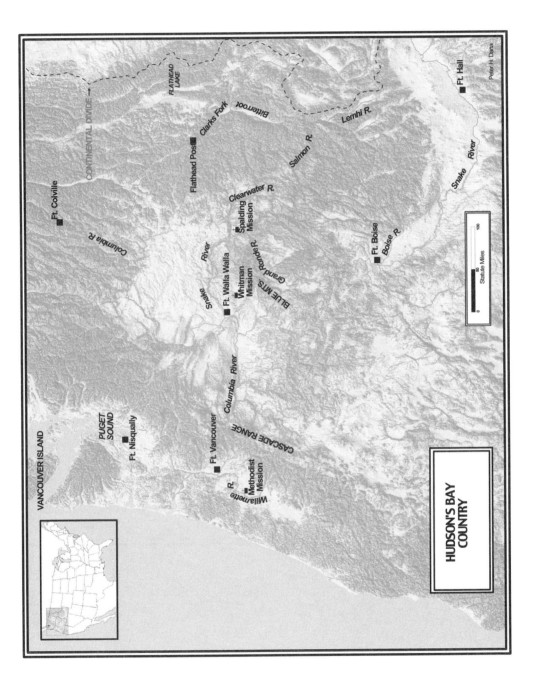

HUDSON'S BAY
COUNTRY

Peter H. Dana

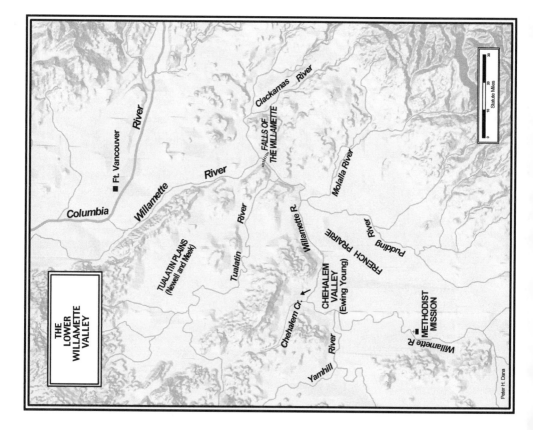

THE LOWER WILLAMETTE VALLEY

Columbia

Willamette River

Ft. Vancouver

River

Clackamas River

FALLS OF THE WILLAMETTE

Molalla River

TUALATIN PLAINS (Newell and Meek)

Tualatin River

Willamette R.

Pudding River

Chehalem Cr.

FRENCH PRAIRIE

CHEHALEM VALLEY (Ewing Young)

Yamhill River

Willamette R.

METHODIST MISSION

Statute Miles

Peter H. Dana

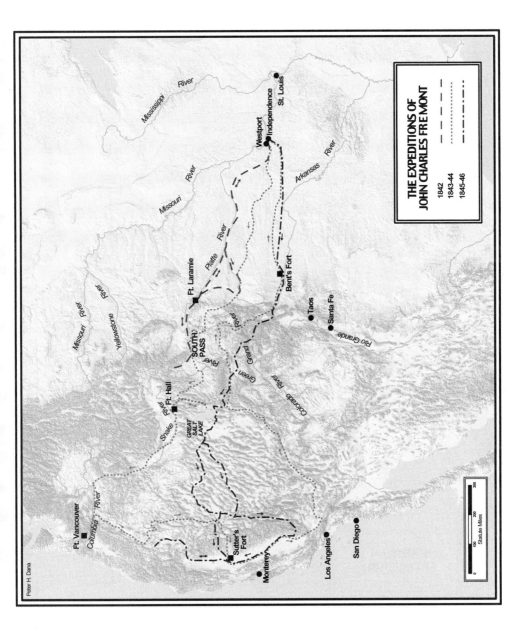

Peter H. Dana

THE EXPEDITIONS OF
JOHN CHARLES FRÉMONT

1842
1843-44
1845-46

St. Louis
Independence
Westport
Mississippi River
Missouri River
Arkansas River
Bent's Fort
Ft. Laramie
Platte River
SOUTH PASS
Taos
Santa Fe
Rio Grande
Sweetwater River
Green River
Grand River
Colorado River
Missouri River
Yellowstone River
Ft. Hall
Snake River
GREAT SALT LAKE
Ft. Vancouver
Columbia River
Sutter's Fort
Monterey
Los Angeles
San Diego

0   100   200   300
Statute Miles

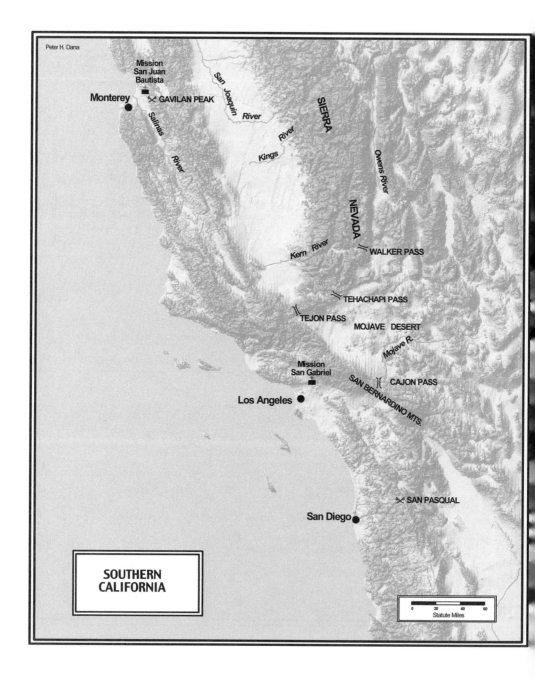

Peter H. Dana

Mission
San Juan
Bautista

Monterey ● ✂ GAVILAN PEAK

San Joaquin

River

Salinas

River

Kings *River*

SIERRA

Owens River

NEVADA

Kern *River* ✂ WALKER PASS

✂ TEHACHAPI PASS

TEJON PASS ✂

MOJAVE DESERT

Mojave R.

Mission
San Gabriel

SAN BERNARDINO MTS. ✂ CAJON PASS

Los Angeles ●

✂ SAN PASQUAL

San Diego ●

SOUTHERN
CALIFORNIA

0   20   40   60
Statute Miles

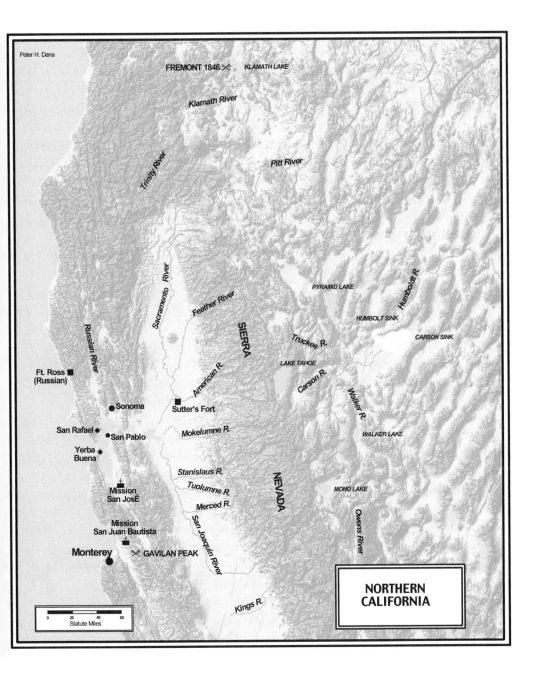

Peter H. Dana

FREMONT 1846 ✕   *KLAMATH LAKE*

Klamath River

Trinity River

Pitt River

Sacramento River

Feather River

PYRAMID LAKE

Humboldt R.

SIERRA

Truckee R.

HUMBOLT SINK

CARSON SINK

LAKE TAHOE

Ft. Ross ■
(Russian)

Russian River

American R.

● Sonoma

■ Sutter's Fort

Carson R.

Walker R.

San Rafael ●
● San Pablo

Mokelumne R.

WALKER LAKE

Yerba ●
Buena

NEVADA

Stanislaus R.

✚
Mission
San JosÈ

Tuolumne R.

MONO LAKE

Merced R.

Owens River

Mission
San Juan Bautista

San Joaquin River

✚
Monterey ●
✕ GAVILAN PEAK

Kings R.

0 20 40 60
Statute Miles

**NORTHERN
CALIFORNIA**

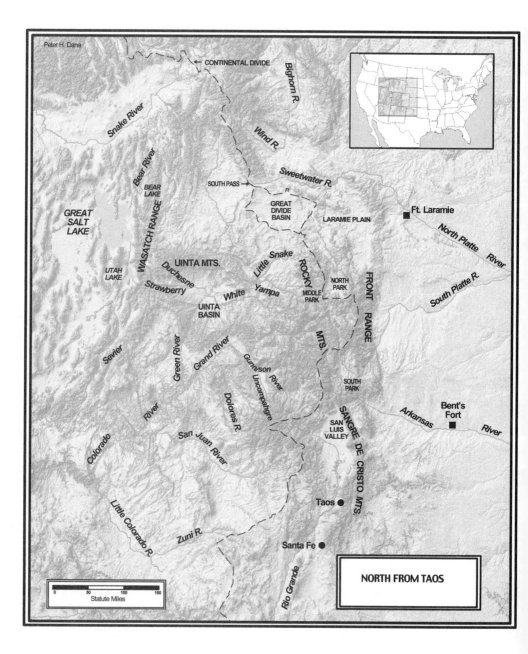

Peter H. Dana

CONTINENTAL DIVIDE

Bighorn R.

Snake River

Wind R.

Sweetwater R.

SOUTH PASS →

Bear River

BEAR LAKE

GREAT DIVIDE BASIN

LARAMIE PLAIN

Ft. Laramie

North Platte River

GREAT SALT LAKE

WASATCH RANGE

UINTA MTS.

Little Snake

ROCKY

NORTH PARK

FRONT RANGE

South Platte R.

UTAH LAKE

Duchesne

Strawberry

White

Yampa

MIDDLE PARK

UINTA BASIN

Sevier

Green River

Grand River

Gunnison River

Uncompahgre

MTS.

SOUTH PARK

Arkansas

Bent's Fort

River

River

Colorado

Dolores R.

San Juan River

SANGRE DE CRISTO MTS.

SAN LUIS VALLEY

Little Colorado R.

Zuni R.

Taos ●

Santa Fe ●

Rio Grande

0   50   100   150
Statute Miles

NORTH FROM TAOS

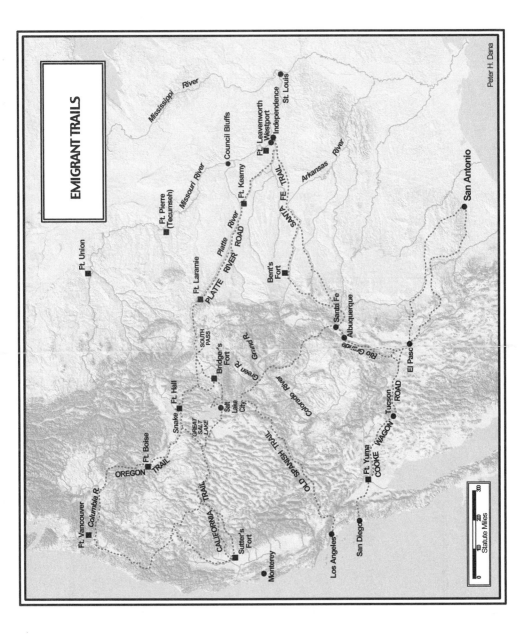

EMIGRANT TRAILS

Peter H. Dana

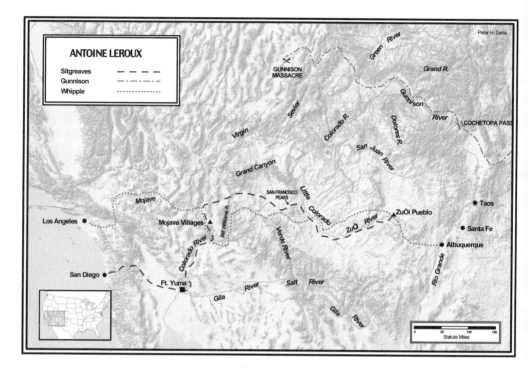

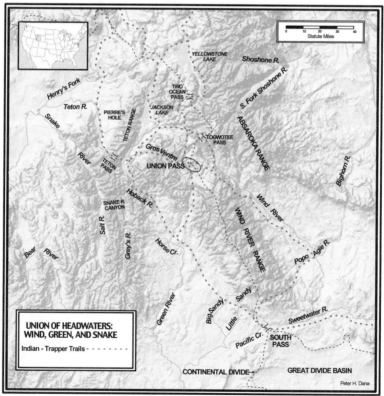

15

JOE MEEK AND DOC NEWELL:

TRAPPERS AS COLONISTS

STOUT, FUN-LOVING JOSEPH L. MEEK, nineteen years of age, came to the mountains with the Sublette caravan of 1829. His Missouri friends and neighbors, Robert "Doc" Newell and George Ebbert, went with the same train. Over the next decade all three developed into superb mountain men. They came to know the Rockies in intimate detail, took beaver and fought Blackfeet with the best, and won the respect of such giants as the Sublettes, Bridger, and Fitzpatrick. Meek enlarged his experience and geographic knowledge in 1833, when he enlisted in Joseph Walker's expedition to California. "Meek was a droll creature," remembered an acquaintance, "a tall man, of fine appearance—a most genial, kind, and brave spirit. He had in his composition no malice, no envy, and no hatred." All three friends left a mark on history, but Joe Meek found an amanuensis to portray his exploits, buffoonery, and genuine accomplishments in such graphic (and often embroidered) narrative as to convince posterity that the Old West boasted "no man like Joe."[1]

Doc Newell was no man like Joe. While matching Joe in mountain skills, Doc was less flamboyant, less given to hyperbole, and better educated. He claimed, besides, a steadier temperament and superior judgment. Newell, recalled an Oregon friend, "was of medium height, stout frame, and fine face. He was full of humanity, good-will, genial feeling, and frankness." Doc and Joe had married daughters of a Nez Perce chief. Doc it was who proposed, after the rendezvous of 1840, that the two pack their families down to the Willamette and take up farming; and Doc it was who organized the move.[2]

This occurred at Fort Hall in September 1840. Three Protestant missionary couples in two wagons had accompanied Andrew Drips's supply train to rendezvous. Black Harris had brought them to the Green River but demanded an exorbitant fee to take them on to Fort Hall. They turned instead to Newell, whose consent so provoked the volatile Harris that he fired a rifle ball in Newell's direction and backed off only when Drips intervened. At Fort Hall, the missionaries decided to speed their journey by switching to pack mules and turned over their two wagons to Newell, probably in payment for his guide services. Also at Fort Hall were the two light wagons the Joel Walker family had brought this far and abandoned in favor of pack animals.

Newell decided to attempt the journey to the Willamette by wagon. In this he received warm encouragement and aid from Fort Hall's chief factor, Francis Ermatinger, who would greatly benefit from a wagon road connecting his post with the Hudson's Bay Company posts of Fort Boise and Fort Walla Walla. Newell had assembled a small party of mountain men who had also decided to carve out a new future, among them Joe Meek, Bill Craig, Caleb Wilkins, and Jack Larison.

With their Indian families and scanty possessions loaded in three wagons, the little expedition got under way on September 27, 1840. The Snake River Plain persuaded everyone that the venture had been a ghastly mistake. Packing people and outfit on the mules, they discarded the wagon beds and pushed forward, the running gear of the wagons bouncing over the black lava rock and sagebrush often as high as a mule's back. Beyond Fort Boise and the Snake, the Blue Mountains proved equally daunting, but at length the group reached Marcus Whitman's mission near Fort Walla Walla.

When Newell voiced regret at his resolve to come through with wagons, Whitman responded: "O, you will never regret it. You have broken the ice, and when others see that wagons have passed they too will pass, and in a few years the valley will be full of our people."[3]

With the rainy season coming on, Newell feared that he could not get his wagons over the Cascade Mountains. He left them at Fort Walla Walla. Here too Craig and Larison parted company, to live with their wives' people in the Nez Perce country. Newell, Meek, and their companions floated down the Columbia to seek new homes and new occupations.

In April 1841 Doc Newell returned to Fort Walla Walla and retrieved one of his wagons. In his mind it was a symbol of achievement as well as of the future Marcus Whitman had predicted. The wagon reached the Willamette on a boat rather than its own wheels, but even so Newell could jot proudly (if somewhat too singularly) in his "Memoranda": "This is to be remembered that I Robert Newell was the first who brought waggons across the rocky mountains."[4]

Just above the falls of the Willamette, where the Tualatin River flows in from the west, the entourage of Meek, Newell, and Wilkins fell in with two old comrades from the Rockies, William Doughty and George Ebbert, the latter the friend who had joined Newell and Meek with the Sublette caravan of 1829. Doughty and Ebbert had preceded the others as Oregon settlers, but all passed a bleak, hungry, wet, cold winter. They lived mostly on boiled wheat, dried salmon skin, and the occasional charity of the Methodist mission and the Hudson's Bay Company. In the spring of 1841, they took up homesteads a short distance up the Tualatin River, on the Tualatin Plain. Newell proved a good enough risk to borrow seed, draft animals, and implements from the Hudson's Bay Company at Fort Vancouver. The bumptious Meek had no such good fortune. But what was he to do? he asked Dr. McLoughlin. "Go to work! Go to work! Go to work!" replied the canny Scotsman.[5]

Go to work Joe did—for his neighboring mountaineers and anyone else who had labor to be performed. In the summer of 1841, he served as pilot and courier for the exploring expedition of naval lieutenant Charles Wilkes. Joe Meek, Doc Newell, and their trapper companions had become colonists—pioneer American settlers in a new land who would join with the immigrants flowing in over the Oregon Trail to build a new society and ultimately a new polity.

NEWELL, MEEK, AND THE DOZEN OR SO TRAPPERS who came down from the mountains in 1839 and 1840 were not the first mountaineers to help make the Willamette Valley an American enclave in a land wholly British despite the legalism of joint occupation. South across a low ridge of mountains from the Tualatin Plain lay a lush meadow watered by Chehalem Creek. This was the heart of a prosperous agricultural and mercantile domain headed by another American mountain man. Ewing Young had been one of the first of the Taos trappers, had ranged the Uinta Basin and the Gila and its tributaries, had blazed trails from New Mexico to California, had trapped California's Central Valley and its bordering mountains, and had even tried his hand at hunting sea otter. At the head of fourteen other trappers, Young had arrived in Oregon in 1834; they were the first American mountain men to settle permanently on the Willamette.[6]

The stimulus for Young's move from California to Oregon sprang from Hall Jackson Kelley. The visionary champion of an American colony in Oregon needed someone to guide him there for the only visit of his long career

210

as Oregon publicist. The perceptive Young probably recognized Kelley as an eccentric zealot and at first refused. Later, economic prospects bleak, Young agreed. He would gather a herd of horses and sell them at the destination.

With seven men and nearly one hundred horses, Young and Kelley got under way in August 1834. Driving more than fifty horses, another seven men joined as Young and his herd moved north up the Sacramento Valley. Kelley called these men "the marauders," and such they were. Repeatedly they killed, plundered, and raped the Indians, friendly or hostile, who crossed their path. To Kelley, Young made excuses for the marauders; but they were merely applying the same hardfisted policy he himself had visited on the tribes of the Gila and Colorado Rivers.

Aside from his attitude toward Indians, Ewing Young was an honest, principled man. He had fairly purchased the horses he drove over the mountains to the Willamette. Doubtless he suspected the marauders had not, but he did not question them very closely. They had chosen to travel with him, and he forbore to turn them away, even had it been possible. For this he would pay a severe penalty.

Hall Jackson Kelley did not remain long on the Columbia. Ravaged by malaria, coldly received by a McLoughlin aware of the calumnies Kelley had rained on the Hudson's Bay Company for years, he passed the winter recuperating in a cabin outside Fort Vancouver. In the spring of 1835, he left Oregon by ship, never to return.

Not Ewing Young. Captivated by the rich pasturage and fertile soil of the Willamette, he had left his men and horses in the Chehalem Valley and come to Fort Vancouver to make his peace with Dr. McLoughlin. There he encountered the awesome power of the Hudson's Bay Company. The governor of California had reported Young as a horse thief, which placed him beyond the benevolent acquiescence with which McLoughlin greeted all other newcomers. Young could expect nothing, in purchase, trade, loan, or charity, from the farms and stores of Fort Vancouver.

The ban imposed indirect consequences as well. Across the Willamette from the Chehalem Valley lay French Prairie, home to thirteen families of French Canadian retirees from the company. On the southern edge of French Prairie, even as Young stubbornly planted himself west of the river, Jason and Daniel Lee began constructing the log buildings of the Methodist mission. Company retirees and missionaries alike depended on the company. Any aid too openly extended to Young would cast the dark cloud of McLoughlin's displeasure over their communities.[7]

Although McLoughlin put out some tentative peace feelers, Young angrily rejected them. In contrast to all other Oregon residents, he would stand up to the Hudson's Bay Company. As the years passed, he heaped abuse on McLoughlin to all who would listen. At the same time, he and his men did well enough to survive. They tended their horses, hunted game, fished the streams and ponds, and trapped the Coast Range for beaver. They traded their furs to the masters of American vessels on the Columbia. Before his own enterprise collapsed, Nathaniel Wyeth took out a load of Young's furs. At the same time, the Methodists and the French Canadians relaxed enough to have occasional dealings with him.

Still Young raged at McLoughlin and sought some way to dent the company's monopoly. In the spring of 1836 he found a way. Nathaniel Wyeth, for two years based on an island at the mouth of the Willamette, gave up his ambitious scheme for connecting fur to salmon to farming and went home to his Boston ice business. From Wyeth, Young bought one of the cauldrons used to pickle salmon for the ocean voyage to Boston. At the mouth of Chehalem Creek, confident that they could manufacture a product that would undermine the power of the company with all but the Methodists, Young and one of his men began construction of a still.

The Methodists took alarm. In January 1837, they convened the Oregon Temperance Society, which adopted a formal resolution asking Young to scrap the venture and offering to reimburse him for his investment. As intended, the Hudson's Bay Company also took alarm. Young's whiskey would find a market among the French Canadians and eventually debauch the Indians on whom the company's trade depended.

That same January, the resolution of the issue paddled up the Willamette in the person of William A. Slacum, purser in the U.S. Navy and a representative of President Andrew Jackson commissioned to report on affairs in Oregon. Slacum brought assurance from Duncan Finlayson, acting for an absent McLoughlin, that if Young would abandon his whiskey project he could trade at Fort Vancouver on the same terms as all other residents. Young readily agreed.

Slacum also gave impetus to another measure necessary to loosen the chains that bound people to the company. McLoughlin allowed Willamette residents to borrow cattle for work and milk, but all calves had to be returned to the company. In other words, the farmers could not also become stockmen. While negotiating an end to the whiskey threat, Young and Slacum talked of the need for cattle owned by the settlers rather than the company. Young said that California contained plenty of cheap cattle that could be driven over the mountains to the Willamette, just as his horses had in 1834. Slacum offered his chartered brig, anchored on the Columbia, to take men to California for this purpose. A meeting at the Methodist mission gave birth to the Willamette Cattle Company. Slacum and Jason Lee drew up the papers, and Ewing Young was chosen to captain the eleven men who would make the drive. To everyone's surprise, John McLoughlin and two of his lieutenants invested more than eight hundred dollars in the enterprise. The Hudson's Bay Company also needed cattle.[8]

Jason Lee's appeal "for the Divine blessing" launched the expedition to California. And blessed with success it was. Nine months later, in October 1837, Young and his tired, bedraggled cowboys herded 630 lean Spanish cattle into a corral on Young's Chehalem Valley pasture. The Willamette farmers now also became stockmen. The Methodist mission received 80 head. Young's share was 135. He had shown the way, moreover, for in years to come many a herd followed the Siskiyou Trail from California to Oregon.

The impasse with the Hudson's Bay Company broken, cordial relations established with the Methodists and the French Canadians, prosperity grounded in horses and cattle thriving under the prod of ambition, energy, and an acute business sense, Ewing Young, mountain man, emerged as the first citizen of the Willamette Valley. In 1838 he erected a sawmill where the distillery had begun to rise two years before. By 1840, his domain had become the economic center of the Willamette Valley. As a close student has concluded, "because of his untiring activity Ewing Young's establishment during these years served for the community as virtually a market place, a store, a bank and a factory as well as the largest farm."[9]

By 1840 too, as Doc Newell and Joe Meek settled across the mountain to the north, Ewing Young's health had begun to fail. He could not know that in death he would make a final contribution to the welfare of his community.

EWING YOUNG'S DEATH on February 15, 1841, highlighted the nearly total absence of law and government in the Willamette Valley. He died intestate, and no probate court stood ready to dispose of his ample estate. Three days later a public meeting, chaired by the Reverend David Leslie, selected a probate judge but in addition, as a follow-up to a meeting chaired by Jason Lee the day before, named a committee to consider what further elements of government the Willamette colony required. In later years, Oregon pioneers looked back on the meetings prompted by Ewing Young's death as the catalyst of a sequence of exercises in democracy that led to the formation of a provisional government. The reality was more complicated.[10]

The charter of the Hudson's Bay Company gave it complete governmental power over all British citizens in jointly occupied Oregon. And if that did not suffice, the company's complete economic power made the difference. As British citizens, the company retirees on French Prairie looked to John McLoughlin for law and order, from which he shrank not in dispensing. Their ties to his authority grew even firmer in 1838, with the appearance of Father Francis Blanchet to minister to the spiritual wants of the Catholic French Canadians. Deeply troubling their allegiance, however, all knew that sooner or later the territory south of the Columbia would fall to the United States. Would the new government honor preemption rights to their land? The navy's Purser Slacum tried to reassure them in 1837, but many recognized the wisdom of harmonizing with the Americans.[11]

By 1841, about five hundred settlers made their homes in the Willamette Valley and along its western tributaries. About half the 125 families were French Canadian, the balance American. Of the latter, a few were ex-sailors, remnants of Wyeth's two expeditions, and immigrants who had traveled overland. The rest consisted of about thirty mountain men and their Indian families, five independent Protestant missionaries and their wives, and the people of the Methodist mission. Two Methodist reinforcements, both in 1837, had been followed by the "Great Reinforcement" of 1840, brought by Lee himself by ship after a trek eastward across the continent in 1838. In all, the Methodist establishment numbered nearly one hundred men, women, and children, although some operated other stations that Lee had organized outside the Willamette Valley.[12]

By 1841, the Willamette mission had grown increasingly secular. With few Indians left in the valley to convert, the large mission staff occupied itself chiefly with agricultural and economic affairs. It remained, however, the only organized entity south of the Columbia and played an influential role in all the affairs of the valley.

Beginning even before the meeting assembled in February 1841 to deal with Ewing Young's estate, the movement toward a government independent of the Hudson's Bay Company played out against a background of bitter rivalry between Methodist Minister Lee and Catholic Father Blanchet. Aside from doctrinal conflict, the two clashed on the government issue. As the only true organization in the valley, the Methodist mission took the lead. In 1839, with Lee absent in the East, acting superintendent David Leslie set himself up as justice of the peace—whether duly elected or merely unopposed by the people remains obscure. Thus a government of sorts already existed when Ewing Young died, and as justice of the peace Leslie chaired the meeting of February 18 that established a probate court and called for consideration of adopting a code of law and enlarging this government.

By contrast, Father Blanchet (firmly bolstered by John McLoughlin) considered his flock well served by Hudson's Bay Company authority and wanted no additional power certain to be dominated by Methodists contemptuous of Catholic teachings. Even so, in a bid for French Canadian backing, the chairmanship of Leslie's committee fell to Father Blanchet. He never called a meeting and in June resigned, clearly signaling that his constituency would join in no further move toward local government.

Lee himself seems to have regarded his own movement useful less for its ostensible purpose than for cutting the tentacles of the Hudson's Bay Company south of the Columbia—specifically for detaching the French Canadians from company domination. With that purpose unattainable for the present, he lost interest in the project.

Nonetheless, a new committee formed, with a mandate to report in October 1841. It did not, mainly because the naval explorer Charles Wilkes showed up in the summer of 1841 and, charmed by McLoughlin, disparaged the idea. Meeting with the committee in August 1841, Wilkes declared that "moral authority" sufficed—Catholic for the French Canadians, Methodist for the Americans. "I further advised them," he wrote, "to wait until the Government of the United States should throw its mantle over them."[13]

Although mountain man Ewing Young had set off this year of discord, the Willamette mountain men took little interest in it. They may have recognized it for what it chiefly was—a battle between Jason Lee and his missionaries, on the one hand, and Father Blanchet and John McLoughlin, on the other. Doc Newell and Joe Meek, at least, had all they could do simply to keep food on the table. By the spring of 1843, however, when the issue surfaced again, they had become substantial citizens, eager to exercise their citizenship. By this time, moreover, the Elijah White train of 1842 had deposited 140 emigrants from the East in the valley, and the "Great Migration" of 1843, with 900 more, was organizing on the Missouri frontier. The Willamette population verged on a dramatic shift to American preponderance.

Doc Newell dated his own interest in local government from 1842. On the Tualatin Plain, an Indian cleaned out the household of one of the Protestant missionaries Newell had piloted from Green River to Fort Hall in 1840. With Joe Meek, Caleb Wilkins, and others, Newell caught and punished the offender. The incident led Newell to ponder the need for law and the machinery to enforce it in similar cases and thus to his involvement in a new push for government. Although Newell's motives may have owed as much to a shrewd assessment of economic possibilities under a new regime, he became one of the most active players in the game that unfolded in 1843.[14]

The fresh public focus on government grew out of a "lyceum" that Newell helped to organize in 1842 and that provided a forum for debates on the future of the colony. The failure of the United States to address the needs of Americans in Oregon had been the subject of reproachful rhetoric in the Congress and the press for twenty years, and the colonists themselves had twice petitioned Washington for action.[15] A topic fiercely debated in the lyceum turned on whether Willamette settlers should imitate their countrymen in Texas and declare an independent republic.

In later years pioneer Oregonians would look back on two "wolf meetings" called in February and March 1843 as the genesis of the drive for a provisional government. They were not, but rather simply what they purported to be: an effort to devise means of reducing the menace to livestock of wolves and other predators. The genesis sprang rather from a lyceum debate at the falls of the Willamette in the middle of March 1843. On this occasion, with Newell one of those in attendance, settlers voted to adopt a code of laws and form a government headed by a governor. They appointed May 2 as the date for another public meeting to carry this resolution into effect.

Hanging over these deliberations was the persistent question of independence. Lansford Hastings, a lawyer who had arrived with the White emigrant train and now represented Dr. McLoughlin in a dispute with the Methodists over property at the falls of the Willamette, moved that the projected government be independent. Such was disgust with Washington that the motion carried. Hastening to repair the damage, George Abernathy, a lay worker at the Methodist mission, offered a resolution to seek independence only after the United States had been afforded four years to extend its jurisdiction over the Willamette. Since the settlers still felt patriotic allegiance to the mother country, they adopted that resolution, which canceled the first.[16]

At public meetings at Champoeg on May 2 and July 5, 1843, Willamette settlers adopted a provisional government. For reasons stemming in part from the legal contest with McLoughlin over the falls property, Jason Lee had lost interest in any government at all. Few Methodists attended either meeting.

Among the most influential participants were the former mountain men, who followed the leadership of Doc Newell. The "Newell party" favored the smallest possible government—one that would cost little but would respond to minor issues that arose from time to time and stand ready to deal with any Indian troubles. Above all, Americans to the core, Newell and his friends opposed any forms that would even imply a movement toward independence.

Here, then, was the central issue: big government and eventually an independent republic like Texas, or small government and eventually inclusion in the American nation. Enough favored independence to make the conflict intense and the division close. At the heart of the debate lay the organization proposed by the March lyceum meeting, which included a governor. Eliminate the governor, and the Newell faction would prevail.

Joe Meek is given the dramatic role of shouting for a division on the issue, all favoring the Newell position to line up behind him, all opposed to line up opposite.[17] That probably did not happen, although its persistence in the literature testifies to the prominence Meek had begun to assume in the Willamette community. Less colorfully, however, the vote gave Newell victory. Many of the French Canadians, alert to the threat big government and independence posed to their interests, crossed the line and supported Newell. Instead of a constitution, there would be a simple code of laws. Instead of a governor, there would be a three-man executive committee.

The provisional government of July 1843 has been called a "nongovernment," which it very nearly was and which its architects intended. It served the needs of the moment, before the "Great Migration" of this same year and the others of following years, carving the Oregon Trail into a wagon road, poured thousands more settlers into the Willamette Valley. Then the provisional government would assume new forms and meet new needs.[18]

Mountain men had played prominent parts in the formation of the provisional government, and they continued to furnish leadership that highlighted a transition from trapper to state builder. Doc Newell, chosen a member of the legislative committee at the May 2 meeting, remained a member after the ratification meeting of July 5 and in the spring election of 1844 won a seat in the provisional legislature. Joseph Gale, a Wyeth brigade leader in the Rockies, took a seat on the executive triumvirate, to be replaced in the 1844 election by another former trapper of note, Osborne Russell.

Joe Meek may not have shouted "Who's for a divide!" and then rejoiced with a "Three cheers for our side!" But he played his usual noisy part in the proceedings. Participants lost no time in recognizing his rising stature by anointing him sheriff under the new government. Reelected in 1844, Sheriff Meek would take rank with the other trappers turned political leaders and also compile a record of vigor and whimsy rivaling his Rocky Mountain career.

NEARLY A DECADE BEFORE the last rendezvous sent Rocky Mountain trappers in search of new occupations, California had offered an alluring alternative to the hard, uncertain life of the beaver hunter. Followers of Ewing Young and Joseph R. Walker observed a land rich in natural resources, benign in climate, and the scene of a seemingly idyllic pastoral lifestyle. The coast teemed with sea otter, the hills with game, and the grasslands with rangy Spanish cattle that took care of themselves until vaqueros stripped off their hides to ship to Boston aboard Yankee trading vessels. Some of the men who arrived with Young and Walker stayed. Young himself came, to remain until moving on to Oregon in 1834. Other Taos trappers, disgruntled with capricious New Mexican officialdom, turned to California.

As Jedediah Smith and James O. Pattie had discovered, California officialdom could be as fickle as New Mexican. Like New Mexico, California lay distant from Mexico City and neglected by the central authority. Factional feuds, vendettas, and comic-opera revolutions fed almost constant turmoil. The ex-trappers could not avoid buffeting by the erratic political winds. The more pugnacious plunged into the contentions and earned acclaim as patriots or scorn as freebooters. Yet others made good citizens, deferring to governmental authority, marrying Mexican women, submitting to Catholic forms, and contributing to the economic welfare of the province. No less American in sentiment than their brethren in Oregon, so long as Mexico ruled they suppressed the impulse to agitate for union with their motherland. When union came, however, they proved as constructive in their American citizenship as Newell and Meek in Oregon.

Exemplifying this class were William Wolfskill and George Yount. Taos trappers, in 1830 they opened the Old Spanish Trail, which evolved into a major trading thoroughfare linking Santa Fe and Los Angeles. Both liked what they saw and stayed.

Already a Mexican citizen, "Don Guillermo" Wolfskill planted himself in the center of the little pueblo of Los Angeles and, launching a dazzling career as a cultivator of grapes, quickly became a leading citizen of the province. Joined by his brother John in 1838, Wolfskill expanded his holdings, eventually assembling 145 acres and by 1846 tending thirty-two thousand vines. He also experimented successfully with groves of orange, lemon, and lime trees. In 1841 Don Guillermo married into a prominent Mexican family and began siring a large family to carry on his agricultural enterprises. In the same year, he and John turned their ambitions north, to San Francisco Bay. Aided by Jacob Leese, a former mountain man who had married the governor's daughter, they gained a grant of eighteen thousand acres on the western edge of the Sacramento Valley. Under John's oversight, his ranch sprouted grains, vegetables, and grapes and pastured cattle and horses by the thousand.[19]

Just across the mountains to the west, in the Napa Valley, lay another large ranch, presided over by George Yount. After arriving in California, he had parted with Wolfskill and headed north, where he soon made close friends with General Mariano Vallejo, commandant of the northern district at Sonoma. Yount's mountain skills, especially in fighting off Indian aggressions from the north, gained their reward in 1836 with the grant of nine thousand acres at the head of the Napa Valley. As legally required, he submitted to Mexican citizenship and Catholicism. By the early 1840s, when the Wolfskills became his neighbors, George de la Concepcion Yount raised grain, vegetables, fruits, and berries, grazed livestock, and operated a sawmill and gristmill. He made his home in a sprawling house of log and adobe. Nearby stood a blockhouse, evidence of his pledge to Vallejo to hold back the Indians of the north.[20]

Others of the Wolfskill and Yount stamp included George Nidever, Job Francis Dye, and Jacob Leese. Nidever, veteran of the Battle of Pierre's Hole in 1832, came to California in 1834 with Joseph Walker's pioneering expedition across the Nevada desert and the Sierras. He stayed, to gain renown as a rifle marksman and famous hunter of sea otter and grizzly bears. He married a Mexican woman but never became a Mexican citizen or a Catholic.[21]

Dye arrived in California as a member of Ewing Young's expedition of 1831–32. He dabbled in ranching, operated a gristmill and distillery, and in 1837 married the niece of Governor Juan Bautista Alvarado. Thereafter, as a Mexican citizen and a Catholic, his fortunes prospered.[22]

Another of the Taos trappers, Leese came to California in 1833 and, after setbacks in trying to drive horses and mules to New Mexico, turned to merchandising. In 1836 he erected a home and store in the newly platted pueblo of Yerba Buena on the western rim of San Francisco Bay, the second citizen to establish himself in what one day would become San Francisco.[23]

Representing another breed of mountain man, Isaac Graham reached California with Joe Walker in 1834. With Nidever, Dye, Leese, and others who settled in California, Graham had begun his trapping career with the ill-fated Bean-Sinclair party out of Fort Smith, Arkansas, in 1830.[24] With Nidever, he had fought at the Battle of Pierre's Hole in 1832. In California he did not give up fighting—or making trouble. With gusto, this "stout, sturdy backwoodsman" plunged into the revolutionary ferment of 1836. At the head of *Los Rifleros Americanos,* forty or fifty roughnecks who numbered ex-trappers in their ranks, he proved the decisive element in Juan Bautista Alvarado's revolutionary bid for the governorship.

But in California politics neither loyalties nor governments remained stable for long. Within two years Alvarado, probably with good reason, had turned on Graham. With forty-five others, both English and American, he was convicted of high treason and banished to a prison in Mexico. Portrayed in the United States as a freedom-loving frontiersman such as had died at the Alamo in Texas, Graham won release in 1841 and returned to

California. As a lumberman and stockman, he gained prosperity, but he had not learned his lesson. Again in 1845 he brought his *rifleros* to a revolutionary cause but picked the losing side. Thereafter, he seems to have kept out of trouble.[25]

Kindred Americans, however, would soon make trouble for their Mexican rulers. Unlike Oregon, California was part of a foreign nation. Foreigners lived there at the sufferance of Mexico. Those who became citizens and played constructive parts in economic and social life did well enough, although none entirely avoided legal or economic torment by capricious authorities. American emigrants who began to arrive in 1841 found welcome and aid in the homes of men like Wolfskill and Yount, and death found them respected leaders of American California.

George Yount died in his big adobe home on October 5, 1865, which prompted a Napa Valley newsman to observe that "Many of us will miss his genial, kind and cordial welcome at his old home." Two days short of a year later, William Wolfskill died in Los Angeles. "When he arrived in this place, the thousands of acres that are now covered with vines loaded with delicious grapes were then but a sandy desert," recalled a city editor. Wolfskill "was truly one of the pioneers of California."[26]

"BEAVER HAS SO DEPRECIATED IN VALUE within the last few years that trapping has been almost abandoned," observed the English traveler George Frederick Ruxton after passing through New Mexico in 1846. Yet Taos remained the base of such mountain men as Kit Carson, Antoine Robidoux, Antoine Leroux, and others. They lived now mainly by trading, sometimes in furs taken by the Indians but mainly in a product for which their community became renowned throughout the West: Taos Lightning. In Taos Ruxton observed several distilleries.

> Most of them belong to Americans, who are generally trappers and hunters, who having married Taos women have settled here. The Taos whisky, a raw fiery spirit which they manufacture, has a ready market in the mountains amongst the trappers and hunters, and the Indian traders, who find the "firewater" the most profitable article of trade with the aborigines, who exchange for it their buffalo robes and other peltries at a "tremendous sacrifice."[27]

Along the Missouri frontier, years of effort to limit the flow of whiskey to Indians had begun to take effect, but now, thanks to the Taos distillers, traders still found a ready source. The channel of this trade ran north from

Taos to the Arkansas River, where ex-trappers had founded two rude communities in 1843 and 1844. At Pueblo and nearby Hardscrabble, they occupied themselves in farming and trading, obtaining Taos Lightning from the south and exchanging it for furs and robes with the Plains Indians to the north and east.

Ruxton observed this traffic at Pueblo, where he met Mark Head, "one of the most daring and successful trappers that ever followed this adventurous mountain life." Head and a companion were off to Taos with a load of pelts and would return with kegs of the potent brew—"a very profitable article of trade amongst the mountain men." (It was Head's last journey. He and his comrade blundered into the Taos revolt of 1847, were shot in the back, stripped, mutilated, and thrown to the wolves.)[28]

American mountain men had been colonists in New Mexico ever since their advent in the early 1820s. They made Taos their base, a fixed rendezvous instead of the annual fairs of the northern Rockies. Many married Mexican women, took the Catholic vows, and became Mexican citizens. Yet they continued to be Americans in spirit, as much so as their brethren in California and Oregon. Few contributed as constructively to the economic and social welfare as William Wolfskill or Robert Newell. But influential colonists they had been from the first, and influential citizens they remained for the rest of their lives.

THE WEAK PROVISIONAL GOVERNMENT crafted by Doc Newell and his followers in 1843 proved adequate for that year. But as the "Great Migration" of 1843 brought nine hundred immigrants from the East and the influx of 1844 another twelve hundred, the political and social dynamics of the Willamette settlement changed rapidly. Farmers, lawyers, merchants, and all the other elements of the communities from which they had come wanted the stronger forms of government they had known at home. Parties took shape: American and Independent, the latter still striving for a republic that could deal with both Britain and the United States. The advocates of *provisional* government—one merely to hold Oregon for union with the United States—at length prevailed. Taxes were imposed, and in 1845 the three-man executive gave way to an elected governor, George Abernathy. The old mountain men continued to be respected and valued members of the community, but no longer did they exert their earlier influence.[29]

The American presidential election of 1844 held forth new hope to Willamette settlers. Democrat James K. Polk won the White House on an expansionist platform. "Fifty-Four Forty or Fight," ran the slogan of one faction of Polk's party, referring to the southern boundary of Russian

Alaska at 54° 40' of north latitude. Polk cannot have seriously thought that goal attainable or worth fighting for, but boundary negotiations sputtered sporadically through 1845 and into 1846. By June 1846, after bouts of jingoism on both sides of the Atlantic, negotiators concluded a treaty. England yielded the only territory truly in dispute and agreed to an international boundary extending the forty-ninth parallel all the way to the Pacific.[30]

Then and ever after, Oregon pioneers congratulated themselves that they had ordained the contents of the treaty simply by taking possession of the land. In fact, they had only minor influence. The land they took possession of lay south of the Columbia, where Britain had long since stood ready to yield all claim. The true roots of the Oregon treaty reached into purely British politics and diplomacy that had little to do with the issues on the Columbia. Not even the interests of the Hudson's Bay Company weighed heavily with the Foreign Office. For the United States, moreover, the stakes embraced the harbor of Puget Sound as much as the people of the Willamette Valley.

Still, Oregon settlers brought some influence to bear. Their growing population kept alive the possibility of a war that neither Britain nor the United States wanted and may have made the solution palatable to a British public opinion that would have earlier rejected it. Most importantly, the burgeoning Willamette settlement forced the Hudson's Bay Company to assess its true interest on and north of the Columbia. By 1845, under the continual prodding of George Simpson, who intensely disliked and distrusted the Americans, John McLoughlin had moved company headquarters from Fort Vancouver to Vancouver Island, north of the forty-ninth parallel. The company's southern frontier no longer rested on the Columbia River.[31]

Although now unquestionably within the limits of the United States, Oregonians had to operate under the provisional government while Washington tarried in creating a territory. Joe Meek continued as sheriff, collecting taxes, summoning juries and witnesses, arresting miscreants, and even taking a census. In 1846, little more than a week before diplomats signed the Oregon boundary treaty, Meek won election to the provisional legislature.

Increasingly a public figure of consequence, Meek lost none of his colorful personality. When he spoke for temperance and took office as president of the Washington Temperance Society, his actions belied his professions. And there were those who doubted the depth of his conviction when, after a Methodist baptismal ceremony in 1844, he declared: "Tell everyone you see that Joseph Meek, that old Rocky Mountain sinner, has turned to the Lord."[32]

Joe Meek's time of glory arrived in 1848. On November 29, 1847, Cayuse Indians descended on the Whitman Mission and butchered Marcus and Narcissa Whitman together with twelve others, including Meek's daughter. War fever swept Oregon, and the legislature instructed the governor to raise a body of militia to quell the uprising. At the same time, the legislature resolved to send a messenger to Washington "for the purpose of soliciting the Immediate influence and protection of the U.S. Government in our internal affairs."

The messenger the legislators selected was their colleague Joseph L. Meek. He traveled up the Columbia with a militia column and helped rebury the victims of the massacre, whose remains had been unearthed by wolves. With nine companions, including his old friend George Ebbert, he set forth across the continent. By early May he was in St. Louis, and he reached Washington on May 28. There he laid the legislature's memorial before the Congress and spent two hours with President Polk. On prancing steeds, Meek and General Winfield Scott escorted the presidential carriage in the Independence Day parade and helped lay the cornerstone of the Washington Monument.

On August 14, 1848, Polk signed legislation creating the Territory of Oregon. And Oregon's "ambassador" to Washington returned home bearing a commission signed by the president of the United States appointing Joseph L. Meek United States Marshal for the Territory of Oregon.

For Oregonians, there truly was "no man like Joe."[33]

16

KIT CARSON: FRÉMONT'S
THIRD EXPEDITION

K IT CARSON SPENT the winter of 1844–45 based in Taos with Josefa but doubtless ranging widely as his restless nature dictated. In Taos he fell in with an old comrade with whom he had trapped off and on since 1835, Richard Owens. Josefa's quiet influence may have helped them decide that, "as we had rambled enough, that it would be advisable for us to go and settle on some good stream and make us a farm." In March 1845, they crossed the Sangre de Cristo Mountains eastward to the edge of the plains and, along the Little Cimarron River, began erecting adobe huts and putting in crops.

The undertaking lasted less than six months. Early in August, an express specially dispatched from Bent's Fort arrived with word that Frémont was there. The previous year Carson had promised his chief that, if ever wanted for another exploration, he stood ready to join. Now Frémont wanted him. The partners sold their nascent ranch for half their investment and hurried to Bent's Fort. "This was like Carson," noted Frémont, "prompt, self-sacrificing, and true." Josefa would not see her husband for two years.

At Bent's Fort, Carson and Owens found Frémont camped with an impressive company of sixty men, including a dozen Delaware Indians and many of their friends from earlier expeditions. Among them were Lucien Maxwell, Basil Lajeunesse, and Alexis Godey. Frémont took an immediate liking to Dick Owens and hired him too. "Cool, brave, and of good judgment," thought Frémont; "a good hunter and good shot; experienced in mountain life; he was an acquisition, and proved valuable throughout the campaign." In fact, on the trio of Carson, Godey, and Owens, Frémont bestowed the ultimate military tribute:

> The three, under Napoleon, might have become Marshals, chosen as he chose men. Carson, of great courage; quick and complete perception, taking in at a glance the advantages as well as the chances for defeat; Godey, insensible to danger, of perfect coolness and stubborn resolution; Owens, equal in courage to the others, and in coolness equal to Godey, who had the *coup-d'ôeil* of a chess-player, covering the whole field with a glance that sees the best move.[1]

Captain Frémont (his achievements recognized by a brevet rank in which he now served, even though still in regular rank a second lieutenant) carried written orders directing him to survey the Arkansas and Red Rivers but not to stray beyond a "reasonable distance" from Bent's Fort and to return home by the end of 1845. Later instructions, Texas having advanced a notch more toward annexation, directed him to detach a party at Bent's Fort to survey south of the Arkansas River.[2]

Kit Carson and Dick Owens did not give up their ranch to explore the neighborhood of Bent's Fort and return home in four months. Like all the others, they enlisted to go to California. Frémont's destination was no secret. In early May, newspapers proclaimed that he would march all the way to the Pacific and remain out for three years. "Those who have a taste for danger and bold daring adventure, may now have a chance." In St. Louis, hundreds of eager applicants literally mobbed the young officer for a place in the ranks.[3]

Carson and his fellow "Marshals" had enlisted in a campaign that would serve their country's growing sense of Manifest Destiny.

FRÉMONT'S THIRD EXPEDITION had the usual scientific purposes, but it had political and possibly military aims as well. Its enlarged scope drew on no officially recorded sanction, although his superiors undoubtedly understood and probably approved the intent. Sanction, rather, lay in the designs of a handful of highly placed officials and the acquiescence of all others when newspapers publicized the undertaking as a government exploring expedition to California. Where the scientific might give way to the political or military depended on developments none could predict with certainty and on the judgment of a young officer whose judgment had not always proved sound.

Elected on an expansionist platform in November 1844, the administration of James K. Polk took office on March 4, 1845, less than a month after Colonel Abert signed the orders for Frémont's survey of the Arkansas River. Three days earlier, a joint resolution of the Congress had opened the way for bringing the Republic of Texas into the American union, once Texas accepted the invitation. Mexico, still denying Texan independence a decade after Texans won at San Jacinto, promptly broke off diplomatic relations with the United States. War threatened, especially as the long-festering issue of the southern boundary of Texas—the Nueces or the Rio Grande—took rank with all the other issues dividing the two nations.

Polk also had designs on California and New Mexico, which he thought he could buy from Mexico. Both provinces dangled by the slenderest thread from the central authority. Both contained many citizens who welcomed American traders and immigrants and even hinted at welcoming American rule.

Great Britain kept the pot bubbling. Her diplomats had intrigued to prevent annexation of Texas. Polk's advisers (wrongly) believed the Royal Navy poised to seize California on any pretext, an act that the United States must exert every effort to head off. Americans in Oregon portrayed the Hudson's Bay Company in villainous terms and demanded an end to joint occupation, fueling boundary negotiations that would excite tempers on both sides of the Atlantic for a year until producing the Treaty of 1846.

Against this background, Captain Frémont (and Jessie) completed the monumental report of the second expedition and basked in national acclaim. Issued by the Congress in ten thousand copies on the eve of the third expedition, the publication (which also included the report of the first expedition) would attain fame as a story of drama and inspiration and as a veritable "trail bible" for overland emigrants.

Through his father-in-law, Frémont also plunged into the intrigues of the new administration. Senator Benton wanted California even more than the president, and so did the newly appointed Secretary of the Navy, historian-turned-cabinet minister George Bancroft. These two, together with Frémont, seem to have reshaped the captain's limited mission. "It was decided," Frémont later wrote, that he would cross the Rockies, reexamine Great Salt Lake, and look for wagon roads across the deserts and mountains to the Pacific.

"And in arranging this expedition," Frémont added, "the eventualities of war were taken into consideration."

For me, no distinct course or definite instruction could be laid down, but the probabilities were made known to me as well as what to do when they became facts. The distance was too great for timely communication; but failing this I was given discretion to act. . . . These frequent discussions among the men who controlled the action of the Government, gave to me the advantage of knowing more thoroughly what were its present wishes, and its intentions in the event of war.

And so the scientific purpose of the third expedition merged with the political and military. Frémont's "it was decided" left the decision makers nameless. Neither Bancroft nor Benton had the authority to make such a decision, and to what extent those who did share in the decision can only be guessed. Frémont's own enigmatic explanation, penned forty years after the events, probably approaches the truth as closely as posterity is likely to get.[4]

REPEATING SCENES of the spring of 1844, the prairies beyond Westport, Independence, and St. Joseph hummed with activity as the grass greened in 1845. Long before Frémont camped at Westport with his entourage in June, the white-topped wagons had begun to assemble at the jump-off places. During the summer of 1845, some five thousand emigrants responded to the waves of publicity portraying Oregon and California as lands of opportunity. The continentalist rhetoric of Polk's electoral drive, combined with the stirring impulses soon to be defined as Manifest Destiny, gave biblical and patriotic rationale to economic self-interest.

Sharing the overland trails with the emigrant wagons that summer were three hundred United States dragoons under Colonel Stephen Watts Kearny. Their mission was to show the flag and the military power of the Great Father to the Indian tribes and warn them to leave the white travelers alone. Guided by Tom Fitzpatrick, the dragoons rode as far as South Pass, then swung south along the Front Range of the Rockies to return to their base at Fort Leavenworth by way of Bent's Fort and the Santa Fe Trail. Although Kearny led a purely military expedition, one of Colonel Abert's officers, Lieutenant William B. Franklin, went along to record scientific data and add his own map to the growing cartographic library of the Topographical Engineers.[5]

From an assembly camp near Independence, an emigrant portrayed the self-image of his fellow travelers and captured the chauvinistic spirit that animated much of the American populace in the spring of 1845. "The whole form as nervous, intelligent, brave and determined a body as ever launched themselves upon the hazard of an untried and arduous enterprise," he wrote. This day a rumor of war with England reached the camp.

All declared their determination "to settle and to conquer. Should they be called to rally around the Star Spangled Banner, and plant the national standard *forever firmly* on the sublime heights that overlook the Pacific, we shall know that truer hearts or better soldiers never primed a rifle or drew a deadlier bead."

"It is a wonderful impulse this," concluded the writer, "combined of patriotism, curiosity, and a warlike spirit of adventure, which is pressing our people onwards to the Western Seas."[6]

Captain John Charles Frémont shared the sentiment and counted himself among its most vigorous practitioners.

WHILE AWAITING KIT CARSON at Bent's Fort, Frémont organized the survey south of the Arkansas River directed in his second set of orders. He had been assigned two young lieutenants so that one might lead this expedition. Instead, he sent both, thus perhaps intentionally preserving his status as the single military figure on his own expedition. The two were Lieutenants James W. Abert, the colonel's son, and William G. Peck. Abert commanded.

Frémont reached Bent's Fort on August 2 by a route north of the Santa Fe Trail. He thus missed Colonel Kearny and his dragoons, who had passed Bent's Fort on the way home a few days previously. Frémont sent an express to overtake Kearny and enlist his guide, Tom Fitzpatrick, as guide for Abert and Peck.

Fitzpatrick knew little of the country to be covered. He had followed the Cimarron Cutoff of the Santa Fe Trail in 1831, when Jedediah Smith lost his life, and that was the limit of his experience. William Bent therefore lent two of his hunters to see the explorers as far as one of his satellite trading posts on the Canadian River, then return to the Arkansas. One was the celebrated John Hatcher, the other named Greenwood (not the famous Caleb "Old" Greenwood, as usually assumed). After that, Fitzpatrick would have to lead the way.

With 33 men, 63 horses and mules, and 4 wagons, the Abert-Peck expedition got under way on August 15, a day before Frémont's own departure from Bent's Fort. Tracing the Santa Fe Trail over Raton Pass, they struck the Canadian and turned east across the Texas Panhandle and into the Indian Territory. The way led through the range of the Kiowa and Comanche Indians, not noted for their friendship for any white people and deadly in their hatred of Texans. Hatcher's Kiowa wife eased the threat, but the travelers did not feel secure until they had left these belligerent tribes behind.

After Bent's men turned back, Fitzpatrick remained the sole "guide." His task was not so much to guide—the Canadian led directly to the intended destination—as to instruct the inexperienced lieutenants in the "mode of voyaging" on the plains. His many gently demonstrated lessons impressed the officers. "These things may appear trifling," they wrote, but on the plains they took on crucial importance. Without incident, the party arrived at Fort Gibson, Indian Territory, on October 21. As for Fitzpatrick, noted the lieutenants, "The preservation of our party was due to his vigilance and discretion."

Again, the union of mountain man with topographical engineer had demonstrated its potential. Under Fitzpatrick's oversight, Abert and Peck had for the first time taken wagons over a route that would achieve secondary importance as an overland trail. Their report described the country and the Indians and provided travelers with locations of water, timber, and grass. Their distinguished map, executed by Charles Preuss, set forth the Canadian River country for the first time in accurate detail.[7]

FRÉMONT RELIED on an abundance of noted mountain men as he moved quickly toward Great Salt Lake. In addition to Maxwell, Lajeunesse, and his three "Marshals," at Pueblo Frémont took on Old Bill Williams (and his Indian family). After ascending the Arkansas to its source and crossing Tennessee Pass to the drainage of the Grand, the expedition picked up the westward-flowing White River and followed it down to the Green. On the White, Joseph R. Walker waited. Apparently he had made the same promise as Carson, to serve again if Frémont came west in 1845. How Walker knew where and when to meet the expedition remains a puzzle, but his knowledge of the Great Basin proved as valuable this year as last.[8]

Frémont's chief interest lay west of the Wasatch Range, in that land of interior drainage that he had named the Great Basin and that appeared as a large white space on Preuss's map. Walker had described the contents of the Great Basin the year before, but Frémont wanted to see for himself. Also, he hoped a reconnaissance might identify feasible wagon routes to California across the basin and the Sierra Nevada barrier on its western edge.

First, however, for twelve days in October Frémont indulged his fascination with Great Salt Lake. Petulant, comfort-loving Charles Preuss had not come this year, but his replacement, Edward Kern, took astronomical readings and sketched scenes along the south shore. A large island, almost a peninsula at low water, drew attention. Carson and a few others accompanied their chief in a horseback ride to the island, the water lapping at the animals' stomachs as their feet sank into twelve inches of spongy salt that formed the lake bottom. This island proved more hospitable than the smaller Frémont Island of the year before, with fresh water, grass, and herds of antelope. For two days the hunters laid in game before returning to the mainland, where an ancient Ute Indian demanded payment for the meat taken from his island. Frémont paid and named the Indian's property Antelope Island.[9]

To the west stretched the daunting obstacle of the Great Salt Lake Desert—a sheet of glaring white salt, utterly lacking water or vegetation, extending in the distance to a low range of mountains on its western rim. The southern reaches of this desert had almost claimed Jedediah Smith's life in 1827. Walker had worked around its northwestern edge in 1833, as had the Bidwell-Bartleson emigrant train of 1841. To cross it directly from the southwestern corner of the lake was much more dangerous. "Frémont was bound to cross," recalled Carson. "Nothing was impossible for him to perform if required in his explorations."[10] Appalled at such recklessness, Old Bill Williams quit and turned back—hardly a loss in view of his curmudgeonly temperament.

Carson led the advance guard. With Maxwell, Lajeunesse, and Auguste Archambeau, he set forth in the last days of October to seek water at the base of a snowy peak on the horizon. A mule packed water and food. A smoke signal would alert Frémont to success. "We travelled on about 60 miles," according to Carson; "no water or grass, not a particle of vegetation could be found, as level and bare as a barn floor, before we struck the mountains."[11] There they found wood, water, and grass and sent up a column of smoke. Frémont and the company and mule train crossed in two days, with one overnight camp on the salt flats.

"To the friendly mountain I gave the name of Pilot Peak," wrote the captain.[12] For emigrant trains that followed, including the ill-fated Donner party, Pilot Peak would serve as a beacon marking the course across the table of salt. Not all would make the journey as easily as Frémont and his wilderness veterans.

On November 9, across the narrow Toano Range to the west, Frémont divided his command. Theodore Talbot, the educated young health seeker who had regained his health on the second expedition, would take the main party west to the headstreams of the Humboldt. With Walker as guide and Kern as topographer, this group would follow the newly emerging emigrant road down the Humboldt to its sink. Meantime, Frémont and fifteen men, including Carson and the other favorites, would swing south and west to examine the tangled terrain Jedediah Smith had attacked in 1827. The two parties would reunite on the shore of a large lake at the base of the Sierras south of the Humboldt Sink. In tribute to his veteran guide, Frémont named it Walker Lake. (At the same time, he renamed Mary's or Ogden's River in honor of the great German cartographer, Baron Alexander von

Humboldt—a name that would endure despite the more fitting tribute to Peter Skene Ogden.)[13]

In the next three weeks, Frémont saw for himself the topography that should fill the blank spaces of Preuss's map. Narrow mountain ranges and intervening desert valleys rippled in north-south configuration all the way to the Sierras, forcing the travelers into a tortuous course. Closely adhering to Indian trails, however, they usually found springs and camping sites adequate for their small numbers, an experience in contrast to Jedediah Smith's eighteen years earlier. By November 24, they had threaded the maze and camped at Walker Lake. Three days later the Talbot-Walker train arrived.[14]

Frémont's detour, which also exposed Carson to new country, unfolded a geographic revelation for the earnest explorer. He wrote Jessie two months later that he had crossed this land represented on all maps as parched, sandy plain. "Instead of a barren country, the mountains were covered with grasses of the best quality, wooded with several varieties of trees, and containing more deer and mountain sheep than we had seen in any previous part of our voyage." He looked on himself as the first explorer, and when Charles Preuss published a new map in 1848 he serrated this area with the ranges that had so amazed Frémont.[15]

With winter snows already overdue in the Sierras, Walker counseled against trying to get the pack train across. Once again, therefore, Frémont divided the command. Talbot, Walker, and Kern would take the main body and the train around the southern tip of the Sierras, while Frémont and his fifteen trailbreakers would dash across the Sierras. The two parties would rejoin at the head of the San Joaquin Valley.

Fortune continued to favor the explorer. Winter snows held off as he and his fifteen men, still including Carson, made their way toward the Sierra summit. This year Frémont found a route superior to the dreadful crossing of 1844—up the Truckee River and across what would soon take the name Donner Pass, in recognition of the horrors that occurred nearby in the winter of 1846–47. On December 9, sunshine still lighting the Sierra peaks, the men hitched their horses at Captain Sutter's fort.

Frémont could not claim discovery of the Sierra crossing that yielded the principal emigrant trail into California and ultimately carried highway and railroad. That honor belonged to the Stevens emigrant party of 1844, which with much suffering but no loss of life got wagons and families across the mountains. Not even mountain men deserved the credit, although three doubtless contributed to the crucial decisions. One was Old Greenwood—genuinely old by 1844, counting mountain experience dating from Manuel Lisa and 1812. But Caleb Greenwood had never been in the

Sierras, and like the rest he could only listen to the Indian guide, Chief Truckee. When Truckee turned out to be right, the grateful pioneers named the river that opened the way in his honor.[16]

For Frémont a month of confusion, extending into the new year, ensued as he tried to find the Talbot-Walker party at the head of the San Joaquin Valley. He thought he had arranged the rendezvous on the "Lake Fork" of Tulare Lake, now the King's River, and he even ascended this river to the Sierra summit, in January buried in snow. This exploit cost him all the cattle he had been driving to succor the Talbot group. Below, moreover, Indians made the foothills dangerous. His Delawares, fierce fighters, together with Carson, Owens, Godey, and Maxwell, fought off constant harassment and killed five of the aggressors before they kept a more cautious distance. Even so, Frémont gave up the search and headed back to Sutter's Fort.

Not until early February 1846 did Talbot and the main party emerge from the mountains into the San Joaquin Valley. After parting with Frémont, they had descended the long, mountain-girt basin of the river that Frémont named for Dick Owens, crossed the Sierras at Walker Pass, and camped at the forks of the Kern River. They thought they were on Frémont's Lake Fork but were a hundred miles too far south. After idling for three weeks, they broke camp, crossed a spur of mountains, and started down the valley toward Sutter's Fort. Frémont, meantime, had moved his small party to the coast. On February 11 Carson and Owens, driving fresh horses, intercepted their comrades at the mouth of the Calaveras River and conducted them to San José for the long-deferred reunion with their chief.[17]

Frémont had not completed the scientific aspects of the third expedition, but his appearance at the coastal towns marked the beginning of his immersion in the turmoil afflicting Mexican California. By February 1846, whatever contingencies and opportunities he had discussed with Senator Benton and Secretary Bancroft shadowed the further prosecution of his topographical mission.

As if sensing the shift in his preoccupations, in late January 1846 Frémont recounted his adventures in a letter to Jessie. She was to pass on to her father several things of importance, including, referring to the Indian troubles on the San Joaquin, "that I have something handsome to tell him of some exploits of Carson and Dick Owens." But the most astonishing declaration lay in a single sentence: "By the route that I have explored I can ride in thirty-five days from the *Fontaine qui Brouit* River [Fountain Creek, on the Arkansas River at Pueblo] to Captain Sutter's; and, for wagons, the road is decidedly far better."[18]

To the United States consul in Monterey, Thomas O. Larkin, Frémont spoke in even more expansive language, as Larkin advised his superiors early in March.

> Captain Frémont passed three degrees South of Fort Hall, having taken a route supposed to be a desart, which made his distance to California, eight or nine hundred miles less. He considers the distance from Independence to Monterey, about one thousand nine hundred miles. He describes the new route he followed as preferable, not only on account of the less distance, but less mountainous, with good pasture and well watered.[19]

If read literally, Frémont's letter to his wife and Larkin's report of what Frémont told him describe the route Frémont himself had explored, although endowing it with attractions hardly deserved. It originated at Bent's Fort on the Santa Fe Trail, climbed one of the highest passes in the Rockies, wended its way across the Uinta Basin and over the Wasatch Range to Great Salt Lake. It spanned the terrible salt desert west of the lake and traced a crazy pattern among the parallel ranges south of the Humboldt. It then surmounted the Sierras by the Truckee River, already the entry for emigrants but nonetheless deadly if reached too late in the season.

That so experienced an explorer as Frémont could have indulged such fancy defies reason, although his career did not lack other such fancies. To place a charitable mantle on his rhetorical ebullience, maybe he had in mind not the exact route he himself had followed but a shortening of the emigrant route already taking shape. Perhaps he did not truly mean for wagon trains to cross the Rockies and the Uinta Basin on his trail or to reach the Truckee River pathway to the Sierra summit by any way other than the Humboldt.

If valid, such a construction leaves his fine words to center on a cutoff south of Great Salt Lake. Instead of following the Oregon Trail to Fort Hall before turning southwest toward California, emigrants could eliminate a northward swing from their journey by crossing the Wasatch southwest of Bridger's Fort, tracing Great Salt Lake on the south, and making their way across the salt desert to strike the road from Fort Hall on the upper Humboldt. If this more limited interpretation is what Frémont meant (which may stretch charity too far), he still stands convicted of fancy. A few computations on his own map would have demonstrated that the route was a cutoff but not a shortcut. If the traveler had decided to bypass Bridger's Fort by taking the difficult Greenwood (or Sublette) Cutoff directly west from South Pass, the route did save 150 miles (not 900); if the traveler went by way of Bridger's Fort, which most did, it saved no miles at all. And besides, it forced an 80-mile passage of the ghastly Great Salt Lake Desert.[20]

Fortunately for Frémont, the cutoff would not bear his name. The culprit turned out to be Lansford W. Hastings, a vigorous California promoter as impulsive and fanciful as Frémont himself. He had gone to Oregon in 1842 and then to California, from which he returned home in 1844 by sea and across Mexico. In 1845 he published *The Emigrants' Guide to Oregon and California,* a successful book that motivated many to go west. Although the book referred vaguely to a new and shorter path to California, it gave no particulars. When Hastings returned to California in 1845, he went the usual way via Fort Hall. At Sutter's Fort early in 1846, he met Frémont and learned of the explorer's traverse south of Great Salt Lake. Returning east that spring in a party that included the old Ashley veteran Jim Clyman, Hastings followed Frémont's route around the south edge of the lake. Clyman was appalled that anyone could think of taking wagons this way, but the ever optimistic Hastings persuaded a number of emigrant parties and turned back to lead one himself. The Donner Party, following too far in the rear, got tangled in the Wasatch canyons, suffered appallingly on the salt desert, and reached the Sierras too late. Trapped high in the mountain snows, they endured one of the great tragedies of western history. The Hastings Cutoff fell at once into disfavor, although not entirely into disuse.[21]

ALLOWING EVEN the most expansive interpretation of what Frémont believed his government expected of him, his course in the early months of 1846 is hard to make sense of. His habit of going where and doing what he pleased, his exaggerated sense of both national and personal honor, his inflated ego, his ethnocentric contempt for native Californians, perhaps even confused uncertainty—all may have played a part. No one has ever convincingly uncovered his motives.

Frémont's appearance found California authorities feeling more than usually insecure. A revolt had expelled the governor appointed by Mexico City, Manuel Micheltorena, and substituted native Californians. The central government, feeble and torn by strife of its own, had apparently acquiesced. Pío Pico assumed the governorship in Los Angeles, while General José Castro reigned as military commandant in the north. They and lesser officials quarreled and schemed among themselves, worried that Mexico City would attempt to reassert central authority, debated what to do about the American immigrants descending from the Sierras to take up new (and illegal) homes in California, and fretted over rumors of the imperial ambitions of England, France, and the United States. And now, uninvited, came Captain Frémont, an officer of the United States Army commanding men said not to be soldiers but clearly a force of fierce, heavily armed fighters. Little wonder that California authorities reacted with suspicion.

On January 27, 1846, Frémont called on Thomas O. Larkin, Monterey merchant who doubled as United States consul in California. The next day, Larkin took Frémont to meet with General Castro and other officials. The captain explained his character as an explorer and his wish to reprovision, camp for the rest of the winter in the San Joaquin Valley distant from the settlements, and in the spring depart for home. Castro readily and courteously assented, but did not put it into writing. Even so, Frémont and Larkin regarded permission as having been granted.[22]

By mid-February, Frémont had refitted and, ignoring his assurances to Castro, set forth with this band of armed foreigners on a tour of the settlements—San José, the ocean at Santa Cruz, and the area east of Monterey in the lower Salinas Valley. This was hardly the unpeopled country of the San Joaquin Valley, and toward the inhabitants Frémont and his men acted with rough insensitivity. What he had in mind, not even Larkin could guess.

Nor could General Castro, who regarded the spectacle as insulting and, in view of the rumors of war between the United States and Mexico, provocative. On March 5 he sent an officer to order the Americans to leave California at once. Frémont affected "astonishment at General Castro's breach of good faith" and instructed the officer to return with word that "I peremptorily refused compliance to an order insulting to my Government and myself."[23]

That night Frémont led his men to the summit of a nearby mountain at the north end of the Gavilan Range. Here, overlooking the Salinas Plain and Monterey Bay, they threw up a log fort and on a sapling thrust into the soil of Mexico unfurled an American flag. "If we are unjustly attacked," Frémont advised Larkin in a penciled note slipped out on March 9, "we will fight to extremity and refuse quarter, trusting to our country to avenge our death."[24]

The affair ended as it had begun, in farce. Castro mobilized several hundred men, but mainly for show. He could not overrun the tough marksmen barricaded behind their logs with any number of men, and he never really intended to. At the same time, while Castro maneuvered and brought up cannon, Frémont awakened to the enormity of his offense. An officer of the United States had hoisted his nation's flag over foreign territory, deployed some fifty riflemen under his command, and defied the legitimate authorities to force him from their jurisdiction. That could get even a certified hero into serious trouble. Many American settlers wanted to join him, but that would have made him a revolutionist and worsened the indignity. Late on March 9, after a wind toppled the sapling, Frémont pronounced it an omen, abandoned the fort, and withdrew to the San Joaquin Valley.

The defenders of the little fort lacked Frémont's understanding of the niceties of international relations. They had cheered at the flag raising, wanted to take on the Mexicans, and saw themselves as patriots stirring a revolt of American settlers against Mexican tyranny. Some were furious at what they believed a cowardly retreat. Joe Walker quit in a rage, never to serve Frémont again. Years later, Kit Carson covered his disappointment by remarking that they left because they "had become tired of waiting for the attack of the valiant Mexican General."[25]

THE EXPEDITION RESUMED its scientific mission, moving up the Sacramento Valley with the objective of seeking a better wagon road into the Willamette Valley than afforded by the Oregon Trail. "In this way," Frémont had written Jessie on January 24, "I shall have explored from the beginning to end *this road to Oregon*."[26] After that, "we turn our faces homeward." Such may have been his intent, although he left Larkin and others with the impression that he meant to go home by way of the Colorado and Gila Rivers. Or he may have been stalling, even as he made his way slowly up the Sacramento, in hopes that events would open new opportunities to further his government's territorial ambitions.

By March 30, 1846, the expedition approached the northern limits of the Central Valley and camped at the ranch of Peter Lassen, a Dane who had settled on Deer Creek, in the shadow of Mount Lassen, two years earlier. Lassen's was but one of a series of ranches Frémont examined as he moved north along the western foothills of the Sierras and forded the numerous rivers and creeks dumping the spring runoff into the Sacramento. Although some claimed Mexican citizenship, all were of American or European origin and had begun raising crops and livestock on this remote Mexican frontier only within the past five or six years. One, Samuel Neal, had served in Frémont's second expedition and at Sutter's Fort persuaded his chief to let him stay behind as a California settler.[27]

Frémont tarried most of April at Lassen's ranch. He camped there from March 30 to April 5, took a circular six-day tour of the northern reaches of the Sacramento Valley, then camped at Lassen's for another two weeks, until April 24. Possibly he was waiting for the snow to go out of the high country, possibly for further developments in the low country.

Sometime during this period, some American settlers approached Frémont for help in attacking Indians said to be plotting a war on the valley
ranchers. Exactly what happened remains vague and confused. As Kit Carson recalled it:

> He [Frémont] and party and some few Americans that lived near
> started for the Indian encampment. Found them to be in great force,
> as was stated. They were attacked. The number killed I cannot say. It
> was a perfect butchery. Those not killed fled in all directions, and we
> returned to Lawson's [Lassen's]. Had accomplished what we went for
> and given the Indians such a chastisement that [it] would be long be-
> fore they ever again would feel like attacking the settlements.

Whether or not the Indians actually meant war cannot be known. The
attackers supposedly came on the quarry in the midst of a war dance,
which inflamed antagonisms already aroused. Contrary to Carson's memory, Frémont almost certainly did not participate, although he may have
given his men permission to volunteer if they wanted. All but four, who remained as camp guards, were said to have ridden with the settlers.

Kit Carson's unfeeling recital of the event betrays his own attitude toward Indians and doubtless that of his comrades. Ever since Jedediah
Smith's time, travelers through the mountains between the Sacramento
and the Willamette, even the Hudson's Bay trappers, had tangled with the
small tribes that lived along the way. Each side perpetrated aggressions on
the other, and each remained wary of the other. With settlers now invading
the upper Sacramento Valley, the Indians must have felt doubly threatened
and may have intended violence. Such slaughter, however, prefigured the
indiscriminate carnage that, with the onset of the gold rush three years
later, nearly annihilated the Indian population of California.[28]

Taking leave of Peter Lassen on April 24, Frémont and his men crossed
the northern spurs of the Sierras to the plains beyond, a rough country
spotted with plateaus, buttes, tule marshes, and lava flows. Turning north,
they struck the upper Pit River, which in its course to the Sacramento separates Mount Shasta and the Cascade Range from the Sierras. On farther
north, in early May they came to Klamath Lake. Frémont had sought it un-
successfully in 1843. Now he identified it as the source of the Klamath
River, which scours a tortuous gorge north of Mount Shasta to reach the
ocean just south of the California boundary. In 1827 Jedediah Smith had
found its lower course a traveler's nightmare.

Frémont intended to camp on the western shore of Klamath Lake until
the snow receded on the Cascade Range, rising immediately to the west. He

wanted to explore, map, and have Kern sketch these rugged slopes, hitherto known only to Indians and Hudson's Bay Company brigades.

Klamath Lake, full of fish and attracting game, supported a sizable population of Klamath Indians. They had shadowed the expedition but had not caused trouble. The whites had even conducted a trading session with them, although neither side relaxed vigilance. Frémont regarded them as unfriendly.

On the night of May 8, two exhausted men dragged into camp on exhausted horses. One was Samuel Neal, Frémonter turned rancher; the other was Levi Sigler. They had ridden one hundred miles in two days with word that a United States officer followed with a pouch of dispatches. He was Lieutenant Archibald H. Gillespie of the U.S. Marine Corps, and he had arrived at Lassen's ranch eight days after Frémont's departure. Aware of Indian dangers, Neal, Lassen, Sigler, and two others had volunteered to escort Gillespie to Frémont, and Neal and Sigler had rushed ahead to overtake him. En route, Indians had given chase, which seemed ominous for Gillespie and the three men with him. Neal and Sigler believed it already too late to save them.

Hastily, Frémont assembled a relief party and at dawn dashed off to Gillespie's succor. Riding with him were Carson, Owens, Godey, Lajeunesse, Maxwell, Joseph Stepperfeldt, and four Delawares.[29] By afternoon, after a ride of forty-five miles, they halted in a forest-bordered meadow opening on Klamath Lake. This was the first water Gillespie would find on Frémont's trail, and Frémont knew he must come here, as in fact he and his companions did only hours later.

That night the two officers sat at the campfire as the marine related all he knew. He had left Washington the previous November and traveled incognito across Mexico, then sailed in a U.S. naval vessel by way of the Sandwich Islands to Monterey, which he reached on April 17. War had not broken out when he left Mexico, but it seemed imminent. Commodore John D. Sloat, commander of the navy's Pacific Squadron, had orders to seize California's ports if war erupted. Moreover, Gillespie had delivered a message from Secretary of State James Buchanan to Consul Larkin appointing him a "confidential agent" with instructions to keep a close eye on the British and spread word among the Californians that they "would be received as brethren" into the American union should they so desire. What else Gillespie related to Frémont, and what the packet of letters from Benton and Jessie contained, have been fiercely debated ever since.[30]

Far into the night, Frémont sat at the campfire studying the letters from home and pondering what he had learned from Gillespie. Once, alerted by restless mules, he went to check the stock. Back at the fire he made his decision, as he recalled it forty years later:

> I saw the way opening clear before me. War with Mexico was inevitable; and a grand opportunity now presented itself to realize in their fullest extent the far-sighted views of Senator Benton, and make the Pacific Ocean the western boundary of the United States. I resolved to move forward on the opportunity and return forthwith to the Sacramento valley in order to bring to bear all the influences I could command.[31]

His course decided, Frémont rolled into his blanket under overhanging cedar boughs and drifted toward sleep. Except for the night on Antelope Island in Great Salt Lake, he later ruefully conceded, this was the only night he had ever failed to post guards in Indian country.

IN THE CHILL NIGHT Kit Carson and Dick Owens lay wrapped in their saddle blankets next to one of the three campfires. Aroused by a thumping sound nearby, Carson called to ask what was the matter. He saw at once, and he and Owens jumped up and shouted, "Indians!" Everyone rolled out and scrambled for their weapons. One of the Delawares seized an unprimed rifle and tried to fire into the darkness as five arrows smashed into his chest.

Led by a chief brandishing a tomahawk, Klamaths charged into the camp circle. Carson fired his pistol, but the ball only severed the cord holding the tomahawk. Maxwell fired and hit the chief in the leg, and as he turned Stepperfeldt sent a ball through his back and into his heart. Their chief dead, the rest of the attackers hastily retreated. "He was the bravest Indian I ever saw," said Carson.

For the rest of the night, the Klamaths shot arrows into the camp, most of which were deflected by blankets hung for the purpose. Owens had run out and driven the mules within rifle range, and the warriors left them alone. Several times, however, they tried to retrieve the body of their chief, but each time fell back before the rifle fire of the defenders.

By dawn the Klamaths had vanished, and the whites counted their casualties—three killed and one wounded. The most grievous loss was Basil Lajeunesse, veteran of all three Frémont expeditions, skilled mountaineer, and valued friend of all. The sound of an axe splitting his skull had awakened Carson to give the alarm. Enraged, Carson seized the chief's tomahawk and smashed in his head, while the Delaware chief Sagundai ripped off his scalp.[32]

"The event cast an angry gloom over our little camp," wrote Frémont. "For the moment I threw all other considerations aside and determined to square accounts with these people before I left them."

He did. Retracing the trail to the base camp, Frémont mobilized his little army and circled around the north shore of Klamath Lake, heading for the principal Klamath town. It lay on the lakeshore across a river entering from the north. Approaching on the morning of May 13, Frémont sent Carson and Owens with nine men to reconnoiter. The warriors already waited in defensive positions as this advance guard forded the river. A storm of arrows greeted them, and they could not respond because they had got their powder wet in the river. Frémont and the main command, however, charged into the fray. Arrows proved no match for the rifles, and soon the warriors ran from the field, leaving fourteen dead behind. The victors fired the village and food stocks of the Klamaths.

In the afternoon, the Frémonters made camp on the east side of Klamath Lake. Someone reported Indians in the nearby forest. Frémont took Carson, Sagundai, and three others to investigate. In a grove of timber, they came suddenly on a Klamath warrior. He stood with a poison-tipped arrow drawn tautly in his bow and aimed directly at Carson's chest. Carson drew down on the Indian, but his rifle snapped. Frémont fired but missed. Instantly the captain's renowned white horse, Sacramento, leaped on the Indian and threw him to the ground. The arrow went wild. Sagundai slipped swiftly off his horse and clubbed the Klamath to death. "It was the work of a moment," wrote Frémont, "but it was a narrow chance for Carson. The poisoned arrow would have gone through his body."[33]

On this very day, May 13, 1846, a continent away, President James K. Polk signed a declaration of war on Mexico.

17

KIT CARSON:

THE CONTINENT SPANNED

IT CARSON'S LOYALTY to John C. Frémont knew no limits. He served his chief capably, faithfully, courageously—and unquestioningly. So did the rest of the Frémonters, former trappers and voyageurs of the beaver era. Only Joe Walker had exhibited a tendency to independence, which blew up with finality after the affair on Gavilan Mountain. Carson, Owens, and Godey appealed to Frémont's romantic instincts, and his prose (and Jessie's) bathed them in a heroic glow that made Carson, at least, a national idol.

Nor were the tributes self-serving press-agentry. Frémont and Carson esteemed each other's special talents, and their shared hardships, dangers, and tilts with death had cemented bonds of friendship.

On three expeditions, Carson had contributed to Frémont's success. He had shown the way as well as how to live in comparative comfort along the way. He had scouted ahead for campsites and eligible trails in deserts, plateaus, canyons, and mountains. He had braved extremes of weather and terrain ranging from the shimmering salt flats to the snow-choked Sierras. And he had fought Indians with consummate skill, sometimes with warrant, sometimes without.

In Frémont's triumphs of 1842–46, Kit Carson played a distinguished part. Now, with his chief, he shed the mantle of explorer and donned the mantle of imperialist. Carson's role now was to aid Frémont, in whatever way directed, to "make the Pacific Ocean the western boundary of the United States."

Kit Carson (right) *and John C. Frémont* (left) *exemplified the union of mountain man and professional military topographer. The mountain man possessed the ability to pilot the scientific cartographer throughout the West. Through the army specialist, therefore, the knowledge of the mountain specialist reached the outside world. Carson served Frémont in his expeditions of 1842, 1843–44, and 1845–46. The two became fast friends, and Frémont's publications made Carson a national hero. Engravings from Frémont's memoirs.* COURTESY DENVER PUBLIC LIBRARY, WESTERN HISTORY DEPARTMENT.

THE MEXICAN WAR sprang mainly from the quarrel over Texas. With the annexation of Texas early in July 1845 and the posting of General Zachary Taylor's army to Corpus Christi, the United States acquired a land Mexico still claimed. When Taylor moved to the Rio Grande in March 1846, he took new positions 150 miles south of the line Mexico regarded as the southern boundary of Texas.

The insult was too grievous to be borne. On April 25, 1846, a Mexican force bloodied a contingent of United States dragoons on the north side of the Rio Grande, and on May 8–9 the two armies collided in the battles of Palo Alto and Resaca de la Palma. On May 11, word of the attack on the dragoons having reached Washington on the eighth, Polk sent a message to Congress alleging that Mexico had "shed American blood on American soil" and calling for a declaration of war.

On May 13, 1846, as Frémont and Kit Carson fought Klamath Indians on the other side of the continent, James K. Polk signed the declaration of war on Mexico.[1]

Polk badly wanted California, less to satisfy the land hunger of agrarian emigrants than to serve maritime interests by extending American sovereignty over the great harbors of San Francisco and San Diego. For decades, New England traders and navigators had understood, and conveyed to national leaders, their nation's vital stake in the California ports and, in the Oregon country, Puget Sound. The power that controlled those harbors would dominate the lucrative trade of the Orient. Even as war erupted with Mexico, Puget Sound lay at the heart of negotiations for an Oregon boundary treaty. New Mexico's value, aside for the commerce of the Santa Fe Trail, lay largely in establishing a land connection with the distant California ports. Before the outbreak of war, Polk had tried to buy California and New Mexico, but political turmoil in Mexico City made it increasingly evident that no Mexican government could part with Mexican territory and remain in power.

Although Polk could be charged with unduly provoking Mexico, he could justify a war over Texas, now plainly American territory. He could not, however, openly avow California and New Mexico as war aims. Public opinion and party politics condoned purchase but not military conquest. Never, therefore, did Polk admit any other objective of the war than the reestablishment of peace. His hope, instead, was that the war would produce a peace in which California and New Mexico fell to the United States not by conquest but by purchase—in dollars, in reparations for a war begun by Mexico, in assumption of the claims of American citizens against Mexico, or in a combination of all. This goal would best be served if the Mexican citizens themselves declared independence and sought union with the United States—a fair prospect in California if not in New Mexico. Failing that, American conquerors would avoid any suggestion of annexation and simply set up temporary governments to rule until a peace treaty resolved the issue of sovereignty.[2]

In distant California, Polk's blueprint fell victim to the political turbulence of native Californios, the anxieties and pugnacity of American immigrants, and the clashing egos and ambitions of American military leaders. In the forefront of the last rode Captain John C. Frémont. At his side rode Kit Carson, drawn by no motive more complicated than loyal obedience to his chief.

RETURNING FROM THE KLAMATH COUNTRY late in May 1846, Frémont injected himself into political chaos. Factions of native Californians intensified their usual quarrels: General Castro versus Governor Pico, north versus south, civil versus military, and increasingly California versus Mexico City. With the central government distracted by its own revolutionary tumult and entangled in an emotional confrontation with the United States, to many the time seemed ripe for breaking away from Mexico.

The American presence heightened tensions. "Confidential Agent" Larkin quietly encouraged leading Californios to declare independence and peacefully join with the United States—an effort already overtaken by the war of which none yet knew. U.S. warships lay at anchor in Monterey and San Francisco Bays, ominous reminders of American power. Lieutenant Gillespie's cover as an American businessman fooled no one. When he set out in pursuit of Frémont, none doubted that his assignment was to recall the explorer to a military mission. And when Frémont camped on May 30 at the "Three Buttes," in the Sacramento Valley fifty miles north of Sutter's Fort, none doubted that he had thrown himself into the seething mix.

American immigrants spotted the neighborhood of Sutter's Fort, uncertain of their future. Rumors boiling out of the coastal settlements proclaimed that General Castro was inciting the Indians to attack them and, even more alarming, gathering a force to expel them from California. Instead, he was mobilizing to topple Governor Pico, but the rumors gained credibility because the immigrants had in fact entered California illegally. The Americans looked to Captain Frémont for leadership and protection.[3]

Probably by early June 1846, Frémont and Gillespie had agreed to do what they could to stir up a revolution, preferably by goading Castro into a rash move that would justify an organized self-defense. They would move discreetly and ambiguously in case war failed to erupt and ratify their actions. If Frémont urged his countrymen to take up arms, he did it quietly and deniably. His very presence with a tough, well-armed force, however, persuaded the Americans of his sympathy and emboldened them to act before Castro swooped down on them.

The immigrants near Sutter's Fort were a diverse lot. Many were would-be farmers who had trekked overland from Missouri or come down from Oregon. Others were sailors who had jumped ship. But many too were old mountaineers, seeking new lives now that the beaver no longer sustained their way of life. Job Dye, once a mountaineer himself but now a substantial California citizen, characterized them as "dare-devil hunters and trappers . . . who had no care on their minds and nothing to lose, in a free fight or a footrace. These men were inured to the toils and hardships of a Pioneer life and were, withal, genuine Americans, ever vigilant to the honor of the 'Old Flag' and the interests of Uncle Sam."[4]

Such were Kit Carson, Alexis Godey, and Dick Owens, and such were others of the Frémonters. The former mountaineers joined with the overlanders to make a farcical revolution but then, under United States authority, helped engineer the American conquest of California.

One of these ex-trappers was Ezekiel Merritt—"Stuttering Merritt," Job Dye called him. "Fearless and simple," said Frémont, "and not given to asking questions when there was something he was required to do. Merritt was my Field-Lieutenant among the settlers."[5]

As Frémont's unquestioning lieutenant among the settlers, "Captain" Merritt must have borne his blessing when he set forth with a squad of twelve men to thwart Castro's supposed design. On June 10 they fell on a small detachment of soldiers driving two hundred horses from Sonoma by way of Sutter's Fort to Castro's headquarters in Santa Clara. Rumor said Castro intended to mount his long-expected offensive against the Americans, although the horses were instead part of the mobilization against Governor Pico. Merritt's men happily made off with the horses while sending the escort to invite the general, if he wanted them back, to come get them. The revolution had begun.[6]

Next, according to Frémont, "I sent Merritt into Sonoma instructed to surprise the garrison at that place."[7] At dawn on June 14, his force now grown to thirty, Merritt trotted into Sonoma. "They were about as rough-looking a set of men as could be imagined," declared one of them.[8] They surrounded the home of General Mariano Guadalupe Vallejo, commandant of the northern frontier and the best friend Americans had among the Californios. He favored annexation to the United States. The insurgents, vague in their objectives, spent much of the day talking with Vallejo and gulping his brandy. Jacob Leese, ex–mountain man and brother-in-law of Vallejo, interpreted. Finally, seizing all the arms and horses they could find, Merritt and about half of the Americans packed Vallejo, Leese, and several others off to Frémont's camp, now on the American River near Sutter's Fort.

In Sonoma, leadership fell to William B. Ide, a New England farmer who had come to California with the immigration of 1845. He promptly drew up a proclamation, like Castro's heavy in rhetoric and light in substance. His men also hoisted over Sonoma a hastily stitched flag bearing the crude design of an animal that the insurgents said was a bear but that locals likened to a pig. The short-lived Bear Flag Republic had been launched—an ironic irrelevancy in light of the outbreak of the Mexican War a month earlier.

To Vallejo, Frémont denied any responsibility for the seizure of Castro's horses, now pastured under Frémont's rifles, or for the descent on Sonoma. At the same time, he ordered Vallejo and his companions confined in Sutter's Fort, where they remained for nearly two months.

Contrary to his disclaimers, Frémont almost certainly sanctioned the raid on the horse herd and the occupation of Sonoma. In capturing and confining Vallejo and other officials, an ignoble action in view of their pro-American sympathies, Frémont apparently hoped to provoke Castro into moving against the Americans and thus justifying an open intervention in behalf of his countrymen. He could then organize the Americans, bolster them with his own men, and take command.[9]

Whether so explicitly plotted, this is the way it worked out. Castro formed three forces, a total of some 260 men, and dispatched them toward Sonoma to attack Ide and his insurgents. Only one, numbering 50 or 60 men under Captain Joaquin de la Torre, actually crossed San Francisco Bay and deployed northward toward Sonoma. The rest gathered at San Pablo. At the same time, another, less disciplined force of about 25 under José Carillo had been ranging west of Sonoma. These two units joined just before an American contingent of 17 attacked at dawn on June 24. After a brief exchange of gunfire, the Mexicans withdrew.

Already, Frémont had judged conditions ripe for his intervention. The day after the skirmish with Torre, Frémont and ninety men rode into Sonoma. Castro had mobilized a major offensive against the Americans, Frémont reasoned, and they had called on him for aid and leadership. He undertook this role, he proclaimed, on his own responsibility, without orders from his government.

For the next week, with Frémont in the lead, the insurgent force marched and countermarched in great confusion in the valleys draining into San Pablo Bay and on the Marin Peninsula. The Mexicans did the same. Finally, Torre embarked at Sausalito and recrossed the bay.

For the moment, at least, the war appeared to be ended. After a rousing Fourth of July celebration at Sonoma, on July 5 the Americans gathered to plan the next step. Frémont took command, and all voted to date California independence from this event rather than the hoisting of the Bear Flag on June 14. With Frémont as "Oso Numero Uno" and Gillespie as second Bear, a four-company battalion was organized. Three, mainly composed of immigrants, elected their captains. To lead the fourth, the mountaineers, Frémont appointed Dick Owens. The battalion, about 225 strong, moved to Frémont's base camp on the American River.

Frémont's luck held. Even the most generous interpretation of what Gillespie may have communicated did not authorize Frémont to lead a filibustering expedition against a foreign government. But fortune relieved him and his government of acute embarrassment. On July 10, a courier rode into Frémont's camp near Sutter's Fort with word that on the seventh Commodore Sloat had raised the American flag over Monterey. The flag also went up at Yerba Buena and Sonoma, where it replaced the short-lived Bear Flag. War, long expected, was now a fact in California.

No longer need Frémont fear for his commission in the United States Army. He had gambled that war would cover his filibustering course, and he had won.

IN THE SHORT BEAR FLAG INTERVAL, Frémont and Kit Carson shared in a deed that stains the reputation of both. On June 19 Ide sent two men, George Fowler and Thomas Cowie, north from Sonoma to obtain gunpowder on the Russian River. José Carillo's partisans captured the pair and put them to death, reportedly with excruciating deliberation. All the Bear Flaggers, including Frémont and Carson, burned for revenge.

Sometime during the late-June maneuvers that ended when the little Californio army withdrew south across San Francisco Bay, a rowboat carrying three men landed at the San Rafael embarcadero, where Frémont had camped. They were an elderly Santa Clara rancher and his twin nephews of twenty years' age. Kit Carson and two Bear Flaggers seized the trio and pronounced them spies bearing a communication from General Castro to Captain de la Torre, which they probably were not. Carson rode to ask Frémont what should be done with them. Frémont answered: "Mr. Carson, I have no use for prisoners—do your duty."

He did. He and his companions promptly shot and killed the three Californios.

Even in the midst of war, and even had the victims been enemy couriers, this act was reprehensible. Rage over the brutal slaying of Fowler and Cowie set the context but hardly excused the offense. Carson's blind loyalty to his chief is a factor, but only scant mitigation. As the responsible commander, Frémont bears the heaviest guilt, but enough splashes on Carson to brand him the perpetrator of an iniquitous deed.[10]

ON JULY 19, 1846, Bear Flagger No. 1 paraded his motley battalion in the streets of Monterey—two companies of immigrants and one of Frémonters, about 170 strong. Frémont rode at their head with an escort of Delaware Indians, followed by his mountaineers. A naval officer recorded the scene in his diary:

They defiled, two abreast, through the principal street of the town. The ground seemed to tremble under their heavy tramp. The citizens glanced at them through their grated windows. Their rifles, revolving pistols, and long knives, glittered over the dusky buckskin which enveloped their sinewy limbs, while their untrimmed locks, flowing out from under their foraging caps, and their black beards, with white teeth glittering through, gave them a wild savage aspect.[11]

An English naval officer was similarly impressed. "Here were true trappers," he marveled, "the class that produced Fenimore Cooper's best works." Among them, he noted, were some "who enjoy a high reputation in the Prairies. Kit Carsons is as well known there as the Duke [of Wellington] is in Europe."[12]

Frémont's interview with Commodore Sloat went badly. Elderly, ill, and overly cautious, Sloat had procrastinated in occupying Monterey, and now he was appalled to learn that Frémont had incited an American uprising without proper authority. Moreover, Sloat had no plans to operate ashore, which left no role for Frémont.

The prospect, however, was hardly grim. Sloat's replacement, Commodore Robert F. Stockton, had already arrived in the Monterey harbor. (He had come to act as second-in-command, only to learn of Sloat's resolve to relinquish command and go home to retirement.) Bold, decisive, vain, abrasive, and politically well connected, the new naval commander meant to conquer and rule California in the fullest sense. He approached this self-defined mission without regard for the lawful limits of his own authority or the sensibilities of the proud Californios. His bellicose proclamation on assuming command, in contrast to Sloat's moderation, dashed the hopes of Sloat and Larkin for a peaceful transfer of sovereignty.

Unlike Sloat, Stockton did intend to operate on land, with his own sailors and marines and whatever volunteers Frémont could enlist. On July 23 the commodore established the "California Battalion of United States Troops," with Frémont as major and Gillespie as captain and second-in-command. This arrangement mobilized a land force under naval authority and subordinated an army officer to a naval superior, which would later beget severe complications in both California and Washington. More to the point, in each other Stockton and Frémont found kindred souls.[13]

Stockton's challenge lay in southern California, less sympathetic to Americans than northern. Castro had hurried to Los Angeles, made his peace with Governor Pico, and tried to gather an army. Because Castro lacked money and the support of the central government, this proved impossible. Castro offered to negotiate, but Stockton set unacceptable conditions. The navy landed Frémont's battalion at San Diego and a contingent of sailors and marines at San Pedro. Early in August the two forces advanced inland as Castro and Pico fled toward Sonora. On August 13 both forces paraded in the streets of Los Angeles.

As John Bidwell summed up the services of the California Battalion, "We simply marched all over California from Sonoma to San Diego and raised the American flag without opposition or protest. We tried to find an enemy, but could not."[14]

California had fallen, Stockton exulted in a personal letter to President Polk penned at Los Angeles on August 26. "My word is at present the law of the land. My person is more than regal." Preparing to embark his squadron soon (he did not divulge his scheme to land a force at Acapulco, on the west coast of Mexico, and drive toward Mexico City), he said he intended to appoint Frémont governor of the territory and Gillespie secretary. "They both understand the people and their language and I think are eminently qualified to perform the duties." Frémont, Stockton concluded, "will send this letter with my despatches to the Secretary of the Navy, by Express over the mountains."[15]

To carry out this daunting mission, Frémont chose Kit Carson, both "to insure the safety and speedy delivery of these important papers, and as a reward for brave and valuable service on many occasions." En route, he could pause briefly in Taos to see Josefa but must travel rapidly enough to reach Washington in sixty days. There he was to call on Senator Benton, who would take him to see the President and the Secretary of the Navy. Thus he could personally fill in all the detail and background left unstated in the official documents. "It was a service of high trust and honor," pronounced Frémont, "but one of great danger also."[16]

On September 5, 1846, with fifteen men and fifty mules loaded with dried meat and corn, Kit Carson rode out of the pueblo of Los Angeles to span the continent.[17]

CARSON HAD TRAVELED the same trail before, with Ewing Young in 1829–31—across the Mojave Desert and the Colorado River, up the Gila to the Santa Rita Copper Mines, and down to the Rio Grande. With his squad of experienced mountaineers, including his old comrade Lucien Maxwell, he made good time. Even so, they pushed hard enough to wear out or slaughter for food thirty-four of the fifty mules.

A month out of Los Angeles, Carson's expressmen descended from the mountains and turned up the Rio Grande. Riding north on the morning of October 6, they had reached a point about three miles south of Socorro when they met a big cavalcade of horsemen advancing through clouds of dust. With a true trapper's greeting, Carson and his men broke into a gallop and yipped and yelled their way to the head of the column.

Three hundred United States dragoons plodded down the valley on mules, followed by a wagon train hauling provisions, and accompanied by a contingent of topographical engineers. Carson and his charging horsemen reined in to be welcomed by Brigadier General Stephen Watts Kearny and his chief guide and scout, Tom Fitzpatrick.

The "Army of the West" had conquered New Mexico. Now it headed west to conquer California.[18]

THE OUTBREAK of the Mexican War in May 1846 found Tom Fitzpatrick in St. Louis, where he eagerly awaited the outcome of Senator Benton's latest effort to have an Indian agency created for the Great Plains and Fitzpatrick appointed agent. Prospects looked promising. War intervened, however, and June found the veteran guide again a guide.

Colonel Stephen Watts Kearny led the Army of the West. A beardless, thin-lipped veteran of thirty-four years in the regular army, a field soldier of outstanding competence, a sagacious leader who could be relied on to accomplish his mission, he had commanded the First Regiment of Dragoons for ten years. The army contained no officer better fitted to head the Army of the West.

As General Zachary Taylor drove deep into Mexico, Kearny had been ordered to march overland to seize New Mexico and California. Throughout the summer of 1846, roiling clouds of dust nearly obscured the Santa Fe Trail as Kearny's army of seventeen hundred regulars and volunteers with artillery, supply wagons, horses, mules, and cattle strung out from Fort Leavenworth to Bent's Fort in units spaced to minimize the impact on grass, timber, and water.[19]

At Bent's Fort, Kearny added Fitzpatrick to his headquarters group; the two had worked well together in the dragoon circuit of the plains in 1845. Here too Fitzpatrick learned that Senator Benton had succeeded. An Upper Platte and Arkansas Indian agency would be created and Fitzpatrick named as agent. That assignment, however, could be delayed if Fitzpatrick wanted to stay with the army. He did, although he predicted "that there would not be a blow struck at santafee whatever may be the case elsewhere."[20]

Fitzpatrick's forecast proved accurate. After a perfunctory effort to organize a defense, Governor Manuel Armijo fled. On August 18, 1846, the advance guard of the Army of the West trooped into the plaza of the New Mexican capital and raised the American flag over the decrepit "Palace of the Governors." Kearny installed a temporary civil government and, muddling presidential policy, proclaimed New Mexico annexed to the United States.[21]

In Santa Fe Fitzpatrick pondered whether to continue with the army to California. The troops, he observed, did not look forward to the hardships of the march, and he thought it would have been better to send an invasion force by sea. Kearny released Fitzpatrick to return and take up the duties of his new post but then changed his mind, and Fitzpatrick resolved to stick with the general as long as his services were wanted. "I hold it a high honor," he declared in burst of sentiment that would have done Frémont credit, "to belong to the advance guard of that American army which will have the glory of planting the stars and stripes on the shores of the Pacific."[22]

Leaving Missouri volunteers to hold New Mexico, Kearny, now a brigadier general, led three hundred dragoons south from Santa Fe on September 25, 1846. Fitzpatrick rode as guide, and Antoine Robidoux, Taos trapper since 1825, as interpreter. On October 6, on the Rio Grande three miles below Socorro, they met Kit Carson and his band of expressmen.

What took place between Kit Carson and General Kearny on that day as the army continued the march down the Rio Grande laid the basis for controversy, confusion, misrepresentation, bitterness, and volumes of verbiage. Carson showed the general his dispatches, especially Commodore Stockton's letter to the president, and related the cheering news that California had fallen to United States forces and Frémont was soon to become governor by appointment of Stockton. Carson's mission now, he emphasized, was to get these dispatches through to the president within the coming month, as he had promised Frémont.

By evening, when the column camped in the valley ten miles below Socorro, Kearny had resolved on a critical change of plans. He no longer needed to take a fighting force across the difficult country to California. Only he, directed by the president to organize a civil government in California, need continue, with a sufficient escort to deter Indian raiders. He would send two hundred dragoons back to Santa Fe and proceed with the remaining one hundred.

Since Carson had just come from California and knew the route intimately, Kearny directed him to hand over the dispatches to Fitzpatrick, who would hasten them to Washington, and turn back to lead the general and his escort to California. Carson objected; Frémont had charged him personally with this mission, and he felt honor-bound to carry it out himself. Kearny insisted, however, and Carson relented.

Later, when Kearny and Frémont collided, with Senator Benton Frémont's shrill advocate, the events of October 6, 1846, became hotly debated issues. How hard Carson resisted, how hard Kearny pressed, and how justified was Kearny's decision stirred angry exchanges. Although Carson clearly wanted to go on to Washington and said so, he did as he was told without unseemly dispute. He could hardly deny Fitzpatrick's competence to complete the assignment, nor his own unique qualifications to guide Kearny over the return trail to California. And although military strategy lay beyond his responsibility, Carson surely recognized the folly of trying to get three hundred dragoons down the Gila and across the California deserts when one hundred would do.[23]

KEARNY'S FIVE-HUNDRED-MILE MARCH from the Rio Grande to the Colorado is less important as a military feat than as a geographical and scientific achievement. Although a punishing ordeal for men and animals, it afforded the Topographical Corps an opportunity to examine and map a country suddenly of strategic importance but hitherto unknown to any but the Indian inhabitants and a handful of Hispanic frontiersmen and American trappers.

Heading the topographical contingent that accompanied Kearny from Fort Leavenworth to Santa Fe was Lieutenant William H. Emory, a distinguished officer destined to rival Frémont in scientific contributions. With impressive red beard, military bearing, and cultured demeanor, he ranked among Colonel Abert's most prominent officers. Reporting to Emory were Lieutenants James W. Abert and William G. Peck, who with the aid of Tom Fitzpatrick had explored the Canadian River in 1845, and Lieutenant William H. Warner. Abert and Peck, ill when Kearny marched for California, stayed behind to prepare a comprehensive map of New Mexico. Warner went with Emory to the Pacific.

One of Kearny's objectives was to open a wagon road to the Pacific. Even in the Rio Grande valley, however, the supply train slowed the march. Carson declared that getting the wagons over the mountains and down the Gila to California would take four months. Reluctantly, the general sent back for packsaddles, had the wagons unhitched and left for later retrieval, and proceeded with a mule train. At the same time, he issued orders for another unit following on his trail to find a way for wagons.

This unit was the Mormon Battalion—four hundred men of the Church of Jesus Christ of Latter Day Saints. They had pledged military service in exchange for passage to California while Brigham Young readied his flock for migration to some corner of the West where the Saints could escape persecution. Captain Philip St. George Cooke, another of the army's brighter lights, commanded the battalion. He was a dragoon, not a topographical engineer, but he claimed a superior intellect and enough engineering skill to gather useful geographical information as he herded his unorthodox, cantankerous battalion across the desert. Besides, he relied on three of the most knowledgeable guides in New Mexico, all veteran trappers: Pauline Weaver, Antoine Leroux, and Jean Baptiste Charbonneau, the last the son of Sacagawea of Lewis and Clark fame.[24]

Even for mules burdened by packs rather than wagons, the march of Kearny's dragoons turned into a test of endurance. Starving on thin grass, struggling in rough, sandy terrain, mules dropped by the dozen. The dragoons walked, leading their emaciated mounts. "The prospect is dreary in the extreme," lamented an officer in his diary on November 6. "Our only hope is to find things better than our guide has represented: although thus far we have found him truthful and trustworthy." Kit Carson was both, and things only got worse.[25]

Indians enlivened the march. Apaches greeted the soldiers cordially. On October 20, near the Copper Mines, Kearny parleyed with the powerful Mimbres chief Mangas Coloradas. They exchanged professions of friendship, and Mangas promised to send some of his young men to guide Captain Cooke's wagon train around the mountains to the south and back to the Gila. Henceforth, the chief pledged, Americans in small parties could travel through Apache country without fear and if in want obtain food and horses from their Indian friends. With twinkling eye, Carson turned to Emory and remarked, "I would not trust one of them."[26]

Down the Gila, where it burst from the mountains and opened on a cactus-studded desert, the soldiers found a warm and more tangible welcome from the Pimas and Maricopas. These friendly agrarian folk shared with the soldiers a bounty of corn, beans, and melons.

For Lieutenant Emory and his topographical unit, the march of Kearny's dragoons led into a singular land that demanded more exhaustive examination than the hurried pace allowed. Emory shot astronomical readings and made notes on the topography, the geology, the soil, the flora and fauna, the Indians, and the remnants of earlier civilizations. Mounds of pottery shards, crumbling adobe structures, and other litter of the past intrigued the officers and prompted speculation on their origins. The imposing Casa Grande ruin in particular impressed them, at once suggesting association with Montezuma. They could find no Indian who had ever heard the word "Montezuma."

Lieutenants Emory and Warner benefited from Kit Carson's knowledge and experience, but he was Kearny's guide, not theirs. Carson rode with and counseled the general, leaving to Emory's men the role he had played with Frémont. Emory relied mainly on one of his mule herders, François de Van Coeur, who had trapped the Gila and Verde Rivers (and fought with Apaches) as recently as 1844.[27]

Emory's scientific interlude, so significant for the postwar years, ended abruptly as the command neared the mouth of the Gila on November 22. A reconnoitering party scooped up four Mexicans driving a horse herd and the next day intercepted an official dispatch rider from Los Angeles to Sonora. Carson could scarcely believe what the captives told and the dispatches confirmed. California had not fallen after all. Californios had risen and thrown off "the detestable Anglo-Yankee yoke."

Henceforth, although Emory continued to record such data as time permitted, Kearny moved swiftly and grimly in discharge of his military assignment.

Meantime, Captain Cooke and the Mormon Battalion labored somewhere in the rear. The Apache guides promised by Mangas Coloradas never appeared, and his own guides turned out to be ignorant of the only country through which wagons could be maneuvered. Leroux, Weaver, and Charbonneau knew the Gila and its northern tributaries but not the upper reaches of its southern tributaries. As the captain wrote in his diary, "Where is water or our most advisable course? Heaven knows! We are exploring an unknown country with wagons."[28]

The true guides appeared two days later in the persons of a Mexican trading party. They told Cooke that he would have to take his wagons on a long swing to the south to get around a series of parallel mountain ranges. Then he could turn back north, by way of the Mexican frontier town of Tucson, and pick up Kearny's trail down the Gila. This is what he did. With some variations, Cooke's Wagon Road would become a major postwar thoroughfare to California.

Lieutenant Emory's work, buttressed by the work of Cooke and Abert and Peck, proved of large significance. No topographical officer had ever surveyed south of the Colorado River, and the descriptions and maps that resulted from these expeditions exposed a vast land virtually unknown to Americans. More immediately, what Emory learned on the Gila and Cooke south of the Gila bore decisively on the boundary negotiations of the Treaty of Guadalupe Hidalgo, ending the war. In this strategic belt of territory, Emory proclaimed, lay the only feasible southern route for a transcontinental railroad.[29]

As General Kearny now knew, California had blown up in Commodore Stockton's face. The arrogant naval officer believed, as he had informed President Polk, that his person was "more than regal" and his word the "law of the land," but he was wrong. Adding further insult to the touchy citizenry, Stockton made Lieutenant Gillespie a captain and placed him in command of U.S. land forces in southern California, with headquarters in Los Angeles. Vain, ambitious, overbearing, with red hair and beard topping a tall frame, he could not have been a worse choice. Like Stockton, Gillespie disdained Mexicans. His administration, a military tyranny fraught with a host of silly regulations, infuriated the firebrands and alienated the compliant. With less than fifty men, mostly sailors and marines, even a benign Gillespie would have had a hard time controlling Los Angeles.

Gillespie could not rely on Frémont for help. Although appointed military commandant for all California, Frémont had marched the California Battalion back to Sutter's Fort to try, vainly, to find another seven hundred men for Stockton's scheme to invade Mexico by way of Acapulco. As Frémont marched north, the commodore sailed north, to concentrate his warships in San Francisco Bay and organize the assault on Acapulco.

Stockton's extravagant plans collapsed in the events of one week at the end of September 1846. On the twenty-third a Californio force of about 150 revolted in Los Angeles. After a week of bloodless maneuvers, Gillespie surrendered, evacuated the pueblo, and embarked his troops on a naval vessel. By October 1, Stockton held northern California, exactly the territory he had held, with the help of the Frémonters and Bear Flaggers, on the summer day when he assumed command from Sloat in Monterey Bay.

By early December, as Kearny and his weary little army of dragoons neared the California settlements, Stockton had made hardly any progress toward recovering his lost domain. He and his shipboard forces held a toehold in San Diego, but an effort to retake Los Angeles had failed. At Monterey, Frémont had filled out his California Battalion to more than four hundred and begun a march southward. (He had also picked up a commission of lieutenant colonel in the regular army, conferred by President Polk, doubtless with some coaching from Senator Benton.) Except for San Diego, therefore, all southern California fell under the military dominion of General José María Flores and about four hundred Californios. Although many of these lacked martial fervor, many too were superb horsemen, poorly equipped with firearms but wielding pennoned lances with deadly skill.[30]

KIT CARSON HAD NEVER FOLLOWED the direct route from the mouth of the Gila to San Diego. With Los Angeles in Mexican control, however, Kearny's course lay this way rather than by the northward circuit to the Mojave Desert and the San Bernardino Valley. From the same Mexican riders who disclosed that the Americans held only San Diego, Carson may have learned the character of this trail. It reached across the ninety-mile waterless desert of the Imperial Valley before winding through the coastal mountains to the hills overlooking San Diego Bay.

The dragoon command was badly used up, the men worn out and underfed, the mules broken down, the arms and equipment of doubtful reliability from lack of care. Part of the men had been mounted on some of the Mexican horses captured on November 23, but they were wild and unbroken, and they weakened crossing the desert. The two twelve-pounder howitzers, laboriously dragged over the mountains and down the Gila, could not be fired without shattering their carriages. Amid the coastal mountains, chill winds blew off snowy peaks, and cold, drenching rain added to the misery of the toiling column.

Despite the weakness of his command, despite his ignorance of conditions in California, Kearny approached San Diego in a combative frame of mind. He thought not of defending himself but of attacking any enemy force that got in his path. Kit Carson has been credited in part with Kearny's overconfidence. From their first meeting on the Rio Grande, Carson had filled the general with stories of how easily California had fallen and how trifling were the fighting qualities of the natives. Reports that the American forces had been thrown out of southern California, even when confirmed by dispatches seized from the Mexican express rider, struck him as incredulous. The Californios would not stand and fight, declared Carson.[31]

On December 5, Kearny and his men joyously welcomed reinforcements. Several days earlier, an English rancher, riding to San Diego anyway, had agreed to carry a message to Commodore Stockton. Now, Stars and Stripes whipping in a windy rain, Captain Gillespie dashed up with a company of thirty-nine volunteers, largely former mountain men. Among them was Carson's old comrade Alexis Godey, now a lieutenant of volunteers. They even brought their own artillery, a little brass four-pounder known as the "Sutter gun." The lord of New Helvetia had acquired it from the Russians when he bought their trading station of Fort Ross in 1841. A detail under Lieutenant Edward F. Beale, scion of a distinguished naval family, served the cannon.[32]

Somewhere en route Gillespie had picked up a report that a Californio force was camped about six miles in Kearny's front. The report was accurate. Captain Andrés Pico, the governor's brother, and about seventy-five lancers lay about the Indian village of San Pasqual, in the narrow valley of the Rio San Bernardo. They knew nothing of Kearny's proximity, only that the hated Gillespie had ridden out of San Diego, probably on a foraging expedition, and might be found and smashed.

Heartily backed by Gillespie, Carson, and most of his officers, Kearny resolved to locate the enemy and attack early the next morning. Despite

Kearny's long record of competence and success, the battle he fought before daybreak on December 6, 1846, ranks among the most mismanaged in U.S. military history. A bungled reconnaissance alerted the enemy. Kearny relegated Gillespie's unit—fit, well mounted, and composed largely of expert riflemen—to a supporting role, along with the Sutter gun, the only artillery in working order. Tired dragoons moved forward on tired horses and mules, their carbines and pistols charged with damp powder, their sabers rusted in their scabbards. Before daylight and in a foggy valley, the advance guard charged before the main force could grope down a dark, brushy ridge to the battleground.

Kearny could have avoided battle altogether by taking the road by which Gillespie had come. Instead, he nearly lost his entire command.

Kit Carson had gravely underrated the foe. Despite mismanagement by their own commander, they fought, maneuvering their mounts with consummate skill and wielding their long, iron-pointed lances with deadly dexterity. The dragoons, their mounts frail, their powder wet, their swords too short to contend with lances, proved no match for the nimble vaqueros. "One shot, and the lance," was the order as the Californios counterattacked. Daylight found the battle over and the lancers withdrawing.

Behind they left Kearny with eighteen dead and seventeen wounded in an assault force that did not exceed fifty men. The dead included three officers, the wounded four. Kearny himself took two severe lance thrusts, one in his arm and the other in a location that made his saddle an instrument of torture. Captain Gillespie, the special nemesis of the natives, received three lance wounds—in his back, chest, and face. Carson's fellow scout, Antoine Robidoux, also lay in the field hospital with lance punctures that nearly killed him.

As for Kit Carson, he charged with the advance guard, about a dozen dragoons led by Captain Abraham Johnston. Nearing the village, however, Carson's horse stumbled and threw him to the ground, breaking his rifle in two. Rolling out of the way of the charging command, he sprang to his feet, "then ran on about 100 yards to where the fight had commenced. A Dragoon had been killed. I took his gun and cartridge box and joined in the melee."[33] Firing from cover, therefore, Carson managed to avoid the lances that brought down so many others. Rifle balls, in fact, accounted for only two of the fatalities; one was Captain Johnston, hit in the forehead an instant after Carson's horse fell.

The Battle of San Pasqual all but wrecked the Army of the West. During the night, scarcely able to transport even the wounded, the troops buried the dead in a common grave. Alexis Godey and two companions slipped into the darkness with a message for Commodore Stockton telling of

Kearny's plight. Lancers still roamed the neighborhood, but the condition of the wounded and the lack of rations made a move toward San Diego imperative.

"Day dawned on the most tattered and ill-fed detachment of men that ever the United States mustered under her colors," recorded Lieutenant Emory.[34] Gillespie's mountaineers showed how to make Indian travois, and in these "ambulances" mules dragged the suffering wounded over the rough ground. At a deserted ranch, the troops commandeered chickens and cattle. Throughout the march, lancers hovered on the flanks. In the evening they occupied the only eligible defensive position. Dragoons drove them off the hill, but in the excitement cattle and chickens both stampeded beyond recapture.

Pico's force had now grown to two hundred, and the beleaguered soldiers on what came to be labeled Mule Hill remained twenty-nine miles short of San Diego. Disheartening word reached them on the morning of December 8, when Pico proposed an exchange of prisoners. The Americans had but one, Pico four. That morning lancers had seized Alexis Godey and his companions returning from San Diego with a dispatch from Stockton. Before capture, they had secreted the document in a tree, but it had been discovered. Pico would trade only one for one, but the freed courier knew what the dispatch contained. Stockton said he had not the animals on which to mount a relief party. Kearny must take care of himself.

That night the officers held a council of war. The army officers agreed that no option remained but to fight their way through, even though the surgeon declared that the wounded could not stand the ordeal. Lieutenant Beale pledged that the navy would not fail the army and volunteered to slip through the enemy lines and bring back help. Kit Carson stepped forward to go too. At first Kearny declared that Carson could not be spared, but relented.

Accompanied by an Indian guide, the pair crept to the foot of Mule Hill. Three lines of mounted sentries ringed the American position. On the rocky ground shoes made too much noise, so Beale and Carson took them off and wedged them under their belts. For two miles, the three men crawled among rocks, brush, and prickly pear until they had put the picket lines behind them. Rising to their feet, Beale and Carson discovered that the shoes had worked loose and fallen behind. They had to hoof their painful way twenty-seven miles to San Diego. More dead than alive, his feet so lacerated he had to be borne on a litter, Beale reached Stockton on the night of December 9. Carson, having taken a longer route, came in the next morning.[35]

The agonizing trek turned out to have been unnecessary. Either Stockton had reconsidered or, more likely, his officers had convinced him of the risk to his own reputation if disaster befell Kearny. After Beale's appearance, but before Carson's, naval lieutenant Andrew Gray led a relief expedition out of San Diego. On Mule Hill, night had fallen on December 10 when the soldiers heard the tramp of marching feet and the challenge of their sentinel. Suddenly their rocky defenses filled with 80 marines and 120 sailors. The siege had been lifted.[36]

The next day, December 11, the combined force took up the march. The lancers had faded into the hills, opening the way for Kearny, with a battered remnant of the Army of the West, to complete the long trek from Fort Leavenworth to the Pacific shore. That afternoon the column ascended a hill from which, Emory recorded, "the Pacific opened for the first time to our view, the sight producing strange but agreeable emotions. One of the mountain men who had never seen the ocean before, opened his arms and exclaimed: 'Lord! there is a great prairie without a tree.' "[37]

CALIFORNIA FELL for the second and final time in January 1847. General Flores and Captain Pico tried to organize a defense of Los Angeles. General Kearny and Commodore Stockton, each with his own orders and ego to serve, tried to sort out their relationship and organize an advance on Los Angeles. They failed in the former but succeeded in the latter. Jointly leading an army of six hundred sailors, marines, dragoons, artillery, and volunteers, with Carson and the scouts well to the front, Stockton and Kearny marched north, up the coast. On January 8, 1847, they routed Flores at the Battle of San Gabriel. Each side maneuvered and fought courageously for an hour and a half, but inflicted few casualties. With even fewer casualties, the two armies clashed the next day on the road to Los Angeles. It was principally an artillery duel and ended in the retreat of Flores. The Americans occupied the pueblo on the tenth.[38]

Meantime, Frémont approached from the north with the California Battalion. Flores turned to cut him off. Offered an opportunity to surrender, he ceded his command to Pico of San Pasqual fame and fled to Sonora. Frémont next granted a truce while surrender terms were worked out by representatives of both sides. On January 13 they signed the "Cahuenga Capitulations," a compact more generous than any Stockton had been willing to grant but one he could hardly repudiate.

Now California had truly fallen to the United States. Who would govern until the war ended and a treaty fixed its future immediately embroiled Stockton, Kearny, and Frémont in a clash of large egos and ambitions and conflicting interpretations of orders. Frémont, acting under Stockton's command for six months, refused to submit to Kearny's authority and claimed the civil governorship of California. Kearny sought to establish his own primacy and was finally provoked by Frémont's insubordination into bringing formal charges. For Californians, the sorry spectacle ended when summer came and the principals departed for Washington to fight out the battle on a national stage. A court-martial convicted Frémont, President Polk suspended the sentence, but in March 1848 the humiliated officer resigned his commission rather than serve under a cloud. During a brief tour in Mexico in the summer of 1848, yellow fever struck General Kearny. Still hounded by Senator Benton and his claque, he died in October. Commodore Stockton left the navy and became a United States senator from New Jersey.

WHEN FRÉMONT and the California Battalion marched into Los Angeles on January 14, 1847, Kit Carson lost no time in rejoining the chief who commanded his true allegiance. Again the mission of dispatch rider to Washington fell to him. The dispatches were urgent only in defending Frémont's course in assuming the civil governorship of California. A long letter to Senator Benton gave his side of the controversy with General Kearny. Another appealed to Secretary of State James Buchanan for funds to support the civil government Frémont conceived himself as heading. This letter was entrusted to Theodore Talbot, veteran of two Frémont expeditions and lately a lieutenant in the California Battalion. Lieutenant Beale, still feeble from his ordeal with Carson to succor the defenders of Mule Hill, carried naval dispatches. But the chief purpose of Carson's overland trek was to provide Benton with ammunition to counter aspersions on Frémont that might find their way east with Kearny emissary Lieutenant Emory and Stockton emissary Lieutenant Gray, both of whom went home by sea.[39]

The ten-man party left Los Angeles on February 25, 1847, and rode quickly up the Gila. Apaches harried the riders, but Carson skillfully eluded an open fight. In Santa Fe by late April, he confronted heartbreaking news that caused a delay of ten days.

Three months earlier, in Taos and other communities of northern New Mexico, a combination of disgruntled Mexicans and Indians had risen against the new American regime. In Taos Charles Bent, governor of New Mexico by Kearny's appointment, and other Americans had been slain. Josefa and her sister, Bent's wife, had barely escaped by digging through an adobe wall even as Bent died in the same room. An American army had marched from Santa Fe, crushed the rebels, and hanged their leaders. After commiserating with Josefa and others of his family, Carson and the couriers resumed their hurried journey.[40]

Carson found Senator Benton in St. Louis and delivered Frémont's letter. Benton asked him to take it on to Washington and show it to the president. By the last week in May, he had reached the capital. Jessie Frémont promptly took him into the Benton household and paraded him before a fascinated Washington officialdom. Ned Beale's prominent family also housed "Don Kit" for a time. Twice Carson and Jessie met with President Polk. Carson gave him Frémont's letter to Benton and filled him in on affairs in California, but the chief executive, who had already decided against Frémont, remained studiedly noncommittal, much to Jessie's frustration. He did, however, on the suggestion of Secretary Buchanan, appoint Carson a second lieutenant in the regular army—in the regiment of which Frémont had been named lieutenant colonel.[41]

Again laden with dispatches, Carson left Washington on June 15, accompanied by Jessie Frémont and Ned Beale, both of whom went only as far as St. Louis. For a second time in 1847, Carson crossed the continent. On the Santa Fe Trail his escort, a company of Missouri volunteers, turned back a determined charge by Comanche warriors.[42] In Santa Fe he saw Josefa briefly, hired another escort, and, to avoid the Apache-infested Gila route, set forth on the Old Spanish Trail. On the Virgin River he encountered Paiutes, the same people who had tormented the Frémont expedition in 1844, and killed one before the others dispersed.

Arriving in Los Angeles in October, Carson found no Frémont, no Kearny, not even Dick Owens or Alexis Godey. Owens, the last commander of the California Battalion, and Godey had accompanied the Kearny-Frémont-Stockton entourage east on the California Trail. Turning north up the coast, Carson headed for the Monterey headquarters of the new military governor of California, Colonel Richard B. Mason.

Mason's aide-de-camp, Lieutenant William Tecumseh Sherman, vividly recalled Kit Carson's arrival in Monterey:

> I well remember the first overland mail. It was brought by Kit Carson in saddle-bags from Taos in New Mexico. We heard of his arrival at Los Angeles, and waited patiently for his arrival at headquarters. His fame then was at its height, from the publication of Frémont's books, and I was very anxious to see a man who had achieved such feats of daring among the wild animals of the Rocky Mountains, and still wilder Indians of the Plains. At last his arrival was reported at the tavern at Monterey, and I hurried to hunt him up. I cannot express my surprise at beholding a small, stoop-shouldered man, with reddish hair, freckled face, soft blue eyes, and nothing to indicate extraordinary courage or daring. He spoke but little, and answered questions in monosyllables. I

asked for his mail, and he picked up his light saddle-bags containing the great overland mail, and we walked together to headquarters, where we delivered his parcel into Colonel Mason's own hands.[43]

The Treaty of Guadalupe Hidalgo, ending the Mexican War and ensuring United States sovereignty over New Mexico and California, remained four months in the future. Yet nothing more perfectly symbolized the realization of the American nation's continental destiny than the arrival in Monterey, in pouches strapped to Kit Carson's saddle, of the first overland mail. Carson, Owens, Godey, the mountaineers of the California Battalion, Robidoux, Weaver, Leroux, and the others who had scouted for Kearny, Emory, and Cooke—all these old trappers had played as vital a role as any soldier, sailor, or marine in fixing the western boundary on the Pacific. When the quiet little mountaineer handed his saddlebag to the tall, red-headed lieutenant in the Monterey plaza late in October 1847, both literally and figuratively the continent had been spanned.

18

JIM BRIDGER:

FILLING IN THE MAP

J IM BRIDGER EXCHANGED the role of trapper for trader only gradually and reluctantly. In the winter of 1844–45 he led a party of thirty
men in a sweep through California, returning in the spring of 1845
by way of the Old Spanish Trail as far as Great Salt Lake. He found plenty
of beaver in California but discovered that no sooner had he set traps than
Indians stole them. He gave up on trapping and turned trader. At Fort
Laramie in September 1845 he sold the fruits of the expedition: beaver and
deerskins, mules and horses, and fourteen hundred California seashells.
The factor allowed five thousand dollars for all but the seashells, which he
did not know how to value.[1]

Even as traders, neither Bridger nor his partner, Louis Vasquez, over-
came their wanderlust. In the summers of 1845 and 1846, emigrants
paused to trade and make repairs at Bridger's Fort on Black's Fork of the
Green River, usually to find the proprietors absent. When there, they
charmed their customers; when not, overlanders recorded dismal impressions of the way station on the trail to Oregon and California.

On June 28, 1847, Bridger and two companions, en route to Fort
Laramie, ascended the Big Sandy toward South Pass. Early in the afternoon, they met advance elements of the year's most distinctive emigrant
train—seventy-two wagons constituting the "Pioneer Party" of the migrat-
ing Church of Jesus Christ of Latter Day Saints. Hounded out of Missouri
and Illinois, their leader slain, the Mormons had turned to a president of
powerful frame and personality, Brigham Young. That day at the mouth of

the Little Sandy, Bridger met Brigham Young and the Council of Twelve Apostles. They had resolved to found a new Zion in the West, somewhere distant from their persecutors. They had read Frémont and Hastings and, though still uncertain, believed that the Salt Lake Valley offered a good prospect. They had planned to stop at Bridger's Fort and question the master of western geography himself. Bridger agreed to pitch camp and share his knowledge with the Mormon elders.[2]

They approached Bridger in a pessimistic frame of mind. They had spent the preceding day with another old trapper, Black Harris, headed east from Oregon to find an emigrant train in need of a guide. Harris had traded with the Mormons—"He sells high," noted the church scribe—and given them a grim picture of their destination. "From his description, which is very discouraging, we have little chance to hope for even a moderately good country anywhere in those regions." Only Cache Valley bore his approval.[3]

Bridger revived hope. He had a long talk with the Council of Twelve and then dined alone with Brigham Young. "We met in council with Mr. Bridger," recorded Apostle Wilford Woodruff, "and found him to be a great traveler, possessing an extensive knowledge of nearly all Oregon and California, the mountains, rivers, lakes, springs, valleys, mines, ore, &c." Contradicting Black Harris, Bridger said the Great Basin was a fine place to settle. He cautioned that frost might nip grains, but otherwise, "He said it was his Paradise, and that if these people settled in it he would settle with them."[4]

Five days later, Bridger and his companions rode down to the North Platte ford, where the Mormons had installed a ferry. He handed the man in charge a message from Brigham Young with instructions to float the party across the river without charge. Bridger, the note added, expected to return from Fort Laramie "in time to pilot the Pioneers through to Salt Lake. He said he could take us to a place that would suit us."[5]

Bridger did not make it back in time. The Mormon advance had to find its own tortuous way down the Wasatch canyons to Great Salt Lake. "This is the place," Brigham Young is said to have proclaimed as he looked out over the great valley. Jim Bridger had played his modest part in getting them to a place that suited them. He did not settle with the Mormons in this "Paradise," as he had promised, but he had not had his last dealings with Brigham Young.

AFTER DELIVERING the first overland mail to Colonel Mason in Monterey in October 1847, Second Lieutenant Christopher Carson found himself assigned to troop duty. His unit, the Regiment of Mounted Riflemen, was in

Mexico, so Lieutenant Sherman had him assigned to a dragoon company in Los Angeles. Commanding twenty-five men, Carson guarded Tejon Pass, the pueblo's strategic gateway northward into the Central Valley and the pathway for Indians driving stolen horses.

While Carson passed the winter of 1847–48 in routine military duty, the Mexican War reached its climax. General Zachary Taylor had thrust into northern Mexico from the Rio Grande, and General Winfield Scott had landed an army at Vera Cruz to fight overland to Mexico City. After a series of hard-fought battles, the capital fell to Scott's troops in September 1847. While Carson idled in Tejon Pass, negotiators gathered at a village outside Mexico City to fashion a peace settlement. On February 2, 1848, they signed the Treaty of Guadalupe Hidalgo. Although they used an inaccurate map that would cause monumental complications when the boundary came to be fixed on the ground, the treaty provided for the cession of New Mexico and Upper California. In return, the United States would pay Mexico fifteen million dollars and assume all claims of American citizens against Mexico. The treaty would not achieve final ratification until July 1848, but questions of sovereignty no longer clouded American possession of the conquered territories, nor of the Pacific Coast with its great harbors of San Diego, San Francisco, and (thanks to the Oregon Boundary Treaty of 1846) Puget Sound.

Nine days before the treaty makers signed their document, on January 24, 1848, an event nearly as far-reaching occurred on the American River forty-five miles upstream from Sutter's Fort. James Marshall had built a sawmill and now worked on a millrace. On this historic day, his eye caught a glint beneath the water flowing in the ditch. He fished out a golden pebble only half the size of a pea. "Then I saw another." The treaty and the pebble combined to set off an explosive movement that swiftly transformed the United States into a continental nation in fact as well as law.

With the onset of spring, Lieutenant Carson found himself the bearer of another overland mail, eastbound. Although news of the gold discovery reached the East a month before Carson completed his journey, he bore pouches full of official reports that underlay President Polk's confirming notice to the Congress in December 1848.

With twenty-seven men, Carson rode out of Los Angeles on May 4, 1848. He took the Old Spanish Trail to Taos. As usual, Paiutes proved a menacing nuisance on the Virgin and Sevier Rivers, but Carson maneuvered through their territory without loss. In the Rockies, the riders courted disaster crossing the Grand River, boiling with the spring runoff. Improvising log rafts on the bank, they struggled to push themselves and their possessions across the freezing torrent. The first effort failed, the second partly succeeded, and the third smashed the raft in midstream with the loss of saddles, ammunition, and food stocks. Two men came close to losing their lives. Later, in the San Luis Valley, the company encountered a band of belligerent Ute and Apache warriors. Carson organized a formidable defense and put on such a convincing display of invincibility that the chiefs withdrew rather than sacrifice their men. On June 14, forty-one days out of Los Angeles, the battered troop rode into Taos.[6]

In Santa Fe Carson learned humiliating news. Although the president had nominated him for his commission in the regular army, the Senate had declined confirmation. Such low-ranking appointments routinely gained Senate approval, but the furor over the Frémont court-martial formed a context in which Carson, a loyal Frémont protégé, probably fell the innocent victim of a barrage aimed at Senator Benton. Carson's friends urged him to let the military authorities in Santa Fe worry about the mail pouches. He refused. It mattered little, he explained, whether he performed this vital public service with the rank of lieutenant or the rank of "experienced mountaineer." He would not forfeit the esteem of his countrymen because the Senate refused to approve an appointment he had not sought and, anyway, would have resigned at war's end.[7]

By August 1848, Kit Carson had delivered his mail pouches at the War Department. He socialized with the Bentons and Frémonts and even his old trapper comrade Joe Meek, in Washington to stir up action in behalf of Oregon in the wake of the Whitman Massacre.

Frémont, now out of the army, planned another western expedition in furtherance of his father-in-law's designs, this one privately financed. Surely he tried to enlist Carson once again as guide and scout, although no surviving record documents such an effort. For Kit Carson, the time had come to curb his roaming ways and pay more attention to Josefa. He would go home to Taos and stay.[8]

THE CALIFORNIA GOLD DISCOVERY filled the overland trails with wagon trains. The California Trail up the Platte and down the Humboldt bore most of the traffic. Many Argonauts, however, reached the Rio Grande on the Santa Fe Trail and two thoroughfares across Texas to unite on variations of the Cooke Wagon Road to California. Others went by sea around the Horn or across the Isthmus. The vast continental interior, however, still held secrets commanding the attention of the federal government. The new boundary had to be fixed on the earth's surface. Forts had to be established and garrisons posted to protect emigrants and campaign against Indians. The best wagon routes west, either new or variants of the old, remained to be determined. And looming ever more darkly in the background, sharpened by regional and commercial rivalries and torn by the sectional clash over slavery, lay the abiding question of the transcontinental railroad. All factions agreed that one had to be built to bind the newly continental nation together. Which way to go fueled controversy for a decade.

The Mexican War and the Oregon Boundary Treaty gave the army much to do in the West—the soldiers of the line as well as Colonel Abert's topographers. The mountaineers of the 1820s and 1830s were still the men who most intimately knew the West. In the prewar years, Kit Carson and John C. Frémont had laid the foundations. In the postwar years, Jim Bridger and Captain Howard Stansbury pointed the way.

Bridger and Vasquez spent the summer of 1849 trading with California-bound forty-niners. In July Bridger witnessed the vanguard of the army in the postwar West. The Regiment of Mounted Riflemen, created in 1846 to police the Oregon Trail, had at last arrived on the Oregon Trail. Under Lieutenant Colonel William W. Loring, it marched the entire length of the trail, posting garrisons along the way. On the main stem of the Platte, Loring established Fort Kearny. Another detachment garrisoned Fort Laramie, purchased from the Chouteau firm and transformed into an army post. Still another contingent wintered at Cantonment Loring, near Fort Hall, but the site afforded only sparse forage and was abandoned in 1850. Finally, the regimental headquarters took station at Fort Vancouver, the old Hudson's Bay Company bastion on the Columbia. The regiment marched in three divisions. Two went by way of Bridger's Fort. The third mistakenly strayed onto Greenwood Cutoff and missed Bridger.[9]

It was not the riflemen who engaged Jim Bridger in his first military service but a topographical unit following in the rear. Colonel Abert had ordered Captain Howard Stansbury to survey the neighborhood of Fort Hall for a suitable location for a fort, then carry out a comprehensive examination of the Great Salt Lake valley. With Lieutenant John W. Gunnison, eighteen men, and five wagons, guided by mountaineer Auguste Archambeau, a Frémont veteran, Stansbury halted at Bridger's Fort on August 11, 1849.[10]

A somewhat pointless mountain excursion through the Wasatch Range introduced Bridger to Stansbury. Their joint contribution to geographical understanding and to westward expansion, however, came later, after Stansbury had completed his valuable survey of the Great Salt Lake valley. Heading for home in September 1850, the captain sought a shortening of the established emigrant trace. He hoped that a direct route might exist from Bridger's Fort to one of the streams draining from the Front Range of the Rockies into the Platte. If so, it would cut off the curve by way of the North Platte and the Sweetwater. Approaching from the east, Frémont had sought a similar shortcut in 1843, but had allowed the Great Divide Basin to deflect his course north to the Sweetwater.

Such a route existed, Bridger assured Stansbury, and he would take time from his trading business to show the way. The two got along famously, and Stansbury learned much about trappers and Indians from his celebrated guide.

The company set out heavily armed and alert to Indian dangers of which Bridger warned. Apprehension mounted only three days out, on September 13, when an Indian war party suddenly charged the camp at daybreak. The attackers turned out to be Shoshones, however, embarrassed to learn that they had swept down on a white bivouac rather than a Ute camp. A visit to the battleground where Henry Fraeb had been killed by Sioux nine years earlier only heightened the fear of Indians.

Skirting the southern edges of the Great Divide Basin, Stansbury's men left it by way of a low portal that came to be known as Bridger's Pass. They forded the North Platte River, rounded the northern tip of the Medicine Bow Mountains, and crawled onto the flat Laramie Plain, brown with autumn grass and carpeted in every direction with herds of buffalo.

With dismay Stansbury observed the wastefulness of mountaineers in times of plenty. Auguste Archambeau worked into a hidden position downwind of a herd and, even though the mules could carry the meat of only one buffalo, calmly brought down four. Stansbury rode to the scene of this "wanton butchery" and watched how mountaineers from the first had dressed meat for the cook fire. With the beast spread-eagled in an upright position on the stomach

> the skinning process commences by making an incision along the top of the backbone, and separating the hide downward, so as to get the more quickly at what are considered the choice parts of the animal. These are the "bass," a hump projecting from the back of the neck just before the shoulders, and which is generally removed with the skin attached: it is about the size of a man's head, and when boiled, resembles marrow, being exceedingly tender, rich, and nutritious. Next comes the "hump," and the "hump ribs," projections of the vertebrae just behind the shoulders, some of which are a foot in length. These are generally broken off by a mallet made of the lower joint of one of the forelegs, cut off for the purpose. After these come the "fleece," portions of flesh covering the ribs; the "depuis," a broad, fat part extending from the shoulders to the tail; the "belly fleece;" some of the ribs, called "side ribs," to distinguish them from the hump ribs; the thigh or marrow-bones, and the tongue. Generally the animal is opened and the tenderloin and tal-

low secured. All the rest, including the hams and shoulders—indeed by far the greater portion of the animal—is left on the ground. When buffalo are plenty, the hump, bass, and tongue—very frequently only the latter—are taken, and occasionally a marrow-bone for a tit-bit.

This, added Stansbury, "is called butchering 'mountain fashion,' and a most barbaric fashion it is." From Archambeau's four kills, only the choice parts were taken from three. The fourth was left untouched. Although the four animals offered meat sufficient to supply a "respectable market" for a week, "it is vain to remonstrate against this wholesale destruction." Few contemporaries, and certainly no mountain men, would have understood Stansbury's point of view.[11]

The Laramie Plain brought on another Indian crisis. The hordes of buffalo had attracted several hundred Oglala Lakota Sioux, the same people who had killed Fraeb in 1841. As they converged on the little band of whites from several directions, Stansbury forted up in a cottonwood grove and prepared for a fight. Thirty rifles, he hoped, would discourage an assault. But it was his defiant gesture of hoisting the American flag that saved him. Bridger walked out alone for a talk and learned that the Oglalas, now regular customers at Fort Laramie, were friends of the white people. Until they saw the Stars and Stripes, they had mistaken Stansbury's men for Crows. Soon Indians and whites mingled in friendly feasting.

That night the captain witnessed a phenomenon even more startling than the "mountain fashion" butchering. He sat with the chiefs around a campfire passing the peace pipe. Bridger, though well known to all the Indians, could speak only Blackfeet and Crow, not Lakota. He was master of the sign language, however, a mode of communication foreign to Stansbury. For more than an hour, he recorded, "our esteemed friend and experienced mountaineer" engaged the entire circle "in a conversation and narrative, the whole of which was carried on without the utterance of a single word. The simultaneous exclamations of surprise or interest, and the occasional bursts of hearty laughter, showed that the whole party perfectly understood not only the theme, but the minutiae of the pantomime exhibited before them. I looked on with close attention, but the signs to me were for the most part altogether unintelligible."[12]

It was a performance George Drouillard would have appreciated.

East of the Laramie Plain, Bridger guided his charges to the head of Lodgepole Creek, which flowed down from the Front Range to the South Platte River. He had, as promised, shown the way.

Stansbury pronounced what came to be known as the Bridger's Pass route a great improvement over the South Pass road. It cut a straight-line

In Taking the Hump Rib *and* Roasting the Hump Rib, *Alfred Jacob Miller depicted two familiar scenes of western life. Miller's patron, Sir William Drummond Stewart, looks on as Indians make the spinal first incision in the process of dressing a buffalo—a sequence that Captain Howard Stansbury later described with fastidious revulsion (p. 268). After roasting, the hump rib rewarded the labor, for it was second only to the tongue as the buffalo's most desirable part.* TAKING THE HUMP RIB COURTESY AMON CARTER MUSEUM, FORT WORTH, TEXAS. *ROASTING THE HUMP RIB* COURTESY WALTERS ART GALLERY, BALTIMORE.

chord across the Sweetwater arc, he reported to Colonel Abert, and short-ened the distance by sixty-one miles. His examination led to the "unhesi-tating conclusion that, in point of diminished distance, easy grades, freedom from serious obstacles, and convenience and abundant supply of materials for construction, the line of this reconnaissance presents a trace for a road that is not only perfectly feasible, but decidedly preferable to the other."[13]

Stansbury wrote not just of a wagon road but a railroad. His report, however, had little influence on the debate over a railroad route across the continent. That was an issue that had to be resolved politically—and mili-tarily—before it could become an engineering issue. But when engineering prevailed, Jim Bridger prevailed. The Overland Mail, the Union Pacific Railroad, and finally Interstate 80 followed the path marked out for Cap-tain Stansbury by Jim Bridger in the autumn of 1850.

ON THE WINTRY NIGHT of January 20, 1849, Kit Carson, Dick Owens, and Lucien Maxwell sat by the fire in Carlos Beaubien's store in Taos, New Mex-ico. They looked up as a pair of men, gaunt, ragged, and exhausted, opened the door. Owens failed to recognize them, but Maxwell exclaimed, "Why don't you know the captain?" The "captain" was John C. Frémont, and ac-companying him was Alexis Godey. The reunion of Frémont, his "three marshals," and the Frémonter Lucien Maxwell brought to an end the cata-strophe of the famous explorer's fourth expedition.[14]

Even as he jumped off on the Santa Fe Trail in September 1848, Fré-mont hoped that somehow Senator Benton could transform his fourth ex-pedition into a government project like the first three. Benton's effort succeeded in the Senate but failed in the House, and no other branch of government stepped forth with a solution. In the end, financing came from private sources, including Frémont's own purse.

The objectives were as ill-defined as the financing. One, however, was to demonstrate the feasibility of a direct railroad route along the thirty-eighth parallel from St. Louis, Benton's home, to California. By surmounting the high peaks around the head of the Rio Grande in midwinter, Frémont could dramatize the advantages of the St. Louis route while burnishing his soiled reputation. To lay his findings before the nation, he had with him some of the best field scientists: Charles Preuss and the three Kern broth-ers—Richard, Edward, and Benjamin.

Although Alexis Godey and other Frémont veterans made up part of the thirty-three men, none knew the mountains toward which the explorer aimed. Kit Carson did, but he had gone home to spend the winter with his family in Taos. At Bent's Fort, John Hatcher and other old hands advised that already, in October, heavy snow lay on the Rockies and warned against trying to cross them. "Uncle Dick" Wooten signed on as guide, but he turned back when he saw how much snow had fallen on the Sangre de Cristos. Finally, at Pueblo, Frémont persuaded a reluctant Old Bill Williams to serve as guide. No former trapper was as vain, eccentric, or cranky as Bill Williams, but he knew the Rockies.[15]

Across the Sangre de Cristos and the San Luis Valley, the expedition endured record snowfall and plunging temperatures. This was no year in which to attempt a crossing of the immense ranges dividing the Rio Grande from the Gunnison and the Grand. Three passes provided portals, but only Cochetopa offered even slight hope of a winter crossing. Frémont and Williams argued over aiming for this or another, farther north, that shortened the route. Which man argued for which pass fell casualty to poor memory and partisan wrangling among the survivors. The choice led north, into the La Garita Mountains. Drifting snow, freezing temperatures, icy walls of rock, deep gorges full of snow, ridge on higher ridge buried in snow and brushed by rolling clouds ravaged men and animals. Mules plunged to their death from narrow ledges, men and mules starved or froze to death, or both. Organization and discipline collapsed. Stubbornly, Frémont refused to admit defeat and turn back. Only after the calamity had exploded into proportions even he could not ignore, after he had sacrificed the lives of ten men to his vainglory, did he and Alexis Godey find their way to Carlos Beaubien's store in Taos.

As Frémont rested and drank hot chocolate in Kit Carson's Taos home, he could claim no such achievements as had crowned his first three expeditions. He could only charge Bill Williams with misleading him and thus bringing on the disaster. Later, dark rumors of cannibalism circulated, and Jessie Frémont attributed to Kit Carson the remark that "In starving times no man who knew him ever walked in front of Bill Williams."[16]

Williams could not defend himself. Within two months, with Dr. Benjamin Kern and others sent to recover cached baggage, he was killed by Ute Indians. He did not lack defenders, however, who contended that Frémont alone caused the tragedy by rejecting the advice of his guide.

For all his foibles, Old Bill Williams takes rank with other former trappers who shared their mental map with trained explorers. His fatal misfortune was to team up with a chief who had shown that he knew how to listen but now, in his rush to restore his heroic image, had forgotten how to pay attention.

IN THE SOUTHWEST, the army found no more reliable and experienced mountain man than Antoine Leroux. A St. Louis native, born about 1801, he had based himself in Taos as early as 1826. South Park, the Western Slope, the Uinta Basin, the San Juan and Gila Valleys—in the rivers and creeks of all he had set his traps. He knew this country as well as Jim Bridger knew the northern Rockies. From the Front Range to the Mojave Desert, Leroux Creeks, Leroux Springs, Leroux Passes, and other landmarks named Leroux recorded his passing.

After New Mexico fell to the United States, no mountain man more freely offered his services to the U.S. Army than Antoine Leroux. In 1846 he helped Captain Philip St. George Cooke blaze the Cooke Wagon Road to California. After the war, field commanders contending with Apache and Ute warriors found him a canny scout and guide and a wise counselor on how to fight Indians. Topographical officers found him a reservoir of knowledge about the lay of the land and its natural and human content.[17]

With public interest focused on wagon and railroad routes to California, Leroux and others believed that a pathway existed farther north than the Gila River trail that Lieutenant William Emory and southern political interests championed. Leroux's conviction and knowledge attained expression on a landmark map compiled in 1851 by Lieutenant James G. Parke. The Parke map drew together all the previous work done in the Southwest. Testifying to the contributions of mountain men, beneath the map's legend Parke credited Old Bill Williams, Ceran St. Vrain, John Hatcher, and Antoine Leroux. To Leroux he attributed the representation of the Colorado River as well as the route of a proposed wagon road from Zuñi to California.[18]

Santa Fean Richard Campbell also believed in such a route. As Ewing Young's comrade in Gila trapping ventures two decades earlier, he knew the country as well as Leroux. He shared his opinion with Lieutenant James H. Simpson, topographical officer for a military campaign against the Navajos in 1849, who urged further exploration of the old trapper trails.[19]

Colonel Abert agreed. He gave the assignment to Captain Lorenzo Sitgreaves, who hired Antoine Leroux as guide and took along Lieutenant Parke to test his map with personal reconnaissance in the field. Richard Kern served as draftsman. The explorers and their fifty-man escort of soldiers gathered at Zuñi Pueblo in September 1851. Leroux led them down the Zuñi and Little Colorado Rivers but, to avoid the depths of the Grand Canyon, turned them west to the San Francisco Peaks. From here the way led around Bill Williams Mountain and across the high, sterile plateaus that had confounded Ewing Young and Kit Carson in 1829.

Despite an infantry escort, Indians plagued the expedition all the way to the Colorado River. They tried to steal stock, fired arrows from a distance, and kept the travelers on constant alert. None dared stray far from the column in search of water, or to vantages from which to scan the deserts for the great river all eagerly sought. On November 3, however, while the command halted to rest exhausted mules, Leroux climbed a nearby height to survey the country. Hiking past an outcropping of rocks, he suddenly walked into a cloud of arrows loosed by Indians concealed among the crags. Three arrows found their mark, one in the wrist, one in the forearm, and one behind an ear. Although gravely wounded, Leroux raised his rifle as the warriors advanced. This scattered them to the cover of rocks, but still they pressed as he backed down the slope. No Indian ventured within rifle range to sacrifice himself to the single ball in the guide's rifle. Comrades raced to the rescue, and the Indians swiftly vanished. The head and arm wounds healed rapidly, but the wrist wound festered, disabling Leroux for the rest of the journey.

Finally striking the Colorado River in the Mojave Valley, the Sitgreaves expedition made its way downstream to find refuge at Fort Yuma, opposite the mouth of the Gila River.

Sitgreaves turned in a report disappointing in many respects. But it did reveal a country hitherto all but unknown and now marked as worthy of consideration for a railroad route. Moreover, it bolstered much of the content of Lieutenant Parke's map.[20]

BY 1853, the controversy over a transcontinental railroad had grown so heated and so dominated by sectional and commercial rivalries that Congress, in desperation, turned to science. Legislation enacted in March 1853 directed the Secretary of War to determine, within ten months, which route offered the best cost and engineering prospects. It was an impossible charge, but Colonel Abert fielded survey parties at once. In the summer and autumn of 1853, they began their hurried work: Isaac I. Stevens, newly appointed governor of Washington Territory, on a line from Lake Superior to Puget Sound; Captain John W. Gunnison on Senator Benton's line along the thirty-eight parallel; Lieutenant Amiel W. Whipple on the thirty-fifth parallel west from Albuquerque, examined by Sitgreaves and Leroux in 1851; and Lieutenants John Pope and John G. Parke on the thirty-second parallel so strongly urged by southern interests. Because of the work of Stansbury and Bridger in 1850, Abert regarded the South Pass area as already covered, although in the end it received no serious consideration.

Their day in the West fast fading, mountain men contributed only marginally to the Pacific Railroad Surveys. Stevens relied heavily on Alexander

Culbertson, the veteran trader at Fort Union, but chiefly to make sure the Blackfeet gave no trouble. Alexis Godey coincidentally turned up to help Lieutenant Robert S. Williamson identify the best passes through the southern Sierra Nevada. But mainly the officers got along with Indian or other local guides where guides were needed at all. By 1853, much of the country to be surveyed had already been mapped and marked with travel routes.

Among mountain men, the Pacific Railroad surveyors counted one bright exception: Antoine Leroux. In two of the surveys, uniting reliable adviser with receptive officers, Leroux played a distinguished part.[21]

BECAUSE OF Senator Benton's noisy advocacy, the Gunnison survey attracted much attention, especially in its charge to find a way through the mountains that had defeated Frémont in 1848. Benton had tried to get Frémont appointed to head this survey. When that failed, he arranged a competing government expedition under Edward F. Beale, en route to California to assume a post as Indian agent obtained for him by Benton. In addition, financed by private interests, Frémont himself took the field for his fifth and final exploring expedition.[22]

For Captain Gunnison, the politically charged part of his mission fell among the passes at the head of the Rio Grande, for here Benton's son-in-law had failed, and here Benton had to demonstrate engineering feasibility. Early in August 1853, in the San Luis Valley, Gunnison sent Lieutenant Edward G. Beckwith to Taos to sign up Antoine Leroux, "the experienced and well-known guide."

Leroux served Gunnison for one month, August 20 to September 22, 1853, long enough to pilot him easily through Cochetopa Pass to the Gunnison River and down to the Grand. From here Gunnison could pick up the Old Spanish Trail across the Uinta Basin and the Wasatch. Even in the terrible winter of 1848–49, Leroux could probably have got Frémont across this pass—if Frémont had heeded him better than he heeded Old Bill Williams.

Less than a month later, on the Sevier River west of the Wasatch Range, Ute Indians fell on Gunnison and part of his men, including the distinguished mapmaker Richard H. Kern. The Gunnison Massacre devolved command of the survey on Lieutenant Beckwith, an artillery officer lacking topographical credentials. Even so, before his death Gunnison had set to paper a fatal blow to Benton's route. The engineering and cost factors of the passes cherished by Benton and Frémont were so adverse that he had not believed them worth calculating. Neither Frémont nor Beale could overcome that judgment.[23]

Leroux had gone no farther with Gunnison because he had promised to guide Lieutenant Whipple's survey of the thirty-fifth parallel, which occupied the entire winter and ended at Los Angeles in March 1854. The key to Whipple's mission lay in the rough dry country between the San Francisco Peaks and the Colorado River, terrain that had baffled Ewing Young in 1829 and Captain Sitgreaves in 1851. Leroux wanted to keep to the north, in high plateau country penetrated by Sitgreaves, but Whipple opted for a more southerly trace. This brought him to the Colorado at the mouth of the Bill Williams River but also got him tangled in canyons plainly unsuited for a railroad. Bowing to Leroux's judgment in this difficult country, Whipple enthusiastically endorsed the thirty-fifth parallel as an "eminently advantageous" railroad route.[24]

Antoine Leroux continued to serve the army on important missions throughout the 1850s, but he had made his contribution to the railroad issue. Although the railroad surveys added much to knowledge of the American West, they exerted little influence on the selection of a line across the continent. Political deadlock produced the surveys, and not until the Civil War broke the deadlock could a route be chosen—and then not on any of those examined by the Pacific Railroad Surveys.

When finally the Santa Fe Railroad was built along the line of the Whipple survey, it bore west and north from the San Francisco Peaks as Antoine Leroux had advised.

LIEUTENANT GOUVERNEUR KEMBLE WARREN exemplified the professional army officers who tapped into the vast body of knowledge stored in the minds of the mountain men and then laid before the public the results of the collaboration between the two. West Point 1850, he gained field experience on the lower Mississippi River before shifting to the Platte and upper Missouri in 1855. For three years, with scientist Ferdinand V. Hayden, Warren concentrated on these rivers and their tributaries. A survey that began in the spring of 1857 ended when Warren bowed to the demand of Sioux chiefs to stay out of the Black Hills.

That old mountain men had much to contribute to Warren's mission he readily acknowledged. He persuaded Jim Baker, Alexander Culbertson, and others to draw sketch maps of the plains and Rockies. He further demonstrated his confidence in them when he concluded the report of his explorations of 1855–57 and urged more fieldwork to clarify the geography of the upper Yellowstone and its tributaries. He wanted to make this examination himself, he wrote, and he had consulted Jim Bridger, Alexander Culbertson, Robert Campbell, and others on the best means of pursuing it. If ordered, he had Bridger's assurance of acting as his guide.[25]

The expedition was ordered, but not with Warren at its head. Assigned to West Point as a mathematics instructor, he had to yield leadership to Captain William F. Raynolds, a dedicated officer though lacking western experience. As promised, Jim Bridger joined for what proved, ironically, a return to country first explored and mapped by Lewis and Clark, with an assist from John Colter and George Drouillard.

JIM BRIDGER HAD LED an active life since showing Captain Stansbury the best route from Bridger's Fort to the South Platte. In September 1851 he served as Shoshone interpreter at the Fort Laramie treaty council. This landmark effort to bring all the Plains tribes into treaty relations with the United States and peace with one another had been organized by Superintendent of Indian Affairs David D. Mitchell (an old mountain man) and Indian Agent Thomas Fitzpatrick (another old mountain man). A collision between the Sioux and Shoshones, traditional enemies, almost launched the peace talks with bloodshed, but the Sioux backed off when they took the measure of Bridger's steadfast and well-armed Shoshones. Bridger renewed old acquaintances, strengthened his friendship with Father De Smet, and impressed the dragoon peacekeepers with his wilderness experience and sage observations on human nature. "He was a genuine article with no alloy," recorded one.[26]

In 1855–57 Bridger attained notoriety as guide for Sir St. George Gore, an Irish nobleman whose passion for hunting and fishing powered a virtual campaign of extermination against western wildlife. With a large entourage of men, animals, carts, and wagons, an extensive and varied arsenal, and the tentage and commissary for a sumptuous outdoor life that made Sir William Drummond Stewart's seem spartan, Gore hunted the Colorado Rockies and the upper Missouri, Yellowstone, Powder, Tongue, and Bighorn Rivers. Indians and Indian agents alike angrily objected to such massive slaughter pursued solely for sport, but he kept at it for three years. By his own count, Gore spent $500,000, traveled 6,000 miles, and killed 2,000 buffalo, 1,600 deer and elk, and 105 bears.[27]

Aside from expert professional services, Bridger regaled the titled Irishman with tales of his mountain adventures, while Gore introduced the unlettered scout to the riches of Shakespeare. After dinner, over wine, Gore read aloud to his guide. Bridger thought the English bard "a leetle too highfalutin for him" and "rayther calculated that thar big Dutchman, Mr. *Full-*

stuff, was a leetle bit too fond of lager beer." Moreover, he avowed, "he be dogoned ef he swallered every thing that thar *Baren* Mountchawson said, and he thought he was a durn'd liar."[28]

Bridger's next adventure involved him in a conflict with people he had dealt with before—the Mormons. In 1847 he had pointed Brigham Young and the Council of Twelve toward the Salt Lake Valley. By 1853, however, the theocracy that had taken root in Salt Lake City extended the jurisdiction of the Territory of Utah to the east and encompassed Bridger's Fort. In the heat of Mormon conflict with the Utes, officials believed Bridger guilty of stirring up and arming the Shoshones as well as other transgressions of territorial law. Alerted to an advancing posse, he fled. Mormons occupied the fort and established other settlements in the neighborhood. Eventually, Bridger and Vasquez negotiated a sale of the post to the church, but Bridger never forgave Brigham Young and his associates.

Payback time came in the spring of 1857, as St. George Gore descended the Missouri and headed for home. Exaggerated reports of Governor Young's tyranny and Mormon aggressions against Gentiles stirred a wave of anti-Mormon sentiment in the East. The new president, James Buchanan, resolved to send an army to impose federal authority on Utah. Colonel Albert Sidney Johnston hired Jim Bridger as chief guide and bestowed on him the title of major.

The Mormons mobilized to defend themselves, and their guerrilla operations so harassed Johnston's army that it could not reach Utah before winter. Stalled at Bridger's Fort, a partly burned ruin since the Mormons had fired it before retreating, Johnston leased a military reservation from Major Bridger and sat out a winter in which the old mountaineer's scouting service demonstrated him worthy of the title. By the spring of 1858, an accommodation had been worked out, and the army marched peacefully through Salt Lake City. Bridger took his discharge, but his fort remained a U.S. Army installation for thirty-two years.

(Bridger's title was cloudy and the lease of dubious legality. When Bridger concluded his contract with Johnston's quartermaster, the property had already been sold to the church even though the money had not been actually paid. The government never paid the rent contracted by the army, and Bridger's claim rocked around the courts and the Congress until long after his death.)[29]

Jim Bridger's conversation with Lieutenant Warren about a government survey of the upper Yellowstone occurred late in July 1856 at the mouth of the Yellowstone, when Warren purchased some of St. George Gore's wagons for his own transportation. By the summer of 1859, when Captain

Raynolds organized the expedition Warren had proposed, Bridger, as promised, was ready to go along as guide.

THE RAYNOLDS EXPEDITION aimed at revealing imperfectly known country and identifying feasible wagon roads linking the Yellowstone and Missouri Rivers to Fort Laramie. Already the War Department foresaw the day when the Yellowstone Basin might attract settlers and form a battleground for the army and the increasingly defiant Sioux. Well stocked with scientists and artists, including Dr. Ferdinand V. Hayden as naturalist and surgeon, the party kept to the field for two years. In the summer and autumn of 1859, the surveyors worked from the Missouri at Fort Pierre overland to the Yellowstone, then turned south along the eastern base of the Bighorn Mountains. After wintering on the North Platte above Fort Laramie, they again took the field in the spring of 1860, this time to scour the headwaters of the Missouri and the Yellowstone. In each season, Lieutenant Henry E. Maynadier led detachments on alternate routes. Military escorts guarded against Indian aggressions.[30]

During his trapping years, Jim Bridger had covered virtually every mile of the field of exploration, but that had been fifteen and more years earlier. As Raynolds noted, he retained an amazing command of the geographical outline but sometimes grew confused about details. More and more, however, Raynolds came to trust Bridger's judgment. As he noted on one such occasion, "This is not in accordance with my pre-conceived plan, but I shall accept his advice out of deference to his remarkable knowledge of the country."[31]

An intensely serious and determined man, the captain was also deeply religious. No more than the overland missionaries could he bring himself to profane the Sabbath. Every Sunday, therefore, the command lay in camp. Three pistol shots substituted for summoning church bells, and the soldiers found the worship service small enough price to pay for a weekly day of rest.

For both Raynolds and Bridger, the severest test occurred in the second summer as they trekked up the Wind River. Lieutenant Maynadier had taken part of the command down the Bighorn and turned west by way of Clark's Fork and the Gallatin to reach a planned rendezvous with Raynolds at the Three Forks. For his part, before joining Maynadier, Raynolds wanted to examine the headwaters of the Yellowstone River and confirm what Bridger had told him of "burning plains, immense lakes, and boiling springs."

Raynolds thought he could simply go up the Wind River and turn north to the head of the Yellowstone. Bridger said this could not be done. Impassable mountains intervened. To reach the Yellowstone, they would have to cross the Continental Divide to the Snake, then recross it to the Yellowstone farther north. The captain remained skeptical until he saw the immense uplift of the Absaroka Range, "rising not less than 5,000 feet above us, its walls apparently vertical with no visible pass nor even cañon."

"Triumphantly and forcibly," Bridger declared: "I told you you could not go through. A bird can't fly over that without taking a supply of grub along." "I had no reply to offer," recorded Raynolds, "and mentally conceded the accuracy of the information of 'the old man of the mountains.' "[32]

Bridger's route lay to the south, to the pass traversed by the Astorians in 1811. As the company began the climb, Bridger remarked that they would camp that night of May 31, 1860, on headwaters of the Columbia and within five miles of the Green. Raynolds partly filled his canteen from the Wind River and vowed to top it off from the Green and the Gros Ventre. He would brew a unique pot of tea.

Now it was the captain's turn to triumph. They had reached the mountains too early in the season. On this same trail, snow had turned back Jedediah Smith in 1824. Now snow slowed, then halted Raynolds's ascent. "Bridger, for the first time, lost heart and declared that it would be impossible to go further." Alone and afoot, Raynolds floundered through the snow to the summit, then returned to push the rest of the men on to the top.

Some ten miles to the east, Raynolds spotted "a bold conical peak." "That peak I regard as the topographical centre of the continent, the waters from its sides flowing into the Gulf of Mexico, the Gulf of California, and the Pacific Ocean. I named it Union peak, and the pass Union pass." From here too he could see the Green River, "but all the romance of my continental tea-party had departed."[33]

Snow and mud exhausted men and animals as they descended the creeks running into the Gros Ventre and down to the Snake in Jackson Hole. Determined to cross back to the Yellowstone, however, Raynolds kept as high as possible and veered north across the drainages. He and Bridger scouted ahead in search of the way back across the Continental Divide. They finally stood in the pass Bridger sought and looked down on the head of the Yellowstone, above Yellowstone Lake. This was Two Ocean Pass, site of the stream that divides to form Atlantic and Pacific Creeks, the place where Bridger told of trout swimming across the Continental Divide.[34]

But the snows were too deep. Raynolds and Bridger had worn themselves out getting this far, and they knew the surveyors, their dragoon escort, and the animals could not make it to the pass. The rendezvous with

Maynadier set for the Three Forks did not afford time to rest. Sadly, they turned the column back to the Gros Ventre and down to Jackson Hole. On the morning of June 9, rising above "a ragged cliff of brilliant red," they glimpsed "the snow-covered peaks of the Great Teton, dazzling in the clear atmosphere, with the reflected rays of the newly-risen sun."[35]

Raynolds hurried to the union with Maynadier. The swollen Snake River presented a formidable barrier. Bridger crafted a rude bullboat from willows covered with the lodge skin of his tepee coated with pine resin. Across the Snake, the contingent climbed over Teton Pass to Pierre's Hole and ascended Henry's Fork. An easy pass led to the head of the Madison and the easy descent to the Three Forks. Raynolds named it Low Pass. Later it became Raynolds Pass.

For the rest of the summer of 1860, Raynolds and two detachments covered a vast territory, but it was an anticlimax. One month later, in July rather than June, Bridger could have conducted the Raynolds expedition across Two Ocean Pass. To him rather than others a decade later (including Ferdinand Hayden) would have fallen the credit of unveiling the thermal wonderland that became Yellowstone National Park.

The Raynolds expedition fell short of some of its goals, notably the pioneering of wagon road routes. But the report and maps brought into focus the contents of a country known only in fuzzy outline to all but Jim Bridger and his comrades who had trapped it thirty years earlier. Old Gabe had helped fill in some of the remaining gaps in the map of the American West.[36]

FOR JIM BRIDGER, another eight years of strenuous service to the army followed the Raynolds survey. He guided and counseled military commanders in the opening campaigns of the wars with the Sioux anticipated by the Raynolds expedition. On December 21, 1866, he stood with Colonel Henry B. Carrington in the frigid stockade of Fort Phil Kearny as Captain William J. Fetterman led his eighty men to death. At seventy-seven, in 1881, Jim Bridger died on his Missouri farm, one of the last survivors of the generation of mountain men.

Tom Fitzpatrick had preceded Bridger in death by twenty-seven years. As Indian agent for the Upper Platte and Arkansas Agency, he had brought his long experience with Indians to bear on the unfolding policy of his government toward the Indians of the Great Plains. He advocated both benevolence and firmness, reward for compliance, military punishment for resistance. The first treaties with the Plains Indians were his inspiration— Fort Laramie in 1851, Fort Atkinson in 1853. He framed many thoughtful recommendations for Indian policy, most of which had no effect. Not surprisingly, he dealt more comfortably and influentially with the Indians than with the political spoilsmen charged with policy and administration. If he failed to perceive the true magnitude of the "Indian problem," still his ideas held more promise than most that floated around the bureaucratic offices of the capital.

Tom Fitzpatrick did not live to witness the tragic unfolding of his government's relations with the western tribes, nor the failure of the two treaties he had negotiated. For thirty years, he had eluded death by Blackfeet arrows and mountain wilderness. On February 7, 1854, in Brown's Hotel on Pennsylvania Avenue in Washington, D.C., pneumonia struck him dead at the age of fifty-five—in a bed, far from the scenes of his perilous life.[37]

Joe Walker never lost the impulse to explore, or simply wander. He tried his hand at mining and ranching, guiding military expeditions, hunting, and simply traveling—all over the West he knew so well. In a last grand adventure, in 1863 he led an expedition into the Apache country north of the Gila River and opened the rich mines that gave birth to Prescott and brought hundreds of gold seekers to the newly organized Territory of Arizona. In 1867, Walker returned to the family ranch, Manzanita, on the slopes of Mount Diablo east of San Francisco Bay. There, at the age of seventy-eight, he died on October 27, 1876—according to his biographer, "from nothing more or less, it seems, than having lived long enough."[38]

After retiring from the mountains in 1835, both William L. Sublette and Robert Campbell prospered as St. Louis merchants. In a last western fling, Sublette accompanied Sir William Drummond Stewart on the Scottish lord's nostalgic final hunting trip to the Green River in 1843. Sublette also farmed and engaged heavily in politics. On July 23, 1845, anticipating Fitzpatrick, Sublette died of tuberculosis in a Pittsburgh hotel room. Campbell continued to thrive as a St. Louis banker and merchant, colonel of Missouri militia, and sometime consultant to government officials on Indian affairs. A bronchial malady took his life at Saratoga Springs, New York, on October 16, 1879.[39]

The man who had fixed the pattern for the collaboration of official explorer and mountain man failed at everything he tried after the age of forty. John C. Frémont's fifth expedition, undertaken in 1853 to bolster his father-in-law's St. Louis–based railroad route, ended his career as an explorer. In the mountains that had vanquished him in 1848, he simply followed the trail blazed two months earlier by Captain Gunnison. The transcontinental trek ended in California with a notable absence of the publicity that had bathed his earlier adventures. The coolly professional conclusion of the martyred Captain Gunnison discredited the hyperbole with which Benton and Frémont had championed the thirty-eighth-parallel route.[40]

The failure of the fifth expedition foreshadowed Frémont's remaining thirty-seven years. As the new Republican Party's first presidential candidate in 1856, he went down to defeat in the contest with James Buchanan. As a Union major general in the first years of the Civil War, he so repeatedly demonstrated his incompetence that he snapped even the elastic tolerance of Abraham Lincoln, who happily complied when the general's offended ego prompted a request to be relieved of command. Business ventures failed. Land speculation failed. Writing undertakings failed. A term as governor of the Territory of Arizona failed. On his deathbed in 1890, he could look back with pride on significant achievements before 1846, but none since.

Frémont's protégé, Kit Carson, fared better. From his base in Taos, he continued throughout the 1850s to scout for the army in campaigns against the Indians. Ironically, however, this celebrated Indian fighter, who in his long career as a mountaineer had taken countless scalps, turned into an Indian sympathizer as well. From 1853 to 1861, he served as U.S. Indian agent for the Ute Indians. He was conscientious, honest, and truthful; he knew the language, thought, and customs of his charges; he listened attentively to their problems; and he reasoned and counseled with them. In return, they accorded him trust and affection.

When war came in 1861, Carson turned soldier. As colonel of the First New Mexico Volunteers, he fought Confederates at the Battle of Valverde. Thereafter, for the rest of the war years, he reverted to Indian fighter. Under the guidance of General James H. Carleton, an old dragoon accorded all the loyalty once lavished on Frémont, he campaigned against Apaches and Navajos with conspicuous success. Later generations of Navajos would call him a butcher, but he waged war with as much humanity as war allows. He took few lives, but by destroying subsistence and property he destroyed the will to resist. At war's end, the government recognized his services with the brevet of brigadier general—a rare attainment for an unlettered old trapper and a fitting climax to a distinguished career. He died in 1868, beloved by all who knew him, venerated by countrymen to whom he was still the legendary hero portrayed by Frémont.[41]

AS THE GENERATION of mountain men died out, so too did the generation of topographical officers. For Captain Raynolds, Jim Bridger had guided the final western survey of the Corps of Topographical Engineers. The Civil War ended their era. Five months after Fort Sumter, Colonel Abert retired after fifty-three years of active service. He died in January 1863, two months before the Congress, responding to wartime conditions, merged the Corps of Topographical Engineers back into the Corps of Engineers. As the army's elite, many of the topographical officers quickly gained general's stars, although few triumphed on the battlefield.

In the postwar years, the further exploration of the American West would be dominated by civilian agencies. The army did not abandon the field altogether, but the work of John Wesley Powell overshadowed the work of Lieutenant George M. Wheeler. Neither, of course, drew on the knowledge of mountain men. Their generation had vanished.

As the time of the military topographer and his mountaineer guide drew to a close, a single young officer created a monument to what they had accomplished. The Pacific Railroad Surveys failed to yield a Pacific railroad, but they prompted Secretary of War Jefferson Davis to charge Lieutenant Gouverneur K. Warren, twenty-four, with preparing a map of the American West to illustrate the reports. He began work in 1854 and, even though seasonally interrupted by field labors on the Missouri and the Platte, completed it in 1857. Accompanied by an extensive "memoir" on method and sources, the map was published in 1859 in the eleventh volume of the *Pacific Railroad Reports*.

Today a bronze General Warren gazes over the Gettysburg battlefield from the eminence of Little Round Top, a monument to the quick action that saved the Union from another crushing defeat by Confederates. The Warren map of 1857 endures as an even more imposing monument, both to Warren's cartographic excellence and to the exploratory achievements of his fellow officers.

The Warren map summed up the work of half a century. As antecedents, the map claimed the work of Lewis and Clark, Zebulon Pike, and Stephen H. Long. But it rested more solidly on the surveys by the corps' officers since 1838—surveys of various corridors and regions of the West anchored on astronomical determinations; surveys that highlighted the names of Frémont, Emory, Stansbury, Gunnison, Whipple, Parke, Sitgreaves, Abert, Peck, Williamson, Warner, McClellan, Meade, Ives, Pope, and dozens of others who wore the emblem of the Topographical Corps. Warren's map contained spaces labeled simply "unexplored," but for the first time the United States had a comprehensive map of the entire nation, essentially correct in topography, and compiled from data gathered in the field according to scientific techniques. After Warren, it remained only to fill in the details.[42]

The Warren map also recorded the outcome of another of the corps' aspirations—national expansion. The international boundaries depicted on this map differed dramatically from those traced on the maps the corps began to build on in 1838. Then the western boundary lay on the Continental Divide in the Rocky Mountains and snaked down the Red River and the Sabine to the Gulf of Mexico. Beyond lay the disputed Oregon country, Mexican California and New Mexico, and the independent Republic of Texas. By 1857, all these lands had been absorbed into the Union, the western boundary rested on the Pacific Ocean, and the United States had fulfilled the continental destiny foreseen by the officers of the corps.

The Warren map symbolized not only the achievements of the Corps of Topographical Engineers. In its carefully penned rivers, mountains, plains, and deserts, it recorded a debt to another body of specialists, fully as expert in their profession as the topographers in theirs—the mountain men. And in its continental boundaries the map recorded still another debt to these specialists. Jim Bridger and his comrades had helped fill in the map of the United States. They had also helped to enlarge the boundaries of the United States. As vanguards of empire, the mountain men had played their part in achieving America's continental destiny.

THE MAPS

PETER H. DANA

THE MAPS that accompany this book are the result of a collaboration between the author of the book and the mapmaker that was so complete as to make us true coauthors of each of these maps. Indeed, the maps would be very different, and we think less effective, without this close working relationship between historian and geographer.

These maps are computer generated. Products of digital technology, their purpose is to illustrate the terrain and waterways of the Trans-Mississippi West and the relationship between landforms and the mountain men who played such a large role in defining the perceptions of the geography of the West during the early nineteenth century. The maps are an attempt to portray, on as realistic and accurate a topographic surface as possible, the routes and places, some real and some imagined, that concerned these explorers.

Most of these maps are shaded relief maps. At one time shaded relief was in many respects more art than science. The cartographer, in attempting to portray terrain surfaces as they might appear from above, makes use of a combination of techniques including contour lines, shading, hachures (lines that follow the steepest slope), and hypsographic tinting (representing elevations with color). Hachures in particular were brought to a true merging of art and science by Swiss mapmakers in the 1940s in their portrayals of the Alps on topographic maps. From the forties through the sixties Erwin Raisz and others incorporated air photographs, satellite imagery, and field data into hand-drawn landform maps of most of the world that remain a standard for their level of accurate and dramatic views of terrain. Raisz's combination of hachuring and shading is distinctive and effective and is still used for base maps and depictions of physiographic divisions. Bob Utley considered the Raisz maps as potential base maps for this book before deciding on computer-generated shaded relief.

The fundamental idea behind shaded relief, produced painstakingly by hand or within a few minutes by computer, is very simple. The idea is to make a map that looks as terrain might when illuminated from above. Shadows and light are manipulated to show terrain variation without respect to specific elevations. That is, if a ridge rises 3,000 feet above a low coastal plain it will appear the same as another ridge rising 3,000 feet above a plateau at a base elevation of a mile. It is the relative slope in local areas that defines the amount of light reflected from the surface that forms the basis for shaded relief.

The shaded relief maps in this book were produced from digital elevation models (DEMs) created and distributed by the United States Geological Survey (USGS). DEMs are grids of elevation values for positions at regular coordinate intervals. The files are the result of the long-term effort to provide digital mapping data for the United States and the world. There are three DEM types that are commonly used for elevation mapping. There is a set of DEMs, arranged in files according to the USGS 7.5-minute quadrangle (1:24,000 scale) maps of the United States. These 50,000 or so data files are registered in meters of Universal Transverse Mercator coordinates and have elevation points about 100 feet apart. The next smallest scale DEMs are produced from the USGS 1:250,000-scale topographic maps. These DEM files are about 9 megabytes in size and are registered in latitude and longitude coordinates with 1,200 latitude rows and 1,200 longitude columns (one data point for every 3-arc seconds of latitude and longitude). Each elevation point is located horizontally about 300 feet from the next. The smallest scale DEMs are the 1:1,000,000-scale files produced from the National Imagery and Mapping Agency (formerly the Defense Mapping Agency) Digital Chart of the World database with a map source in the DMA Operational Navigation Chart (ONC) series. These DEMs are very large (it takes four 80-megabyte files to cover the United States) and have an elevation data point for every 30 seconds of latitude and longitude (about every half mile). The 3-arc second and 30-arc second DEMs are available without charge from the Global Land Information System Internet site maintained by the USGS.

We began the process of making the smaller-scale shaded relief maps in the book by downloading the four DCW DEMs that cover North America from the USGS GLIS World Wide Web site. Using a "C" program written for the project, we extracted 16-bit elevation values from rectangular areas defined in latitude and longitude space, and reprojected the data (through the simplest of nearest value methods) into a new grid file registered in equally spaced coordinates in an Albers Equal Area map projection. While most of the maps are made with the 30-arc second DEMs in this Albers projection, one map, the Lower Willamette Valley map, was made from four merged larger-scale 3-arc second DEM files and was produced using a simple cylindrical projection.

Two commercial microcomputer programs were used for most of the process of making these maps. Golden Software, of Golden, Colorado, produces MapViewer, a desktop thematic mapping program, and Surfer, a contouring and three-dimensional surface-rendering program. Both are moderately priced and have acquired a good reputation over the years as simple and reliable programs for personal computer platforms. Both are Windows programs. Part of the challenge of this project was to produce maps using easily available data, hardware, and software.

We used Surfer to produce shaded relief maps of the required areas. This process requires selection from a list of methods for determining the gradient that controls smoothness of reflected light, the shading method that selects from a number of algorithms for computing the amount of reflected light from each DEM cell, the horizontal azimuth angle from which the simulated sunlight will come, the elevation angle of the light source, and the vertical scale. For these maps, both color hue and saturation were used as visual clues to luminescence. A light yellow indicates much reflected light, while a light green indicates little reflected light. The result is a landform portrayal that shows, in a natural-looking color, terrain-slope variation in as much detail as the scale of the DEMs allows.

Digital line graphs (DLGs) are files of coordinates that define line segments representing curved lines or regions. To delineate streams, rivers, and the borders of water bodies, DLGs originating from USGS were used on these maps. Golden Software provides to registered customers a set of thinned (to 10% of their original USGS file size) DLGs that can be downloaded from their computers over the telephone. These files can be directly imported into MapViewer and Surfer. Because these maps are projected in an Albers Equal Area Projection and because we required selected streams and water bodies for these maps, we selected the required line segments and water body boundary lines in MapViewer, converted them to the same Albers projection, and exported them in Albers coordinates for importation into Surfer.

The production of detailed route maps was perhaps the most interesting part of the mapping process. In Surfer, we first made a shaded-relief map of the entire area, then exported it as a raster image file (a file of pixels, rather than a vector file of elevations, coordinates, and lines segment end points). The raster image was then imported into MapViewer as a layer and calibrated as an Albers projection. In another MapViewer layer we imported a file of all available rivers and streams. Calling on Bob Utley's familiarity with the terrain and his knowledge of the explorations, we used MapViewer tools to place, move, insert, and delete nodes representing the routes until the connected line segments traced the path around peaks and down drainages that Bob (and history) required. Occasionally we imported (on new layers), state boundaries, city centroid locations, water bodies, or other routes to aid in the process of determining the correct path. When the routes were sufficiently correct, the other layers were deleted and the finished route saved as a properly georeferenced and projected vector file for importation into Surfer.

The Continental Divide serves as a good example of the route georeferencing process. We began above the Canadian border on the MapViewer relief image. On one layer, we traced between the headwaters of the streams bound for the Pacific and Atlantic, keeping to the ridges of the dividing terrain in another layer, and continued to follow the course of the divide southward, around Wyoming's Great Divide Basin, across the Rockies, and on into Mexico. It is difficult to imagine a more appropriate technique for registering a line in geographic coordinates based on the landforms and streams that form the dividing line that played such an important part in the geographic consciousness of early westward expansion.

In Surfer, we overlaid each shaded relief layer with the appropriate rivers, water bodies, and routes. Then we imported a mask layer made in MapViewer from a region with transparent holes for the land surfaces and a solid color for the oceans and the Great Lakes. Rivers were colored and their line widths were adjusted appropriately. Water bodies were color-filled, and each map was then annotated with text and symbols. Locator maps were inserted where appropriate, using the mask layer, state boundaries, and a miniature version of the shaded relief for the mapped area.

Three maps, printed in black and white, also use shaded relief in three different shades to represent the extent of geographic knowledge at different points in history. These too were produced in Surfer, and then cut and merged together in an image-processing package. Three other maps are line drawings taken from existing period maps. In these cases, rough drawings were converted to uniform vector files by scanning the rough maps, then extracting vector-line information using a raster-to-vector converter that "traces" lines in the image. These vector files were then imported into MapViewer and edited, then exported for importation into Surfer, where the final text and symbols were added. One additional map is simply a scanned image of an existing period map, image-processed to reduce the creases and other artifacts, then saved as a raster image file.

These maps of the past were all made using microcomputers and inexpensive software and were all printed from digital files. Mapping the past was the link between the mapmaker and the author of this book. Reading the 1992 article "Mapping the Past: A Survey of Microcomputer Cartography" by Dr. Kenneth E. Foote, Department of Geography, the University of Texas at Austin (Volume 25 of *Historical Methods*), prompted Bob Utley to contact Dr. Foote to ask if indeed "computer technology had reached a state where truly innovative historical mapping is possible." Ken Foote referred Bob Utley to me, and while some of our early dreams of oblique three-dimensional views of the West have not yet made it to print, and while we have sometimes been less than innovative, we think we have effectively portrayed the relationship between landforms and explorers and the resulting growth of geographic knowledge in the early West. I hope too that we have come close to Ken Foote's vision of using readily available microcomputer technologies to map the past in new ways.

Peter H. Dana
Department of Geography
University of Texas at Austin
January 10, 1997

ACKNOWLEDGMENTS

A S ALWAYS, my severest and most constructive critic is my wife, Melody Webb. All my books owe her influence an incalculable debt, and *A Life Wild and Perilous* follows in this tradition. For the mountain man book, however, the debt is twofold. For four years, 1992–96, while she served as assistant superintendent of Grand Teton National Park, I had the privilege of living in a big log home at the very foot of the Grand Tetons. Each day (in nice weather), I sat at my desk with the Grand Teton itself looming over my computer monitor. No setting could be more inspirational for taking on the mountain men than Jackson Hole, "the crossroads of the fur trade," and its surrounding mountains. Beyond the inspiration, this mountain residence afforded me the opportunity to master the complex geography of the northern Rockies, the heartland of the fur trade. For a book such as mine, these outdoor archives proved nearly as critical as the indoor archives preserving the all-too-scarce documentation of this important phase of the American experience. To Melody and her boss, Superintendent Jack Neckels, I am grateful for the chance to have lived in so beautiful and historic a place.

To two unsurpassed specialists in the mountain men and the fur trade I express heartfelt appreciation for reading and commenting on the entire manuscript. Professor James P. Ronda of the University of Tulsa and Professor William R. Swagerty of the University of Idaho saved me from errors of fact and interpretation and provided badly needed reassurance that

I was on the right track. Professor Mary Lee Spence of the University of Illinois, coeditor of the Frémont papers, performed the same service for the three chapters on Kit Carson and John C. Frémont, for which I am thankful.

This is a very different book than I started to write, and the final incarnation is much reshaped from earlier versions. Even the title has gone through mutations beyond count. I have learned through experience that the skills and instincts of my agent, Carl Brandt, and my editor, Jack Macrae, nearly always move me in the right direction. I salute them for the close attention they have given this project and the forthright advice they have not hesitated to express.

I am very proud of the maps. I felt that computer technology must have advanced far enough to yield new looks at the topography so vital to an understanding of the mountain man story. Ron Tyler of the Texas State Historical Association put me in touch with Kenneth Foote of the University of Texas Geography Department who put me in touch with my Georgetown neighbor, Peter Dana. Our collaboration has been exciting and productive for us both. The shaded relief maps show more precisely than conventional generalized maps the topography the mountain men confronted. For readers who want to know how these maps were created entirely on a computer screen and printed entirely from computer disk, Peter has provided a separate essay.

Libraries and library staffs are indispensable to any historical work. I acknowledge my debt to the following: Utah State University at Logan—Bradford R. Cole, Keeper of Manuscripts, and Clyde A. Milner and Anne Butler of the *Western Historical Quarterly;* Harold B. Lee Library of Brigham Young University, Provo, Utah—David J. Whittaker and staff; Denver Public Library Western History Department—Eleanor P. Gehres, A. D. Mastrogiuseppe, Barbara Walton, Kathey Swan, and Philip Panum; Colorado Historical Society, Denver—David Halaas; Bancroft Library, University of California, Berkeley—Bonnie Hardwick; Huntington Library, San Marino, California—Peter Blodgett; American Heritage Center, University of Wyoming—Michael J. Devine; staff of Utah State Historical Society, Salt Lake City; staff University of Texas Library, Austin. I am especially grateful to the staff of the Teton County Library in Jackson, Wyoming, for unfailing efforts to help me find obscure books rarely shelved in a local library.

Finally, I gratefully acknowledge the constructive contributions of the following individuals: Susan Badger Doyle (Sheridan, Wyoming), William H. Goetzmann (University of Texas), Fred Gowans (Brigham Young University), James S. Hutchins (Smithsonian Institution), Janet Lecompte (University of Idaho), Eli Paul (Nebraska State Historical Society), B. Byron Price (Buffalo Bill Historical Center, Cody, Wyoming), Dan Provo (National Museum of Wildlife Art, Jackson, Wyoming), William B. Resor (Jackson, Wyoming), Marc Simmons (Cerillos, New Mexico), Erwin N. Thompson (Golden, Colorado).

SOURCES

Most of the mountain men were illiterate, or at least not literate enough to leave a written record of their lives. A handful of exceptions, most of them published, provide the best contemporary view of trapper life. They are included in the following bibliography. Prominent and obscure alike claim biographies of widely varying merit. The single most valuable source for these men is the monumental compilation edited by LeRoy R. Hafen, *Mountain Men and the Fur Trade of the Far West,* 10 vols. (Glendale: Arthur H. Clark Co., 1965–72).

The Missouri Historical Society in St. Louis provides the richest single depository of manuscript sources of the fur trade on the Missouri River and in the Rocky Mountains. I have accessed the Chouteau Collection by microfilm, in the excellent edition compiled and edited by William R. Swagerty. This is titled "Papers of the St. Louis Fur Trade," issued by University Publications of America, Bethesda, Maryland. Part 1 is the Chouteau Collection, 1752–1925. Part 2 is Fur Company Ledgers and Account Books, 1802–1871. For my purposes, Part 1 has been the most useful. The Missouri Historical Society is also the home of the Sublette and Campbell Collections, which are not included in the microfilm publication of the Papers of the St. Louis Fur Trade.

This brings me to Dale L. Morgan, that exceptional and indefatigable scholar of the fur trade and many other western topics. Morgan's papers at the Bancroft Library, University of California, Berkeley, contain transcripts of documents from the Sublette and Campbell Collections. Because they are on microfilm, I have used his transcriptions rather than the originals.

An indispensable source for fur-trade history is newspapers, especially the St. Louis newspapers. Again Dale Morgan has done much of my research for me. He made transcripts of nearly every item bearing on the history of the West in the newspapers of twenty-four states. Where my notes credit no other source for a newspaper citation, a Morgan transcript is the source. Copies of many of these transcripts (but not all) are in the Dale Morgan Collection at the Utah State Historical Society in Salt Lake City.

Morgan's interests and research ranged widely, and his papers contain other important items that I have used. The Morgan Collection is available on microfilm, in eighty reels. Most of the papers are correspondence files, for he conducted an extensive correspondence with leading historians of his time. His research data are on reels 69–79.

Finally, the official records of the St. Louis Superintendency of Indian Affairs, held throughout most of the years of this book by William Clark, provide critical source material. These records are available on microfilm from the National Archives and Records Service as Record Group 75, Records of the Bureau of Indian Affairs, Letters Received from the St. Louis Superintendency, 1824–1851, M234, reels 747–56.

PUBLISHED SOURCES

Abel, Annie H., ed. *Chardon's Journal at Fort Clark, 1834–39*. Pierre: South Dakota State Historical Society, 1932.

———. "General B. L. E. Bonneville." *Washington Historical Quarterly* 16 (July 1927): 207–30.

Abert, James W. *Through the Country of the Comanche Indians in the Fall of the Year 1845: The Journal of a U.S. Army Expedition Led by Lieutenant James W. Abert*. Ed. John Galvin. San Francisco, 1970. (See also U.S. Serial 477.)

Allen, A. J. *Ten Years in Oregon: Travels and Adventures of Doctor E. White and Lady West of the Rocky Mountains*. Ithaca, N.Y., 1848.

Allen, John L. *Passage through the Garden: Lewis and Clark and the Image of the American Northwest*. Urbana: University of Illinois Press, 1975. Reprinted as *Lewis and Clark and the Image of the American Northwest*. New York: Dover Publications, 1991.

Alter, J. Cecil. *James Bridger: A Historical Narrative*. Salt Lake City: Shephard Book Co., 1925. Reprinted as *Jim Bridger*. Norman: University of Oklahoma Press, 1962.

Ambrose, Stephen E. *Undaunted Courage: Meriwether Lewis, Thomas Jefferson, and the Opening of the American West*. New York: Simon & Schuster, 1996.

Ames, George Walcott, Jr. "Gillespie and the Conquest of California." *California Historical Society Quarterly* 17 (September 1938): 271–81.

Anderson, Harry H. "The Letters of Peter Wilson, First Resident Agent among the Teton Sioux." *Nebraska History* 42 (December 1961): 237–64.

Anderson, Maybelle Harmon. *Appleton M. Harmon Goes West*. Berkeley: University of California Press, 1946.

Atkinson, Henry. "Journal of the Atkinson-O'Fallon Expedition." Ed. Russell Reid and Clell G. Gannon. *North Dakota Historical Quarterly* 4 (October 1929): 5–56.

Ball, John. "Across the Continent 70 Years Ago: Extracts from the Journal of John Ball of his Trip Across the Rocky Mountains and Life in Oregon." *Oregon Historical Quarterly* 3 (March 1902): 82–104. Reprinted in *John Ball's Autobiography*. Glendale, Calif.: Arthur H. Clark Co., 1927.

———. Letter, October 14, 1874. *Montana Historical Society Contributions* 1 (1876): 111–12.

———. Letters of 1832–33. In Archer B. Hulbert, *The Call of the Columbia, 1830–35*. Colorado Springs and Denver: Stewart Commission of Colorado College and Denver Public Library, 1934.

Barry, J. Neilson. "Captain Bonneville." *Annals of Wyoming* 8 (April 1932): 610–33.

Barry, Louise, ed. "William Clark's Diary, May 1826–February 1831." *Kansas Historical Quarterly* 16 (1948): 1–40, 136–75, 274–306, 384–411.

Batman, Richard. *James Pattie's West: The Dream and the Reality.* Norman: University of Oklahoma Press, 1986.

Bauer, K. Jack. *The Mexican War, 1846–1848.* New York: Macmillan, 1974. Lincoln: University of Nebraska Press, 1992.

Beidleman, Richard G. "Nathaniel Wyeth's Fort Hall." *Oregon Historical Quarterly* 58 (September 1957): 197–250.

Bek, William G., trans. and ed. "First Journey to North America in the Years 1822 to 1824 [Prince Paul Wilhelm]." *South Dakota Historical Collections* 19 (1938): 7–474.

Benton, Thomas Hart. *Thirty Years View: A History of the Working of the American Government for Thirty Years, 1820–1850.* 2 vols. New York: D. Appleton & Co., 1854.

Berry, Don. *A Majority of Scoundrels: An Informal History of the Rocky Mountain Fur Company.* New York: Harper & Bros., 1961.

Bidwell, John. "Frémont and the Conquest of California." *Century Magazine* 41 (February 1891): 518–25.

Bieber, Ralph P., ed. *Exploring Southwestern Trails, 1846–1854.* Glendale, Calif.: Arthur H. Clark Co., 1938.

Binns, Archie. *Peter Skene Ogden, Fur Trader.* Portland, Ore.: Binfords & Mort, 1967.

Blackwelder, Bernice. *Great Westerner: The Story of Kit Carson.* Caldwell, Idaho: Caxton Printers, 1962.

Blair, Walter, and Franklin J. Meine, eds. *Half Horse Half Alligator.* Chicago: University of Chicago Press, 1956.

Boggs, William M. "Manuscript about Bent's Fort, Kit Carson, the Far West and Life among the Indians." Ed. LeRoy R. Hafen. *Colorado Magazine* 7 (March 1930): 45–69.

Bonner, Thomas D. *The Life and Adventures of James P. Beckwourth.* Ed. Delmont R. Oswald. Lincoln: University of Nebraska Press, 1972.

Bonneville, B. L. E. Letter to Montana Historical Society. *Montana Historical Society Contributions* 3 (1900): 105–10.

Brackenridge, Henry M. *Views of Louisiana Together with a Journal of a Voyage up the Missouri River in 1811.* Pittsburgh: Cramer, Spear & Eichbaum, 1814.

Brackett, William S. "Bonneville and Bridger." *Montana Historical Society Contributions* 3 (1900): 175–200.

Bradbury, John. *Travels in the Interior of America in the Years 1809, 1810, and 1811.* Liverpool: Smith and Glaway, 1817. In Reuben Gold Thwaites, *Early Western Travels* 5.

Brandon, William. *The Men and the Mountain: Frémont's Fourth Expedition.* New York: William Morrow, 1955.

Brewerton, George D. "A Ride with Kit Carson." *Harper's Magazine* 7 (August 1853): 306–34. Reprinted as *Overland with Kit Carson: A Narrative of the Old Spanish Trail in '48.* Lincoln: University of Nebraska Press, 1993.

Bright, Verne. "Black Harris, Mountain Man, Teller of Tales." *Oregon Historical Quarterly* 52 (March 1951): 3–20.

Brooks, George R., ed. *The Southwest Expedition of Jedediah S. Smith: His Personal Account of the Journey to California, 1826–1827.* Glendale, Calif.: Arthur H. Clark Co., 1977. Lincoln: University of Nebraska Press, 1989.

Brosnan, Cornelius J. *Jason Lee: Prophet of the New Oregon.* New York: Macmillan, 1932.

———. "The Oregon Memorial of 1838." *Oregon Historical Quarterly* 34 (March 1933): 68–87.

Brown, David L. *Three Years in the Rocky Mountains.* New York: privately published, 1950. Reprinted from *Cincinnati Atlas*, 1845.

Bryant, Edwin. *What I Saw in California . . .* [in 1846–47]. New York: D. Appleton & Co., 1848. Lincoln: University of Nebraska Press, 1985.

Burnett, Peter H. "Recollections of an Old Pioneer." *Oregon Historical Quarterly* 5 (1904): 64–99, 151–98, 272–305, 370–402.

Calvin, Ross, ed. *Lieutenant Emory Reports: A Reprint of Lieutenant W. H. Emory's Notes of a Military Reconnoissance*. Albuquerque: University of New Mexico Press, 1951.

Camp, Charles L., ed. *George C. Yount and His Chronicles of the West*. Denver: Old West Publishing Co., 1966.

————, ed. *James Clyman, American Frontiersman; The Adventures of a Trapper and Covered-Wagon Migrant as Told in His Own Reminiscences and Diaries*. Portland, Ore.: Champoeg Press, 1960.

————. "Jedediah Smith's First Far Western Expedition." *Western Historical Quarterly* 4 (April 1973): 151–70.

————. "Kit Carson in California." *California Historical Society Quarterly* 1 (October 1922): 111–15.

Campbell, Robert. "Correspondence of Robert Campbell, 1834–1845." Ed. Stella M. Drumm. Missouri Historical Society, *Glimpses of the Past* 8 (January–June 1941): 1–65.

————. "The Private Journal of Robert Campbell." Ed. George R. Brooks. *Missouri Historical Society Bulletin* 20 (October 1963–January 1964): 3–24, 107–18.

————. *The Rocky Mountain Letters of Robert Campbell*. New York: privately printed, 1955. Reprinted from Philadelphia *National Atlas*.

Carey, Charles H., ed. *The Journals of Thedore Talbot, 1843 and 1849–52, with the Frémont Expedition of 1843 and with the First Military Company in Oregon Territory, 1849–1852*. Portland, Ore.: Metropolitan Press, 1931.

Carleton, James H. *The Prairie Logbooks: Dragoon Campaigns to the Pawnee Villages in 1844, and to the Rocky Mountains in 1845*. Ed. Louis Pelzer. Chicago: Caxton Club, 1943. Lincoln: University of Nebraska Press, 1983.

Carriker, Robert C. *Father Peter John De Smet, Jesuit in the West*. Norman: University of Oklahoma Press, 1995.

Carter, Harvey L. *"Dear Old Kit": The Historical Christopher Carson*. Norman: University of Oklahoma Press, 1968.

————. "The Divergent Paths of Frémont's 'Three Marshals.' " *New Mexico Historical Review* 48 (January 1973): 5–25.

Carter, Harvey L., and Marcia C. Spencer. "Stereotypes of the Mountain Men." *Western Historical Quarterly* 6 (January 1975): 17–32. (See also Goetzmann, William H.)

Chalfant, William Y. *Dangerous Passage: The Santa Fe Trail and the Mexican War*. Norman: University of Oklahoma Press, 1994.

Chittenden, Hiram M. *The American Fur Trade of the Far West*. 2 vols. Stanford, Calif.: Academic Reprints, 1954.

Chittenden, Hiram M., and A. D. Richardson, eds. *Life, Letters and Travels of Father Pierre-Jean De Smet. . . .* 4 vols. New York: Francis D. Harper, 1905.

Clark, Charles G. *The Men of the Lewis and Clark Expedition: A Biographical Roster of the Fifty-One Members and a Composite Diary of their Activities from all Known Sources*. Glendale, Calif.: Arthur H. Clark Co., 1970.

Clarke, Dwight L. *Stephen Watts Kearny: Soldier of the West*. Norman: University of Oklahoma Press, 1961.

Clayton, H. J. Recollections of James Bridger. *San Francisco Daily Alta California*, April 21, 1872.

Clayton, William. *William Clayton's Journal*. Salt Lake City: Deseret News, 1921.

Cleland, Robert G. *This Reckless Breed of Men: The Trappers and Fur Traders of the Southwest*. New York: Alfred A. Knopf, 1950.

Cline, Gloria Griffen. *Exploring the Great Basin*. Norman: University of Oklahoma Press, 1963.

———. *Peter Skene Ogden and the Hudson's Bay Company*. Norman: University of Oklahoma Press, 1975.

Clokey, Richard M. *William H. Ashley: Enterprise and Politics in the Trans-Mississippi West*. Norman: University of Oklahoma Press, 1979.

Colton, Walter. *Deck and Port, or, Incidents of a Cruise in the United States Frigate "Congress" to California*. New York: A. S. Barnes, 1850.

Conrad, Howard L. *Uncle Dick Wooton: The Pioneer Frontiersman of the Rocky Mountain Region*. Lincoln: University of Nebraska Press, 1980.

Cooke, Philip St. George. *The Conquest of New Mexico and California: An Historical and Personal Narrative*. New York: G. P. Putnam's Sons, 1878.

———. *Scenes and Adventures in the Army*. Philadelphia, 1859. New York: Arno Press, 1973.

Coues, Elliott, ed. *History of the Expedition under the Command of Lewis and Clark*. 4 vols. in 3. 1893. Reprint, New York: Dover Publications, 1964.

Cox, Ross. *The Columbia River*. Ed. Edgar I. and Jane R. Stewart. Norman: University of Oklahoma Press, 1957.

Crampton, C. Gregory, and Gloria G. Griffen. "The San Buenaventura: Mythical River of the West." *Pacific Historical Review* 25 (May 1956): 163–71.

Crawford, Medorem. "The Journal of Medorem Crawford." *Sources of the History of Oregon* 1 (Eugene: State Job Office, 1897): 1–23.

Cutright, Paul Russell. *Lewis and Clark, Pioneering Naturalists*. Urbana: University of Illinois Press, 1969. Lincoln: University of Nebraska Press, 1989.

———. "Lewis on the Marias, 1806." *Montana the Magazine of Western History* 18 (Summer 1968): 30–43.

Dale, Harrison C., ed. *The Ashley-Smith Explorations and the Discovery of a Central Route to the Pacific, 1822–1829*. Glendale: Arthur H. Clark Co., 1941. Reprinted as *The Explorations of William H. Ashley and Jedediah Smith, 1822–1829*. Lincoln: University of Nebraska Press, 1991.

DeLand, Charles E. "Basil Clement (Claymore)." *South Dakota Historical Collections* 11 (1922): 245–389.

Denig, Edwin. *Five Indian Tribes of the Upper Missouri: Sioux, Arikaras, Assiniboines, Crees, Crows*. Ed. John C. Ewers. Norman: University of Oklahoma Press, 1961.

De Smet, Pierre Jean, S.J. *Letters and Sketches, with a Narrative of a Year's Residence among the Indian Tribes of the Rocky Mountains*. Philadelphia: M. Fithian, 1843. In Reuben Gold Thwaites, *Early Western Travels* 27.

DeVoto, Bernard. *Across the Wide Missouri*. Boston: Houghton Mifflin Co., 1947.

———. *The Course of Empire*. Boston: Houghton Mifflin Co., 1952.

———. "An Inference Regarding the Expedition of Lewis and Clark." *Proceedings of the American Philosophical Society* 99 (August 1955): 185–94.

———. *The Year of Decision, 1846*. Boston: Houghton Mifflin Co., 1942.

Dodge, Grenville M. *Biographical Sketch of James Bridger, Mountaineer*. New York: Unz & Co., 1905. Reprinted in Alter, J. Cecil, 1925 edition.

Drumm, Stella M., ed. "Reports of the Fur Trade and Inland Trade to Mexico, 1831." Missouri Historical Society, *Glimpses of the Past* 9 (January–September 1941): 1–86.

Drury, Clifford M. *Elkanah and Mary Walker: Pioneers among the Spokanes*. Caldwell, Idaho: Caxton, 1940.

———, ed. *Diaries and Letters of Asa Bowen Smith, Regarding the Nez Perce Mission, 1838–1842*. Glendale, Calif.: Arthur H. Clark Co., 1958.

————, ed. *First White Women over the Rockies: Diaries, Letters, and Biographical Sketches.* Glendale, Calif.: Arthur H. Clark Co., 1966.

————. *Henry Harmon Spalding.* Caldwell, Idaho: Caxton, 1936.

————. *Marcus Whitman, M.D.: Pioneer and Martyr.* Caldwell, Idaho: Caxton, 1937.

Dunwiddie, Peter W. "The Nature of the Relationship between the Blackfeet Indians and the Men of the Fur Trade." *Annals of Wyoming* 46 (Spring 1974): 23–33.

Dye, Job Francis. *Recollections of a Pioneer, 1830–1852: Rocky Mountains, New Mexico, California.* Los Angeles: Glen Dawson, 1951.

Eaton, W. Clement. "Nathaniel Wyeth's Oregon Expeditions." *Pacific Historical Review* 4 (June 1935): 101–13.

Eells, Mrs. Myra. "Journal." *Transactions of the Oregon Pioneer Association, 1889.* Also in Hafen and Young, *Fort Laramie.*

Elliott, T. C. " 'Doctor' Robert Newell: Pioneer." *Oregon Historical Quarterly* 9 (June 1908): 103–26.

————, ed. "Journal of Alexander Ross—Snake Country Expedition, 1824." *Oregon Historical Quarterly* 14 (December 1913): 366–88.

————, ed. "The Journal of John Work; July 5–September 15, 1826. *Washington Historical Quarterly* 6 (January 1915): 26–49.

————, ed. "Journal of John Work [April 21–July 21, 1831]." *Oregon Historical Quarterly* 14 (September 1913): 280–314.

————, ed. "Journal of John Work [August 22, 1830–March 18, 1831]." *Oregon Historical Quarterly* 13 (December 1912): 361–71.

————, ed. "The Peter Skene Ogden Journals." *Oregon Historical Quarterly* 10 (December 1909): 331–65.

Ellison, Robert S. *Fort Bridger, Wyoming: A Brief History.* Sheridan, Wyo.: privately published, 1938.

Ellison, William H., ed. *The Life and Adventures of George Nidever.* Berkeley: University of California Press, 1937.

Estergreen, M. Morgan. *Kit Carson: A Portrait in Courage.* Norman: University of Oklahoma Press, 1962.

Ewers, John C. "The Indian Trade of the Upper Missouri before Lewis and Clark: An Interpretation." In Ewers, *Indian Life on the Upper Missouri.* Norman: University of Oklahoma Press, 1968.

Farnham, Thomas J. *Travels in the Great Western Prairies, the Anahuac and Rocky Mountains, and in the Oregon Territory [1839–40].* 2 vols. London: Richard Bentley, 1843. In Reuben Gold Thwaites, *Early Western Travels* 28–29.

Favour, Alpheus H. *Old Bill Williams, Mountain Man.* Chapel Hill: University of North Carolina Press, 1936. Norman: University of Oklahoma Press, 1962.

Ferris, Warren A. *Life in the Rocky Mountains: Diary of Wanderings on the Sources of the Rivers Missouri, Columbia, and Colorado from February, 1830, to November, 1835.* Ed. Paul C. Phillips. Denver: Old West Publishing Co., 1940.

Field, Matthew C. *Prairie and Mountain Sketches.* Ed. Kate L. Gregg and John F. McDermott. Norman: University of Oklahoma Press, 1957.

Franchère, Gabriel. *Journal of a Voyage on the North West Coast of North America during the Years 1811, 1812, 1813, and 1814.* Ed. W. Kaye Lamb. Toronto: Champlain Society, 1969.

Frémont, John C. "The Conquest of California." *Century Magazine* 41 (April 1891): 923–24.

————. *Memoirs of My Life.* Chicago and New York: Bedford, Clarke & Co., 1887.

————. *Narratives of Exploration and Adventure.* Ed. Allan Nevins. New York: Longmans, Green, 1956.

Frost, Donald M. *Notes on General Ashley, the Overland Trail, and South Pass.* Worcester, Mass.: American Antiquarian Society, 1945.

Galbraith, John S. *The Hudson's Bay Company as an Imperial Factor, 1821–1869.* Berkeley: University of California Press, 1957.

———. *The Little Emperor: Governor Simpson of the Hudson's Bay Company.* Toronto: Macmillan of Canada, 1976.

Galvin, John, ed. *Through the Country of the Comanche Indians in the Year 1845: The Journal of a U.S. Army Expedition Led by Lieutenant James W. Abert.* San Francisco: John Howell Books, 1970.

Gass, Patrick. *A Journal of the Voyages and Travels of a Corps of Discovery.* 1807. Reprint, Minneapolis: Ross and Haines, 1958.

Ghent, W. J. "A Sketch of John Colter." *Wyoming Annals* 10 (July 1938): 111–16.

Gilbert, Bil. *Westering Man: The Life of Joseph Walker.* New York: Atheneum, 1983. Norman: University of Oklahoma Press, 1985.

Goetzmann, William H. *Army Exploration in the American West, 1803–1863.* New Haven: Yale University Press, 1959.

———. *Exploration and Empire: The Explorer and Scientist in the Winning of the American West.* New York: Alfred A. Knopf, 1966.

———. *The Mountain Man.* Cody, Wyo.: Buffalo Bill Historical Center, 1978.

———. "The Mountain Man as Jacksonian Man." *American Quarterly* 15 (fall 1963): 402–15. (See also Carter, Harvey, and Marcia Spencer.)

Gordon-McCutcheon, R. C., ed. *Kit Carson: Indian Fighter or Indian Killer?* Niwot, Colo.: University Press of Colorado, 1996.

Gowans, Fred R. *Rocky Mountain Rendezvous: A History of the Fur Trade Rendezvous, 1825–1840.* Provo, Utah: Brigham Young University Press, 1976.

Gowans, Fred R., and Eugene E. Campbell. *Fort Bridger: Island in the Wilderness.* Provo, Utah: Brigham Young University Press, 1975.

Graebner, Norman A. *Empire on the Pacific: A Study in American Continental Expansion.* New York: Ronald Press, 1955.

Grant, Louis S. "Fort Hall under the Hudson's Bay Company, 1837–1856." *Oregon Historical Quarterly* 41 (March 1940): 34–39.

Gray, William H. *A History of Oregon.* Portland, Ore.: Harris & Holman; San Francisco: H. H. Bancroft; New York: American News Co., 1870.

———. "Journal of W. H. Gray, from December 28, 1836, to October 15, 1837." *Whitman College Quarterly* 16 (June 1913): 7–76. Reprinted as *Journal of William H. Gray.* ed. Don Johnson. Fairfield, Wash.: Ye Galleon Press, 1980.

Gudde, Ernest G. *Sutter's Own Story: The Life of General John Augustus Sutter and the History of New Helvetia.* New York: G. P. Putnam's Sons, 1936.

Guild, Thelma S., and Harvey L. Carter. *Kit Carson: A Pattern for Heroes.* Lincoln: University of Nebraska Press, 1984.

Hafen, LeRoy R. "The Bean-Sinclair Party of Rocky Mountain Trappers, 1830–32." *Colorado Magazine* 31 (July 1954): 161–71.

———. *Broken Hand: The Life Story of Thomas Fitzpatrick.* Lincoln: University of Nebraska Press, 1980.

———. "The Early Fur Trade Posts on the South Platte." *Mississippi Valley Historical Review* 7 (1925): 334–41.

———. "Fort Davy Crockett, Its Fur Men and Visitors." *Colorado Magazine* 29 (January 1952): 17–33.

———. "Fort St. Vrain." *Colorado Magazine* 29 (October 1954): 241–55.

———. "Fort Vasquez." *Colorado Magazine* 41 (1964): 198–212.

———. "Fraeb's Last Fight and How Battle Creek Got Its Name." *Colorado Magazine* 7 (1930): 97–101.

———. *The Mountain Men and the Fur Trade of the Far West.* 10 vols. Glendale, Calif.: Arthur H. Clark Co., 1965–72.

———, ed. *Ruxton of the Rockies.* Norman: University of Oklahoma Press, 1950.

———. "Thomas Fitzpatrick and the First Indian Agency in Colorado." *Colorado Magazine* 6 (March 1929): 53–62.

Hafen, LeRoy R., and Ann W. Hafen, eds. *Frémont's Fourth Expedition: A Documentary Account of the Disaster of 1848–49.* Glendale, Calif.: Arthur H. Clark Co., 1960.

———. *The Old Spanish Trail.* Glendale, Calif.: Arthur H. Clark Co., 1954.

———, eds. *Rufus B. Sage: His Letters and Papers, 1846–1847.* Glendale, Calif.: Arthur H. Clark Co., 1956.

———, eds. *To the Rockies and Oregon, 1839–1842.* Glendale, Calif.: Arthur H. Clark Co., 1955.

Hafen, LeRoy R., and Francis M. Young. *Fort Laramie and the Pageant of the West, 1834–1890.* Glendale, Calif.: Arthur H. Clark Co., 1938.

Hague, Harlan, and David J. Langum. *Thomas O. Larkin: A Life of Patriotism and Profit in Old California.* Norman: University of Oklahoma Press, 1990.

Haines, Francis D. "Pioneer Portrait: Robert Newell." *Idaho Yesterdays* 9 (Spring 1965): 2–9.

———, ed. *The Snake Country Expedition of 1830–31: John Work's Field Journal.* Norman: University of Oklahoma Press, 1971.

Hammond, George P., ed. *The Adventures of Alexander Barclay, Mountain Man: A Narrative of His Career, 1810–1855: His Memorandum Diary, 1845–1850.* Denver: Old West Publishing Co., 1976.

———. *The Larkin Papers: Personal, Business, and Official Correspondence of Thomas Oliver Larkin, Merchant and United States Consul in California.* 10 vols. Berkeley: University of California Press, 1951–64.

Harlow, Neal. *California Conquered: War and Peace on the Pacific, 1846–1850.* Berkeley: University of California Press, 1982.

Harris, Burton. *John Colter: His Years in the Rockies.* New York: Charles Scribner's Sons, 1952. Lincoln: University of Nebraska Press, 1993.

Heap, Gwinn Harris. *Central Route to the Pacific . . .* Ed. LeRoy R. Hafen. Glendale, Calif.: Arthur H. Clark Co., 1957.

Herr, Pamela. *Jessie Benton Frémont: A Biography.* New York: Franklin Watts, 1987. Norman: University of Oklahoma Press, 1988.

Hill, Joseph J. "Ewing Young in the Fur Trade of the Far Southwest, 1822–1834." *Oregon Historical Quarterly* 24 (March 1923): 1–35.

———. "New Light on Pattie and the Southwestern Fur Trade." *Southwestern Historical Quarterly* 26 (April 1923): 243–54.

———. "Spanish and Mexican Exploration and Trade Northwest from New Mexico into the Great Basin, 1765–1853." *Utah Historical Quarterly* 3 (January 1930): 3–23.

Hine, Robert V. *Edward Kern and American Expansion.* New Haven: Yale University Press, 1962. Reprinted as *In the Shadow of Frémont: Edward Kern and the Art of American Exploration, 1845–1860.* Norman: University of Oklahoma Press, 1981.

Hine, Robert V., and Savoie Lottinville, eds. *Soldier in the West: The Letters of Theodore Talbot during His Services in California, Mexico, and Oregon, 1845–53.* Norman: University of Oklahoma Press, 1972.

Hollman, Frederick V. *Dr. John McLoughlin, The Father of Oregon.* Cleveland: Arthur H. Clark Co., 1907.

Holloway, Drew Allen, ed. *A Narrative of Colonel Robert Campbell's Experiences in the Rocky Mountain Fur Trade from 1825 to 1835*. Fairfield, Wash.: Ye Galleon Press, 1991.

Holmes, Frederick V. "A Brief History of the Oregon Provisional Government and What Caused Its Formation." *Oregon Historical Quarterly* 13 (June 1912): 89–139.

Holmes, Kenneth L. *Ewing Young: Master Trapper*. Portland, Oreg.: Binfords & Mort, 1967.

Holmes, Reuben. "The Five Scalps." Missouri Historical Society, *Glimpses of the Past* 5 (January–March 1938): 3–54.

Hulbert, Archer B. *The Call of the Columbia: Iron Men and Saints Take the Oregon Trail, 1830–35*. Colorado Springs and Denver: Stewart Commission of Colorado College and Denver Public Library, 1934.

———, ed. *Southwest on the Turquoise Trail: The First Diaries on the Road to Santa Fe*. Colorado Springs and Denver: Stewart Commission of Colorado College and Denver Public Library, 1933.

Hulbert, Archer B., and Dorothy P. Hulbert, eds. *Marcus Whitman, Crusader*. 3 vols. Colorado Springs and Denver: Stewart Commission of Colorado College and Denver Public Library, 1936–41.

———. *The Oregon Crusade: Across Land and Sea to Oregon, 1830–1840*. Colorado Springs and Denver: Stewart Commission of Colorado College and Denver Public Library, 1935.

Husband, Michael B. "Senator Lewis Linn and the Oregon Question." *Missouri Historical Review* 66 (October 1971): 1–19.

Hussey, John A. *Champoeg: Place of Transition*. Portland: Oregon Historical Society, 1967.

———. "The Origin of the Gillespie Mission." *California Historical Society Quarterly* 19 (March 1940): 43–58.

Ide, Simeon. *The Conquest of California: A Biography of William B. Ide*. Oakland: California Biobooks, 1994.

Immel, Michael E. "Deposition and Interrogation of . . . , June 25, 1821." *Missouri Historical Society Bulletin* 4 (1948): 78–81.

Irving, Washington. *The Adventures of Captain Bonneville, U.S.A., in the Rocky Mountains and the Far West*. Ed. Edgeley W. Todd. Norman: University of Oklahoma Press, 1986.

———. *Astoria, or Anecdotes of an Enterprise beyond the Rocky Mountains*. 2 vols. Philadelphia: Carey, Lee & Blanchard, 1836. Reprint, Norman: University of Oklahoma Press, 1964.

Jackson, Donald. *Letters of the Lewis and Clark Expedition with Related Documents, 1783–1854*. 2d ed. 2 vols. Urbana: University of Illinois Press, 1978.

———. *Thomas Jefferson and the Stony Mountains: Exploring the West from Monticello*. Urbana: University of Illinois Press, 1981.

Jackson, Donald, and Mary Lee Spence, eds. *The Expeditions of John Charles Frémont*. 4 vols. Urbana: University of Illinois Press, 1970–84.

Jackson, John C. *Shadow on the Tetons: David E. Jackson and the Claiming of the American West*. Missoula, Mont.: Mountain Press Publishing Co., 1993.

James, Thomas. *Three Years among the Indians and Mexicans*. Ed. Walter B. Douglas. St. Louis: Missouri Historical Society, 1916.

Jeffrey, Julie Roy. *Converting the West: A Biography of Narcissa Whitman*. Norman: University of Oklahoma Press, 1991.

Johansen, Dorothy O., ed. *Robert Newell's Memoranda: Travels in the Teritory of Missourie; Travel to the Kayuse War; together with A Report on the Indians south of the Columbia River*. Portland, Ore.: Champoeg Press, 1959.

Johansen, Dorothy O., and Charles M. Gates. *Empire on the Columbia: A History of the Pacific Northwest*. New York: Harper & Brothers, 1957.

Johnson, Donald R., ed. *William H. Gray: Journal of His Journey East, 1836–37.* Fairfield, Wash.: Ye Galleon Press, 1980.

Josephy, Alvin M., Jr. *The Nez Perce Indians and the Opening of the Northwest.* New Haven: Yale University Press, 1965.

Kearny, Thomas. "Kearny and 'Kit' Carson, as Interpreted by Stanley Vestal." *New Mexico Historical Review* 5 (January 1930): 1–16.

Kennerly, James. "Diary of . . . 1823–1826." Ed. Edgar B. Wesley. *Missouri Historical Society Collections* 6 (October 1928): 41–97.

Killoren, John J. *"Come, Blackrobe": De Smet and the Indian Tragedy.* Norman: University of Oklahoma Press, 1994.

Kroeber, Clifton, ed. "The Route of James O. Pattie on the Colorado in 1826: A Reappraisal by A. L. Kroeber." *Arizona and the West* 6 (Summer 1964): 119–36.

Lass, William E. *A History of Steamboating on the Upper Missouri River.* Lincoln: University of Nebraska Press, 1962.

Lavender, David. *Bent's Fort.* New York: Doubleday, 1954.

———. *Fist in the Wilderness.* Garden City, N.Y.: Doubleday, 1964.

———. *Westward Vision: The Story of the Oregon Trail.* New York: McGraw-Hill, 1963. Lincoln: University of Nebraska Press, 1985.

Lecompte, Janet. "The Chouteaus and the St. Louis Fur Trade." In William R. Swagerty, ed. *A Guide to the Microfilm Edition of Papers of the St. Louis Fur Trade.* Bethesda, Md.: University Publications of America, 1991: xiii–xx.

———. *Pueblo, Hardscrabble, Greenhorn: Society on the High Plains, 1832–1856.* Norman: University of Oklahoma Press, 1978.

Lee, Jason. [Abstract of overland journal, April 28–June 29, 1834; July 2, 1834–February 6, 1835.] *New York Christian Advocate and Journal,* October 3, 1834, October 30, 1835. Reprinted in Hulbert and Hulbert, *Oregon Crusade.*

———. "Diary of Rev. Jason Lee." *Oregon Historical Quarterly* 17 (June–December 1916): 116–46, 240–66, 397–430.

Leonard, Zenas. *Adventures of Zenas Leonard, Fur Trader.* Ed. John C. Ewers. Norman: University of Oklahoma Press, 1959.

Loewenberg, Robert J. "Creating a Provisional Government in Oregon: A Revision." *Pacific Northwest Quarterly* 68 (January 1977): 13–24.

———. *Equality on the Oregon Frontier: Jason Lee and the Methodist Mission, 1834–43.* Seattle: University of Washington Press, 1976.

Lowe, Percival G. *Five Years a Dragoon ('49 to '54) and Other Adventures on the Great Plains.* Ed. Don Russell. Norman: University of Oklahoma Press, 1965.

McDermott, John Francis, ed. *The Frontier Reexamined.* Urbana: University of Illinois Press, 1967.

Maloney, Alice B. "The Richard Campbell Party of 1827." *California Historical Society Quarterly* 17 (December 1939): 347–54.

Marcy, Randolph B. *Thirty Years of Army Life on the Border.* New York: Harper & Brothers, 1866. Philadelphia: J. B. Lippincott, 1962.

Marsh, James B. *Four Years in the Rockies: or, The Adventures of Isaac P. Rose. . . .* New Castle, Pa.: W. B. Thomas, 1884. Columbus, Ohio: Long's College Book Store, n.d.

Marshall, Thomas M., ed. "The Journals of Jules de Mun." *Missouri Historical Society Collections* 5 (1928): 167–208, 311–27.

———. "St. Vrain's Expedition to the Gila in 1826." In H. Morse Stephens and Herbert E. Bolton, eds. *The Pacific Ocean in History.* New York: Macmillan, 1917: 429–38.

Marti, Werner H. *Messenger of Destiny: The California Adventures, 1846–1847, of Archibald H. Gillespie, U.S. Marine Corps.* San Francisco: John Howell Books, 1960.

Mattes, Merrill J. *Platte River Road Narratives: A Descriptive Bibliography of Travel over the Great Central Route.* . . . Urbana: University of Illinois Press, 1988.

Maximilian, Prince of Wied. *Travels in the Interior of North America.* London, 1843. In Reuben Gold Thwaites, *Early Western Travels* 24.

McDermott, John Francis. "Washington Irving and the Journal of Captain Bonneville." *Mississippi Valley Historical Review* 43 (December 1956): 459–67.

McDonald, Lois Halliday. *Fur Trade Letters of Francis Ermantinger.* Glendale, Calif.: Arthur H. Clark Co., 1980.

McLoughlin, John. *Letters of John McLoughlin from Fort Vancouver to the Governor and Committee, First Series, 1825–1838.* Ed. E. E. Rich. London and Toronto: Hudson's Bay Record Society, 1941.

———. *Letters of John McLoughlin from Fort Vancouver to the Governor and Committee, Second Series, 1839–44.* Ed. E. E. Rich. London: Hudson's Bay Record Society, 1943.

———. *Letters of John McLoughlin from Fort Vancouver to the Governor and Committee, Third Series, 1844–46.* Ed. E. E. Rich. London: Hudson's Bay Record Society, 1944.

Meek, Stephen Hall. *The Autobiography of a Mountain Man.* Ed. Arthur Woodward. Pasadena: Glen Dawson, 1948. From *Golden Era,* April 1885.

Meinig, D. W. *The Great Columbia Plain: A Historical Geography, 1805–1910.* Seattle: University of Washington Press, 1968.

Merk, Frederick. *Fur Trade and Empire: George Simpson's Journal . . . 1824–1825.* Cambridge: Harvard University Press, 1931.

———. *Manifest Destiny and Mission in American History: A Reinterpretation.* New York: Alfred A. Knopf, 1963.

———. *The Oregon Question: Essays in Anglo-American Diplomacy and Politics.* Cambridge: Belknap Press of Harvard University Press, 1946.

———. "Snake Country Expedition, 1824–25: An Episode of Fur Trade and Empire." *Mississippi Valley Historical Review* 21 (June 1934): 49–75.

Methodist Mission. "The Mission Record Book of the Methodist Episcopal Church, Willamette Station, Oregon Territory, North America, Commenced in 1834." *Oregon Historical Quarterly* 23 (September 1922): 248–52.

Miller, Alfred Jacob. *The West of Alfred Jacob Miller.* Ed. Marvin C. Ross. Norman: University of Oklahoma Press, 1968.

Miller, David E., ed. "Peter Skene Ogden's Journal of His Expedition to Utah, 1825." *Utah Historical Quarterly* 20 (April 1952): 159–86.

———. "Peter Skene Ogden's Trek into Utah, 1828–29." *Pacific Northwest Quarterly* 51 (January 1960): 16–25.

Moody, Marshall D. "Kit Carson, Agent to the Indians of New Mexico." *New Mexico Historical Review* 28 (January 1953): 1–20.

Morgan, Dale L. *The Great Salt Lake.* Indianapolis: Bobbs-Merrill Co., 1947. Lincoln: University of Nebraska Press, 1986.

———. *The Humboldt: Highroad of the West.* New York: Farrar & Rinehart, 1943. Lincoln: University of Nebraska Press, 1985.

———. *Jedediah Smith and the Opening of the West.* Indianapolis: Bobbs-Merrill Co., 1953. Lincoln: University of Nebraska Press, 1964.

———, ed. *Overland in 1846: Diaries and Letters of the California-Oregon Trail.* 2 vols. Georgetown, Calif.: Talisman Press, 1963. Lincoln: University of Nebraska Press, 1993.

———, ed. *The West of William H. Ashley.* Denver: Old West Publishing Co., 1964.

Morgan, Dale L., and Eleanor T. Harris, eds. *The Rocky Mountain Journals of William Marshall Anderson: The West in 1834.* San Marino, Calif.: Huntington Library, 1967. Lincoln: University of Nebraska Press, 1987.

Morgan, Dale L., and Carl I. Wheat. *Jedediah Smith and His Maps of the American West.* San Francisco: California Historical Society, 1954.

Moulton, Gary E., ed. *The Journals of the Lewis and Clark Expedition.* 10 vols. Lincoln: University of Nebraska Press, 1983–96.

Munger, Asahel. "Diary of Asahel Munger and Wife." *Oregon Historical Quarterly* 8 (1907): 387–405.

Myers, John Myers. *Pirate, Pawnee, and Mountain Man: The Saga of Hugh Glass.* Boston: Little, Brown, & Co., 1963. Reprinted as *The Saga of Hugh Glass.* Lincoln: University of Nebraska Press, 1976.

Nasatir, A. P. "The International Significance of the Jones and Immell Massacre and the Aricara Outbreak in 1823." *Pacific Northwest Quarterly* 30 (January 1939): 77–108.

Nesmith, James W. "Diary of the Emigration of 1843." *Oregon Historical Quarterly* 7 (December 1906): 329–59.

Nevins, Allan. *Frémont: Pathmarker of the West.* New York: Longmans, Green & Co., 1955.

———. "Kit Carson, Bayard of the Plains." *American Scholar* 8 (Summer 1939): 333–49.

Nichols, Roger L. *General Henry Atkinson: A Western Military Career.* Norman: University of Oklahoma Press, 1965.

Nidever, George. *Life and Adventures of George Nidever.* Ed. W. H. Ellison. Berkeley: University of California Press, 1937.

Nunis, Doyce B., Jr. "The Fur Men: Key to Westward Expansion." *Historian* 23 (February 1961): 167–90.

Oglesby, Richard E. *Manuel Lisa and the Opening of the Missouri Fur Trade.* Norman: University of Oklahoma Press, 1963.

Oliphant, J. Orin, ed. "A Letter by Henry H. Spalding from the Rocky Mountains." *Oregon Historical Quarterly* 51 (June 1950): 127–33. From *New York Evangelist,* October 22, 1836.

O'Meara, Walter. *Daughters of the Country: The Women of the Fur Traders and Mountain Men.* New York: Harcourt, Brace & World, 1968.

Osgood, Ernest S. *Field Notes of Captain William Clark.* New Haven: Yale University Press, 1964.

Palmer, Joel. *Journal of Travels over the Rocky Mountains to the Mouth of the Columbia River . . . [1845–46].* Cincinnati: J. A. & U. P. James, 1847. In Reuben Gold Thwaites, *Early Western Travels* 30.

Parker, Samuel. *Journal of Exploring Tour Beyond the Rocky Mountains.* Ithaca, N.Y.: Andrus, Woodruff & Gauntlett, 1842. 4th ed., 1844.

———. "Letter, Green River, August 17, 1835." *Missionary Herald* 32 (February 1836): 70–72.

———. [Report to the American Board of His Tour to Oregon and Back, 1835–37.] Boston, June 25, 1837. Printed in Archer B. Hulbert and Dorothy P. Hulbert, eds. *Marcus Whitman, Crusader.*

Parkhill, Forbes. *Blazed Trail of Antoine Leroux.* Los Angeles: Westernlore Press, 1965.

Phillips, Catherine Coffin. *Jessie Benton Frémont: A Woman Who Made History.* San Francisco: J. H. Nash, 1935. Lincoln: University of Nebraska Press, 1995.

Phillips, Paul C. *The Fur Trade.* 2 vols. Norman: University of Oklahoma Press, 1961.

Pike, C. J. "Petitions of Oregon Settlers, 1838–48." *Oregon Historical Quarterly* 34 (September 1933): 216–35.

Pletcher, David M. *The Diplomacy of Annexation: Texas, Oregon, and the Mexican War.* Columbia: University of Missouri Press, 1973.

Point, Nicholas. *Wilderness Kingdom: Indian Life in the Rocky Mountains, 1840–1847, The Journals and Paintings of Nicholas Point, S.J.* Trans. Joseph P. Donnelly. New York: Holt, Rinehart and Winston, 1967.

Pomeroy, Earl. *The Pacific Slope: A History.* Seattle: University of Washington Press, 1965.

Porter, Kenneth W. *John Jacob Astor, Business Man.* 2 vols. Cambridge: Harvard University Press, 1931.

———. "Roll of the Overland Astorians, 1810–12." *Oregon Historical Quarterly* 34 (1933): 103–12.

Porter, Mae Reed, and Odessa Davenport. *Scotsman in Buckskin: Sir William Drummond Stewart and the Rocky Mountain Fur Trade.* New York: Hastings House, 1963.

Pratt, Julius W. "John L. O'Sullivan and Manifest Destiny." *New York History* 14 (July 1933): 213–34.

Preuss, Charles. *Exploring with Frémont.* Ed. and Trans. E. G. Gudde and E. K. Gudde. Norman: University of Oklahoma Press, 1958.

Prucha, Francis Paul. *The Sword of the Republic: The United States Army on the Frontier, 1783–1846.* New York: Macmillan, 1969.

Quaife, Milo M., ed. *The Journals of Captain Meriwether Lewis and Sergeant John Ordway.* Madison: Historical Society of Wisconsin, 1916.

Ray, Arthur J. *Indians in the Fur Trade: Their Role as Trappers, Hunters and Middlemen in the Lands Southwest of Hudson's Bay, 1660–1870.* Toronto: University of Toronto Press, 1974.

Raynolds, W. F. *Report on the Exploration of the Yellowstone River.* Washington, D.C.: GPO, 1868.

Reed, Henry E., ed. "Lovejoy's Pioneer Narrative, 1842–48." *Oregon Historical Quarterly* 31 (September 1930): 237–60.

Reed, James Frazier. "Letter from Fort Bridger, July 31, 1846." *Springfield Sangamon Journal*, November 5, 1846. Reprinted in *Utah Historical Quarterly* 19 (1951): 192–94.

Reid, Russell, and C. G. Gannon, eds. "Journal of the Atkinson-O'Fallon Expedition." *North Dakota Historical Quarterly* 4 (October 1929): 5–56.

Rich, E. E. *The Fur Trade and the Northwest to 1857.* Toronto: McClelland and Stewart, 1967.

———. *The History of the Hudson's Bay Company, 1670–1870.* 2 vols. London: Hudson's Bay Record Society, 1958–62.

———, ed. *Part of Dispatch from George Simpson, Esqr., Governor of Rupert's Land to the Governor and Committee of the Hudson's Bay Company, London.* London: Hudson's Bay Record Society, 1947.

———, ed. *Peter Skene Ogden's Snake Country Journals, 1824–25 and 1825–26.* London: Hudson's Bay Record Society, 1950.

Richardson, Albert D. *Beyond the Mississippi . . . 1857–1867.* Hartford: American Publishing Co., 1867.

Robb, John S. [Solitaire, pseud.]. "Major Fitzpatrick, the Discoverer of the South Pass." *St. Louis Weekly Reveille*, March 1, 1847, reprinted as Appendix B in Hafen, *Broken Hand.*

Robinson, Doane, ed. "Fort Tecumseh and Fort Pierre Journal and Letter Books." *South Dakota Historical Collections* 9 (1918): 69–239.

Rolle, Andrew. *John Charles Frémont: Character as Destiny.* Norman: University of Oklahoma Press, 1991.

Rollins, Philip Ashton, ed. *The Discovery of the Oregon Trail: Robert Stuart's Narrative of His Overland Trip Eastward in 1812–13.* New York: Charles Scribner's Sons, 1935. Lincoln: University of Nebraska Press, 1995.

Ronda, James P. *Astoria and Empire.* Lincoln: University of Nebraska Press, 1990.

———. "Dreaming the Pass: The Western Imagination and the Landscape of South Pass." In Leonard Engel, ed. *The Big Empty: Essays on Land as Narrative.* Albuquerque: University of New Mexico Press, 1994.

———. *Lewis and Clark among the Indians.* Lincoln: University of Nebraska Press, 1984.

Ross, Alexander. *Adventures of the First Settlers on the Oregon or Columbia River.* 1849: Reprint, Lincoln: University of Nebraska Press, 1986.

———. *The Fur Hunters of the Far West. . . .* 2 vols. London: 1855. Revised ed., ed. Kenneth A. Spaulding. Norman: University of Oklahoma Press, 1956.

Rowe, David C. "Government Relations with the Fur Trappers of the Upper Missouri, 1820–1840." *North Dakota History* 25 (Spring 1968): 481–505.

Ruby, Robert H., and John A. Brown. *A Guide to the Indian Tribes of the Pacific Northwest.* Norman: University of Oklahoma Press, 1986.

Rusling, James F. *Across America, or, The Great West and the Pacific Coast.* New York: Sheldon & Co., 1874.

Russell, Carl P. *Firearms, Traps and Tools of the Mountain Men.* New York: Alfred A. Knopf, 1967. Albuquerque: University of New Mexico Press, 1977.

Russell, Osborne. *Journal of a Trapper, or Nine Years in the Rocky Mountains.* Ed. Aubrey L. Haines. Lincoln: University of Nebraska Press, 1955.

Ruxton, Frederick. *Life in the Far West.* Ed. LeRoy R. Hafen. Norman: University of Oklahoma Press, 1951.

Sabin, Edwin L. *Kit Carson Days, 1809–1868.* 2 vols. New York: Press of the Pioneers, 1935. Lincoln: University of Nebraska Press, 1995.

Saum, Lewis O. *The Fur Trader and the Indian.* Seattle: University of Washington Press, 1965.

Scaglione, John. "Ogden's Report of His 1829–30 Expedition." *California Historical Society Quarterly* 28 (June 1949): 117–24.

Schubert, Frank N., ed. *March to South Pass: William B. Franklin's Journal of the Kearny Expedition of 1845.* Washington, D.C.: Office of the Chief of Engineers, 1979.

Sellers, Charles G. *James K. Polk, Continentalist, 1843–1846.* Princeton, N.J.: Princeton University Press, 1966.

———. *James K. Polk, Jacksonian.* Princeton, N.J.: Princeton University Press, 1957.

Settle, Raymond W., ed. *The March of the Mounted Riflemen: From Fort Leavenworth to Fort Vancouver, May to October 1849.* Glendale, Calif.: Arthur H. Clark Co., 1940. Lincoln: University of Nebraska Press, 1989.

Sherman, William T. *Memoirs of William T. Sherman.* Bloomington, Indiana, Civil War Centennial Series: Indiana University Press, 1957.

Shotwell, A. J. "James Bridger: The Greatest Rocky Mountain Scout." *Old Santa Fe* 3 (July 1916): 258–66.

Simpson, James H. *Journal of a Military Reconnaissance from Santa Fe, New Mexico, to the Navajo Country . . . in 1849.* Philadelphia, 1852.

Sitgreaves, Lorenzo. *Report of an Exploration down the Zuñi and Colorado Rivers.* Washington, D.C.: Beverly Tucker, 1854.

Skarsten, M. O. *George Drouillard: Hunter and Interpreter for Lewis and Clark and Fur Trader, 1807–1810.* Glendale, Calif.: Arthur H. Clark Co., 1964.

Sketch of the Life of Com. Robert F. Stockton. New York: Derby & Jackson, 1856.

Slacum, William A. "Slacum's Report on Oregon." *Oregon Historical Quarterly* 13 (June 1912): 175–224.

Spence, Clark C. "A Celtic Nimrod in the Old West." *Montana the Magazine of Western History* 9 (April 1959): 56–66.

Stansbury, Howard. *Exploration of the Valley of the Great Salt Lake of Utah.* Philadelphia: Lippincott, Grambo & Co., 1852. Washington, D.C.: Smithsonian Institution Press, 1988.

Stenberg, Richard R. "The Failure of Polk's Mexican War Intrigue of 1845." *Pacific Historical Review* 32 (February 1957): 5–11.

———. "Polk and Frémont, 1845–1846." *Pacific Historical Review* 7 (1938): 211–27.

Stewart, George R. *The California Trail: An Epic with Many Heroes.* New York: McGraw-Hill, 1962. Lincoln: University of Nebraska Press, 1983.

Stewart, William Drummond. *Edward Warren.* Ed. Winfred Blevins. London, 1854; Missoula, Mont.: Mountain Press Publishing Co., 1986.

Sublette, William L. [Account of the Battle of Pierre's Hole]. *Missouri Republican,* October 16, 1832. *Missouri Intelligencer,* October 20, 1832.

Sullivan, Maurice S., ed. *The Travels of Jedediah Smith.* Santa Ana, Calif.: Fine Arts Press, 1934. Lincoln: University of Nebraska Press, 1992.

Sunder, John E. *Bill Sublette, Mountain Man.* Norman: University of Oklahoma Press, 1959.

———. *The Fur Trade on the Upper Missouri, 1840–1865.* Norman: University of Oklahoma Press 1965.

———. *Joshua Pilcher: Fur Trader and Indian Agent.* Norman: University of Oklahoma Press, 1968.

Swagerty, William R. "Marriage and Settlement Patterns of Rocky Mountain Trappers and Traders." *Western Historical Quarterly* 11 (April 1980): 159–79.

———. "The Upper Missouri Outfit: The Men and the Fur Trade in the 1830s." *Fort Union Fur Trade Symposium Proceedings, September 13–15, 1990.* Williston, N.D.: Friends of Fort Union Trading Post, 1994: 25–42.

———. "A View from the Bottom Up: The Work Force of the American Fur Company on the Upper Missouri in the 1830s." *Montana the Magazine of Western History* 43 (Winter 1993): 18–33.

Swagerty, William R., and Dick A. Wilson. "Faithful Service under Different Flags: Socioeconomic Profile of the Columbia District, Hudson's Bay Company and the Upper Missouri Outfit, American Fur Company, 1825–1835." In Jennifer S. H. Brown, W. J. Eccles, and Donald P. Heldman, eds. *The Fur Trade Revisited: Selected Papers of the Sixth North American Fur Trade Conference, Mackinac Island, Michigan, 1991.* East Lansing: Michigan State University Press, 1994: 243–67.

Talbot, Vivian Linford. *David E. Jackson: Field Captain of the Rocky Mountain Fur Trade.* Jackson, Wyo.: Jackson Hole Historical Society and Museum, 1996.

Taylor, Emerson Gifford. *Gouverneur Kemble Warren: The Life and Letters of an American Soldier, 1830–1882.* Boston: Houghton Mifflin Co., 1932.

Tays, George. "Frémont Had No Secret Instructions." *Pacific Historical Review* 9 (May 1940): 157–71.

Thomas, Alfred B. "Spanish Expeditions into Colorado." *Colorado Magazine* 1 (November 1924): 289–300.

Thompson, Erwin N. *Fort Union Trading Post: Fur Trade Empire on the Upper Missouri.* Medora, N.D.: Theodore Roosevelt Nature and History Association, 1986.

Tobie, Harvey E. *No Man like Joe.* Portland, Ore.: Binford and Morts, 1949.

Townsend, John K. *Narrative of a Journey across the Rocky Mountains, to the Columbia River . . . [1833–34].* Philadelphia: Henry Perkins, 1839. In Reuben Gold Thwaites *Early Western Travels* 21.

Turner, Henry Smith. *The Original Journals of Henry Smith Turner.* Ed. Dwight L. Clarke. Norman: University of Oklahoma Press, 1966.

Tyler, Ron, ed. *Alfred Jacob Miller: Artist on the Oregon Trail.* Fort Worth: Amon Carter Museum, 1982.

Ulibarri, George S. "The Chouteau-Demunn Expedition to New Mexico, 1815–16." *New Mexico Historical Review* 36 (October 1961): 263–73.

U.S. Serial 17. *House Executive Documents*. 15th Congress, 2d session, no. 25, 1818. Indians and the fur trade.

U.S. Serial 89. *Senate Executive Documents*. 18th Congress, 1st session, no. 1 (1823).

U.S. Serial 108. *Senate Executive Documents*. 18th Congress, 1st session, no. 7 (1825).

U.S. Serial 203. *Senate Executive Documents*. 21st Congress, 2d session, no. 39. 1831. Ashley, Pilcher, and others on fur trade.

U.S. Serial 213. *Senate Executive Documents*. 22d Congress, 1st session, no. 1, 1831.

U.S. Serial 470. Stephen W. Kearny. *Report of a Summer Campaign to the Rocky Mountains in 1845, Senate Executive Documents*. 29th Congress, 1st session, no. 1, 1846.

U.S. Serial 477. *Senate Executive Documents*. 29th Congress, 1st session, no. 438, 1846. *Journal of Lt. James W. Abert from Bent's Fort to St. Louis, in 1845*.

U.S. Serial 503. *Senate Executive Documents*. 30th Congress, 1st session, no. 1, 1847. Kearny's Mexican War reports.

U.S. Serial 517. *House Executive Documents*. 30th Congress, 1st session, no. 41, 1847. Lieutenant Abert's report.

U.S. Serial 956. *House Executive Documents*. 35th Congress, 1st session, no. 71, 1858. Utah Expedition.

U.S. Serial 975. *Senate Executive Documents*. 35th Congress, 2d session, no. 1, 1858. Utah Expedition.

U.S. Serial 1317. *Senate Executive Documents*. 40th Congress, 1st session, no. 77, 1868. Raynolds Expeditions.

U.S. Serial 2913. *Senate Reports*. 52d Congress, 1st session, no. 625, 1892. Fort Bridger.

U.S. War Department. *Reports of Explorations and Surveys to Ascertain the Most Practicable and Economical Route for a Railroad between the Mississippi River and the Pacific*. 12 vols. Washington, D.C.: various printers, 1855–60.

Vandiver, Clarence. *The Fur Trade and Early Western Exploration*. Cleveland: Arthur H. Clark Co., 1929.

Van Kirk, Sylvia. *Many Tender Ties: Women in Fur Trade Society, 1670–1870*. Norman: University of Oklahoma Press, 1983.

Victor, Frances Fuller. *The River of the West: Life and Adventure in the Rocky Mountains and Oregon. . . .* Hartford and Toledo: R. W. Bliss & Co., 1870. Reprint, 2 vols. Eds. Winfred Blevins and Lee Nash. Missoula, Mont.: Mountain Press Publishing Co., 1983, 1987.

Vinton, Stallo. *John Colter*. New York: Edward Eberstadt, 1926.

Waldo, William. "Recollections of a Septuagenarian." Missouri Historical Society, *Glimpses of the Past* 5 (April–June 1928): 59–94.

Walpole, Frederick. *Four Years in the Pacific in Her Majesty's Ship "Collingwood."* 2 vols. London: Richard Bentley, 1849.

Warner, Ted J., ed. *The Domínguez-Escalante Journal: Their Expedition through Colorado, Utah, Arizona, and New Mexico in 1776*. Provo, Utah: Brigham Young University Press, 1976.

Warren, G. K. *Explorations in the Dacota Country in the Year 1855*. Washington: A. O. P. Nicholson, 1856. *Senate Executive Documents*. 34th Congress, 1st session, no. 76.

———. *Preliminary Report of Explorations in Nebraska and Dakota in the Years 1855–'56–'57*. Washington, D.C., 1859.

Weber, David J., ed. *The Californios versus Jedediah Smith, 1826–1827*. Spokane: Arthur H. Clark Co., 1990.

————. *The Taos Trappers: The Fur Trade in the Far Southwest, 1540–1846.* Norman: University of Oklahoma Press, 1971.

Wheat, Carl I. *Mapping the Transmississpi West, 1540–1861.* 6 vols. San Francisco: Institute of Historical Cartography, 1957–63.

White, Linda Harper, and Fred R. Gowans. "Traders to Trappers: Andrew Henry and the Rocky Mountain Fur Trade." *Montana the Magazine of Western History* 43 (Winter 1993): 58–65.

Whitman, Marcus. "Journal and Report of Dr. Marcus Whitman." *Oregon Historical Quarterly* 28 (September 1927): 239–51.

Williams, Glyndwr, ed. *Peter Skene Ogden's Snake Country Journals, 1827–28 and 1828–29.* London: Hudson's Bay Record Society, 1971.

Williams, Joseph. *Narrative of a Tour from the State of Indiana to the Oregon Territory in the Years 1841–2.* Cincinnati: J. B. Wilson, 1848. Reprint, New York: Edward Eberstadt, 1921. In Hafen, *To the Rockies*, 199–287.

Wilson, Iris H. *William Wolfskill, 1798–1866: Frontier Trapper to California Ranchero.* Glendale, Calif.: Arthur H. Clark Co., 1965.

Wilson, Elinor. *Jim Beckwourth: Black Mountain Man and War Chief of the Crows.* Norman: University of Oklahoma Press, 1972.

Wishart, David J. *The Fur Trade of the American West, 1807–1840: A Geographical Synthesis.* Lincoln: University of Nebraska Press, 1979.

Wislizenus, F. A. *A Journey to the Rocky Mountains in the Year 1839.* St. Louis: Missouri Historical Society, 1912. Glorieta, N.M.: Rio Grande Press, 1969.

Woodward, Arthur. "Lances at San Pascual." *California Historical Society Quarterly* 25 (December 1946): 289–308; and 26 (March 1947): 21–62.

Wyeth, John B. *Oregon: or, a Short History of a Long Journey from the Atlantic Ocean to the Region of the Pacific, by Land.* Cambridge, Mass.: privately published, 1833. In Reuben Gold Thwaites, *Early Western Travels* 21.

Young, F. G., ed. "The Correspondence and Journals of Captain Nathaniel Wyeth, 1831–6." *Sources of the History Oregon* 1. Eugene: University Press, 1899.

————. "Ewing Young and His Estate: A Chapter in the Economic and Community Development of Oregon." *Oregon Historical Quarterly* 21 (September 1920): 172–315.

————, ed. "Journal and Report of Dr. Marcus Whitman of His Tour of Exploration with Rev. Samuel Parker in 1835 Beyond the Rocky Mountains." *Oregon Historical Quarterly* 28 (September 1927): 239–51.

NOTES

INTRODUCTION

1. Charles Francis Adams, ed., *The Memoirs of John Quincy Adams*, 12 vols. (Philadelphia: J. P. Lippincott, 1874–77), 4:438–39.

CHAPTER 1

1. The transfer ceremonies are described in Hiram M. Chittenden, *The American Fur Trade of the Far West*, 3 vols. (New York: Francis P. Harper, 1902), 1:104–05. This classic of the fur trade, still a basic history nearly a century later, has appeared in many editions. Mine is Stanford, Calif.: Academic Reprints, 1954. Most readily available is a Bison Book edition with an excellent foreword by William R. Swagerty, 2 vols. (Lincoln: University of Nebraska Press, 1986).

2. Most of what is known of Colter comes from Thomas James, *Three Years among the Indians and Mexicans*, ed. Walter B. Douglas (1846; St. Louis: Missouri Historical Society, 1916), or is inferred from references in the journals of Lewis and Clark. There are two accepted biographies: Stallo Vinton, *John Colter* (New York: E. Eberstadt, 1926) and Burton Harris, *John Colter: His Years in the Rockies* (New York: Charles Scribner's Sons, 1952). Harris is generally considered the superior, although heavily speculative in his reconstructions. Consult especially the Bison Book edition (Lincoln: University of Nebraska Press, 1993); it contains Harris's addenda as incorporated in a subsequent edition (Casper, Wyo.: Big Horn Book Co., 1983) and an introduction by David Lavender that identifies the strengths and weaknesses of the book. I have found the most authoritative and informative account of Colter to be Aubrey L. Haines, "John Colter," in LeRoy R. Hafen, ed., *Mountain Men and the Fur Trade of the Far West*, 10 vols. (Glendale: Arthur H. Clark Co., 1965–72), 8:73–85. This

monumental compilation will appear frequently in my citations. Finally, see also W. J. Ghent, "A Sketch of John Colter," *Wyoming Annals* 10 (July 1938): 111–16.

3. M. O. Skarsten, *George Drouillard: Hunter and Interpreter for Lewis and Clark and Fur Trader, 1807–1810* (Glendale: Arthur H. Clark Co., 1964), 18. Skarsten also wrote the sketch of Drouillard in Hafen, *Mountain Men,* 4:69–82. Lewis notes the engagement of Drouillard in his journal. He was hired as an interpreter at Fort Massac, on the Illinois side of the Ohio River, on November 11, 1803. The original sources for the Lewis and Clark expedition are many, the journals of both offering the greatest riches. Most books cite Reuben Gold Thwaites, ed., *Original Journals of the Lewis and Clark Expedition,* 8 vols. (New York: Dodd, Mead and Co., 1904). However, the journals and other original sources have been edited in a new and much improved edition: Gary E. Moulton, ed., *The Journals of the Lewis and Clark Expedition,* 10 vols. (Lincoln: University of Nebraska Press, 1983–96). Vol. 1 is the *Atlas of the Lewis and Clark Expedition.* I have used Moulton rather than Thwaites. Other sources are: Donald Jackson, ed., *Letters of the Lewis and Clark Expedition with Related Documents, 1783–1854,* 2d ed., 2 vols. (Urbana: University of Illinois Press, 1978); Ernest S. Osgood, ed., *Field Notes of Captain William Clark, 1803–05* (New Haven: Yale University Press, 1964); Patrick Gass, *A Journal of the Voyages and Travels of a Corps of Discovery* (1807; reprint, Minneapolis: Ross and Haines, 1958); Elliott Coues, ed., *History of the Expedition under the Command of Lewis and Clark,* 4 vols. in 3 (1893; reprint, New York: Dover Publications, 1964); and Milo M. Quaife, ed., *The Journals of Captain Meriwether Lewis and Sergeant John Ordway* (Madison: Historical Society of Wisconsin, 1916). Among many histories of the Lewis and Clark expedition, that by Bernard DeVoto still stands out: *The Course of Empire* (Boston: Houghton Mifflin Co., 1952). Although dated in some respects, it retains the vigor of thoughtful scholarship and compelling prose. Emphasizing scientific aspects but also of great value for the geography of the route by one intimately acquainted with the country is Paul Russell Cutright, *Lewis and Clark, Pioneering Naturalists* (Urbana: University of Illinois Press, 1969; Lincoln: University of Nebraska Press, 1989).

4. Lewis is the subject of a recent biography that is also an outstanding history of the Lewis and Clark expedition and deserves prominent recognition among the sources in the previous footnote: Stephen E. Ambrose, *Undaunted Courage: Meriwether Lewis, Thomas Jefferson, and the Opening of the American West* (New York: Simon & Schuster, 1996). Strangely, William Clark, the more significant of the two in the long term, awaits an authoritative biographer. James P. Ronda will undoubtedly gain that distinction.

5. Donald Jackson argues persuasively against the usual interpretation that Jefferson was already planning the expedition when he chose Lewis: *Thomas Jefferson and the Stony Mountains: Exploring the West from Monticello* (Urbana: University of Illinois Press, 1981), 117–21.

6. This background is ably sketched in Jackson, *Thomas Jefferson and the Stony Mountains,* chaps. 7 and 14. Interesting perspectives on Jefferson's geopolitical design are in Bernard DeVoto, "An Inference Regarding the Expedition of Lewis and Clark," American Philosophical Society *Proceedings* 99 (August 1955): 185–94.

7. The development of this image through French and English literature and cartography, and its exact content as absorbed by Jefferson and Lewis on the eve of the Lewis and Clark expedition, is brilliantly explored in John L. Allen, *Passage through the Garden: Lewis and Clark and the Image of the American Northwest* (Urbana: University of Illinois Press, 1975). Reprinted as *Lewis and Clark and the Image of the American*

Northwest (New York: Dover Publications, 1991). Consult also Jackson, *Thomas Jefferson and the Stony Mountains.*

8. Dated June 20, 1803, the instructions appear in Jackson, *Letters of the Lewis and Clark Expedition,* 1:61–66.

9. Moulton, 3:336. See also Skarsten, *George Drouillard,* 323–25.

10. This and other passages touching relations with Indian tribes draw heavily on a brilliant study of the subject from both white and Indian perspectives: James P. Ronda, *Lewis and Clark among the Indians* (Lincoln: University of Nebraska Press, 1984). The crucial Shoshone and Flathead meetings are detailed in chap. 6.

11. Moulton, *Journals of the Lewis and Clark Expedition,* 8:127–39. Skarsten, *George Drouillard,* chap. 20. Ronda, *Lewis and Clark among the Indians,* 238–44. Paul Russell Cutright, "Lewis on the Marias, 1806," *Montana the Magazine of Western History* 18 (summer 1968): 30–43. Ambrose, *Undaunted Courage,* chap. 29, gives an excellent reconstruction of the Marias incident.

12. Historians long ascribed the unrelenting hostility of the Blackfeet solely to the incident on the Marias. Recent scholarship, however, attributes it more to Colter, Drouillard, and their companions of 1810–11 than to Lewis. For perceptive analyses of the complex factors underlying the hostility, see Ronda, 243–44, and Alvin M. Josephy, Jr., *The Nez Perce Indians and the Opening of the Northwest* (New Haven: Yale University Press, 1965), 651–53.

CHAPTER 2

1. Gary E. Moulton, ed., *The Journals of the Lewis and Clark Expedition,* 10 vols. (Lincoln: University of Nebraska Press, 1983–96), 7:302. Lewis's entry of August 15, 1806. Burton Harris, *John Colter: His Years in the Rockies* (New York: Charles Scribner's Sons, 1952; Lincoln: University of Nebraska Press, 1993) remains the standard authority on Colter, although one must dig through a tangle of verbiage and digression to find the factual nuggets. They are there, however, together with extended quotations from the few primary sources bearing on Colter's adventures.

2. The standard biography, a thorough and sound work, is Richard E. Oglesby, *Manuel Lisa and the Opening of the Missouri Fur Trade* (Norman: University of Oklahoma Press, 1963).

3. The financial motive is most clearly articulated by William H. Goetzmann, "The Mountain Man as Jacksonian Man," *American Quarterly* 15 (fall 1963): 402–15. This article inspired a rejoinder from Harvey L. Carter and Marcia C. Spencer, "Stereotypes of the Mountain Man," *Western Historical Quarterly* 6 (January 1975): 17–32, in which they argued that Goetzmann's "expectant capitalist" diminished the heroic mold in which mountain men should also be seen. For other commentary on this controversy, see William R. Swagerty, "The Upper Missouri Outfit: The Men and the Fur Trade in the 1830s," *Fort Union Fur Trade Symposium Proceedings, September 13–15, 1890* (Williston, N.D.: Friends of Fort Union Trading Post, 1994): 25–42; John Francis McDermott, "The Frontier Reexamined," in McDermott, ed., *The Frontier Reexamined* (Urbana: University of Illinois Press, 1967): 12; and Richard E. Oglesby, "The Fur Trade as Business," in ibid., 127.

4. The process is described and illustrated in Carl P. Russell, *Firearms, Traps, and Tools of the Mountain Men* (New York: Alfred A. Knopf, 1967; Albuquerque: University of New Mexico Press, 1977), 6–7.

5. The traps and the process are described and illustrated in ibid., chap. 3.

6. Ibid., 151–60.

7. Washington Irving, *The Adventures of Captain Bonneville, U.S.A., in the Rocky Mountains and the Far West*, ed. Edgeley W. Todd (Norman: University of Oklahoma Press, 1986), 70.

8. Warren A. Ferris, *Life in the Rocky Mountains: Diary of Wanderings on the Sources of the Rivers Missouri, Columbia, and Colorado from February, 1830, to November, 1835*, ed. Paul C. Phillips (Denver: Old West Publishing Co., 1940), 103–04.

9. Harris, *John Colter*, examines all the evidence in chap. 5. He brought to his analysis the strengths of a native of the Bighorn Basin thoroughly familiar with all the topography. As a self-taught historian, however, he was weak in the handling of evidence. The documentary evidence consists of a tantalizingly brief passage in Henry M. Brackenridge, *Views of Louisiana Together with a Journal of a Voyage up the Missouri River in 1811* (Pittsburgh, 1814); and a line drawn on William Clark's map, as discussed later in this chapter. Thus an intimate knowledge of the country such as Harris possessed, together with a sense of what was possible and plausible in the winter, are vital ingredients in the analysis. Another self-taught historian (although he taught himself better than Harris) was Aubrey L. Haines, who as a longtime employee of Yellowstone National Park knew the country as well as Harris. His "John Colter" in LeRoy R. Hafen, ed., *Mountain Men and the Fur Trade of the Far West*, 10 vols. (Glendale: Arthur H. Clark Co., 1965–72), 8:73–85, is an essential part of the literature, for he repudiates two items of presumed evidence that Harris and other writers relied on. One was the "Colter Stone," found in Pierre's Hole west of the Tetons in 1931, bearing Colter's name and the date 1808. The other was a tree blazed with his name, spelled Coulter, north of Jackson Lake. The stone was one of many inscribed with historic names found in the area and was probably created as "campfire doodling" by members of the Hayden survey of 1872. The blazed tree stood on a stream later named Coulter Creek, for a Chicago botanist who fished on it and doubtless carved his name on the tree. "Colter's Hell," a highly active thermal area in Colter's time but now inactive, occupied a stretch of the Shoshone River on the western edge of present Cody, Wyoming.

10. M. O. Skarsten, *George Drouillard: Hunter and Trader for Lewis and Clark and Fur Trader, 1807–1810* (Glendale: Arthur H. Clark Co., 1964), chap. 23. As with Colter, the main evidence is cartographic, to be dealt with later in this chapter.

11. There are two credible sources for this affair. Thomas James, *Three Years among the Indians and Mexicans*, ed. Walter B. Douglas (1846; St. Louis: Missouri Historical Society, 1916), 52–53, is the most reliable because he got it directly from Colter while standing on the battleground itself two years later, although he wrote of it more than thirty years afterward. A confirmatory account appeared in an extensive report on the upper Missouri fur trade penned by Major Thomas Biddle to Colonel Henry Atkinson, Camp Missouri, October 29, 1819, in *American State Papers, Indians Affairs*, 2:201. In this letter, Biddle ascribes the origins of Blackfeet hostility to Colter's part in this fight and specifically exempts Lewis's action on the Marias in 1806. My account differs somewhat from most others, including Harris and Haines. Colter is usually portrayed as being sent by Lisa to open trade with the Blackfeet at the Three Forks. He fell in with Flathead and Crow hunters and was with them when the Blackfeet attacked. This version, however, ignores James's subsequent remarks about the Flatheads: "At the time of this well fought battle, Colter was leading them to Manuel's Fort to trade with the Americans, when the Black Feet fell upon them in such numbers as seemingly to make their destruction certain."

12. This was the thesis of Major Thomas Biddle, as cited in the previous note. Although Colter's violent confrontations with Blackfeet precipitated open war between Americans and the tribe, they did not, of course, cause the war. Blackfeet motives sprang from two sources: anger over whites arming their traditional foes, and anger over whites themselves trapping fur animals the Blackfeet regarded as their own. A good analysis is Peter W. Dunwiddie, "The Nature of the Relationship between the Blackfeet Indians and the Men of the Fur Trade," *Annals of Wyoming* 46 (spring 1974): 23–33.

13. Again James, 64–65, is the authority. Colter recounted the adventure at the Three Forks in 1810.

14. Oglesby, *Manuel Lisa*, chap. 3. James, 35, is the authority for Colter's presence with Vasquez. James was with the expedition.

15. For Menard, see sketch by Richard Oglesby in Hafen, *Mountain Men*, 6:307–18; for Henry, sketch by Louis J. Clements in ibid., 173–84.

16. Again the principal source is James, *Three Years among the Indians and Mexicans*, 66–93, although James was with the party that worked down the Missouri. See also Menard to Pierre Chouteau, Three Forks, April 21, 1810, in Hiram M. Chittenden, *The American Fur Trade of the Far West*, 2 vols. (Stanford, Calif.: Academic Reprints, 1954), 2:897–98; and Oglesby, *Manuel Lisa*, 93–98.

17. James, 65.

18. James, 80. Interview with Menard, *St. Louis Louisiana Gazette*, July 26, 1810, in ibid., 283–85.

19. April 21, 1810, in Chittenden, *Fur Trade*, 2:897–98.

20. The principal source for what happened to Henry after Menard left is a report from Bradbury and Brackenridge, returning from the Mandan villages, that appeared in the *St. Louis Louisiana Gazette*, August 8, 1811, quoted in Dale L. Morgan, *The West of William H. Ashley* (Denver: Old West Publishing Co., 1964), xxxiv–xxxv. Apparently Henry was led to cross to the Snake drainage by a report of Peter Weiser, a Lewis and Clark veteran and one of the Fort Raymond trappers of 1808–10, that he had been to this country and found it not only rich in beaver but the domain of friendly Shoshone and Flathead Indians. The expedition crossed the Continental Divide at Raynolds Pass, a low and easy transit from the upper Madison to the head of Henry's Fork of the Snake.

21. The evolution of Clark's map and the contributions of Drouillard and Colter are set forth in John L. Allen, *Passage through the Garden: Lewis and Clark and the Image of the American Northwest* (Urbana: University of Illinois Press, 1975), 378–79; Moulton, *Journals of the Lewis and Clark Expedition*, 1:12–13; and Carl I. Wheat, *Mapping the Transmississippi West, 1540–1861*, 6 vols. (San Francisco: Institute of Historical Cartography, 1957–63), 2:31, 40–43, 49, 51–57. There is disagreement over whether Drouillard actually drew one of the two maps that date from 1808. Moulton believes that both were jointly prepared by Lewis and Clark, with Drouillard's participation. Wheat attributes the rough sketch map to Drouillard and the larger, more detailed map to Clark, "doubtless with Drouillard looking over his shoulder." The two authorities, however, do not differ on the importance of Drouillard's contribution. Wheat further comments on the two 1808 maps: "These maps are most revealing. They show a knowledge of the intricate waterways of the mountains that was not equaled on the published maps for many years. Since these maps were in Captain Clark's possession, it is interesting to note that on both the published map and the manuscript map [of 1810] he used the geography provided by Drouillard, mistaking only the upper waters of the Green for those of the Rio Grande."

22. Lisa's interest is sketched in Oglesby, *Manuel Lisa*, 35 et seq. The 1808 sketch map touched on in the previous note bore an inked notation along the Bighorn River "the road to the Spanish settlements," and at Lisa's Fort Raymond another, "from this establishment a man on horseback can travel to the Spanish country in 14 days."

23. Pike is quoted and discussed in Wheat, *Mapping the Transmississippi West*, 2:18, 20–21, 26–27.

24. Harris, *John Colter*, chap. 8.

CHAPTER 3

1. John Bradbury, *Travels in the Interior of America in the Years 1809, 1810, and 1811* (Liverpool: Smith and Galway, 1817), in Reuben Gold Thwaites, ed., *Early Western Travels*, 5:98. Bradbury, an English naturalist traveling with Wilson Price Hunt's westbound Astorians (see below), met all three but described only Robinson.

2. See chapter 2. Richard E. Oglesby, *Manuel Lisa and the Opening of the Missouri Fur Trade* (Norman: University of Oklahoma Press, 1963), 45 n. 20, 93, 96–97. Although not naming the three Kentuckians, the principal source for the Three Forks story is Thomas James, *Three Years among the Indians and Mexicans*, ed. Walter B. Douglas (St. Louis: Missouri Historical Society, 1916), chaps. 1 and 2. See also Hiram M. Chittenden, *The American Fur Trade of the Far West*, 2 vols. (Stanford, Calif.: Academic Reprints, 1954), 1:141–46. A convenient summary of the three trappers is Harvey L. Carter, "John Hoback, Jacob Reznor, and Edward Robinson," in LeRoy R. Hafen, ed., *Mountain Men and the Fur Trade of the Far West*, 10 vols. (Glendale: Arthur H. Clark Co., 1965–72), 9:211–14.

3. For the demise of the one company and the birth of the other under the stimulus of Manuel Lisa, see Oglesby, *Manuel Lisa*, chap. 4. For a sketch of Henry, see Louis J. Clements, "Andrew Henry," in Hafen, *Mountain Men*, 6:173–84.

4. Bradbury, 98.

5. For more than a century and a half, the standard and highly readable authority on Astoria has been Washington Irving's *Astoria, or Anecdotes of an Enterprise beyond the Rocky Mountains*, 2 vols. (Philadelphia: Carey, Lee & Blanchard, 1836). It has appeared in many subsequent editions, but the best is edited and with an introduction by Edgeley W. Todd (Norman: University of Oklahoma Press, 1964). Irving's work still is indispensable, for he had access to sources that no longer exist. The best modern study, a thorough and well-written work, is James P. Ronda, *Astoria and Empire* (Lincoln: University of Nebraska Press, 1990). The standard biography of Astor is Kenneth W. Porter, *John Jacob Astor, Business Man*, 2 vols. (Cambridge: Harvard University Press, 1931). Hunt's own journal of the westbound Overland Astorians is a translation of a brief French version that is printed as an appendix to the chronicle of the eastbound Astorians: Philip Ashton Rollins, ed., *The Discovery of the Oregon Trail: Robert Stuart's Narrative of His Overland Trip Eastward in 1812–13* (New York: Charles Scribner's Sons, 1935; Lincoln: University of Nebraska Press, 1995). This version of Hunt's journal is disappointing, but the original seems not to have survived. Ramsay Crooks, one of the company partners with Hunt, wrote a brief account for Bradbury that appears in Bradbury's journal and narrative in Thwaites, *Early Western Travels*, 5:228–34. An excellent, well-documented account of the Hunt expedition is William Brandon, "Wilson Price Hunt," in Hafen, *Mountain Men*, 6:185–206. My account of Astor's inspiration for Astoria is drawn from Ronda, *Astoria and Empire*, chap. 1, and differs from most earlier, and simpler, interpretations.

6. Ronda, *Astoria and Empire*, 128–30, 140–41.

7. Ibid., 149–51. Irving, *Astoria*, 175–78. This was in May 1811. The version of Hunt's journal published as an appendix of Rollins, *Discovery of the Oregon Trail*, does not begin until July.

8. At this point Hunt's journal and Crooks's account as cited in the previous note begin. See also Kenneth W. Porter, "Roll of the Overland Astorians, 1810–12," *Oregon Historical Quarterly* 34 (1933): 103–12, which names and briefly sketches all members of the expedition.

9. Reuben Holmes, "The Five Scalps," ed. Stella M. Drumm, Missouri Historical Society, *Glimpses of the Past* 5 (January–March 1938): 3–54.

10. Hunt's journal, 284–85. Ronda, 173–74. Irving, 246–50. For a sketch of Rose, whose contribution to this book is not finished, see Willis Blenkinsop, "Edward Rose," in Hafen, *Mountain Men*, 9:335–45.

11. Irving, 256–57. Hunt, 286–87.

12. On August 17, 1996, piloted by historian-geographer William B. Resor, I retraced the Astorian route from the Wind River to the upper Green. Resor knows these mountains intimately and has studied all the historic documents and maps tracing travel routes through them. Union Pass is not even recognizable as a pass but is a broad, uneven meadow perhaps ten miles in diameter. In this miniature version of Pike's "grand reservoir of snows and fountains" are headstreams of river systems that find their way to the Pacific, the Gulf of California, and the Gulf of Mexico. For horsemen, Union Pass offered superior routes connecting the Gros Ventre (a tributary of the Snake), the upper Green, and the upper Wind. Forest Service roads traverse the Union Pass area, but the modern highway from Jackson Hole to the upper Wind uses Togwotee Pass. Indians and trappers used this route too, but it compared unfavorably with Union Pass. Togwotee was steep, thickly clad with pines (and thus fallen timber), endowed with sparse grass for forage, and clogged with deep snow for most of the year. Union Pass and the Hoback will recur later in this book.

13. Hunt, 288–89. Ronda, 177–79. Irving, 262–68. Actually, Teton Pass divides the Teton Range from the Snake River Range, which parallels the Snake River in its northwesterly course to the confluence with Henry's Fork. Snake River Canyon in turn separates the Snake River Range from a series of north-south ranges on the south.

14. Hunt, 255–56. Irving, chaps. 32–38. Crooks in Bradbury, 231–34. Brandon, "Wilson Price Hunt," 196–206.

15. The adventures of Robinson, Hoback, and Reznor from October 1811 to August 1812 were recounted for Stuart and his associates at the time of their meeting. What Stuart recorded in his journal and what Irving later wrote based on this and other sources are the principal evidence of what the trappers did and where they went. Irving, 370–73. Rollins, *Discovery of the Oregon Trail*, 86–87. Important also are the annotations of Edgeley W. Todd in the former and Philip Ashton Rollins in the latter. They make sense of the cryptic accounts in terms of modern geography. Irving himself, better informed after his work on Captain Bonneville, added geographical information (e.g., Great Salt Lake) that had become available by the 1830s.

16. Alexander Ross, *Adventures of the First Settlers on the Oregon or Columbia River* (1849; Lincoln: University of Nebraska Press, 1986), 223. This is a reprint, with foreword by James P. Ronda, of the version in Thwaites, *Early Western Travels*, 7.

17. Stuart in Rollins, chap. 5. Irving, 374–75. Ross, 223.

18. Stuart in Rollins, 134. Irving, 379–85. Irving adds considerable colorful detail to Stuart's brief entry; whether from true sources or his own imagination is unknown.

19. Most historians believe he was, that the route up the Hoback was dictated by the Shoshone's revelation. I doubt it. I suspect that not until the upper Green did Stuart conceive of departing from routes Miller had traveled. Perhaps then the Indian's words about a southern pass caused him to keep to the southeast, along the western base of the Wind River Mountains, rather than retrace Hunt's route back to the upper Wind River by way of Union Pass.

20. Stuart in Rollins, chap. 7. Irving, chap. 48.

21. Rollins, *Discovery of the Oregon Trail*, lxvii–lxviii, reprints part of the *Gazette*'s article of May 15, 1813, and lists the other papers in which it appeared, including the influential *National Intelligencer* of Washington, D.C., Baltimore's *Niles's Weekly Register*, three New York City papers, and one in Boston. A fine summary of the history and significance of South Pass is James P. Ronda, "Dreaming the Pass: The Western Imagination and the Landscape of South Pass," in Leonard Engel, ed., *The Big Empty: Essays on the Land as Narrative* (Albuquerque: University of New Mexico Press, 1994), 7–25.

22. For the activities of David Thompson and his associates, see E. E. Rich, *The Fur Trade and the Northwest to 1857* (Toronto: McClelland and Stewart, 1967), 198–202; and Paul C. Phillips, *The Fur Trade*, 2 vols. (Norman: University of Oklahoma Press, 1961), 2:284–91.

23. Ronda, *Astoria and Empire*, chap. 9.

24. The forty-ninth parallel is the present boundary separating Canada from Montana and North Dakota. The forty-second parallel is the present northern boundary of California, Nevada, and Utah. The short southern border of Alaska, ending on the east in the Canadian province of British Columbia, conforms to 54° 40′.

25. The tortuous course of Oregon diplomacy is traced in a series of essays by Frederick Merk consolidated in *The Oregon Question: Essays in Anglo-American Diplomacy and Politics* (Cambridge: Harvard University Press, 1967). Pertinent to the above paragraphs are the first three essays.

26. Ross, *Adventures of First Settlers*, 223.

27. Irving, chap. 52.

28. Alternatively, one died after falling from his horse, the other slain by Indians. The principal sources for these events, which do not always agree, are Irving, *Astoria*, 498–500; Ross, *Adventures of First Settlers*, 265–70; Ross Cox, *The Columbia River*, ed. Edgar I. Stewart and Jane R. Stewart (1831; Norman: University of Oklahoma Press, 1957), 51–54; and Gabriel Franchère, *Journal of a Voyage on the North West Coast of North America during the Years 1811, 1812, 1813, and 1814*. The last has appeared in several editions, including Thwaites, *Early Western Travels*, 6. The best is W. Kaye Lamb, ed. (Toronto: Champlain Society, 1969). See also Harriet D. Munnick, "Pierre Dorion," in Hafen, *Mountain Men*, 8:107–12.

29. All accounts are drawn from the seemingly very coherent account of Dorion's wife. In Ross, she says she remained with Reed until early January. In Irving, she is represented as accompanying her husband. I accept Ross, who gives her account supposedly verbatim.

30. One suspects Ross of embroidering the actual words of the woman, but the thought is true. Irving tells the story in more detail and with some important differences. There seems some question whether the Indians involved were Snakes (that is, Shoshones) or Bannocks. Dorion's wife clearly identifies them as Dog Rib Snakes.

CHAPTER 4

1. Carl I. Wheat, *Mapping the Transmississippi West, 1549–1861*, 6 vols. (San Francisco: Institute of Historical Cartography, 1957-63), 2:chap. 16. C. Gregory Crampton and Gloria G. Griffen, "The San Buenaventura, Mythical River of the West," *Pacific Historical Review* 25 (May 1956): 163–71. See also Dale L. Morgan, *The Great Salt Lake* (Indianapolis: Bobbs-Merrill Co., 1947; Lincoln: University of Nebraska Press, 1986), 60–64. The route of Domínguez and Escalante formed the eastern half of what later became the Old Spanish Trail. See LeRoy R. Hafen and Ann W. Hafen, *The Old Spanish Trail: Santa Fe to Los Angeles* (Glendale, Calif.: Arthur H. Clark Co., 1954; Lincoln: University of Nebraska Press, 1993), chap. 2. For the Domínguez-Escalante expedition, see Ted J. Warner, ed., *The Domínguez-Escalante Journal: Their Expedition through Colorado, Utah, Arizona, and New Mexico in 1776* (Provo, Utah: Brigham Young University Press, 1976).

2. The quotation is from an anonymous friend writing a eulogy, "Jedediah Strong Smith," *Illinois Monthly Magazine* 2 (June 1832), reprinted as Appendix I in Edwin L. Sabin, *Kit Carson Days, 1809–1868*, 2 vols. (New York: Press of the Pioneers, 1935), 2:821–26. The standard biography of Smith, a seminal work of fur-trade history, is Dale L. Morgan, *Jedediah Smith and the Opening of the West* (Indianapolis: Bobbs-Merrill Co., 1953), and my story of Smith draws heavily on Morgan's impeccable scholarship. Both Sabin and Morgan have been reprinted as Bison Books by the University of Nebraska Press and are readily available.

3. Morgan, 26.

4. Francis Paul Prucha, *The Sword of the Republic: The United States Army on the Frontier, 1783–1846* (New York: Macmillan, 1969), chap. 8. Roger L. Nichols, *General Henry Atkinson: A Western Military Career* (Norman: University of Oklahoma Press, 1965), chap. 4.

5. Morgan, *Jedediah Smith*, chap. 1 and endnotes, covers these firms most clearly, but see also, under relevant index entries, Hiram M. Chittenden, *The American Fur Trade of the Far West*, 2 vols. (Stanford, Calif.: Academic Reprints, 1954); and Paul C. Phillips, *The Fur Trade*, 2 vols. (Norman: University of Oklahoma Press, 1961). The activities of the Missouri Fur Company are especially well presented in John E. Sunder, *Joshua Pilcher: Fur Trader and Indian Agent* (Norman: University of Oklahoma Press, 1968), chap. 3. Sunder places Immell and Jones on the Yellowstone in 1821. Morgan does not think they got there until 1822. I favor Sunder.

6. Virtually all the documentation of Ashley's years in the fur trade, including Smith's activities, was assembled and published in Dale L. Morgan, ed., *The West of William H. Ashley* (Denver: Old West Publishing Co., 1964), a monumental compilation with extensive annotation. Many newspaper items appear both in Morgan and in Donald McKay Frost, *Notes on General Ashley, the Overland Trail, and South Pass* (Worcester, Mass.: American Antiquarian Society, 1945). All newspaper citations unattributed in my notes to the publications of either Morgan or Frost I have consulted in the voluminous transcripts typed by Dale Morgan and now preserved with his papers at the Bancroft Library, University of California, Berkeley. Many of these transcripts are part of another Dale Morgan Collection at the Utah Historical Society in Salt Lake City.

7. Maurice S. Sullivan, ed., *The Travels of Jedediah Smith: A Documentary Outline Including the Journal of the Great American Pathfinder* (Santa Ana, Calif.: Fine Arts

Press, 1934; Lincoln: University of Nebraska Press, 1992), 1. Smith's laboriously compiled records were lost to fire or other causes after his death, but a copy of important
portions turned up a century later in a branch of the Smith family and was published
by Sullivan in 1934. Morgan's *Jedediah Smith and the Opening of the West* remains the
ultimate authority on all aspects of Smith's life.

8. *Niles's Weekly Register* (Baltimore), June 8, 1822, repeating *New York Commercial
Advertiser.*

9. Nowhere in the contemporary documents is Jackson mentioned by name as a member of the 1822 expedition, but a legal document in April 1822, transferring his stock
to his brother's care "for the term of three years or untill his Return from the Expedition he is about to take up the Missouri," seems sufficient evidence. John C. Jackson,
Shadow on the Tetons: David E. Jackson and the Claiming of the American West (Missoula: Mountain Press Publishing Co., 1993) draws on family papers and tradition
and other material collected by David Jackson's great-grandson, Carl D. W. Hays,
who wrote the sketch of Jackson in LeRoy R. Hafen, ed., *Mountain Men and the Fur
Trade of the Far West*, 10 vols. (Glendale: Arthur H. Clark Co., 1965–72), 9:215–44, and
intended to write a biography himself. Better documented than either is Vivian Linford Talbot, *David E. Jackson: Field Captain of the Rocky Mountain Fur Trade* (Jackson, Wyo.: Jackson Hole Historical Society and Museum, 1996).

10. Grenville M. Dodge, *Biographical Sketch of James Bridger, Mountaineer* (New York:
Unz & Co., 1905), reproduced in J. Cecil Alter, *James Bridger: A Historical Narrative*
(Salt Lake City: Shephard Book Co., 1925), 522. The standard biography of Bridger is
Alter, reissued in a revised edition as *Jim Bridger* (Norman: University of Oklahoma
Press, 1962), but omitting the Dodge sketch. Despite its status, Alter's work is badly
flawed, both stylistically and in his handling of evidence.

11. All relevant documents are in Morgan, *West of William H. Ashley:* Atkinson to Cal-
houn, St. Louis, January 25, 1822, 1; O'Fallon to Calhoun, St. Louis, April 9, 1822, 6;
Calhoun to Clark, Washington, D.C., July 1, 1822, 17; Clark to Calhoun, St. Louis,
August 9, 1822, 18. Records of the Ashley-Henry trading license are in ibid., 1–2.

12. The principal source for the Ashley terms is Thomas Hempstead to Joshua Pilcher,
St. Louis, April 3, 1822, in Morgan, *West of William H. Ashley*, 3–4. Hempstead was
acting partner of the Missouri Fur Company and was reporting what he had heard in
St. Louis on the eve of the departure of the Ashley-Henry expedition. Both here and
in his biography of Smith, 28–29, Morgan quotes but does not elaborate on Hempstead's description, which does not clearly indicate whether the hunters and trappers
received their supplies and equipment as part of the terms of engagement or had to
buy them on credit. Ashley's biographer, however, citing the same source, writes that
on the voyage upriver the hunters and trappers would do whatever was needed in exchange for transportation but that once in the field they would have to purchase all
their supplies from the firm on credit. Richard M. Clokey, *William H. Ashley: Enterprise and Politics in the Trans-Mississippi West* (Norman: University of Oklahoma
Press, 1980), 68. The Rocky Mountain free trapper of later years, of course, had to
buy everything from the company.

13. Henry's departure is noted in Hempstead's letter of April 3 cited in the previous note.
Without specifying the date, the departure is also reported in *St. Louis Enquirer*, April
13, 1822, printed in Frost, *Notes on General Ashley*, 68–69; and in Morgan, *West of
William H. Ashley*, 6–7. For the second boat, see Sullivan, *Travels of Jedediah Smith*,
1–2; and *St. Louis Enquirer*, June 3, 1822, and *St. Louis Missouri Republican*, June 5,
1822, in Frost, 69.

14. The fort and the site as they appeared in 1825 are described in Russell Reid and Clell G. Gannon, eds., "Journal of the Atkinson-O'Fallon Expedition," *North Dakota History* 4 (October 1929): 41. Clark to Calhoun, St. Louis, January 14, 1824, in Morgan, *West of William H. Ashley*, 69–71, contains a statement by Ashley and Henry of their losses on the upper Missouri, together with a deposition of Joshua Griffith, January 12, 1824, detailing the Assiniboine theft. Griffith was a member of Henry's party.

15. Clokey, 76–77. Smith wrote that Ashley descended the river in a pirogue, and Morgan repeats it. Although his source is obscure, Clokey's version makes more sense. Henry needed neither the boatmen nor the keelboats. Strangely, St. Louis newspapers seem not to have reported Ashley's arrival from the Yellowstone.

16. Sullivan, *Travels of Jedediah Smith*, 8–10. At this point the surviving part of Smith's account ends, not to resume for three and one-half years. In none of the contemporary documents does Weber's name appear in these events, but his role has been clearly established. How long his party remained on the Yellowstone and Powder in 1822–23, however, is lost to history. For a summary of what is known of Weber, see LeRoy R. Hafen, "John H. Weber," in Hafen, *Mountain Men*, 9:379–84.

17. Daniel T. Potts to "Dear and Respected Brother," Rocky Mountain [Cache Valley Rendezvous], July 16, 1826, *Philadelphia Gazette and Daily Advertiser*, November 14, 1826, in Frost, *Notes on General Ashley*, 60.

18. Walter Blair and Franklin J. Meine, eds. *Half Horse Half Alligator* (Chicago: University of Chicago Press, 1956), bring together all the references, credible and mythical, on Mike Fink. Fink's death is noted in *St. Louis Missouri Republican*, July 16, 1823, in Frost, *Notes on General Ashley*, 82. Morgan, *Jedediah Smith*, tells the story in detail, 46–49.

19. The only details of this episode are contained in a deposition of Hugh Johnson, St. Louis, January 13, 1824, in Morgan, *West of William H. Ashley*, 72.

20. The best account was penned by survivor William Gordon in a letter to Joshua Pilcher written at the Mandan villages on June 15, 1823, two weeks later. It was quoted at length in Pilcher to O'Fallon, Fort Recovery (Cedar Fort), July 23, 1823, in turn published in the *Washington National Intelligencer*, September 24, 1823, reprinted in Frost, *Notes on General Ashley*, 90–94. Gordon provided another account in 1831: *Senate Executive Documents*, 22d Congress, 1st session, no. 90 (serial 213), 26–27. Additional details are in a letter from Pilcher to Hempstead from which extracts were published in the *Franklin Missouri Intelligencer*, September 30, 1823, in Frost, 94–95. See also *St. Louis Missouri Republican*, July 16, 1823, in ibid., 81–82. See also O'Fallon to Clark, Fort Atkinson, July 3, 1823, in Morgan, *West of William H. Ashley*, 44–45. The Indians sold their booty at the Hudson's Bay Company post of Edmonton Factory. For this and other particulars from British sources, see A. P. Nasatir, "The International Significance of the Jones and Immell Massacre and of the Aricara Outbreak in 1823," *Pacific Northwest Quarterly* 30 (January 1939): 77–108.

21. In a letter of June 4, 1823, published in the *St. Louis Missouri Republican*, July 9, in Morgan, *West of William H. Ashley*, 25, Ashley tells of receiving an express from Henry asking him to purchase all the horses he could on the way up. Morgan, *Jedediah Smith*, 49–50, deduces the identity of the courier from the fact that Smith was with Ashley when he reached the Arikara villages on May 30. The reasoning is more clearly set forth in Morgan and Carl I. Wheat, *Jedediah Smith and His Maps of the American West* (San Francisco: California Historical Society, 1954), 47. Where Smith met the Ashley expedition is unknown.

22. *St. Louis Missouri Republican,* January 15 and 22, 1823; *St. Louis Enquirer,* February 1, 1823, in Frost, *Notes on General Ashley,* 70–71.

23. Charles L. Camp, ed., *James Clyman, Frontiersman: The Adventures of a Trapper and Covered-Wagon Emigrant as Told in His Own Reminiscences and Diaries* (Portland, Ore.: Champoeg Press, 1960), 7–8. See also Charles L. Camp, "James Clyman," in Hafen, *Mountain Men,* 1:233–52. Clyman is a central character, used to personalize larger themes, of Bernard DeVoto's *The Year of Decision, 1846* (Boston: Houghton Mifflin Co., 1942). The expedition's departure was reported by the *St. Louis Missouri Republican,* March 12, 1823, and the *Franklin Missouri Intelligencer,* April 1, 1823, in Frost, *Notes on General Ashley,* 71–72.

24. Sources bearing on the events at the Arikara villages are voluminous and are all reprinted in Morgan, *West of William H. Ashley,* book 1. Most important are three detailed letters penned by Ashley himself immediately after the episode. The first two were written aboard the *Rocky Mountains* on June 4, one addressed to the *St. Louis Missouri Republican* (which appeared in the issue of July 9), the other to Indian Agent Benjamin O'Fallon and Colonel Henry Leavenworth, commander of Fort Atkinson. The third, addressed to a friend in Franklin and published in that town's *Missouri Intelligencer,* July 8, was dated June 7 opposite the mouth of Cheyenne River. All are in ibid., 25–31. Graphic also is Jim Clyman's account in Camp, *James Clyman,* 8–12.

25. Both quotations are Clyman's in Camp, 9.

26. The quotation and description are by an unidentified participant on one of the keelboats, in a letter to a friend in Washington, D.C., dated at Fort Kiowa, June 17, 1823, printed in the *National Intelligencer,* September 3, 1823, in Morgan, *West of William H. Ashley,* 31–34. Ashley's three letters cited above cover all events in detail.

27. Eulogy cited in note 2, above. The Ashley quotation is from his letter of June 4, 1823, in Morgan, *West of William H. Ashley,* 27. The dead and wounded are named here also.

28. Clyman names Smith and mentions his companion. Camp, *James Clyman,* 12. Smith is said to have stepped forward to volunteer, much to Ashley's astonishment. William Waldo, "Recollections of a Septuagenarian," Missouri Historical Society *Glimpses of the Past* 5 (April–June 1938), 83. It seems more likely that Smith, as a Henry man knowledgeable about the upriver country and as the courier who brought Henry's request for horses, struck Ashley as the most qualified man for the job.

29. Reprinted in Morgan, *West of William H. Ashley,* 31. The original is in the South Dakota Historical Society, Pierre.

30. Ashley's third letter describing the battle with the Arikaras was written here on June 7 and addressed to a friend in Franklin. It appeared in the *Franklin Missouri Intelligencer,* July 8. Morgan, *West of William H. Ashley,* 29–31.

31. O'Fallon to Ashley, Fort Atkinson, June 20, 1823, in ibid., 35–36. O'Fallon reported Ashley's disaster and the plans under way at Fort Atkinson to Superintendent of Indian Affairs William Clark in St. Louis by letters of June 24 and July 3, and Clark passed them on to Secretary of War Calhoun on July 4 and July 18, ibid., 36–37, 44–47.

32. Clyman in Camp, *James Clyman,* 13. One Samuel Smith, who came down with Henry, continued to St. Louis and related some details of the voyage to General Atkinson, who reported them to his superior, General Edmund Gaines, on August 15, Morgan, *West of William H. Ashley,* 240 n. 137, and *Senate Executive Documents,* 18th Congress, 1st session, no. 1 (serial 89), 83.

33. Ashley to John [not Benjamin] O'Fallon, Fort Brassaux, July 19, 1823, in Morgan,

West of William H. Ashley, 47–48. Fort Brassaux or Brazeau was another name for Fort Kiowa, also known as Fort Lookout.

34. The Leavenworth expedition produced mountains of paper, both documentation and recrimination. Some, with annotation, is contained in Morgan, *West of William H. Ashley*, 51 ff. More is included in Frost, *Notes on General Ashley*, 96–129. Most of the official reports were printed in *Senate Executive Documents*, 18th Congress, 1st session, no. 1, 1823 (serial 89), 55–108; and some of these in *South Dakota Historical Collections* 1 (1902): 181–233. See also Camp, *James Clyman*, 13–15.

35. Angus McDonald and William Gordon of the Missouri Fur Company set fire to the villages. McDonald explains why and gives his account of the expedition in a letter to the editor published in the *Washington (D.C.) Gazette*, September 13, 1824.

36. Leavenworth's Order No. 145, Fort Atkinson, August 29, 1823, in *Franklin Missouri Intelligencer*, September 30, 1823. The long-term effect on the Indians of the upper Missouri was stated by a veteran trader at Fort Union writing in the 1850s: Edwin Thomas Denig, *Five Indian Tribes of the Upper Missouri: Sioux, Arickaras, Assiniboines, Crees, Crows*, ed. John C. Ewers (Norman: University of Oklahoma Press, 1961), 56–57.

37. Ashley to John O'Fallon, Fort Brassaux (or Brazeau) [Kiowa], July 19, 1823, in Morgan, *West of William H. Ashley*, 47–48.

CHAPTER 5

1. "Solitaire" remembered this number, Clyman eleven. "Solitaire" [John S. Robb], "Major Fitzpatrick: The Discoverer of South Pass!" *St. Louis Weekly Reveille*, March 1, 1847, reprinted in LeRoy R. Hafen, *Broken Hand: The Life of Thomas Fitzpatrick, Mountain Man, Guide and Indian Agent* (Denver: Old West Publishing Co., 1931; Lincoln: University of Nebraska Press, 1973), 338–42. Charles L. Camp, ed., *James Clyman, Frontiersman: The Adventures of a Trapper and Covered-Wagon Emigrant as Told in His Own Reminiscences and Diaries* (Portland, Ore.: Champoeg Press, 1960), 15. Dale L. Morgan, *Jedediah Smith and the Opening of the West* (Indianapolis: Bobbs-Merrill Co., 1953; Lincoln: University of Nebraska Press, 1964), 80, favors sixteen.

2. Washington Irving, *The Adventures of Captain Bonneville, U.S.A., in the Rocky Mountains and the Far West*, ed. Edgeley W. Todd (Norman: University of Oklahoma Press, 1961), 166–67.

3. Only two primary sources support the first stages of Smith's expedition, although much can be inferred from other sources. The two are the recollections years later of James Clyman and Thomas Fitzpatrick (mixed with those of newsman Charles Keemle, who shared some of the adventures as a member of a Missouri Fur Company expedition with the same objective): Camp, *James Clyman*, 15–26, 49–52, 264–65; and "Solitaire" [John S. Robb], "Major Fitzpatrick: The Discoverer of South Pass!" *St. Louis Weekly Reveille*, March 1, 1847, reprinted in Hafen, *Broken Hand*, 338–42. This and tangential evidence is presented and ably analyzed in Dale L. Morgan, ed., *The West of William H. Ashley* (Denver: Old West Publishing Co., 1964), 77–78; and in Morgan, *Jedediah Smith*, 78–89. The route of Smith's party is traced in Dale L. Morgan and Carl I. Wheat, *Jedediah Smith and His Maps of the American West* (San Francisco: California Historical Society, 1954), 49–50; and in Charles L. Camp, "Jedediah Smith's First Far-Western Expedition," *Western Historical Quarterly* 4 (April 1973): 151–70.

4. Camp, *James Clyman*, 18.

5. U.S. Highway 14 roughly traces the Smith party's route across the Bighorn Mountains while U.S. 16, to the south, approximates the Astorian route of 1811.

6. Henry's misfortunes were recounted by three of Henry's men who descended the Missouri the following December, one of whom was almost certainly Moses "Black" Harris. Their account is recorded in Colonel Henry Leavenworth to General Alexander Macomb, Fort Atkinson, December 20, 1823, which in turn was abstracted in the *Franklin Missouri Intelligencer*, January 22, 1824. The former is in Morgan, *West of William H. Ashley*, 68–69, the latter in Donald McKay Frost, *Notes on General Ashley, the Overland Trail, and South Pass* (Worcester, Mass.: American Antiquarian Society, 1945), 127–29. The circumstances of the Mandan attack on Henry were recounted by Mandan chiefs to General Henry Atkinson in July 1825. Russell Reid and Clell G. Gannon, eds., "Journal of the Atkinson-O'Fallon Expedition," *North Dakota History* 4 (October 1929): 35–36.

7. Charles L. Camp, ed., *George C. Yount and His Chronicles of the West* (Denver: Old West Publishing Co., 1966), 197.

8. The identification of Bridger hangs by a slender thread, but one persuasive enough to convince nearly all serious students, including this one. However, J. Cecil Alter, Bridger's first biographer, could not bring himself to believe his hero the one who remained with Fitzgerald, or indeed that the incident claimed much veracity at all beyond Glass's active imagination: *Jim Bridger* (1925, 1950; Norman: University of Oklahoma Press, 1962), chap. 9. I have examined the principal sources for the Glass episode, but they are conveniently brought together and analyzed in John Myers Myers, *The Saga of Hugh Glass: Pirate, Pawnee, and Mountain Man* (New York: Little, Brown, 1963; Lincoln: University of Nebraska Press, 1976), chaps. 4 and 5. Morgan, *Jedediah Smith*, 390–91, succinctly identifies and evaluates the primary sources.

9. Duncan Finlayson, Edmonton Factory Journal, January 23, 1824, in A. P. Nasatir, "The International Significance of the Jones and Immell Massacre and the Aricara Outbreak in 1823," *Pacific Northwest Quarterly* 30 (January 1939): 85.

10. Reuben Holmes, "The Five Scalps," ed. Stella M. Drumm, Missouri Historical Society, *Glimpses of the Past* 5 (January–March 1938): 48. To Clyman's account another source for these events was added when Weber arrived. Daniel T. Potts, last noted with Smith at the mouth of the Musselshell in the winter of 1822–23, provides a few details—tantalizingly few. Potts to "Dear and Respected Brother," Rocky Mountain [Cache Valley Rendezvous], July 16, 1826, *Philadelphia Gazette and Daily Advertiser*, November 14, 1826, in Morgan, *West of William H. Ashley*, 80–81. Strangely, Smith's chronicler, Clyman, does not mention the Weber party or the Keemle-Gordon party. Potts, who was with Weber, mentions neither of the other two. Keemle ("Solitaire," in Hafen, *Broken Hand*, 338–42) does mention Smith, and from the description all three give of the country there can be no question that they all gathered in the upper Wind River valley.

11. "Solitaire," as cited in note 1 above. This source and Clyman remain the only primary documentation for the further adventures of the Smith expedition, and "Solitaire" tells disappointingly little.

12. Camp, *Clyman*, 264–65. This quotation is not in Clyman's main narrative of the expedition but in a fragmentary diary copied by a researcher for Hubert H. Bancroft in 1871.

13. Since Clyman went with Fitzpatrick, Smith's hunt to the south is undocumented.

14. The adventures of both Clyman and Fitzpatrick are recounted in Camp, *James*

Clyman, 28–29. Clyman, however, has Fitzpatrick's bullboat grounded by falling water before leaving the Sweetwater and the furs cached near the great granite hump later named Independence Rock. The swamping of the bullboat occurred as stated in the North Platte canyon, but after the furs had been cached. I have relied instead on Fitzpatrick's memory as recorded in the "Solitaire" account cited above. Morgan, *Jedediah Smith,* 112, places the boat disaster in Devil's Gate of the Sweetwater, above Independence Rock. This is incompatible with the low water Clyman describes; but more persuasive is Fitzpatrick's recollection of the site of his boat swamping when the same thing happened to Frémont nearly twenty years later. See Camp's note 24, p. 310. In his later *West of William H. Ashley,* 96, Morgan seems to change his mind and concede the North Platte canyon as the site of the disaster.

15. See documents and analysis by Morgan in *West of William H. Ashley,* 96–97.

16. In his diary, Fort Atkinson's sutler James Kennerly recorded Ashley's arrival at Council Bluffs on October 21, "destined for the Spanish Country," and Fitzpatrick's arrival at Bellevue on October 26. Morgan, *West of William H. Ashley,* 98.

17. *St. Louis Enquirer,* August 30, 1824, repeated in *Arkansas Gazette,* September 21, 1824; *Arkansas Gazette,* November 16, 1824, repeating *Enquirer* dispatch of unspecified date. Morgan, *West of William H. Ashley,* 87, 97. The quotation attained national prominence in *Niles's Weekly Register* (Baltimore), December 4, 1824.

18. *St. Louis Enquirer,* June 17, 1824, in Morgan, *West of William H. Ashley,* 76.

19. Myers, *Saga of Hugh Glass,* 179–85. Morgan, *West of William H. Ashley,* 76–77.

20. The activities of Henry and his men during the winter of 1823–24 are sparsely documented and depend on much inference. A letter of Daniel Potts cited in note 10 above provides some details. Potts wrote another letter from Henry's Fort on July 7, 1824, on the eve of Henry's departure and his own with Weber's party, in which he gives additional information. The relevant portions of both are reprinted in Morgan, *West of William H. Ashley,* 79–80.

21. Quoted in Hiram M. Chittenden, *The American Fur Trade of the Far West,* 2 vols. (Stanford, Calif.: Academic Reprints, 1954), 1:252. For Henry's career, see Linda Harper White and Fred R. Gowans, "Traders to Trappers: Andrew Henry and the Rocky Mountain Fur Trade," *Montana the Magazine of Western History* 43 (Winter 1993): 58–65.

22. U.S. Indian Agent Benjamin O'Fallon to Superintendent of Indian Affairs William Clark, Council Bluffs, July 9, 1824, in Morgan, *West of William H. Ashley,* 82–83.

23. Clark to Calhoun, St. Louis, September 18, 1823, in Morgan, *West of William H. Ashley,* 61.

24. *Niles's Weekly Register* (Baltimore), August 23, 1823.

25. Leavenworth to General Henry Atkinson, Fort Atkinson, November 11, 1823, in Morgan, *West of William H. Ashley,* 64–67.

26. Francis Paul Prucha, *The Sword of the Republic: The United States Army on the Frontier, 1783–1846* (New York: Macmillan, 1969), 157–62.

27. The episode is treated in the expedition's journal for August 5, 1825. This document is most conveniently accessed as Russell Reid and Clell G. Gannon, eds., "Journal of the Atkinson-O'Fallon Expedition," *North Dakota History* 4 (October 1929): 5–56. Extracts covering August 14 to September 19 are in Morgan, *West of William H. Ashley,* 130–36. For the expedition report, November 23, 1825, see *House Executive Documents,* 19th Congress, 1st session, no. 17, March 6, 1826 (serial 136). For the text of the treaties, see Charles J. Kappler, comp., *Indian Affairs: Laws and Treaties,* 2 vols. (Washington: Government Printing Office, 1904), 2:225–62.

28. Prucha, *Sword of the Republic*, 237.

29. T. C. Elliott, ed., "Journal of Alexander Ross—Snake Country Expedition, 1824," *Oregon Historical Quarterly* 14 (December 1913), 385–86. See also Alexander Ross, *The Fur Hunters of the Far West*, ed. Kenneth A. Spaulding (Norman: University of Oklahoma Press, 1956), 284–85; Morgan, *Jedediah Smith*, 128–32; and Morgan and Wheat, *Jedediah Smith and His Maps of the American West*, 52–53.

CHAPTER 6

1. The first quotation is from Nicollet's official report, reproduced in *South Dakota Historical Collections* 10 (1920):112–13. The second is from Marvin C. Ross, ed., *The West of Alfred Jacob Miller* (Norman: University of Oklahoma Press, 1968), 76. The third is from William Drummond Stewart, *Edward Warren*, ed. Winfred Blevins (London, 1854; Missoula: Mountain Press Publishing Co., 1986), 143, 144. The fourth is from Berthold to J. P. Cabanné, December 29, 1826, in Dale L. Morgan, ed., *The West of William H. Ashley* (Denver: Old West Publishing Co., 1964), 309–10. Provost has no full-length biography. See LeRoy R. Hafen, "Étienne Provost," in Hafen, *The Mountain Men and the Fur Trade of the Far West*, 10 vols. (Glendale: Arthur H. Clark Co., 1965–72), 6:371–85; and biographical sketch in Dale L. Morgan and Eleanor Towles Harris, *The Rocky Mountain Journals of William Marshall Anderson* (San Marino, Calif.: Huntington Library, 1967; Lincoln: University of Nebraska Press, 1987), 343–51.

2. Trapping and trading ventures toward New Mexico during the Spanish period are summarized in David J. Weber, *The Taos Trappers: The Fur Trade in the Far Southwest, 1540–1846* (Norman: University of Oklahoma Press, 1970), chap. 3. For the Chouteau–de Mun story, see Thomas M. Marshall, ed., "The Journals of Jules de Mun," *Missouri Historical Society Collections* 5 (1928): 167–208, 311–27. The journals are only fragmentary, but this source also reprints de Mun to Governor William Clark, St. Louis, November 25, 1817, telling his story in detail. A deposition setting forth the tribulations of eleven of the men, including Provost, is reprinted in Robert Glass Cleland, *This Reckless Breed of Men: The Trappers and Fur Traders of the Southwest* (New York: Alfred A. Knopf, 1950; Lincoln: University of Nebraska Press, 1992), 124–25. Chouteau recounts the story briefly in A. P. Chouteau to Secretary of War Lewis Cass, Western Creek Agency, November 12, 1832, Missouri Historical Society Papers of the St. Louis Fur Trade Part 1, microfilm reel 19, frame 47. See also Morgan, *West of William H. Ashley*, xliii–xlvii; and George S. Ulibarri, "The Chouteau-Demunn Expedition to New Mexico, 1815–16," *New Mexico Historical Review* 36 (October 1961): 263–73.

3. LeRoy R. Hafen, "Joseph Bissonet, dit Bijou," in Hafen, *Mountain Men*, 9:27–32; and Morgan, *West of William H. Ashley*, xliv–xlv. Another Joseph Bissonette was prominent in the later years of the fur trade. The de Mun journal contains implications that his men did not venture west of the Continental Divide. For Spanish penetrations, see Alfred B. Thomas, "Spanish Expeditions into Colorado," *Colorado Magazine* 1 (November 1924): 289–300.

4. Weber, *Taos Trappers*, chaps. 4 and 5.

5. Ibid., chap. 2. Joseph J. Hill, "Spanish and Mexican Exploration and Trade Northwest from New Mexico into the Great Basin, 1765–1853," *Utah Historical Quarterly* 3 (January 1930): 3–23. Leland H. Creer, "Spanish-American Slave Trade in the Great

Basin, 1800–1853," *New Mexico Historical Review* 24 (July 1949): 171–83. LeRoy R. Hafen and Ann W. Hafen, *Old Spanish Trail: Sante Fe to Los Angeles* (Glendale, Calif.: Arthur H. Clark Co., 1954; Lincoln: University of Nebraska Press, 1993).

6. The movement across the Continental Divide from Taos is contemporaneously noted by William Huddart and William Becknell in the *St. Louis Missouri Intelligencer,* April 19 and June 25, 1825; and in a letter of Augustus Storrs to Senator Thomas Hart Benton written at Franklin, Missouri, in November 1824, reproduced in *Niles's Weekly Register,* January 15, 1825, and in *Senate Executive Documents,* 18th Congress, 2d session, no. 7 (serial 108), 11. Reprinted in Archer B. Hulbert, ed., *Southwest on the Turquoise Trail: The First Diaries on the Road to Santa Fe* (Colorado Springs and Denver: Stewart Commission of Colorado College and Denver Public Library, 1933), 77–98. The best reconstruction of the Provost-Leclerc activities, with analysis of evidence, is Morgan, *West of William H. Ashley,* 277–79. See also Weber, *Taos Trappers,* 70–72.

7. The story is told in detail by trapper Warren A. Ferris, *Life in the Rocky Mountains,* ed. Paul C. Phillips (Denver: Old West Publishing Co., 1940), 308–09. Ferris numbers the party at fifteen and the victims at eleven or twelve. Other sources give lesser numbers of which mine, also accepted by Dale Morgan (in sketch of Provost in *Rocky Mountain Journals of William Marshall Anderson,* 344), is a rough average. The Indian Bureau's tabular statement of persons killed and robbed in the Indian country, compiled in 1831, lists seven men of Provost and Leclerc killed by Snakes (Shoshones) at "Reta" Lake. Record Group 75, Bureau of Indian Affairs (BIA) Letters Received, St. Louis Superintendency, M234, microfilm reel 749 (1829–31), National Archives and Records Service (NARS). In the summer of 1824 the Hudson's Bay Company Snake Country Expedition under Alexander Ross had a run-in with Shoshones, precipitated by some of Ross's own men, that ended in the death of a Shoshone chief. The Indians' vengeance fell on Provost's Americans. Frederick Merk, ed., "Notes and Documents: The Snake Country Expedition Correspondence, 1824–1825," *Mississippi Valley Historical Review* 21 (June 1934): 67–68.

8. Warren Ferris's map of the Rocky Mountains, discussed later in this book, identifies today's Jordan River as "Prouvau's River," from which it may be inferred that this was the scene of the massacre he described in the source cited in the previous note. If he got this far, Provost must have got to Great Salt Lake.

9. The principal source for Weber's movements are the cryptic jottings of Daniel Potts in a letter to his brother, Cache Valley, July 16, 1826, in Donald McKay Frost, *Notes on General Ashley, the Overland Trail, and South Pass* (Worcester, Mass.: American Antiquarian Society, 1945), 61–63.

10. Compiling his monumental geographical memoir of the West in 1857, Lieutenant G. K. Warren of the Topographical Corps queried the veteran trapper and trader Robert Campbell about the discovery of Great Salt Lake. Campbell replied on April 4, 1857, that fortuitously the letter had arrived while both Bridger and Samuel Tulloch, another of Weber's men, were present in Campbell's St. Louis office. Both agreed on the circumstances of Bridger's discovery. The letter appeared in Warren's Memoir in the *Pacific Railroad Reports,* vol. 11, but is more easily consulted in J. Cecil Alter, *Jim Bridger* (Salt Lake City, 1925; Norman: University of Oklahoma Press, 1962), 59–60. Bridger also gave this account in an interview appearing in the *Denver Rocky Mountain News,* May 15, 1861.

11. Simpson's inspection is recorded in Frederick Merk, ed., *Fur Trade and Empire: George Simpson's Journal* (Cambridge: Harvard University Press, 1931).

12. The people and events treated in this section are admirably presented from the British perspective in E. E. Rich, *The History of the Hudson's Bay Company, 1670–1870*, 2 vols. (London: Hudson's Bay Record Society, 1947), 2:chap. 22. See also E. E. Rich, *The Fur Trade and the Northwest to 1857* (Toronto: McClelland and Stewart, 1967), chaps. 13 and 14.

13. Merk, *Fur Trade and Empire*, 43.

14. Simpson to Ogden, Fort George, March 14, 1825, in E. E. Rich, ed., *Peter Skene Ogden's Snake Country Journals, 1824–25 and 1825–26* (London: Hudson's Bay Record Society, 1950), 253. For Ogden, see Gloria Griffin Cline, *Peter Skene Ogden and the Hudson's Bay Company* (Norman: University of Oklahoma Press, 1975); and Archie Binns, *Peter Skene Ogden, Fur Trader* (Portland, Ore.: Binfords & Mort, 1967).

15. Nearly all that is known of Provost and the events following his appearance in Ogden's camp comes from British sources, mainly the journals of Ogden and his clerk, William Kittson. Rich, *Peter Skene Ogden's Snake Country Journals*. The relevant sections of Ogden's journal are on pp. 48–53. Kittson's journal is printed as Appendix A, the pertinent entries on pp. 233–35. See also Frederick Merk, "Snake Country Expedition, 1824–25: An Episode of Fur Trade and Empire," *Mississippi Valley Historical Review* 21 (June 1934): 49–61. An annex to this article, "Notes and Documents: The Snake Country Expedition Correspondence, 1824–1825," 62–75, prints important letters. See also Ogden to Governor, Chief Factor, and Chief Traders, Snake River Plain, June 27, 1825, in E. E. Rich, ed., *Letters of John McLoughlin from Fort Vancouver to the Governor and Committee, First Series, 1825–1838* (London and Toronto: Hudson's Bay Record Society, 1941), 296–99.

16. In addition to sources cited in the previous note, see Dale L. Morgan, *Jedediah Smith and the Opening of the West* (Indianapolis: Bobbs-Merrill Co., 1953; Lincoln: University of Nebraska Press, 1964), chap. 7; and Dale L. Morgan and Carl I. Wheat, *Jedediah Smith and His Maps of the American West* (San Francisco: California Historical Society, 1954), 54.

17. William H. Ashley to William Orr, *Missouri Observer*, October 31, 1827, in Morgan, *West of William H. Ashley*, 176–77.

18. Rich, *Peter Skene Ogden's Snake Country Journals*, 48–49, places these events on the south fork of Ogden River, which Ogden himself named the New River. However, Morgan, *West of William H. Ashley*, 277–78, 311; and David E. Miller, ed., "Peter Skene Ogden's Journal of His Expedition to Utah, 1825," *Utah Historical Quarterly* 20 (April 1952): 159–86, fix the site on the Weber River near present Mountain Green, Utah, which is about fifteen miles upstream from present Ogden, the approximate site of Weber's camp. Miller, based at the University of Utah in Salt Lake City, carefully related the Ogden and Kittson journals and the Kittson map to the actual terrain, and his conclusions outweigh Rich's. Miller believes that Ogden mistook the Weber for the south fork of his "New River." After debouching from the mountains, the two rivers unite before flowing into Great Salt Lake. Ogden, however, could not have known this, since he did not descend either to the lake.

19. Carl I. Wheat, *Mapping the Transmississippi West, 1540–1861*, 6 vols. (San Francisco: Institute of Historical Geography, 1957–63), 2:112–16.

20. The events of the next month involving the Ashley and Provost men must be gleaned from a narrative and diary authored by Ashley. The diary was long credited to William L. Sublette but was positively identified as Ashley's by Dale L. Morgan. Morgan, *West of William H. Ashley*, contains both, integrated chronologically and with extensive and authoritative annotation. The narrative, a long letter from Ashley

to General Henry Atkinson, December 1825, may be consulted in its unbroken entirety in Harrison C. Dale, ed., *The Ashley-Smith Explorations and the Discovery of a Central Route to the Pacific, 1822–1829* (Glendale, Calif.: Arthur H. Clark Co., 1941), reprinted as *The Explorations of William H. Ashley and Jedediah Smith, 1822–1829* (Lincoln: University of Nebraska Press, 1991). As will develop in the next few paragraphs of my narrative, Provost set out to find Ashley, which means that he learned about Ashley while in Weber's camp. He could have obtained this information only from Zachariah Ham. Morgan raises a possibility—remote, I think—that it came from Ham via some Ute Indians.

21. Morgan, *West of William H. Ashley*, 105, 265–67.

22. Beckwourth's autobiography, first published in 1856, is best consulted in tandem with his biography, which attempts to sort the truth out from the fiction. Thomas D. Bonner, *The Life and Adventures of James P. Beckwourth*, introduction, notes, and epilogue by Delmont R. Oswald (Lincoln: University of Nebraska Press, 1972). Elinor Wilson, *Jim Beckwourth: Black Mountain Man and War Chief of the Crows* (Norman: University of Oklahoma Press, 1972).

23. Morgan, 269. Ashley's adventures in 1824–25 are authoritatively chronicled in Richard M. Clokey, *William H. Ashley: Enterprise and Politics in the Trans-Mississippi West* (Norman: University of Oklahoma Press, 1980), chap. 7.

24. Bonner, *Life and Adventures of James P. Beckwourth*, 57–61.

25. Ashley's adventures from May 3 to June 7 are in Morgan, *West of William H. Ashley*, 108–16, 283–84.

26. Charles L. Camp, ed., *James Clyman, Frontiersman* (Portland, Ore.: Champoeg Press, 1960), 38. Beckwourth was present and gave an account portraying himself as the hero. Bonner, *Life and Adventures of James P. Beckwourth*, 63–65. LaBarge Creek and LaBarge, Wyoming, recall the event and the site.

27. Ashley's diary ends abruptly on June 27, 1825, but he touches on the rendezvous in his narrative; and his accounts, listing names, merchandise and prices, and beaver skins purchased, tell much about the rendezvous and the economics of the mountain trade. Morgan, *West of William H. Ashley*, 118–30. Beckwourth was there, and his overblown account, giving himself a conspicuous part, yields a few plausible glimpses. Bonner, chap. 7. Ashley says only that he chose a new site twenty miles upstream from the original site, without identifying which stream. Twenty miles up the Green, however, does not yield an eligible site, while twenty miles up Henry's Fork provides an ideal site. See Fred R. Gowans, *Rocky Mountain Rendezvous* (Layton, Utah: Peregrine Smith Books, 1985), 14–23. See also Don Berry, *A Majority of Scoundrels: An Informal History of the Rocky Mountain Fur Company* (New York: Harper & Brothers, 1961), chaps. 7 and 8; and Clokey, *William H. Ashley*, 159–63.

28. Besides Ashley's accounts, see Morgan, *Jedediah Smith and the Opening of the West*, 171–72. The evolution of the Rocky Mountain trapping system is competently treated in David J. Wishart, *The Fur Trade of the American West, 1807–1840* (Lincoln: University of Nebraska Press, 1979), chaps. 4 and 5.

29. For Provost's subsequent career, see Hafen, "Étienne Provost," 376–85.

CHAPTER 7

1. Ashley's narrative carries the story from rendezvous to the mouth of the Yellowstone, where he met the Atkinson-O'Fallon expedition on August 17. Thereafter, the

expedition's journals carry the story down to Fort Atkinson. Newspapers noted Ashley's arrival in St. Louis: *Franklin Missouri Intelligencer,* October 7, 1825, and *Missouri Advocate and St. Louis Advertiser,* October 8, 1825. All these documents are printed in Dale L. Morgan, ed., *The West of William H. Ashley* (Denver: Old West Publishing Co., 1964), 129–37. Jim Beckwourth was one of the twenty-five men who accompanied Ashley all the way to St. Louis. With his usual mix of fact, fancy, and hyperbole, he tells the story in Thomas D. Bonner, *The Life and Adventures of James P. Beckwourth,* ed. Delmont R. Oswald (Lincoln: University of Nebraska Press, 1972), chap. 7. See also Richard M. Clokey, *William H. Ashley: Enterprise and Politics in the Trans-Mississippi West* (Norman: University of Oklahoma Press, 1980), 163–67.

2. The first quotation is from Alfred Jacob Miller, *The West of Alfred Jacob Miller,* ed. Marvin C. Ross (Norman: University of Oklahoma Press, 1968), 67. The second is from George Frederick Ruxton, *Life in the Far West,* ed. LeRoy R. Hafen (Norman: University of Oklahoma Press, 1951), 7. "Boudins" were buffalo sausages encased in buffalo intestines and roasted over a fire. See also Jerome Peltier, "Moses 'Black' Harris," in LeRoy R. Hafen, ed., *Mountain Men and the Fur Trade of the Far West,* 10 vols. (Glendale, Calif.: Arthur H. Clark Co., 1965–72), 4:103–17.

3. These events were brought into focus by Dale Morgan's discovery of an account dictated in 1870 by Robert Campbell, a participant, partly printed in Morgan, *West of William H. Ashley,* 143–44, and in its entirety as Drew Allen Holloway, ed., *A Narrative of Colonel Robert Campbell's Experiences in the Rocky Mountain Fur Trade from 1825 to 1835* (Fairfield, Wash.: Ye Galleon Press, 1991). The original is in the Campbell Papers, Missouri Historical Society, St. Louis. Campbell's revelations supersede Morgan's earlier rendition of this and events in the mountains as given in *Jedediah Smith and the Opening of the West* (Indianapolis: Bobbs-Merrill Co., 1953), chap. 9, which is erroneous.

4. *Missouri Advocate and St. Louis Enquirer,* March 11, 1826, in Morgan, *West of William H. Ashley,* 140–41. The Indians doubtless referred to the Humboldt, which rises more than a hundred miles west of the lake and which had yet to be discovered by whites. The Humboldt, of course, loses itself in sinks at the eastern base of the Sierra Nevada.

5. *Missouri Herald and St. Louis Advertiser,* November 8, 1826, in Morgan, *West of William H. Ashley,* 153–54. In note 313, p. 304, Morgan identifies and discusses the fragmentary sources for the boat trip around the lake. Again, discovery of the Campbell narrative, together with other new findings, invalidates the passages in Morgan's biography of Smith ascribing to Smith rather than Sublette and Jackson the spring 1826 expedition northwest of Great Salt Lake and thence to the Snake. James Clyman and Henry Fraeb were probably two of the four men.

6. Bonner, *Life and Adventures of James P. Beckwourth,* 107. See also Fred R. Gowans, *Rocky Mountain Rendezvous: A History of the Fur Trade Rendezvous, 1825–1840* (Layton, Utah: Peregrine Smith Books, 1985), 24–32.

7. The articles of agreement, July 18, 1826, are printed in Morgan, *West of William H. Ashley,* 150–52.

8. An especially good overview of the mountain men, succinct yet comprehensive, is William H. Goetzmann, *The Mountain Man* (Cody, Wyo.: Buffalo Bill Historical Center, 1978). The following works are among the best in conveying the essence of the mountain man. Washington Irving, *The Adventures of Captain Bonneville, U.S.A., in the Rocky Mountains and the Far West,* ed. Edgeley W. Todd (Norman: University of Oklahoma Press, 1986). Frances Fuller Victor, *The River of the West: Life and Adven-*

ture in the Rocky Mountains and Oregon. . . . (Hartford and Toledo: R. W. Bliss & Co., 1870). This has been reprinted in two volumes (Missoula: Mountain Press Publishing Co., 1983, 1987), the first volume, *The Mountain Years,* ed. Winfred Blevins; the second volume, *The Oregon Years,* ed. Lee Nash. I find this edition much more convenient to use because of the editorial annotations, and all citations are from it. W. A. Ferris, *Life in the Rocky Mountains: Diary of Wanderings on the Sources of the Rivers Missouri, Columbia, and Colorado from February, 1830, to November, 1835,* ed. Paul C. Phillips (Denver: Old West Publishing Co., 1940). Zenas Leonard, *Adventures of a Mountain Man: The Narrative of Zenas Leonard,* ed. Milo M. Quaife (Lincoln: University of Nebraska Press, 1978); and also as *Adventures of Zenas Leonard, Fur Trader,* ed. John C. Ewers (Norman: University of Oklahoma Press, 1959). John K. Townsend, *Narrative of a Journey across the Rocky Mountains, to the Columbia River . . . [1833–34]* (Philadelphia: Henry Perkins, 1839), in Reuben Gold Thwaites, ed., *Early Western Travels,* 21. Dale L. Morgan and Eleanor Towles Harris, eds., *The Rocky Mountain Journals of William Marshall Anderson: The West in 1834* (San Marino, Calif.: Huntington Library, 1967; Lincoln: University of Nebraska Press, 1987). Osborne Russell, *Journal of a Trapper,* ed. Aubrey L. Haines (Lincoln: University of Nebraska Press, 1965); Marvin C. Ross, ed. *The West of Alfred Jacob Miller* (Norman: University of Oklahoma Press, 1968). Hiram M. Chittenden, *The American Fur Trade of the Far West,* 2 vols. (1902; Stanford, Calif.: Academic Reprints, 1964).

9. An excellent overview of the Rocky Mountain trapping system is David Wishart, *The Fur Trade of the American West, 1807–1840* (Lincoln: University of Nebraska Press, 1979), chaps. 4 and 5. A contemporary overview of great value is Joshua Pilcher's report to President Andrew Jackson in *Senate Executive Documents,* 22d Congress, 1st session, 1831 (serial 213), but more readily accessed and explained in Stella M. Drumm, ed., "Reports of the Fur Trade and Inland Trade to Mexico, 1831," Missouri Historical Society, *Glimpses of the Past* 9 (January–September 1941): 11–25.

10. For a statistical view of ethnicity as well as other social and economic factors, see Janet Lecompte's introduction to *French Fur Traders and Voyageurs in the American West: Twenty-five Biographical Sketches* [from Hafen's *Mountain Men and the Fur Trade*] (Spokane: Arthur H. Clark Co., 1995; Lincoln: University of Nebraska Press, 1997), 9–26. Lecompte shows how previous historians have not only minimized French numbers and contributions but also indulged inaccurate French stereotyping. See also William R. Swagerty, "A View from the Bottom Up: The Work Force of the American Fur Company on the Upper Missouri in the 1830s," *Montana the Magazine of Western History* 43 (Winter 1993): 18–33; Swagerty and Dick A. Wilson, "Faithful Service under Different Flags: A Socioeconomic Profile of the Columbia District of the Hudson's Bay Company and the Upper Missouri Outfit, American Fur Company, 1825–1835," in Jennifer S. H. Brown, W. J. Eccles, and Donald P. Heldman, eds., *The Fur Trade Revisited: Selected Papers from the Sixth North American Fur Trade Conference, Mackinac Island, Michigan, 1991* (East Lansing: Michigan State University Press, 1994): 243–67; and Swagerty, "The Upper Missouri Outfit: The Men and the Fur Trade in the 1830s," *Fort Union Fur Trade Symposium Proceedings September, 13–15, 1990* (Williston, N.D.: Friends of Fort Union Trading Post, 1994): 25–42.

11. Irving, *Adventures of Captain Bonneville,* 155–56.

12. Victor, *River of the West,* 1:50.

13. For the role of women, see Sylvia Van Kirk, *Many Tender Ties: Women in Fur-Trade Society, 1670–1870* (Norman: University of Oklahoma Press, 1980); Walter O'Meara, *Daughters of the Country: The Women of the Fur Traders and Mountain Men* (New

York: Harcourt, Brace & World, 1968); and William R. Swagerty, "Marriage and Settlement Patterns of Rocky Mountain Trappers and Traders," *Western Historical Quarterly* 11 (April 1980): 159–79.

14. Irving, 10–11.

15. Both Smith and his clerk, Harrison G. Rogers, kept journals and memoranda. For the journey of 1826–27, the source to consult is George R. Brooks, ed., *The Southwest Expedition of Jedediah S. Smith: His Personal Account of the Journey to California, 1826–1827* (Glendale: Arthur H. Clark Co., 1977; Lincoln: University of Nebraska Press, 1989). This is drawn from a contemporary copy of the lost original that turned up only in 1967. Harrison Rogers's daybook is also included. The whole is superbly edited by Brooks. The Rogers daybook was originally published in 1918 by Harrison C. Dale, *The Ashley-Smith Explorations and the Discovery of a Central Route to the Pacific, 1822–1829* (rev. ed., Glendale, Calif.: Arthur H. Clark Co., 1941; Lincoln: University of Nebraska Press, 1989). The Brooks transcription and editing are superior. Maurice S. Sullivan, *The Travels of Jedediah Smith: A Documentary Outline, Including His Journal* (Santa Ana, Calif.: Fine Arts Press, 1934; Lincoln: University of Nebraska Press, 1992) contains journal entries beginning only near the end of the 1826–27 journey but carries the record forward to July 1828. Brooks includes these final days, but thereafter one must turn to Sullivan, whose editing is inferior to Brooks's.

    Scholars have debated Smith's intention when he set forth on this expedition. Some find intimations in his journal that he meant to reach California, and some even postulate that his objective from the beginning was the Columbia. I take the journal at face value—that until circumstance dictated otherwise Smith planned to return to Cache Valley for the winter of 1826–27.

16. Brooks, 37.

17. Ibid., 66.

18. Ibid., 77–78.

19. In addition to the Smith and Rogers journals in ibid., Smith wrote two letters bearing on his California troubles, one to the U.S. minister in Mexico City from San Diego, December 16, 1826; and another to General William Clark, Superintendent of Indian Affairs in St. Louis, from the rendezvous on Bear Lake, July 12, 1827. Both are reprinted in Morgan, *Jedediah Smith and the Opening of the West*, Appendix A. For the Mexican perspective, not unreasonable in the circumstances, see David J. Weber, ed., *The Californios versus Jedediah Smith, 1826–1827: A New Cache of Documents* (Spokane: Arthur H. Clark Co., 1990).

20. Brooks, 178.

21. Ibid., 193.

22. Ibid., 197.

23. As I state in chapter 2, I believe that in 1808 John Colter traced the north shore of Yellowstone Lake and then descended the Yellowstone River, circling the Upper and Lower Falls, and crossing the river below Tower Falls. Almost certainly he did not see the geyser basins of the Firehole and Gibbon Rivers on the west side of the park. See Aubrey Haines, "John Colter," in Hafen, *Mountain Men*, 8:78–80. Principal sources for the Jackson-Sublette expedition of 1826 are Daniel Potts's letter to his brother, written at the Bear Lake rendezvous on July 8, 1827, in Morgan, *West of William H. Ashley*, 161–62; and Holloway, *Colonel Robert Campbell's Experiences*. Potts described Yellowstone Lake and the thermal features at West Thumb and on the north shore, where he had probably been preceded by Colter. But the trappers then turned northwest to reach the Three Forks by way of the Gallatin. The likeliest routes from Yel-

lowstone Lake to the head of the Gallatin River would have revealed one or both of the great geyser basins on the Firehole and Gibbon Rivers, which join to form the Madison River. Potts does not mention the Gallatin; that comes from the Campbell Manuscript.

24. Ashley's accounts in Morgan, *West of William H. Ashley,* 171–74. Jackson, *Shadow on the Tetons,* chaps. 9–10. Gowans, *Rocky Mountain Rendezvous,* 33–38. Holloway, *Colonel Robert Campbell's Experiences.* The ordeal of Sublette and Harris in hiking to St. Louis in midwinter was related by Sublette to newsman Matthew Field in 1843: *Prairie and Mountain Sketches,* ed. Kate L. Gregg and John Francis McDermott (Norman: University of Oklahoma Press, 1957), 165–66.

25. Sullivan, *Travels of Jedediah Smith,* 26. Brooks having ended with the 1827 rendezvous, Sullivan is now the authority for the further travels of Smith.

26. Sullivan, 31. Smith's journal contains a blank page and a half followed by two missing pages. Omitted is his account of the river crossing and the initial attack. The journal resumes with the events on the west bank. Over the signature of the three partners, Smith wrote an account of his 1827–28 adventures for General William Clark, entitled "A brief sketch of accidents, misfortunes, and depredations committed by Indians, &c. on the firm of Smith, Jackson & Sublette, Indian traders on the East & west side of the Rocky Mountains, since July 1826 to the present [December?] 24th, 1829." The Mojave incident is dealt with only briefly: "Mr. Smith and his party in attempting to cross the river on rafts, was attacked by those Indians and completely defeated with a loss of 10 men and 2 women (taken prisoners) the property all taken or destroyed." The full document is printed in Morgan, *Jedediah Smith,* 337–43. The Mojaves seem to have been thrown into a foul mood by a recent encounter with trappers based in New Mexico, treated in the next chapter.

27. Sullivan, 30.
28. Ibid., 40.
29. Again the plausible Mexican perspective is revealed in Weber, *Californios versus Jedediah Smith.*
30. Smith's journal ends with the entry of July 3. Harrison Rogers's journal continues until July 13, the day before the massacre in which he perished. The Smith journal is in Sullivan, but the Rogers journal must be consulted in Dale, *Ashley-Smith Explorations,* 242 ff. This work is more readily available under the title *The Explorations of William H. Ashley and Jedediah Smith, 1822–1829* (Lincoln: University of Nebraska Press, 1991). Such details of the massacre as are known come from the lone survivor, Arthur Black, and Smith himself as related to John McLoughlin of the Hudson's Bay Company. McLoughlin to Governor and Committee, Fort Vancouver, August 10, 1828, in E. E. Rich, ed., *Letters of John McLoughlin from Fort Vancouver to the Governor and Committee, First Series, 1825–1838* (London and Toronto: Hudson's Bay Record Society, 1941), 68–70. Much also was learned by Alexander McLeod, who led a Hudson's Bay expedition in search of Smith's property. His journal is printed in Sullivan, 112–35. Fortunately for history, among the booty recovered by McLeod were the papers of Smith and Rogers that are printed in Sullivan and Dale. Sullivan and Morgan call the Indians Kelawatsets, but see Robert H. Ruby and John A. Brown, *A Guide to the Indian Tribes of the Pacific Northwest* (Norman: University of Oklahoma Press, 1986), 97–99.
31. Simpson to McLoughlin, York Factory, July 9, 1827, in E. E. Rich, ed., *Part of Dispatch from George Simpson Esq. . . . [March 1, March 24, June 5, 1829]* (London: Hudson's Bay Record Society, 1947), 155–56. For developments in the Columbia

Department, see this report and Rich's introduction, and also E. E. Rich, *The History of the Hudson's Bay Company, 1670–1870,* 2 vols. (London: Hudson's Bay Record Society, 1959), 2:chaps. 22–23. See also Rich's introduction to *Letters of John McLoughlin from Fort Vancouver.* For the boundary negotiations of 1827, see Frederick Merk, *The Oregon Question: Essays in Anglo American Diplomacy and Politics* (Cambridge: Harvard University Press, 1967), chaps. 8–9.

32. McLoughlin to Governor and Committee, Fort Vancouver, August 10, 1828, in Rich, *Letters of John McLoughlin,* 68–70.

33. McLeod's journal is printed in Sullivan, *Travels of Jedediah Smith,* 112–35.

34. The deal is set forth in two long letters from Simpson to Smith, Fort Vancouver, December 26 and 29, 1828, printed in Sullivan, 136–42; and in Frederick Merk, ed., *Fur Trade and Empire: George Simpson's Journal* (Cambridge: Harvard University Press, 1931), 302–06.

35. Rich, *Part of Dispatch from George Simpson,* 66–67.

36. *Philadelphia National Gazette,* November 26, 1830, quoting *Cincinnati Commercial Advertiser,* repeating *St. Louis Beacon,* in Donald McKay Frost, *Notes on General Ashley, the Overland Trail, and South Pass* (Worcester, Mass.: American Antiquarian Society, 1945), 152–53. See also *Columbia Missouri Intelligencer and Boon's Lick Advertiser,* October 9, 1830, and *St. Louis Missouri Republican,* October 19, 1830, ibid.

37. The personal letters of Jedediah Smith and his family are reprinted as Appendix B of Morgan, *Jedediah Smith.*

38. Ibid., 323–24. The course of the fall and spring hunt may be followed in the accounts of two participants, Joe Meek and Robert Newell. Frances Fuller Victor, *The River of the West: Life and Adventure in the Rocky Mountains and Oregon....* (Hartford and Toledo: R. W. Bliss & Co., 1870); Reprint, Winfred Blevins, ed., *The River of the West: The Adventures of Joe Meek,* 2 vols. (Missoula: Mountain Press Publishing Co., 1983, 1987), 83–85. Dorothy O. Johansen, ed., *Robert Newell's Memoranda....* (Portland, Ore.: Champoeg Press, 1959), 31.

39. Morgan, *Jedediah Smith,* 316–21. Don Berry, *A Majority of Scoundrels: An Informal History of the Rocky Mountain Fur Company* (New York: Harper & Bros., 1961), chap. 16.

40. Morgan, *Jedediah Smith,* 325–30. Details of Smith's death came from Mexican traders with the Comanches. Morgan discusses his sources at length in his citations, 435–36.

41. Carl I. Wheat, *Mapping the Transmississippi West, 1540–1861,* 6 vols. (San Francisco: Institute of Historical Cartography, 1957–63), 2:167–68. My account of the Smith maps is based on this monumental study and Dale L. Morgan and Carl I. Wheat, *Jedediah Smith and His Maps of the American West* (San Francisco: California Historical Society, 1954).

42. Wheat, 2:116.

43. The story of the Smith-Frémont-Gibbs map is told in Wheat, 2:119–38; and Morgan and Wheat, chaps. 2–4.

44. Wheat, 2:119.

CHAPTER 8

1. An excellent biography is Kenneth L. Holmes, *Ewing Young, Master Trapper* (Portland, Ore.: Binfords & Mort, 1967). Authoritative though brief is Harvey L. Carter, "Ewing Young," in LeRoy R. Hafen, ed., *Mountain Men and the Fur Trade of the Far West,* 10 vols. (Glendale, Calif.: Arthur H. Clark Co.,1965–72), 2:379–401.

2. Wolfskill is the authority for the quotation, in Holmes, 20. For Wolfskill, see Iris Higbie Wilson, *William Wolfskill, 1798–1866* (Glendale, Calif.: Arthur H. Clark Co., 1965).
3. The story is hard to piece together because it rests on the recollections years later of two participants, George Yount and Pegleg Smith, and on the celebrated contemporary account of a third, James Ohio Pattie, which has long been a subject of confusion and debate. Mexican sources have added much, but prodigies of deduction and speculation are still necessary. Holmes and Wilson both have accounts, but the best, drawing heavily on Mexican sources, is David J. Weber, *The Taos Trappers: The Fur Trade in the Far Southwest, 1540–1846* (Norman: University of Oklahoma Press, 1968), chap. 8. Less satisfactory but also tapping Mexican archives is Robert Glass Cleland, *This Reckless Breed of Men: The Trappers and Fur Traders of the Southwest* (New York: Alfred A. Knopf, 1950; Lincoln: University of Nebraska Press, 1992), chaps. 4 and 5. The first venture into Mexican sources was Thomas Maitland Marshall, "St. Vrain's Expedition to the Gila in 1826," in H. Morse Stephens and Herbert E. Bolton, eds., *The Pacific Ocean in History* (New York: Macmillan, 1917): 429–38. A dated but valuable item is Joseph J. Hill, "Ewing Young in the Fur Trade of the Far Southwest, 1822–1834," *Oregon Historical Quarterly* 24 (March 1923): 1–35. See also Hill's "New Light on Pattie and the Southwestern Fur Trade," *Southwestern Historical Quarterly* 26 (April 1923): 245–54. Pattie's story, first published in 1831 as told to Timothy Flint, is available in many editions, most notably as edited by Reuben Gold Thwaites in *Early Western Travels* 18, and as edited by Milo M. Quaife in a 1930 Lakeside Classic. However, Pattie's narrative is such an extraordinary mix of fact and fancy that his genuine contributions are best drawn from an astute study by Richard Batman, *James Pattie's West: The Dream and the Reality* (Norman: University of Oklahoma Press, 1986). Smith's reminiscences are in "Sketches from the Life of Pegleg Smith," *Hutchings' Illustrated California Magazine* 5 (nos. 4–9, October–March 1860–61); and "The Story of an Old Trapper: Life and Adventures of the Late Peg-Leg Smith," *San Francisco Evening Bulletin*, October 26, 1866. For Yount, see Charles L. Camp, ed., *George C. Yount and His Chronicles of the West* (Denver: Old West Publishing Co., 1966). The identification of St. Vrain's partner as "Old Bill" Williams, among other possible Williamses, is authoritative speculation.
4. The standard biography is Alpheus H. Favour, *Old Bill Williams, Mountain Man* (Norman: University of Oklahoma Press, 1962). See also Frederic E. Voelker, "William Sherley (Old Bill) Williams," in Hafen, *Mountain Men*, 8:365–94.
5. An excellent sketch is Doyce B. Nunis, Jr., "Milton Sublette," in Hafen, *Mountain Men*, 4:331–49.
6. Alfred Glen Humphreys, "Thomas L. (Peg-leg) Smith," ibid.,4:311–30. See also biographical sketch in Camp, *George C. Yount*, Part 10.
7. That the Indians were Apaches or Yavapais was the conclusion of anthropologist A. L. Kroeber, with whom I agree. "The Route of James O. Pattie on the Colorado in 1826: A Reappraisal by A. L. Kroeber," with comments by Robert C. Euler and Albert H. Schroeder, ed. Clifton Kroeber, *Arizona and the West* 6 (Summer 1964): 119–36. The year was 1827, not 1826. Pattie's chronology was off by a year, as demonstrated by Batman and others. Batman, 168–74, conjectures that Pattie may not have been with Robidoux but with Young from the beginning, and that his account of the adventures of Robidoux's group was contrived. George Yount identified the Indians as Pimas and Maricopas, which seems as unlikely as Pattie's Papagos. Camp, *George C. Yount*, 31–32.
8. Camp, *George C. Yount*, 32–33, 37.

9. J. P. Cabanné to Pierre Chouteau, Jr., Council Bluffs, July 17, 1825, Missouri Historical Society Papers of the St. Louis Fur Trade Part 1, microfilm reel 12. See also David J. Weber, "Sylvester S. Pratte," in Hafen, *Mountain Men*, 6:359–70.

10. Weber, "Pratte," and Harold H. Dunham, "Ceran St. Vrain," in Hafen, *Mountain Men*, 5:297–316. The story of this expedition is engagingly recounted in David Lavender, *Bent's Fort* (New York: Doubleday, 1954), chap. 4.

11. The only authoritative source for this event is Smith himself, as told and perhaps embroidered years later, in "Sketches from the Life of Peg-leg Smith," *Hutchings' Illustrated California Magazine* 5 (March 1861): 420. But see also Weber, *Taos Trappers*, 170; Humphreys, "Thomas L. (Peg-leg) Smith," 323–25; and Lavender, *Bent's Fort*, 74–76.

12. Weber, *Taos Trappers*, 170–73.

13. Alice B. Maloney, "The Richard Campbell Party of 1827," *California Historical Society Quarterly* 17 (December 1939): 347–54. As will appear in a later chapter, in 1850 Campbell, a resident of Santa Fe, described his 1827 route for army topographer Lieutenant James H. Simpson. Some of the topography is confused, but Zuñi Pueblo, the Zuñi River, and "El Vado de los Padres," the Crossing of the Fathers, are identified. The last was one of the few places between the Grand Canyon and the Uinta Basin where the Colorado River could be forded. Quoted in full ibid., 350–51. In his journal of 1827 Jedediah Smith mentions a report, obtained from Governor Echeandía, of an American trapping party on the upper San Joaquin. This would have been Campbell. Maurice S. Sullivan, ed., *The Travels of Jedediah Smith: A Documentary Outline* (Santa Ana, Calif.: Fine Arts Press, 1934; Lincoln: University of Nebraska Press, 1992), 42. See also Weber, *Taos Trappers*, 134–36.

14. Again, rather than Pattie's original narrative, I prefer to work from the excellent analysis by Richard Batman in *James Pattie's West*, chaps. 10–15. The descent of the Gila, before the breakup of the company, is recorded by George Yount, one of those who parted with the main group, apparently because of Sylvester Pattie's tyranny. Camp, *George Yount*, 43–46. The Yount group turned up the Colorado and eventually returned to Taos by the Campbell route through Zuñi. See also Weber, *Taos Trappers*, 136–41.

15. Carson's memoirs are the principal source for the Young expedition. They have been published in many editions, but the best is Harvey L. Carter, ed., *"Dear Old Kit": The Historical Christopher Carson* (Norman: University of Oklahoma Press, 1968). Laden with extensive annotations, this edition also makes sense of Carson's often confused chronology. There have also been many biographies of Carson, but the best (though still flawed) is Thelma S. Guild and Harvey L. Carter, *Kit Carson: A Pattern for Heroes* (Lincoln: University of Nebraska Press, 1984). Scholars impatiently await the truly authoritative treatment of Carson by Marc Simmons. The Young expedition is also treated in Holmes, *Ewing Young*, chap. 4; Hill, "Ewing Young in the Fur Trade of the Far Southwest," 23–27; and Weber, *Taos Trappers*, 141–44.

16. Carter, *"Dear Old Kit,"* 44.

17. Ibid., 46. The desert crossing followed a route roughly approximating the present line of the Santa Fe Railroad from Seligman, Arizona, through Kingman, to the Colorado at Toprock.

18. For Ogden see John Scaglione, "Ogden's Report of His 1829–30 Expedition," *California Historical Society Quarterly* 28 (June 1949): 117–24. Carson implies that the two groups parted on the lower Sacramento while Ogden says the upper. See Holmes, *Ewing Young*, 50, for a resolution of the conflict.

19. Carter, *"Dear Old Kit,"* 47. Holmes, *Ewing Young,* 50–52, and Hill, "Ewing Young in the Far Southwest," 24–26, citing Mexican documents, establish that the mission involved was San José, not, as Carson stated, San Rafael.

20. Carter, *"Dear Old Kit,"* 48.

21. Wilson, *William Wolfskill,* chap. 3, treats the expedition in detail. Yount's reminiscences are in Camp, *George Yount,* part 5. See also LeRoy R. Hafen and Ann W. Hafen, *Old Spanish Trail, Santa Fe to Los Angeles* (Glendale, Calif.: Arthur H. Clark Co., 1954; Norman: University of Nebraska Press, 1993), 140–54.

22. Holmes, *Ewing Young,* chap. 5. Weber, *Taos Trappers,* 145–52. Hill, "Ewing Young in the Fur Trade of the Far Southwest," 29–31. John C. Jackson, *Shadow on the Tetons: David E. Jackson and the Claiming of the American West* (Missoula, Mont.: Mountain Press Publishing Co., 1993), chaps. 13 and 14. Vivian Linford Talbot, *David E. Jackson: Field Captain of the Rocky Mountain Fur Trade* (Jackson, Wyo.: Jackson Hole Historical Society and Museum, 1996), chap. 4. The account of one of Young's men is Job Francis Dye, *Recollections of a Pioneer, 1830–1852* (Los Angeles: Glen Dawson, 1951).

23. Quoted in Holmes, 92.

24. Weber, *Taos Trappers,* 190.

CHAPTER 9

1. Bil Gilbert, *Westering Man: The Life of Joseph Walker* (New York: Atheneum, 1983; Norman: University of Oklahoma Press, 1985), is an excellent biography, perhaps the best biography of any mountain man. As Gilbert demonstrates, contrary to most usage, his subject's name was Joseph *Rutherford* Walker, not Joseph *Reddeford* Walker.

2. Walker's character is exceptionally well drawn throughout Gilbert's *Westering Man.* A good appraisal by one of his men is in William H. Ellison, ed., *The Life and Adventures of George Nidever* (Berkeley: University of California Press, 1937), 34.

3. Gilbert, 96.

4. Washington Irving, *The Adventures of Captain Bonneville, U.S.A., in the Rocky Mountains and the Far West,* ed. Edgeley W. Todd, foreword by James P. Ronda (Norman: University of Oklahoma Press, 1986), lii, liii, 27. Irving's book, based on Bonneville's journals, was first published in 1837 and has been through many editions since. This edition, with the authoritative introduction and annotations of Edgeley W. Todd, is the best as well as the most readily available. Irving's history, of course, is the most important source for Bonneville's expedition. The journals from which it was drawn have never been found. Irving took an unknown degree of literary license with Bonneville's manuscript, but there is no more authoritative or comprehensive history of the enterprise. In addition, Irving provided posterity with much colorful and accurate detail about trappers and trapping.

5. The issue is sensibly and comprehensively discussed by Gilbert, *Westering Man,* 96–100 and passim, as well as by Todd in the cited edition of Irving, xxiv–xxv. See also William H. Goetzmann, *Exploration and Empire: The Explorer and the Scientist in the Winning of the American West* (New York: Alfred A. Knopf, 1966), 148–50. Gilbert and Goetzmann both believe (as do I) that Bonneville's expedition had official backing, perhaps by President Andrew Jackson himself. Todd is more equivocal, although conceding commerce not to have been the primary purpose. Bonneville's application for leave, May 21, 1831, and General Alexander Macomb's authorization

and instructions, July 29, 1831, are printed in Todd's edition of Irving, xxv–xxvi and 379–80.

6. Warren A. Ferris, *Life in the Rocky Mountains: Diary of Wanderings on the Sources of the Rivers Missouri, Columbia, and Colorado from February, 1830, to November, 1835,* ed. Paul C. Phillips (Denver: Old West Publishing Co., 1940), 206–07. Ferris described the fort at the rendezvous held here in 1833. See Irving, *Adventures of Captain Bonneville,* 49–50. Irving reduces the fort to a "fortified camp" necessary for defense against Blackfeet. Gilbert, *Westering Man,* 111–12, discusses the issue in more realistic terms.

7. This rendezvous benefited from an unusual array of participants who put their observations to paper, among them Bonneville (by way of Irving), Campbell, Ferris, Wyeth, Stewart, and others. They are conveniently brought together in Fred R. Gowans, *Rocky Mountain Rendezvous: A History of the Fur Trade Rendezvous, 1825–1840* (Layton, Utah: Peregrine Smith Books, 1985), 80–99.

8. This is the thesis of Gilbert, *Westering Man,* 111–12. Bonneville's letter to Macomb, "Crow Country, Wind River," July 29, 1833, is printed in the Todd edition of Irving, 381–90. Michael Cerré carried the letter to St. Louis with Bonneville's meager cargo of beaver.

9. John C. Ewers, ed., *Adventures of Zenas Leonard* (Norman: University of Oklahoma Press, 1959), 64.

10. Irving, 162, 296. Gilbert, *Westering Man,* 124–26. Whether the blame rests on Irving or on Bonneville for lying to Irving can be debated. Gilbert argues plausibly for Irving's guilt, while Todd, editor of the authoritative edition of Irving, charges Bonneville. I tend to Gilbert's view because Bonneville's papers, from which Irving worked, must have contained at least the broad outlines of the plan. Or perhaps, as James Ronda has pointed out to me, Irving's literary style required foils and villains, and Walker served a convenient narrative purpose.

11. Irving, *Adventures of Captain Bonneville,* covers the Walker expedition, but only as an indirect source, since he got his information from Bonneville, who got it from Walker. Also, Irving's scapegoating of Walker makes this portion of his book less reliable than other portions. The prime source for the expedition is Walker's clerk, Zenas Leonard: Ewers, *Adventures of Zenas Leonard,* 63–132. Ellison, *Life and Adventures of George Nidever,* 31–35, is the account of another participant, though in less detail and farther removed in time than Leonard. Frances Fuller Victor, *The River of the West: Life and Adventure in the Rocky Mountains and Oregon* (Hartford: R. W. Bliss & Co., 1870), chap. 8, is supposedly Joe Meek's story; but for this adventure one detects more of Washington Irving than Joe Meek. Joe's brother made a disappointingly minuscule contribution in Stephen Hall Meek, *The Autobiography of a Mountain Man, 1805–1889,* ed. Arthur Woodward (Pasadena, Calif.: Glen Dawson, 1948), 5–6. Gilbert, *Westering Man,* 119–52, relates the story with his usual authoritative skill.

12. Gloria Griffen Cline, *Peter Skene Ogden and the Hudson's Bay Company* (Norman: University of Oklahoma Press, 1974). Archie Binns, *Peter Skene Ogden: Fur Trader* (Portland, Oreg.: Binfords & Mort, 1967). Ted J. Warner, "Peter Skene Ogden," in LeRoy R. Hafen, ed., *Mountain Men and the Fur Trade of the Far West,* 10 vols. (Glendale, Calif.: Arthur H. Clark Co., 1965–72), 3:213–38.

13. The Humboldt has its own biographer: Dale L. Morgan, *The Humboldt: Highroad of the West* (New York: Farrar & Rinehart, 1943; Lincoln: University of Nebraska Press, 1985). The best history, however, is Gloria Griffen Cline, *Exploring the Great Basin* (Norman: University of Oklahoma Press, 1963).

14. Ewers, *Adventures of Zenas Leonard*, 71–72.
15. Irving, *Adventures of Captain Bonneville*, 284–85.
16. Contemporary accounts by Leonard, Nidever, and the Meek brothers, as well as Irving, differ in some details, but except for Irving not in interpretation. In addition to sources already cited, see Stephen Hall Meek's account in *Niles's Weekly Register*, March 25, 1837.
17. Ewers, *Adventures of Zenas Leonard*, 94–95.
18. Irving, 296.
19. Ibid., chaps. 42–47.
20. Zenas Leonard clerked for Walker in the hunts of 1834–35 and was present at the meeting between Walker and Bonneville at the 1835 rendezvous. Ewers, *Adventures of Zenas Leonard*, 160–61.
21. Edgeley Todd details the story, as disclosed by official documents of the War Department, in his introduction to Irving.
22. The maps are discussed in Carl I. Wheat, *Mapping the Transmississippi West, 1540–1861*, 6 vols. (San Francisco: Institute of Historical Cartography, 1957–63), 2:158–59. Bonneville's somewhat inflated assessment of his maps and his geographical contributions were set forth in a letter to Lieutenant G. K. Warren of the Topographical Corps, Gila River, New Mexico, August 24, 1857, in Warren's "Memoir to Accompany the Map of the Territory of the United States to the Pacific Ocean," *Pacific Railway Surveys* 11. Bonneville, by then a colonel, was campaigning against Apaches in New Mexico.
23. Todd also discusses the book's significance in his introduction to Irving.

CHAPTER 10

1. The quotation is from Joe Meek in Francis Fuller Victor, *The River of the West: Life and Adventure in the Rocky Mountains and Oregon. . . .* (Hartford and Toledo: R. W. Bliss & Co., 1870); reprint; Winfred Blevins, ed., *The River of the West: The Adventures of Joe Meek*, 2 vols. (Missoula, Mont.: Mountain Press Publishing Co., 1983, 1987), 1:92. A good biography is John E. Sunder, *Bill Sublette, Mountain Man* (Norman: University of Oklahoma Press, 1959).
2. The company's move to the Trans-Mississippi West is detailed in Kenneth W. Porter, *John Jacob Astor, Business Man*, 2 vols. (Cambridge: Harvard University Press, 1931), 2:743–50. A history of the American Fur Company is David Lavender, *Fist in the Wilderness* (Garden City, N.Y.: Doubleday, 1964), which is not as narrowly confined to business affairs as is Porter's biography.
3. A biographical sketch is Ray H. Mattison, "Kenneth McKenzie," in LeRoy R. Hafen, *Mountain Men and the Fur Trade of the Far West*, 10 vols. (Glendale, Calif.: Arthur H. Clark Co., 1965–72), 2:217–24. See also sketch in Annie H. Abel, ed., *Chardon's Journal at Fort Clark, 1834–1839* (Pierre: South Dakota Department of History, 1932), 216–18. An excellent history of Fort Union is Erwin N. Thompson, *Fort Union Trading Post: Fur Trade Empire on the Upper Missouri* (Medora, N.D.: Theodore Roosevelt Nature and History Association, 1986).
4. Construction of Fort Floyd began at the mouth of the Yellowstone in the fall of 1828, and the name was changed to Fort Union in 1829.
5. Glass's mission is described in Hiram M. Chittenden, *A History of the American Fur Trade of the Far West*, 2 vols. (Stanford, Calif.: Academic Reprints, 1954), 1:328, based

on a McKenzie letter that seems no longer to exist. See also John Myers Myers, *The Saga of Hugh Glass: Pirate, Pawnee, and Mountain Man* (Lincoln: University of Nebraska Press, 1976), 214, 216–17.

6. Allen C. Trottman, "Lucien Fontenelle," in Hafen, *Mountain Men*, 5:81–89. Harvey L. Carter, "Andrew Drips," ibid., 8:143–56.

7. Harvey L. Carter, "William H. Vanderburgh," in Hafen, *Mountain Men*, 7:315–20. Carter seems not to have known of the Blackfeet fight, which is documented in the *Missouri Republican*, March 22, 1831, and the *St. Louis Beacon*, March 24 and May 12, 1831. For the replacement horses needed for a spring 1831 hunt, see entries of February 22 and 24, 1831, in Doane Robinson, ed., "Fort Tecumseh and Fort Pierre Journal and Letter Books," *South Dakota Historical Collections* 9 (1918): 147, 148; and Daniel Lamont to Pierre Chouteau, Jr., Fort Tecumseh, April 4, 1831, Fort Tecumseh Letter Book, 33–34, in Missouri Historical Society Papers of the St. Louis Fur Trade Part 1, microfilm reel 17, frame 104.

8. For Indian attitudes in general, and Crow in particular, see especially William Gordon to Secretary of War Lewis Cass, St. Louis, October 3, 1831, in Stella M. Drumm, ed., "Reports of the Fur Trade and Inland Trade to Mexico, 1831," Missouri Historical Society, *Glimpses of the Past* 9 (January–September 1941): 57–61. Gordon had been on the Missouri and in the mountains since 1822 and had participated in the Leavenworth expedition against the Arikaras. In 1832 Blackfeet told Indian Agent John F. Sanford that they wanted to be friends with the Americans but would kill every trapper they could. Traders, they said, had nothing to fear. Sanford to Superintendent of Indian Affairs William Clark, St. Louis, July 17, 1832, Record Group 75, BIA LR St. Louis Superintendency, microfilm M234, reel 750, frame 115, NARS.

9. Lavender, *Fist in the Wilderness*, 393–95, 398. The German nobleman Maximilian, accompanied by artist Karl Bodmer, came up the Missouri to Fort Union on the company's steamboat in 1833 and journeyed on to the new fort in the Blackfeet country. His journal sheds much light on the early history of Fort Piegan/McKenzie. Reuben Gold Thwaites, ed., *Early Western Travels* 23: chaps. 18 and 19. See also McKenzie to Agent American Fur Co., Western Dept., at St. Louis, Fort Tecumseh, June 7, 1831, Fort Tecumseh Letter Book, 42–44, Missouri Historical Society Papers of the St. Louis Fur Trade Part 1, microfilm reel 17, frame 40.

10. *Missouri Republican*, in *Little Rock Arkansas Gazette*, July 25, 1832. Lavender, *Fist in the Wilderness*, 391, 393–94, 397. William E. Lass, *A History of Steamboating on the Upper Missouri River* (Lincoln: University of Nebraska Press, 1962), 7–12.

11. Trapper Warren Ferris records the union with Vanderburgh in March 1832. *Life in the Rocky Mountains: Diary of Wanderings on the Sources of the Rivers Missouri, Columbia, and Colorado from February, 1830, to November, 1835*, ed. Paul C. Phillips (Denver: Old West Publishing Co., 1949), 138. Pierre Chouteau is shrewdly assessed, and his labyrinth of family connections in St. Louis detailed, in Janet Lecompte, "The Chouteaus and the St. Louis Fur Trade," in *Guide to the Microfilm Edition of Papers of the St. Louis Fur Trade* (Bethesda, Md.: University Publications of America, 1991): xiii–xxii.

12. It was also a well-documented rendezvous, and every participant gave a different estimate of the number present. One thousand, including Indians, is Joe Meek's guess, which is as good as any. For Meek see Victor, *The River of the West* (Blevins edition), 1:chap. 6. As previously noted, I prefer the edition edited by Winfred Blevins (Missoula, Mont.: Mountain Press Publishing Co., 1983) because Blevins corrects Meek's sometimes faulty memory for chronology and fact. Besides Ferris, accounts of other

participants are Johansen, *Robert Newell's Memoranda,* 32; William H. Ellison, ed., *The Life and Adventures of George Nidever* (Berkeley: University of California Press, 1937), 24–31; John C. Ewers, ed., *The Adventures of Zenas Leonard, Fur Trader* (Norman: University of Oklahoma Press, 1959), 31–47; F. G. Young, ed., *The Correspondence and Journals of Nathaniel J. Wyeth, 1831–6,* Sources of the History of Oregon, vol. 1 (Eugene, Ore.: University Press, 1899), 158–62; John B. Wyeth, *Oregon: or, A Short History of a Long Journey from the Atlantic Ocean to the Region of the Pacific, by Land* (1833), in Thwaites, *Early Western Travels* 21:60–72; John Ball, "Across the Continent Seventy Years Ago [extracts from his journal, as compiled by his daughter]," *Oregon Historical Quarterly* 3 (March 1902): 89–92; Drew Allen Holloway, ed., *A Narrative of Colonel Robert Campbell's Experiences in the Rocky Mountain Fur Trade from 1825 to 1835* (Fairfield, Wash.: Ye Galleon Press, 1991), 37–42; and (although based on Bonneville, who was not there but talked with many who were) Washington Irving, *The Adventures of Captain Bonneville, U.S.A., in the Rocky Mountains and the Far West,* ed. Edgeley W. Todd (Norman: University of Oklahoma Press, 1961), chap. 6.

13. Wyeth's adventures are well documented in Young, *Correspondence and Journals of Captain Nathaniel J. Wyeth.* Wyeth's blueprint is set forth in the introduction. An especially good discussion of Wyeth's plan in relation to the Hudson's Bay Company is D. W. Meinig, *The Great Columbia Plain: A Historical Geography, 1805–1910* (Seattle: University of Washington Press, 1968), 108–14.

14. Victor, *River of the West,* 110–12 (Blevins edition).

15. Ewers, *Adventures of Zenas Leonard,* 36. Where and by whom Fitzpatrick was found differs from account to account. All the sources for the 1832 rendezvous tell the story of Fitzpatrick in more or less detail. Leonard tells it in great detail, as recounted by Fitzpatrick himself. For an account of his ordeal as synthesized from these sources, see LeRoy R. Hafen, *Broken Hand: The Life of Thomas Fitzpatrick, Mountain Man, Guide, and Indian Agent* (Denver: Old West Publishing Co., 1931; Lincoln: University of Nebraska Press, 1981), chap. 6.

16. For Wyeth's troubles, see Young, *Correspondence and Journals of Captain Nathaniel J. Wyeth,* 158; and John B. Wyeth, *Oregon,* 64–67. John was nephew of Nathaniel and the leader of the revolt, which grew out of resistance to Wyeth's authoritarian style. John wrote this book as an indictment of his uncle.

17. Robert Campbell to Hugh Campbell, Lewis's Fork, July 18, 1832, in Robert Campbell, *The Rocky Mountain Letters of Robert Campbell* (New York: privately published, 1955), 7–11. Robert was writing this letter to his brother when the alarm was raised and finished it after returning from the fight. All the sources cited in previous notes, including Ferris, describe the Battle of Pierre's Hole, with general agreement on details. Another important source is William L. Sublette to W. H. Ashley, Lexington, Missouri, September 21, 1832, in *St. Louis Beacon,* October 11, 1832, reprinted in *Little Rock Arkansas Gazette,* October 31, 1832.

18. John Ball to Dr. Brinsmade, Fort Vancouver, January 1, 1833, in Archer B. Hulbert, *The Call of the Columbia: Iron Men and Saints Take the Oregon Trail, 1830–35* (Colorado Springs and Denver: Stewart Commission of Colorado College and Denver Public Library, 1934), 174.

19. Holloway, *Narrative of Col. Robert Campbell's Experiences,* 44. See also Irving, *Adventures of Captain Bonneville,* 75.

20. Articles of Agreement, "under the Three Tetons," July 25, 1832, Sublette Papers, Missouri Historical Society. My copy comes from the Dale Morgan Papers at the Bancroft

Library, University of California, Berkeley. The document is printed in full in Hafen, *Broken Hand*, 116–18.

21. Irving, 91. Warren Ferris traces the movements, without hinting at their competitive character, in *Life in the Rocky Mountains*, 159–74. See also Fitzpatrick to Robert Campbell, "River Platte," June 4, 1833, Campbell Papers, Missouri Historical Society. My copy is from the Dale Morgan Papers, Bancroft Library. Part of it is reprinted in Hafen, *Broken Hand*, 123–24.

22. The principal source for this affray is Irving, 91–95. Meek gives his version in Victor, *River of the West*, 132–35 (Blevins edition), although Mrs. Victor seems to have got as much of the narrative from Irving as from Meek. Ferris,183–84, only briefly touches on the incident.

23. Ferris, *Life in the Rocky Mountains*, 175–79, 181, 185. *St. Louis Times*, March 23, 1833, reprinted in *New York Evening Courier and New-York Enquirer*, April 10, 1833. See also Harvey L. Carter, "William H. Vanderburgh," in Hafen, *Mountain Men*, 7:315–20. This affair seems to have occurred at the western base of Ennis Pass near the head of Alder Gulch, not far from present Virginia City, Montana.

24. That Vanderburgh had agreed with Fitzpatrick and Bridger to call off the conflict is the thesis of Don Berry in *Majority of Scoundrels*, 286. I agree. Berry also says the Blackfeet cut off Vanderburgh's arms and flaunted them as trophies at Fort McKenzie. He presumably inferred this from the newspaper account cited in ibid., which indeed says "The Blackfeet took his arms to the Blackfeet Fort on the Missouri as a trophy." Later, however, the article indicates the "arms" were a rifle and a pistol.

25. Maximilian, Prince of Wied, *Travels in the Interior of North America* (London, 1843), in Thwaites, *Early Western Travels*, 24:102–04. Maximilian got the story from Gardner when presented with the scalp. See also Superintendent of Indian Affairs William Clark to Commissioner of Indian Affairs Elbert Herring, St. Louis, August 17, 1833, enclosing Agent John F. A. Sanford to Clark, July 20, 1833, RG 75, BIA Letters Received St. Louis Superintendency, microfilm M234, reel 75, frames 416-19, NARS. Myers, *Saga of Hugh Glass,* chap. 7.

26. Articles of copartnership of William L. Sublette and Robert Campbell, December 20, 1832, Sublette Papers, Missouri Historical Society, copy from Dale Morgan Papers, Bancroft Library.

27. Holloway, *Col. Robert Campbell's Experiences*, 42–45. Campbell's experiences throughout 1833 may be followed in George R. Brooks, ed., "The Private Journal of Robert Campbell," *Missouri Historical Society Bulletin* 20 (October 1963–January 1964): 3–24, 107–18; and in a series of letters he wrote to his mother and sister from Fort William during the winter of 1833–34, Campbell Papers, Missouri Historical Society (copies in Dale Morgan Papers, Bancroft Library). See also Robert Campbell to Hugh Campbell, November 16, 1833, in *The Rocky Mountain Letters of Robert Campbell*, 14–16. Wyeth came down from the 1833 rendezvous with Campbell and records events in Young, *Correspondence and Journals of Captain Nathaniel J. Wyeth*, 207–16. Charles Larpenteur also traveled with Campbell, for which see his *Forty Years a Fur Trader on the Upper Missouri* (Chicago: Lakeside Press, 1933; Lincoln: University of Nebraska Press, 1989), 27–40; and Erwin N. Thompson, ed., "White Bear (Mato Washejoe), Upper Missouri Trader: Journals and Notes of Charles Larpenteur between 1834 and 1872" (unpublished MS., c. 1992, from originals in Minnesota Historical Society, copy in Montana Historical Society, my copy courtesy editor). Sunder, *Bill Sublette*, chaps. 7 and 8, covers these events, but does not treat them as explicitly as Berry, *Majority of Scoundrels*, chaps. 22 and 23. Berry's interpretations differ from most treatments, but in general I agree with them.

28. The law was 4 Stat. 729-35 (June 30, 1832). The story may be followed in detail in the official documents of RG 75, BIA Letters Received, St. Louis Superintendency, microfilm M234, reel 750 (1832–35); and the Missouri Historical Society Papers of the St. Louis Fur Trade Part 1, microfilm reels 19–22. Berry, *Majority of Scoundrels*, 299 ff, summarizes it, as does Lavender, *Fist in the Wilderness*, 407–10, 414–17.

29. In addition to the views of McKenzie that Campbell recorded in his diary at Fort William, McKenzie himself was a compulsive letter writer. The story of the competition is set down in detail in his letters to various subordinates and to Pierre Chouteau, Jr., in St. Louis. Most were written in December 1833 at Fort Union. All are in the Missouri Historical Society Papers of the St. Louis Fur Trade Part 1, microfilm reel 22. Many are reprinted in Abel, *Chardon's Journal at Fort Clark*, Appendix F.

30. McKenzie to Tulloch, Fort Union, January 8, 1834, Missouri Historical Society Papers of the St. Louis Fur Trade Part 1, microfilm reel 22, frame 799. Same to same, March 11, 1834, ibid., frame 801. Same to D. D. Mitchell, January 21, 1834, ibid., frame 795. Fitzpatrick to Milton Sublette, Ham's Fork of the Green, November 13, 1833; and same to W. H. Ashley, same date, Sublette Papers, Missouri Historical Society (copies in Dale Morgan Papers, Bancroft Library). Victor, *River of the West*, 160–61 (Blevins edition). Irving, *Adventures of Captain Bonneville*, 207–08. Brooks, "Private Journal of Robert Campbell," 112–13.

31. The story of the still and its political fallout is extensively documented in Papers of the St. Louis Fur Trade Part 1, microfilm reels 22 and 23. In addition to McKenzie's still, the company agent at Council Bluffs, J. P. Cabanné, had taken it on himself to seize the liquor a competitor was smuggling up the river—a clearly illegal act that bought American Fur even more trouble than McKenzie's still. The liquor story is told by Lavender, chap. 25, and Berry, chap. 22.

32. Sunder, *Bill Sublette*, chap. 8. Hugh Campbell to Robert Campbell, Philadelphia, February 14, 1834, Campbell Papers, Missouri Historical Society, quoted in ibid., 135. Berry, 347–48. Porter, *Astor*, 2:769–70.

33. Correspondence between Chouteau, Crooks, and Astor throughout this period appears in Papers of the St. Louis Fur Trade Part 1, microfilm reels 22 and 23. Lavender, chap. 25. Berry, chap. 23. Porter, *John Jacob Astor*, 2:765–71, 776–79.

34. Here I follow and agree with the unconventional interpretation of Don Berry in *Majority of Scoundrels*, chap. 23, which differs sharply from that in Sunder, *Bill Sublette*, chap. 8. The evidence is slender, mostly to be gleaned from cryptic but highly significant remarks in Hugh Campbell to Robert Campbell (still at Fort William), April 5, 1834, Campbell Papers, Missouri Historical Society (copy in Dale Morgan Papers, Bancroft Library). Events as they unfolded lend plausibility to the assumptions. Berry believes that Sublette, in negotiations with American Fur officials in New York, promised the elimination of major competition in the mountains within a year—i.e., that Rocky Mountain would no longer exist.

35. Young, *Correspondence and Journals of Captain Nathaniel J. Wyeth*, 225. The dissolution of the Rocky Mountain Fur Company is recorded in five "notices," all executed on June 20, 1834, in Sublette Papers, Missouri Historical Society (copies in Dale Morgan Papers, Bancroft Library).

36. For Joe Meek, Victor, *River of the West*, 164–65 (Blevins edition). For the establishment of Fort Hall, see Young, 227; and Osborne Russell, *Journal of a Trapper*, ed. Aubrey L. Haines (Lincoln: University of Nebraska Press, 1965), 5–7.

37. Holloway, *Narrative of Colonel Robert Campbell's Experiences*, 45. The standard history of the fort is LeRoy R. Hafen and Francis Marion Young, *Fort Laramie and the Pageant of the West, 1834–1890* (Glendale, Calif.: Arthur H. Clark Co., 1938; Lincoln:

University of Nebraska Press, 1984). However, the authors' account of the founding of Fort William in 1834 is flawed.

CHAPTER 11

1. W. A. Ferris, *Life in the Rocky Mountains: A Diary of Wanderings on the Sources of the Rivers Missouri, Columbia, and Colorado from February, 1830, to November, 1835*, ed. Paul C. Phillips (Denver: Old West Publishing Co., 1940), 1.
2. Paul Phillips's introduction to ibid. contains a biographical sketch of Ferris. See also Lyman Petersen, Jr., "Warren Angus Ferris," in LeRoy R. Hafen, ed., *The Mountain Men and the Fur Trade of the Far West*, 10 vols. (Glendale, Calif.: Arthur H. Clark Co., 1965–72), 2:135–55.
3. *Life in the Rocky Mountains*, 74.
4. Ibid., 150.
5. Ibid., 207–08.
6. Paul Phillips's introduction to *Life in the Rocky Mountains*, xliv–xlv.
7. Phillips relates the story in the preface to ibid.
8. Carl I. Wheat, *Mapping the Transmississippi West, 1540–1861*, 6 vols. (San Francisco: Institute of Historical Cartography, 1957–63), 2:155–57. Phillips evaluates the significance of the map in an introductory chapter to *Life in the Rocky Mountains*, ix–xiv. It is reproduced in a large foldout in the book. The original is now in the Harold B. Lee Library at Brigham Young University, Provo, Utah, where I have examined it.

CHAPTER 12

1. Dale L. Morgan and Eleanor Towles Harris, eds., *The Rocky Mountain Journals of William Marshall Anderson: The West in 1834* (San Marino, Calif.: Huntington Library, 1967; Lincoln: University of Nebraska Press, 1987), 130. John C. Ewers, ed., *Adventures of Zenas Leonard* (Norman: University of Oklahoma Press, 1959), 8–9. F. A. Wislizenus, *A Journey to the Rocky Mountains in 1839* (St. Louis: Missouri Historical Society, 1912; Glorieta, N.M.: Rio Grande Press, 1969), 137–38. Fitzpatrick's biographer, LeRoy Hafen, quotes an 1847 newspaper report of how Fitzpatrick shattered his hand and dates the accident to early 1836. Although the account seems dubiously wild, Hafen is correct in noting that no observer mentions the torn hand before this date. LeRoy R. Hafen, *Broken Hand: The Life of Thomas Fitzpatrick, Mountain Man, Guide and Indian Agent* (Lincoln: University of Nebraska Press, 1973), 150–52.
2. Frances Fuller Victor, *The River of the West: Life and Adventures in the Rocky Mountains and Oregon. . . .* (Hartford and Toledo: R. W. Bliss & Co., 1870). Reprint, Winfred Blevins, ed., *The River of the West: The Adventures of Joe Meek*, 2 vols. (Missoula, Mont.: Mountain Press Publishing Co., 1983, 1987), 1:187. William H. Gray, *History of Oregon* (Portland, Oreg.: Harris and Holman; San Francisco: H. H. Bancroft; New York: American News Co., 1870), 107–08. The best biography of Whitman is Clifford M. Drury, *Marcus Whitman, M.D.: Pioneer and Martyr* (Caldwell, Idaho: Caxton Printers, 1937); but see also Archer B. Hulbert and Dorothy P. Hulbert, *Marcus Whitman, Crusader*, 3 vols. (Colorado Springs and Denver: Stewart Commission of Colorado College and Denver Public Library, 1936–41).

3. Both Parker and Whitman kept journals. The quotation is from Parker, *Journal of an Exploring Tour Beyond the Rocky Mountains* (Ithaca, N.Y.: Andrus, Woodruff & Gauntlert, 1842; 4th ed., 1844), 72. Whitman's journal is less detailed but well backed by the biographies of Drury and the Hulberts. F. G. Young, ed., "Journal and Report by Dr. Marcus Whitman of His Tour of Exploration with Rev. Samuel Parker in 1835 Beyond the Rocky Mountains," *Oregon Historical Quarterly* 28 (September 1927): 239–51.

4. Joseph Williams, *Narrative of a Tour from the State of Indiana to the Oregon Territory in the Years 1841-2* (Cincinnati: J. B. Wilson, 1843), in LeRoy R. Hafen and Ann W. Hafen, eds., *To the Rockies and Oregon, 1839–1842* (Glendale, Calif.: Arthur H. Clark Co., 1955), 221.

5. The most thoroughly researched and authoritatively presented history of the company's handling of the American threat is E. E. Rich, *The History of the Hudson's Bay Company, 1670–1870*, 2 vols. (London: Hudson's Bay Record Society, 1959), 2:chaps. 24–25.

6. Wyeth's adventures are well documented in F. G. Young, ed., *The Correspondence and Journals of Captain Nathaniel J. Wyeth, 1831–36*, Sources of the History of Oregon, vol. 1 (Eugene: University Press, 1899). Wyeth's blueprint is set forth in the introduction. An especially good discussion of Wyeth's plan in relation to the Hudson's Bay Company is D. W. Meinig, *The Great Columbia Plain: A Historical Geography, 1805–1910* (Seattle: University of Washington Press, 1968), 108–14.

7. The sources are synthesized and the story told in authoritative detail in Alvin M. Josephy, Jr., *The Nez Perce Indians and the Opening of the Northwest* (New Haven: Yale University Press, 1965), 93–102.

8. John K. Townsend, *Narrative of a Journey across the Rocky Mountains, to the Columbia River . . . [1833–34]* (Philadelphia: Henry Perkins, 1839), in Thwaites, *Early Western Travels* 21:137. Jason Lee kept a diary, of which there are two versions. The so-called original is in Archer B. Hulbert and Dorothy P. Hulbert, *The Oregon Crusade: Across Land and Sea to Oregon* (Colorado Springs and Denver: Stewart Commission of Colorado College and Denver Public Library, 1935). The expanded version is "Diary of Rev. Jason Lee," *Oregon Historical Quarterly* 17 (June–December 1916): 116–46, 240–66, 397–430. The first and second quotations are from the original, 153, 159; the second from the expanded, 138. See also Cornelius J. Brosnan, *Jason Lee: Prophet of the New Oregon* (New York: Macmillan, 1932), chap. 3.

9. Parker, *Journal of an Exploring Expedition*, 79. See also Young, "Journal and Report by Dr. Marcus Whitman," entry of August 13, 1835, 247. Meek's quotation is from Victor, *River of the West*, 1:187 (Blevins edition).

10. The quotations are from Parker's report to the American Board, Boston, June 25, 1837, in Hulbert, *Marcus Whitman, Crusader*, 1:103. Gray, in *History of Oregon*, 108, contended that the separation occurred not because of an agreement but "because Mr. P. could not 'put up' with the offhand, careless, and, as he thought, slovenly manner in which Dr. Whitman was inclined to travel. Dr. W. was a man that could accomodate himself to circumstances; such as dippling the water from a running stream with his hand, to drink; having but a hunter's knife (without a fork) to cut and eat his food; in short, could *rough it* without qualms of stomach." That is probably how Parker felt about Whitman, but was probably not at the root of the decision. See Drury, *Marcus Whitman*, 104.

11. Parker, *Journal*, 84. Chouinard was long known in the literature only as "Shunar." As noted in Thelma S. Guild and Harvey L. Carter, *Kit Carson: A Pattern for Heroes*

(Lincoln: University of Nebraska Press, 1984), 305 n. 26, Marc Simmons discovered documentation of Shunar's true name. Simmons's biography of Carson is eagerly awaited. I am indebted to William R. Swagerty for a copy of the document, which is an order of Lucien Fontenelle on Pratte, Chouteau & Company, September 17, 1834, to pay a sum of money to Joseph Chouinard. The document is in the Chouteau Collection at the Missouri Historical Society, St. Louis.

12. Parker thoroughly investigated the Snake, Clearwater, and Columbia Rivers and made a detailed record of his observations, together with a thoughtful identification of mission fields and sites. Curiously, then, he did not await the coming of the Whitman party in 1836 or even, much to their surprise and annoyance, send them a written report. His book, including a landmark map, acquainted the literate public with his findings, but appeared years too late to benefit Whitman and his associates. See Meinig, *Great Columbia Plain*, 118–24.

13. Ibid., 88. Victor, *River of the West*, 1:187 (Blevins edition). The words of course are Mrs. Victor's setting to paper what Joe told her, doubtless in more colorful language.

14. A good synthesis of the events of the 1836 rendezvous is Fred R. Gowans, *Rocky Mountain Rendezvous* (Layton, Utah: Peregrine Smith Books, 1985), 130–44. Gray, *History of Oregon*, 121–29, contains an unusually detailed description of the rendezvous' people, events, and setting.

15. The effort is sketchily documented in letters in the Missouri Historical Society Papers of the St. Louis Fur Trade Part 1, microfilm reel 24. I have examined these papers, but they are cited and partly reproduced in Hafen, *Broken Hand*, chap. 8. The details of the transaction remain undocumented. The only direct source is Marcus Whitman: "Major Pilcher joined us at Fort Williams and came on to Rendezvoux, as agent of Pratt, Chouteau & Co., in whose behalf he bought out the 'mountain partners,' so that the whole business now belongs to them." Whitman to Samuel Parker, Fort Vancouver, September 18, 1836, in Hulbert and Hulbert, *Marcus Whitman*, 1:229–32.

16. The experiences of these women and others to follow are well documented in Clifford M. Drury, *First White Women over the Rockies: Diaries, Letters, and Biographical Sketches of the Six Women of the Oregon Mission Who Made the Overland Journey in 1836 and 1838*, 2 vols. (Glendale, Calif.: Arthur H. Clark Co., 1963). See also Hulbert and Hulbert, *Marcus Whitman;* Drury, *Marcus Whitman;* and Drury, *Henry Harmon Spalding* (Caldwell, Idaho: Caxton Printers, 1936).

17. Not without exposing his own prejudices and shortcomings, William H. Gray, one of the Whitman party of 1836, characterized all the major players in the drama. For the Whitmans and Spaldings, see his *History of Oregon*, 109–10. For Narcissa, see Julie Roy Jeffrey, *Converting the West: A Biography of Narcissa Whitman* (Norman: University of Oklahoma Press, 1991).

18. Osborne Russell, *Journal of a Trapper*, ed. Aubrey L. Haines (Lincoln: University of Nebraska Press, 1965), 41. Spalding to "brother Leavitt," Rendezvous, head quarters [waters] of Colorado, Rocky Mountains, July 11, 1836, in J. Orin Oliphant, ed., "A Letter by Henry H. Spalding from the Rocky Mountains," *Oregon Historical Quarterly* 51 (June 1950): 132. Narcissa tells of their reception by the Indians in a letter from rendezvous to her family, in Drury, *First White Women over the Rockies*, 58.

19. Victor, *River of the West*, 1:207 (Blevins edition).

20. A biography of Stewart is Mae Reed Porter and Odessa Davenport, *Scotsman in Buckskin: Sir William Drummond Stewart and the Rocky Mountain Fur Trade* (New York: Hastings House, 1963).

21. Gray, *History of Oregon*, 122.

22. Ibid., 124. Wyeth also gave the missionaries much valuable information and advice about what lay ahead.

23. Drury, *First White Women*, 116. Spalding attributed this remark to McKay many years later. If his memory was correct, writes Drury, McKay was the first to recognize the significance of the presence of the two women at the 1836 rendezvous.

24. Spalding to Leavitt, July 11, 1836, in Oliphant, "Letter by Henry H. Spalding from the Rocky Mountains," 30. Drury, *Marcus Whitman*, 147.

25. Hidden for nearly a century, the Miller paintings came to light in 1935 and were popularized by Bernard DeVoto in *Across the Wide Missouri* (Boston: Houghton Mifflin Co., 1947). They are more completely published, with authoritative commentary, in Ron Tyler, ed., *Alfred Jacob Miller: Artist on the Oregon Trail* (Fort Worth: Amon Carter Museum, 1982). See also Marvin C. Ross, ed., *The West of Alfred Jacob Miller* (Norman: University of Oklahoma Press, 1968), which matches each illustration with Miller's accompanying text.

26. Porter and Davenport, *Scotsman in Buckskin*, 150–51. Ross, *West of Alfred Jacob Miller*, 159.

27. Besides his account in *History of Oregon*, 173, Gray kept a daily journal. It is available in two forms: "The Unpublished Journal of William H. Gray, from December, 1836, to October, 1837," *Whitman College Quarterly* 16 (June 1913): 1–79; and Donald R. Johnson, ed., *William H. Gray: Journal of His Journey East, 1836–37* (Fairfield, Wash.: Ye Galleon Press, 1980). In his own colorful style, and with disdain for Gray, DeVoto gives the story in detail in *Across the Wide Missouri*, 326–33.

28. David L. Brown, *Three Years in the Rocky Mountains* (New York: privately published, 1950), 19. These are Brown's letters as printed in the *Cincinnati Atlas*, 1845. Reverend Asa Smith, one of the 1838 reinforcements, talked to Jim Bridger at that year's rendezvous. Bridger confirmed that he had urged Gray to wait for Fitzpatrick, "that he would certainly be defeated if he went on alone." Smith to Rev. David D. Greene, Wind River, July 10, 1838, in Clifford M. Drury, ed., *The Diaries and Letters of Henry H. Spalding and Asa Bowen Smith Relating to the Nez Perce Mission, 1838–1842* (Glendale, Calif.: Arthur H. Clark Co., 1958), 72.

29. The Reverend Asa Smith, in the letter cited in ibid., writes that "Mr. G. is censured very much by the Company on account of the loss of the Indians last fall." DeVoto, *Across the Wide Missouri*, 326-33, treats this episode in detail. See also Alvin M. Josephy, Jr., *The Nez Perce Indians and the Opening of the Northwest* (New Haven: Yale University Press, 1965), 167–68. According to Josephy, the French Canadian himself, disgusted by Gray's readiness to surrender his Indian charges, spread word back to the mountain men and ultimately to the Nez Perces.

30. Asa and Sarah Smith, Mary Walker, Myra Eells, and Cornelius Rogers kept journals. For Smith, see Drury, *Diaries and Letters of Henry H. Spalding and Asa Bowen Smith;* for the others, see Drury, *First White Women over the Rockies*. The Smith quotation is p. 159 of the former, the Walker quotation p. 85 of the latter. All the original sources are brought together in Gowans, *Rocky Mountain Rendezvous*, 142–84.

31. Smith diary, July 1, 1838, 67. Eells diary, July 5, 1838, 100.

32. Myra Eells diary, July 5, 1838, 99.

33. Smith to Rev. David D. Greene, Rendezvous on Wind River, July 10, 1838, in Drury, *Diaries and Letters of Henry H. Spalding and Asa Bowen Smith*, 70-73.

34. Pilcher to Secretary of War John H. Eaton, undated late 1830, *Senate Executive Documents*, 21st Congress, 2d session, January 26, 1831, no. 39 (serial 203), reprinted in

Donald R. Johnson, ed., *British Establishments on the Columbia and the State of the Fur Trade* (Fairfield, Wash.: Ye Galleon Press, 1981), 32.

35. "Lee and Whitman and their associates were the catalysts of American settlement, and perhaps more." Earl Pomeroy, *The Pacific Slope: A History* (Seattle: University of Washington Press, 1965), 27. The Hudson's Bay Company clearly recognized the dilemma posed by the missionaries. See John McLoughlin to Governor and Committee, Fort Vancouver, November 20, 1840, in E. E. Rich, ed., *Letters of John McLoughlin from Fort Vancouver to the Governor and Committee, Second Series, 1839–44* (London and Toronto: Hudson's Bay Record Society, 1943), 18–19.

CHAPTER 13

1. William H. Gray, *A History of Oregon* (Portland, Oreg.: Harris and Holman; San Francisco: H. H. Bancroft; New York: American News Co., 1870), 125.
2. Grenville M. Dodge, *Biographical Sketch of James Bridger, Mountaineer, Trapper and Guide* (New York: Unz & Co., 1905), reproduced as appendix in the first edition of J. Cecil Alter, *James Bridger* (Salt Lake City, 1925), 507.
3. William S. Brackett, "Bonneville and Bridger," *Montana Historical Society Contributions* 3 (1900): 182.
4. David L. Brown, *Three Years in the Rocky Mountains* [reprinted from *Cincinnati Atlas*, issues of September 1845] (New York: Edward Eberstadt, 1950), 12. See also Gray, *History of Oregon*, 125.
5. J. J. Astor to Pierre Chouteau, Jr., Paris, August 1832; William B. Astor to Chouteau, New York, October 17, 1832, Missouri Historical Society Papers of the St. Louis Fur Trade Part 1, microfilm reel 20, frames 181 and 429. The nutria is a South American aquatic rodent.
6. William Gordon to Secretary of War Lewis Cass, St. Louis, October 3, 1831, in Stella M. Drumm, ed., "Reports of the Fur Trade and Inland Trade to Mexico, 1831," Missouri Historical Society, *Glimpses of the Past* 9 (January–September 1941): 61.
7. William B. Astor to Chouteau, New York, November 19, 1832, Missouri Historical Society Papers of the St. Louis Fur Trade Part 1, microfilm reel 20, frame 558.
8. John E. Sunder, *The Fur Trade on the Upper Missouri, 1840–1865* (Norman: University of Oklahoma Press, 1965), chap. 1. See also David J. Wishart, *The Fur Trade of the American West, 1807–1840* (Lincoln: University of Nebraska Press, 1879), chap. 5.
9. F. A. Wislizenus, *A Journey to the Rocky Mountains in the Year 1839* (St. Louis: Missouri Historical Society, 1912; Glorieta, N.M.: Rio Grande Press, 1969), 86.
10. Francis Fuller Victor, *The River of the West: Life and Adventures in the Rocky Mountains and Oregon. . . . (* Hartford and Toledo: R. W. Bliss & Co., 1870); reprint, Winfred Blevins, ed., *The River of the West: The Adventures of Joe Meek,* 2 vols. (Missoula, Mont.: Mountain Press Publishing Co., 1983, 1987), 1:264.
11. De Smet to Rev. Fr. Verhaegen, St. Louis University, March 11, 1854, in Hiram M. Chittenden and A. D. Richardson, eds., *Life, Letters and Travels of Father Pierre-Jean De Smet,* 4 vols. (New York: Francis D. Harper, 1905), 4:1488–89. John J. Killoren, S. J., *"Come, Blackrobe": De Smet and the Indian Tragedy* (Norman: University of Oklahoma Press, 1994), 58–61, for the meeting with Bridger. In a series of letters written to colleagues in St. Louis in February 1841, De Smet recounted his travels of 1840. While dealing in great detail with Indians, his letters are disappointingly sparse on his white companions. Ibid., 137, 149–53, 160, 202–03, 221, 244. A good biography is

Robert C. Carriker, *Father Peter John De Smet, Jesuit in the West* (Norman: University of Oklahoma Press, 1995).

12. Bridger's movements in 1840–41 are hard to follow. J. Cecil Alter, *Jim Bridger* (Norman: University of Oklahoma Press, 1962), chaps. 33–34, is untrustworthy. Much more reliable is the sketch of Bridger in the appendix to Dale L. Morgan and Eleanor Towles Harris, eds., *The Rocky Mountain Journals of William Marshall Anderson* (San Marino, Calif.: Huntington Library, 1967; Lincoln: University of Nebraska Press, 1967), 265–66. This appendix, "A Galaxy of Mountain Men," occupies nearly 150 pages of the book and is an immensely valuable series of biographical sketches.

13. Joseph Williams, *Narrative of a Tour from the State of Indiana to the Oregon Territory in the Years 1841–2,* in LeRoy R. Hafen and Ann W. Hafen, eds., *To the Rockies and Oregon, 1839–1842* (Glendale, Calif.: Arthur H. Clark Co., 1955), 230.

14. LeRoy R. Hafen, "Fraeb's Last Fight and How Battle Creek Got Its Name," *Colorado Magazine* 7 (May 1930): 97–101.

15. Chittenden and Richardson, 4:1465.

16. Quoted in Hafen, *Broken Hand,* 174–75. For De Smet's recruitment of Fitzpatrick, see Killoren, *"Come Blackrobe,"* 69. Bidwell, De Smet, Point, Mengarini, and others kept diaries or wrote reminiscences, for descriptions of which see Merrill J. Mattes, *Platte River Road Narratives: A Descriptive Bibliography of Travel over the Great Central Route. . . .* (Urbana: University of Illinois Press, 1988), 39–44. The classic history of California emigration is George R. Stewart, *The California Trail* (New York: McGraw-Hill, 1962; Lincoln: University of Nebraska Press, 1983). The 1841 crossing is the subject of chap. 1.

17. De Smet tells the story in detail in a letter to Father Provincial, Beaverhead, September 1, 1841, in Chittenden and Richardson, 1:311. See also Williams's diary entry for June 4, 1841, in *Narrative of a Tour,* 222. Dawson himself recounted his adventure in Charles L. Camp, ed., *Narrative of Nicholas "Cheyenne" Dawson* (San Francisco, 1933).

18. Williams, *Narrative of a Tour,* 270.

19. The story of the White train is engagingly told in David Lavender, *Westward Vision: The Story of the Oregon Trail* (New York: McGraw-Hill, 1963; Lincoln: University of Nebraska Press, 1985), chap. 18. In addition, see White's own reminiscences in A. J. Allen, ed., *Ten Years in Oregon: Travels and Adventures of Dr. E. White and Lady West of the Rocky Mountains* (Ithaca, N.Y., 1848); Medorem Crawford's journal, Sources of the History of Oregon, vol. 1 (Eugene: State Job Office, 1897); and Henry E. Reed, ed., "Lovejoy's Pioneer Narrative, 1842–48," *Oregon Historical Quarterly* 31 (September 1930): 237–60. See also Hafen, *Broken Hand,* 181–84.

20. Allen, *Ten Years in Oregon,* 153.

21. Ibid., 155.

22. So asserted Lieutenant John C. Frémont, then at Fort Laramie, who will make his debut in this book in the next chapter: "From all that I have been able to learn, I have no doubt that the emigrants owe their lives to Mr. Fitzpatrick." Donald Jackson and Mary Lee Spence, eds., *The Expeditions of John Charles Frémont,* 3 vols. (Urbana: University of Illinois Press, 1970–84), 1:223. For this episode, see also Allen, 160 and Crawford, 13.

23. The evolution of Fort Bridger, confusing in its early years, is treated in Fred R. Gowans and Eugene E. Campbell, *Fort Bridger: Island in the Wilderness* (Provo, Utah: Brigham Young University Press, 1975), chap. 1.

24. James Bridger by Edwin Denig to P. Chouteau & Co., Fort Union, December 10,

1843, Missouri Historical Society Papers of the St. Louis Fur Trade Part 1, microfilm reel 28, frame 949.

CHAPTER 14

1. The best biography of Carson is Thelma S. Guild and Harvey L. Carter, *Kit Carson: A Pattern for Heroes* (Lincoln: University of Nebraska Press, 1984). Worthwhile but containing many inaccuracies are M. Morgan Estergreen, *Kit Carson: A Portrait in Courage* (Norman: University of Oklahoma Press, 1962) and Bernice Blackwelder, *Great Westerner: The Story of Kit Carson* (Caldwell, Idaho: Caxton Printers, 1962). Dated and flawed by reliance on an old-timer later exposed as a fraud, yet still containing much of value, is Edwin L. Sabin, *Kit Carson Days, 1809–1868,* first published in 1914, reissued in a revised edition in 1935, and most readily available now in two volumes from the University of Nebraska Press, 1995. Entirely lacking in merit is Stanley Vestal, *Kit Carson, the Happy Warrior of the Old West* (Boston: Houghton Mifflin Co., 1928). Until Marc Simmons completes his long-anticipated biography, Carson until 1856, when he dictated his memoirs, is best documented in Harvey L. Carter, ed., *"Dear Old Kit": The Historical Christopher Carson* (Norman: University of Oklahoma Press, 1968). Although several other editions of Carson's memoirs exist, Carter's is the only one that overcomes Carson's faulty memory for dates and places in his life in an accurate chronological framework. In addition, the work is heavily annotated with data and insights drawn from Carter's lifelong study of Carson.
2. Carter, *"Dear Old Kit,"* 79, 82.
3. Carson does not mention his Indian marriages in his memoirs, which has created much confusion and controversy and necessitated much speculation. I follow Carter's conclusions, based on such evidence as has come to light. Sometimes Waanibe and child traveled with Kit, a common practice in both American and British brigades. At other times she lived with Indian or mixed-blood families at trading posts such as Fort Hall, Fort Davy Crockett, and Fort Robidoux.
4. Carter, *"Dear Old Kit,"* 79, n. 120.
5. Ibid., 81.
6. John C. Frémont, *Memoirs of My Life* (Chicago and New York: Belford, Clarke & Co., 1887), 74.
7. Michael B. Husband, "Senator Lewis F. Linn and the Oregon Question," *Missouri Historical Review* 66 (October 1971): 1–19. See also Frederick Merk, *The Oregon Question: Essays in Anglo-American Diplomacy and Politics* (Cambridge: Harvard University Press, 1967), essay 6: "The Oregon Question in the Webster-Ashburton Negotiations."
8. The connection is lucidly drawn in William H. Goetzmann, *Exploration and Empire: The Explorer and the Scientist in the Winning of the American West* (New York: Alfred A. Knopf, 1966), 240–41.
9. An excellent and comprehensive history of the Corps of Topographical Engineers is William H. Goetzmann, *Army Exploration in the American West, 1803–1863* (New Haven: Yale University Press, 1959).
10. Dated but still standard is Allan Nevins, *Frémont: Pathmarker of the West* (New York: Longmans, Green, 1955). A recent biography highlighting Frémont's rich psychological content is Andrew Rolle, *John Charles Frémont: Character as Destiny* (Norman: University of Oklahoma Press, 1991). For Jessie see Pamela Herr, *Jessie Benton Fré-*

mont: A Biography (New York: Franklin Watts, 1987) and Catherine Coffin Phillips, *Jessie Benton Frémont: A Woman Who Made History* (San Francisco: J. H. Nash, 1935; Lincoln: University of Nebraska Press, 1995).

11. See especially Thomas Hart Benton, *Thirty Years View: A History of the Working of the American Government for Thirty Years, 1820–1850*, 2 vols. (New York: D. Appleton & Co., 1854), 2:478. See also Goetzmann, *Exploration and Empire*, 240.

12. Frémont's orders are Abert to Frémont, Washington, April 25, 1842, in Donald Jackson and Mary Lee Spence, eds., *The Expeditions of John Charles Frémont*, 3 vols. (Urbana: University of Illinois Press, 1970–84), 1:121–22. Unless otherwise cited, my account rests on Frémont's official report printed in this source. A valuable supplement by Frémont's cranky cartographer is Charles Preuss, *Exploring with Frémont: The Private Diaries of Charles Preuss, Cartographer for John C. Frémont on His First, Second, and Fourth Expeditions to the Far West*, trans. and ed. Erwin G. and Elizabeth K. Gudde (Norman: University of Oklahoma Press, 1958).

13. "Mode of voyaging" was a term used by one of Pierre Chouteau's associates, Benjamin Clapp, in a letter written in St. Louis for Frémont to hand to Andrew Drips at Westport. Drips knew the "mode of voyaging" in the West, and Frémont intended to hire him for the post that instead went to Carson. Drips was then taking up a federal appointment to suppress the liquor trade with the Indians and probably would not have accepted. "Mode of voyaging," however, well describes the service former mountain men provided for military and civilian travelers alike. Clapp to Drips, St. Louis, May 30, 1842, in Jackson and Spence, *Expeditions of John Charles Frémont*, 1:125.

14. Preuss, *Exploring with Frémont*, 60.

15. *Report of an Exploration of the Country Lying between the Missouri River and the Rocky Mountains on the Line of the Kansas and Great Platte Rivers*, Senate Executive Documents, 27th Congress, 3d session, no. 243, March 1843 (serial 416). This is reproduced from the original manuscript report, with extensive annotation, in Jackson and Spence, *Expeditions of John Charles Frémont*, 1:168–340. Frémont had not stood on the loftiest peak. Some twenty are higher, and the one he climbed is not the one that now bears his name.

16. Jackson and Spence, 1:180.

17. *Niles's National Register*, May 6, 1843.

18. David Lavender, *Westward Vision: The Story of the Oregon Trail* (New York: McGraw-Hill, 1963; Lincoln: University of Nebraska Press, 1985), chap. 19. For description of all the firsthand sources of travel on the trail in 1843, see Merrill J. Mattes, *Platte River Road Narratives: A Descriptive Bibliography of Travel over the Great Central Overland Route. . . .* (Urbana: University of Illinois Press, 1988), 47–55.

19. George R. Stewart, *The California Trail* (New York: McGraw-Hill, 1962; Lincoln: University of Nebraska Press, 1983), chap. 3. Bil Gilbert, *Westering Man: The Life of Joseph Walker* (New York: Atheneum, 1983; Norman: University of Oklahoma Press, 1985), 188–97.

20. Mae Reed Porter and Odessa Davenport, *Scotsman in Buckskin: Sir William Drummond Stewart and the Rocky Mountain Fur Trade* (New York: Hastings House, 1963), chaps. 22–24. John E. Sunder, *Bill Sublette, Mountain Man* (Norman: University of Oklahoma Press, 1959), chap. 11. Historian of the expedition was a New Orleans journalist: Matthew C. Field, *Prairie and Mountain Sketches*, ed. Kate L. Gregg and John Francis McDermott (Norman: University of Oklahoma Press, 1957).

21. In a letter that has not survived, Benton told Abert what he wanted Frémont to do—doubtless what Benton and Frémont had decided he ought to do—and Abert

forwarded to Frémont a brief "sketch of duties" based on the Benton letter. Abert to Frémont, Washington, March 10, 1843, in Jackson and Spence, 1:160–61.

22. Frémont's official report to Colonel Abert, dated at Washington City, March 1, 1845, was published as *A Report of the Exploring Expedition to Oregon and North California in the Years 1843–44*, in Jackson and Spence, 1:426–806. The quotation is on pp. 445–46.

23. This meeting is the plausible speculation of David Lavender, *Bent's Fort* (Garden City, N.Y.: Doubleday, 1954), 225–26, 402 n. 7. In his memoirs Carson says he reached Bent's Fort to find that Frémont had already passed, and hurried to catch up with him. Carter, *"Dear Old Kit,"* 87. Neither Carter nor any other of Carson's biographers points out that Frémont did not pass Bent's Fort but had crossed the plains farther north. How, then, did Carson know about the Frémont expedition and where to find its chief? As Lavender shows, the timing places Carson and Maxwell on the same trail at the same time traveling in opposite directions. Carson may well have gone on to Bent's Fort, but he already knew where to find Frémont.

24. Unless otherwise noted, what follows is drawn from Frémont's report and Carson's memoirs.

25. Jackson and Spence, 1:452–53. Theodore Talbot, a well-bred eastern health seeker, accompanied the expedition. He traveled with Fitzpatrick when separated from Frémont. He kept an informative journal that unfortunately ends abruptly at Fort Boise on October 14, 1843. Charles H. Carey, ed., *The Journals of Theodore Talbot, 1843 and 1849–52, with the Frémont Expedition of 1843 and with the First Military Company in Oregon Territory, 1849–1852* (Portland, Ore.: Metropolitan Press, 1931).

26. "Nothing doing!" growled Preuss, to endure two weeks of discomfort growing another beard just to have a few dinner invitations. "No! No! I'd rather stay with the Indians in the tent, especially since we have good bread, butter, milk, and potatoes." Preuss, *Exploring with Frémont*, 97–98.

27. The editors of Frémont's papers are persuasively skeptical of the suspenseful search for the Buenaventura set down in Frémont's report. "It is hard to resist the suspicion that Jessie Benton Frémont's flair for the dramatic is somehow involved," they write. Jackson and Spence, 1:574 n. 85. Bear in mind that Frémont's report is a retrospective narrative, not a daily journal. "Great Basin," for example, is not a term he could have used before exploring its edge.

28. Jackson and Spence, 1:607.

29. This paragraph is drawn from the analysis of Jackson and Spence, 1:611 n. 101.

30. Ibid., 1:631.

31. Preuss, *Exploring with Frémont*, 113–14.

32. Sutter tells of meeting Frémont and Kit Carson as they came down from the Sierras in Erwin R. Gudde, *Sutter's Own Story* (New York: G. P. Putnam's Sons, 1936), 99–102.

33. Jackson and Spence, 1:669.

34. Ibid., 1:658.

35. Frémont relates the story in great detail, in Jackson and Spence, 1:677–84, as does Carson, in Carter, *"Dear Old Kit,"* 91–95. For Preuss, see *Exploring with Frémont*, 127–28.

36. Jackson and Spence, map portfolio, map 3. Frémont's ruminations, and his acknowledgment of Joe Walker, are in ibid., 1:693–701. See also Gilbert, *Westering Man*, 198–201.

37. Ibid., 1:720.

38. Carter, *"Dear Old Kit,"* 95.

39. Commentary by Donald Jackson, in introduction to map portfolio of Jackson and Spence, 13. For further assessments, see Carl I. Wheat, *Mapping the Transmississippi West, 1540–1861*, 6 vols. (San Francisco: Institute of Historical Cartography, 1957–63), 2:181, 195–96, 199–200; and Gloria Griffen Cline, *Exploring the Great Basin* (Norman: University of Oklahoma Press, 1963), chap. 10.

40. John L. O'Sullivan in *New York Democratic Review*, July 1845. For a history of the concept see Frederick Merk, *Manifest Destiny and Mission in American History: A Reinterpretation* (New York: Alfred A. Knopf, 1963). See also Julius W. Pratt, "John L. O'Sullivan and Manifest Destiny," *New York History* 14 (July 1933): 213–34. For further evaluation of Frémont, see Goetzmann, *Exploration and Empire*, 248–52; and Goetzmann, *Army Exploration of the American West*, 101–08.

CHAPTER 15

1. Frances Fuller Victor, *The River of the West: Life and Adventure in the Rocky Mountains and Oregon. . . .* (Hartford: R. W. Bliss & Co., 1870; Columbus, Ohio: Long's College Book Store, 1950). The most useful edition is entitled *The River of the West: The Adventures of Joe Meek*, 2 vols. (Missoula, Mont.: Mountain Press Publishing Co., 1983, 1985). The first volume, the mountain years, is edited by Winfred Blevins; the second, the Oregon years, by Lee Nash. The editors correct and enlarge on aspects of the original. Mrs. Victor, a researcher for Hubert H. Bancroft, also ghosted Bancroft's two-volume history of Oregon. A well-researched and -documented biography of Meek is Harvey E. Tobie, *No Man Like Joe* (Portland, Ore.: Binford & Morts, 1949). Tobie also wrote the sketch of Meek in LeRoy R. Hafen, ed., *Mountain Men and the Fur Trade of the Far West*, 10 vols. (Glendale, Calif.: Arthur H. Clark Co., 1965–72), 1:313–35. The quotation is from emigrant Peter H. Burnett, later first governor of American California, in "Recollections of an Old Pioneer," *Oregon Historical Quarterly* 5 (March 1904): 154–55.

2. Biographical data on Newell are in Dorothy O. Johansen, ed., *Robert Newell's Memoranda. . . .* (Portland, Ore.: Champoeg Press, 1959) and T. C. Elliott, " 'Doctor' Robert Newell: Pioneer," *Oregon Historical Quarterly* 9 (June 1908): 103–26. LeRoy Hafen's biographical sketch in Hafen, *Mountain Men and the Fur Trade*, 8:251–76, relies heavily on Johansen but contains useful information. The quotation is from Burnett, "Recollections of an Old Pioneer," 158.

3. Quoted in Elliott, "Robert Newell," 107. The story is pieced together in the sources cited in the previous two notes, but see also David Lavender, *Westward Vision: The Story of the Oregon Trail* (New York: McGraw-Hill, 1963; Lincoln: University of Nebraska Press, 1985), 342–43.

4. Johansen, 39.

5. Burnett, "Recollections of an Old Pioneer," 152. Mrs. Victor tells a variant of this story: "Mr. Joe, Mr. Joe, you must leave off killing Indians, and go to work." *River of the West*, 2:58 (Nash edition). Doughty, Ebbert, and Wilkins all have biographical sketches by Harvey E. Tobie in Hafen, *Mountain Men and the Fur Trade*, 3:81–88, 4:83–96, 3:385–95.

6. Young's story, including the Oregon years, is well set forth in Kenneth L. Holmes, *Ewing Young, Master Trapper* (Portland, Ore.: Binford & Morts, 1967), from which the following account is drawn.

7. Identification of the groups and individuals peopling the Willamette Valley in the 1830s is in John A. Hussey, *Champoeg: Place of Transition* (Portland: Oregon Historical Society, 1967), chaps. 4–5.
8. These events were amply detailed in Slacum's official report, printed as a govenment document but more easily accessed as "Slacum's Report on Oregon, 1836-7," *Oregon Historical Quarterly* 13 (June 1912): 175–224. See also Holmes, *Ewing Young*, chap. 8; "The Mission Record Book of the Methodist Episcopal Church, Willamette Station, Oregon Territory, North America, Commenced in 1834," *Oregon Historical Quarterly* 23 (September 1922): 248–52; and Cornelius J. Brosnan, *Jason Lee, Prophet of the New Oregon* (New York: Macmillan, 1932), 84–87 and Appendix 2.
9. F. G. Young, "Ewing Young and His Estate: A Chapter in the Economic and Community Development of Oregon," *Oregon Historical Quarterly* 21 (September 1920): 183.
10. This and the interpretation of subsequent events that produced a provisional government are explicit in all the early histories of Oregon and persist in more recent texts. A fair sample is Frederick V. Holmes, "A Brief History of the Oregon Provisional Government and What Caused Its Formation," *Oregon Historical Quarterly* 13 (June 1912): 89–139. The standard interpretation, however, has been successfully challenged in a deeply researched study by Robert J. Loewenberg, *Equality on the Oregon Frontier: Jason Lee and the Methodist Mission, 1834–43* (Seattle: University of Washington Press, 1976). The issues pertinent to my text are more succinctly set forth in Loewenberg, "Creating a Provisional Government in Oregon: A Revision," *Pacific Northwest Quarterly* 68 (January 1977): 13–24.
11. "Slacum's Report on Oregon," 197–98.
12. Holman, "Oregon Provisional Government," 93–98, attempts with fair success to name all the Americans who settled in the Willamette Valley before 1841. See also Hussey, *Champoeg*, 128–29, for a discussion of population.
13. Wilkes's report quoted in Holman, "Oregon Provisional Government," 104. See also Loewenberg, *Equality on the Oregon Frontier*, 150–52. Hussey, *Champoeg*, 136–41.
14. Once more, this is not the standard history but the revisionist interpretation of Robert Loewenberg, as cited above. The chief culprit in distorting this history, and perhaps even tampering with the documents, was missionary William H. Gray, who has figured in earlier chapters of this book and whose *History of Oregon* remains a basic source.
15. C. J. Pike, "Petitions of Oregon Settlers, 1838–48," *Oregon Historical Quarterly* 34 (September 1933): 216–35. Cornelius J. Brosnan, "The Oregon Memorial of 1838," ibid. 34 (March 1933): 68–77.
16. This meeting is most clearly reconstructed by Loewenberg in "Creating a Provisional Government in Oregon," 19–20.
17. Victor, *River of the West*, 2:83 (Nash edition).
18. Loewenberg, *Equality on the Oregon Frontier*, chap. 8.
19. Iris Higbie Wilson, *William Wolfskill, 1798–1866: Frontier Trapper to California Ranchero* (Glendale, Calif.: Arthur H. Clark Co., 1965).
20. Charles C. Camp, ed., *George C. Yount and his Chronicles of the West* (Denver: Old West Publishing Co., 1965), xii–xviii and part 6.
21. William H. Ellison, ed., *The Life and Adventures of George Nidever, 1802–1883* (Berkeley: University of California Press, 1937). Margaret E. Beckman and William H. Ellison, "George Nidever," in Hafen, *Mountain Men*, 1:337–66.
22. Job F. Dye, *Recollections of a Pioneer* (Los Angeles: Glen Dawson, 1951). Gloria Griffen Cline, "Job Francis Dye," in Hafen, *Mountain Men and the Fur Trade*, 1:259–71.

23. Gloria Griffen Cline, "Jacob Leese," in Hafen, *Mountain Men*, 3:189–96.
24. LeRoy R. Hafen, "The Bean-Sinclair Party of Rocky Mountain Trappers, 1830–32," *Colorado Magazine* 31 (July 1954): 161–71.
25. Doyce B. Nunis, Jr., "Isaac Graham," in Hafen, *Mountain Men*, 3:141–62.
26. Camp, *George C. Yount*, xiii. Wilson, *William Wolfskill*, 221.
27. LeRoy R. Hafen, ed., *Ruxton of the Rockies* (Norman: University of Oklahoma Press, 1950), 225, 190–91.
28. Ibid., 219. Janet Lecompte, *Pueblo, Hardscrabble, Greenhorn: Society on the High Plains, 1832–1856* (Norman: University of Oklahoma Press, 1978). David J. Weber, *The Taos Trappers: The Fur Trade in the Far Southwest, 1540–1846* (Norman: University of Oklahoma Press, 1968), chap. 13. Harvey L. Carter, "Mark Head," in Hafen, *Mountain Men*, 1:287–93.
29. Dorothy O. Johansen and Charles M. Gates, *Empire on the Columbia: A History of the Pacific Northwest* (New York: Harper & Brothers, 1957), 243–45.
30. The tortured history of the Oregon boundary is authoritatively traced in David M. Pletcher, *The Diplomacy of Annexation: Texas, Oregon, and the Mexican War* (Columbia: University of Missouri Press, 1973), and in the series of essays in Frederick Merk, *The Oregon Question: Essays in Anglo-American Diplomacy and Politics* (Cambridge: Harvard University Press, 1967).
31. Merk, "Pioneers and the Boundary," ibid., essay 8, definitively resolved this issue when first published in 1924.
32. Tobie, *No Man Like Joe*, 114. Tobie's biography is well researched and authoritative, but Victor, *River of the West*, should also be consulted.
33. Tobie, *No Man Like Joe*, chap. 20–21, recounts the Washington experience.

CHAPTER 16

1. From Frémont's memoirs in Mary Lee Spence and Donald Jackson, eds., *The Explorations of John Charles Frémont*, 3 vols. (Urbana: University of Illinois Press, 1970–84), 2:14. See ibid., 13, for the express to Carson. Note that the second volume gives Spence priority. The third volume is entirely Spence's. Embroiled in the court-martial that prompted his resignation from the army, Frémont wrote no official report of the third expedition, and his memoirs, published forty years later but drawn from contemporary notes, are the principal source. Carson treats the farming venture and call from Frémont in his memoirs: Harvey L. Carter, ed., *"Dear Old Kit": The Historical Kit Carson* (Norman: University of Oklahoma Press, 1968), 95–96. See also Harvey L. Carter, "The Three Divergent Paths of Frémont's 'Three Marshals,'" *New Mexico Historical Review* 48 (January 1973): 5–25.
2. Abert to Frémont, February 12 and April 10, 1845, in Jackson and Spence, 1:395, 407.
3. The quotation is from *Niles's National Register*, May 3, 1845. Theodore Talbot, the well-educated young aristocrat who had served capably on the second expedition, recorded the frenzy that swept St. Louis as Frémont openly publicized the true objective of the third expedition. Robert V. Hine and Savoie Lottinville, eds., *Soldier in the West: The Letters of Theodore Talbot during His Services in California, Mexico, and Oregon, 1845–53* (Norman: University of Oklahoma Press, 1972), chap. 1.
4. The quotations from Frémont's memoirs are in Spence and Jackson, 2:3–4. A vast literature deals with the events surrounding the annexation of Texas, the outbreak of the Mexican War, the seizure of California and New Mexico, and the settlement of the

Oregon boundary dispute. I have drawn heavily on David M. Pletcher, *The Diplomacy of Annexation: Texas, Oregon, and the Mexican War* (Columbia: University of Missouri Press, 1973). See also the introduction to Spence and Jackson, 2:xix–xlvii; and Allan Nevins, *Frémont: Pathmarker of the West* (New York: Longman's Green, 1955), chap. 14. Polk's excellent biographer also handles these matters: Charles Sellers, *James K. Polk, Continentalist, 1843–46* (Princeton, N.J.: Princeton University Press, 1966). This is the second volume of the biography; the first is *James K. Polk, Jacksonian, 1795–1843* (Princeton, N.J.: Princeton University Press, 1957).

5. This was a well-documented expedition. See Kearny's *Report of a Summer Campaign to the Rocky Mountains in 1845, Senate Executive Documents*, 29th Congress, 1st session, no. 1 (Serial 470); Frank N. Schubert, ed., *March to South Pass: William B. Franklin's Journal of the Kearny Expedition of 1845* (Washington, D.C.: Office of the Chief of Engineers, 1979); Philip St. George Cooke, *Scenes and Adventures in the Army* (Philadelphia, 1859; New York: Arno Press, 1973), 282–395; and James H. Carleton, *The Prairie Logbooks: Dragoon Campaigns to the Pawnee Villages in 1844, and to the Rocky Mountains in 1845*, ed. Louis Pelzer (Chicago: Caxton Club, 1943; Lincoln: University of Nebraska Press, 1983), 155–280.

6. Dated at Kaw Village, Kansas, May 15, 1845, reprinted from the *Independence Western Expositor* by the *St. Louis Missouri Reporter*, June 3, 1845.

7. John Galvin, ed., *Through the Country of the Comanche Indians in the Year 1845: The Journal of a U.S. Army Expedition Led by Lieutenant James W. Abert. . . .* (San Francisco: John Howell Books, 1970). The quotation is on p. 7. William H. Goetzmann, *Army Exploration in the American West, 1803–1863* (New Haven: Yale University Press, 1959), 123–27. LeRoy R. Hafen, *Broken Hand: The Life of Thomas Fitzpatrick* (Lincoln: University of Nebraska Press, 1981), 218–28. Frémont memoirs and Frémont to Abert, Bent's Fort, August 15, 1845, in Spence and Jackson, 2:7–8 and 11–13. At this time, Caleb Greenwood and his sons were farther north, guiding emigrants and scouting wagon roads to California. Harvey L. Carter, "Caleb Greenwood," in LeRoy R. Hafen, ed., *Mountain Men and the Fur Trade of the Far West*, 10 vols. (Glendale, Calif.: Arthur H. Clark Co., 1965–72), 9:187–92. For Hatcher see Carter's biographical sketch in ibid., 4:125–36.

8. Walker's biographer deals with these matters: Bil Gilbert, *Westering Man: The Life of Joseph Walker* (New York: Atheneum, 1983; Norman: University of Oklahoma Press, 1985), 212. Gilbert can only explain the puzzle with "They met, it seems, by pre-arrangement." Clearly, given Walker's movements in the preceding months, he intended to be on the White River to meet Frémont. Also, without mentioning Frémont, he told Captain Philip St. George Cooke of the dragoon expedition that he was going to California. Expedition member Theodore Talbot twice wrote to his mother that they expected to pick up Walker along the way and later recorded when and where. *Soldier in the West*, 13, 32, 36. So the questions remain unanswered: How did Walker know about the Frémont expedition, when it would pass down the White River, indeed that it would not follow some other course?

9. Primary sources for the third expedition before it arrived in California are Frémont's memoirs in Spence and Jackson, 2:13–30; Carson's memoirs in Carter, *"Dear Old Kit,"* 96–100; Theodore Talbot's letter to his mother, Monterey, July 24, 1846, in *Soldier in the West*, 35–40; and an extensive body of Kern papers in various depositories, on which Robert V. Hine drew for *Edward Kern and American Expansion* (New Haven: Yale University Press, 1962), republished as *In the Shadow of Frémont: Edward Kern and the Art of American Exploration, 1845–1860* (Norman: University of Oklahoma

Press, 1981). For Frémont as well as later historians, the Great Basin exploration is overshadowed by the more dramatic events of California. The most detailed reconstruction of Frémont's two routes across Nevada is in Dale L. Morgan, *The Great Salt Lake* (Indianapolis: Bobbs-Merrill Co., 1947; Lincoln: University of Nebraska Press, 1986), chap. 9.

10. Carter, *"Dear Old Kit,"* 99.
11. Ibid.
12. Spence and Jackson, 2:21.
13. In his memoirs, Frémont says Kern led the Humboldt detachment, but he is contradicted by Carson, Kern, and Frémont himself in a letter to Jessie cited below.
14. Edward Kern kept a diary covering the Talbot-Walker journey down the Humboldt, in Spence and Jackson, 2:48–52.
15. Frémont to Jessie, Yerba Buena, January 24, 1846, in Spence and Jackson, 2:46–48. The Preuss map of 1848 is map 5 in the map portfolio volume of Spence and Jackson.
16. George R. Stewart, *The California Trail: An Epic with Many Heroes* (New York: McGraw-Hill, 1962; Lincoln: University of Nebraska Press, 1983), chap. 4. For Greenwood, see Harvey L. Carter, "Caleb Greenwood," in Hafen, *Mountain Men*, 9:187–92.
17. Kern's diary in Spence and Jackson, 2:52–61.
18. Frémont to Jessie, Yerba Buena, January 24, 1846, in Spence and Jackson, 2:46–48.
19. Larkin to Secretary of State James Buchanan, Monterey, March 6, 1846, in George P. Hammond, ed., *The Larkin Papers: Personal, Business, and Official Correspondence of Thomas Oliver Larkin, Merchant and United States Consul in California*, 10 vols. (Berkeley: University of California Press, 1951–64), 4:232–33.
20. See mileage chart in Stewart, *California Trail*, 135. From Bridger's Fort, the chart counts 475 miles by way of Fort Hall and 485 miles by way of the "cutoff." From the junction of the main trail and the Sublette Cutoff, the distances become 434 via the Sublette Cutoff and Fort Hall, 585 via Bridger's Fort and Fort Hall, and 595 via Great Salt Lake.
21. Stewart, *California Trail*, tells the Hastings story in a sequence of chapters; see index. For the meeting of Hastings and Frémont, see Spence and Jackson, 2:44 n. 11. Jim Clyman tells his story in Charles L Camp, ed., *James Clyman, Frontiersman* (Portland, Ore.: Champoeg Press, 1960), books 8 and 9. For a thoroughly documented presentation, see introduction to Dale L. Morgan, ed., *Overland in 1846: Diaries and Letters of the California-Oregon Trail*, 2 vols. (Georgetown, Calif.: Talisman Press, 1963; Lincoln: University of Nebraska Press, 1993), 1:14–69, 88–117.
22. Extensive correspondence exchanged among Frémont, Larkin, Castro, and others, together with excerpts from Frémont's memoirs, are in Spence and Jackson, 2:63–85. Omitted in favor of more contemporary documents is the portion of the memoirs covering March 3–9, for which see, besides the memoirs themselves, Frémont, *Narratives of Exploration and Adventure*, ed. Allan Nevins (New York: Longmans, Green, 1956), 470–72. For these and subsequent events I rely heavily on Neal Harlow, *California Conquered: War and Peace on the Pacific, 1846–1850* (Berkeley: University of California Press, 1982), chap. 4. See also Harlan Hague and David J. Langum, *Thomas O. Larkin: A Life of Patriotism and Profit in Old California* (Norman: University of Oklahoma Press, 1990), chap. 7.
23. John C. Frémont, *Memoirs of My Life* (Chicago and New York: Belford, Clarke & Co., 1887), 459.
24. Spence and Jackson, 2:81.

25. Gilbert, *Westering Man*, 215. Carter, *"Dear Old Kit,"* 103. Frémont's version is in *Memoirs of My Life*, 459–60.
26. Spence and Jackson, 2:46.
27. Frémont's memoirs, Spence and Jackson, 2:85–128, recount the march up the Sacramento and back in March–May 1846. For these events, Carson's memoirs are more detailed than usual. Carter, *"Dear Old Kit,"* 101–10.
28. Spence and Jackson, 2:124–25, have an excellent analysis of the sparse and vague contemporary evidence. See also Carter, *"Dear Old Kit,"* 102–03 n. 189. One of the participants, quoted by Carter, fixes the site at the point where the Sacramento River issues from the mountains and gives the Indian dead at more than 175. Frémont says nothing about this episode in his memoirs.
29. Frémont's memoirs name the party incorrectly. He or his printer inserted a comma between Basil and Lajeunesse, converting him into two people, and he omitted Maxwell, whom Carson included.
30. The central questions are whether Gillespie relayed instructions from President Polk, with whom he had met on the eve of his departure, for Frémont to play an active military role in California affairs, and whether the private letters from Senator Benton urged such a course. Spence and Jackson, 2:xxvi–xxix, present a good discussion of the issue and the opposing viewpoints. Arguing the affirmative is Richard R. Stenberg, "Polk and Frémont, 1845–1846," *Pacific Historical Review* 7 (September 1938): 211–27; the negative, George Tays, "Frémont Had No Secret Instructions," ibid. 9 (May 1940): 157–71. See also John A. Hussey, "The Origin of the Gillespie Mission," *California Historical Society Quarterly* 19 (March 1940): 43–58. Gillespie relates his journey to overtake Frémont in a letter to Secretary of the Navy Bancroft, Monterey, July 25, 1846, in George Walcott Ames, Jr., "Gillespie and the Conquest of California," ibid. 17 (September 1938): 271–81. This source is a series of Gillespie letters printed in this issue, as well as the preceding and succeeding issues, of the journal. A good discussion of the question is in Werner H. Marti, *Messenger of Destiny: The California Adventures, 1846–1847, of Archibald H. Gillespie, U.S. Marine Corps* (San Francisco: John Howell Books, 1960), chap. 2.
31. Spence and Jackson, 2:111.
32. Both Frémont and Carson describe the fight in detail. Spence and Jackson, 2:112–13. Carter, *"Dear Old Kit,"* 103–04.
33. Spence and Jackson, 2:119.

CHAPTER 17

1. Mexican War literature is voluminous. For the diplomatic story I rely heavily on David M. Pletcher, *The Diplomacy of Annexation: Texas, Oregon, and the Mexican War* (Columbia: University of Missouri Press, 1973); for the military story, K. Jack Bauer, *The Mexican War, 1846–1848* (New York: Macmillan, 1974; Lincoln: University of Nebraska Press, 1992).
2. The importance of the Pacific harbors to Manifest Destiny and U.S. foreign and domestic policy tends to be overshadowed by the westward movement of agrarian emigrants. These paragraphs are drawn principally from the clear exposition of Norman A. Graebner, *Empire on the Pacific: A Study in American Continental Expansion* (New York: Ronald Press, 1955).
3. For these events I rely mainly on Neal Harlow, *California Conquered: War and Peace*

    on the Pacific, 1846–1850 (Berkeley: University of California Press, 1982), chap. 7. See also Harlan Hague and David J. Langum, *Thomas O. Larkin: A Life of Patriotism and Profit in Old California* (Norman: University of Oklahoma Press, 1990), chap. 8.

4. Job Francis Dye, *Recollections of a Pioneer, 1830–1852* (Los Angeles: Glen Dawson, 1951), 53.

5. For Dye, ibid., 54. John C. Frémont, *Memoirs of My Life* (Chicago and New York: Belford, Clarke & Co., 1887), 509. For a more detailed characterization of Merritt, see John Bidwell, "Frémont in the Conquest of California," *Century Magazine* 41 (February 1891): 523.

6. In addition to Harlow, chap. 8, for the Bear Flag Revolt see Simeon Ide, *The Conquest of California: A Biography of William B. Ide* (Oakland, Calif.: Biobooks, 1944), and Edwin Bryant, *What I Saw in California* (New York: D. Appleton, 1848; Lincoln: University of Nebraska Press, 1985), chap. 23. Bryant arrived in California with the 1846 immigration, after the Bear Flag Revolt. His account, however, quotes at length from a participant. The horses, driven by two lieutenants and fourteen soldiers, had to follow this circuitous route from Sonoma to Santa Clara to head the arms of San Francisco Bay reaching out into the Sacramento Valley. The only alternative was to boat or swim them across the bay.

7. Frémont, *Memoirs*, 509.

8. In Bryant, 289.

9. This was William B. Ide's understanding. Simeon Ide, *The Conquest of California*, 82–83.

10. Carson does not touch on this in his memoirs. Frémont in his memoirs blames the slayings on some of his Delaware Indians. The version given here was related by Carson himself and one of the other executioners soon after the event and is set down in LeRoy R. Hafen, ed., "The W. M. Boggs Manuscript about Bent's Fort, Kit Carson, the Far West and Life among the Indians," *Colorado Magazine* 7 (March 1930): 61–63. Boggs told essentially the same story in a letter to Simeon Ide: *Conquest of California*, 45–46. See further discussion and analysis of sources in Carter, *"Dear Old Kit,"* 107 n. 206; and Spence and Jackson, 2:186 n. 6. Gillespie's version has Carson killing the men as soon as they came ashore and then reporting to Frémont, who approved. See Werner H. Marti, *Messenger of Destiny: The California Adventures, 1846–1847, of Archibald H. Gillespie, U.S. Marine Corps* (San Francisco: John Howell Books, 1960), 60–61. For a discussion of all the versions, see Allan Nevins, *Frémont: Pathmarker of the West* (New York: Longmans, Green, 1955), 275–76.

11. Walter Colton, *Deck and Port, or, Incidents of a Cruise in the United States Frigate "Congress" to California* (New York: A. S. Barnes, 1850), 392–93. Gillespie to Secretary of the Navy, July 25, 1846, in George Walcott Ames, Jr., "Gillespie and the Conquest of California," *California Historical Society Quarterly* 17 (September 1938): 277–78.

12. Lieutenant Frederick Walpole, *Four Years in the Pacific in Her Majesty's Ship "Collingwood,"* 2 vols. (London: Richardy Bentley, 1849), 2:215–17.

13. *A Sketch of the Life of Com. Robert F. Stockton* (New York: Derby & Jackson, 1856), 113. See also Marti, *Messenger of Destiny*, 69–70; and Nevins, *Frémont*, 290–91.

14. Bidwell, "Frémont in the Conquest of California," 523. For these and later operations of the battalion, see William H. Ellison, "From San Juan to Cahuenga: The Experiences of Frémont's Battalion," *Pacific Historical Review* 27 (August 1938): 245–62.

15. Stockton to Polk, August 26, 1846, in Spence and Jackson, 2:193–94. For Stockton's plan to invade Mexico, see *Sketch of the Life of Com. Robert F. Stockton*, 125–26.

16. Frémont, *Memoirs*, 567.

17. Carter, *"Dear Old Kit,"* 111 and 112, n. 211.

18. Carson's memoirs in ibid., 11–12, are the only source for the journey from Los Angeles to the meeting with Kearny. The figure thirty-four mules, however, comes from a statement Carson drew up for Senator Benton in 1847 to be used in the conflict between Frémont and Kearny. This appears in Frémont, *Memoirs*, 585.

19. LeRoy R. Hafen, *Broken Hand: The Life of Thomas Fitzpatrick* (Lincoln: University of Nebraska Press, 1981), 229–33. For a brief account of the march of the Army of the West, see Bauer, *Mexican War*, chap. 8. The standard biography of Kearny, which covers the subject in depth, is Dwight L. Clarke, *Stephen Watts Kearny: Soldier of the West* (Norman: University of Oklahoma Press, 1961).

20. Fitzpatrick to Andrew Sublette, Bent's Fort, July 31, 1846, Sublette Papers, Missouri Historical Society (copy in Dale Morgan Papers, Bancroft Library).

21. Secretary of War William L. Marcy's orders to Kearny for the seizure of New Mexico and California, dated June 3, say nothing about annexation but direct him to establish temporary civil governments. Annexation, however, is implicit in instructions to keep in office authorities willing to take the oath of allegiance to the United States, to assure the people that the United States intended to provide them with a free government as soon as possible, "similar to that which exists in our territories," and to alert them that they would be called on "to exercise the rights of freemen in electing their own representatives to the territorial legislature." Although Kearny later came under fire for usurping congressional prerogatives by instituting the enlightened "Kearny Code" for the governance of New Mexico, he was not faulted for actions that amounted to acquisition by military conquest. Marcy's orders are Appendix A of Clarke, *Kearny*.

22. Two letters to Robert Campbell, Santa Fe, August 24 and September 3, 1846, reprinted in Hafen, *Broken Hand*, 236–39.

23. All the evidence is presented and thoughtfully considered in Clarke, *Kearny*, 167–75, who concludes that Carson did not resist so forcefully nor Kearny insist so vehemently and insultingly as Benton and Frémont later contended.

24. For Cooke's march, see his journal in Ralph P. Bieber, ed., *Exploring Southwestern Trails, 1846–1854* (Glendale, Calif.: Arthur H. Clark Co., 1938), 63–240. See also Philip St. George Cooke, *The Conquest of New Mexico and California: An Historical and Personal Narrative* (New York: G. P. Putnam's Sons, 1878), chap. 3. For Emory, see Ross Calvin, ed., *Lieutenant Emory Reports: A Reprint of Lieutenant W. H. Emory's Notes of a Military Reconnoissance* (Albuquerque: University of New Mexico Press, 1951). I also rely on Clarke, *Kearny*, chap. 14 and William H. Goetzmann, *Army Exploration in the American West* (New Haven: Yale University Press, 1959), 127–52. Charbonneau had also been with Abert and Peck in the Canadian River survey of 1845.

25. Dwight L. Clarke, ed., *The Original Journals of Henry Smith Turner with Stephen Watts Kearny to New Mexico and California, 1846–1847* (Norman: University of Oklahoma Press, 1966), 105.

26. Calvin, *Lieutenant Emory Reports*, 100.

27. Ibid., 136. Emory calls him Le Voncoeur, but his roster (p.78) gives the name as rendered in the text.

28. Bieber, *Exploring Southwestern Trails*, 104. Entry of November 18, 1846.

29. Carl I. Wheat, *Mapping the Transmississippi West, 1540–1861*, 6 vols. (San Francisco: Institute of Historical Cartography, 1957–63), 3:8. See also Goetzmann, *Army Exploration*, 142–44.

30. Harlow, *California Conquered*, chaps. 11–12. Marti, *Messenger of Destiny*, chap. 4. Bauer, *Mexican War*, chap. 11. Ellison, "San Juan to Cahuenga."

31. Clarke, *Kearny*, 204–07, for discussion of the matter.

32. Sutter, a commissioned Mexican officer, had taken the gun to Governor Micheltorena to help in his defense against revolutionaries in 1844. With Micheltorena's expulsion, the gun fell to General José Castro, from whom it was seized by the Americans when he and Pico fled Los Angeles in August 1846. Arthur Woodward, "Lances at San Pascual," *California Historical Society Quarterly* 26 (March 1947): 29. This two-part article in ibid. 25 (December 1946): 289–308 and 26 (March 1947): 21–62, is my principal source for San Pasqual. See also Kearny's official reports, San Diego, December 12 and 13, 1846, *Senate Executive Documents*, 30th Congress, 1st session, no. 1 (Serial 503), 513–16; Clarke, *Kearny*, chap. 15; Harlow, *California Conquered*, chap. 12; Calvin, *Lieutenant Emory Reports*, 169–75; Carter, *"Dear Old Kit,"* 112–15; and Marti, *Messenger of Destiny*, chap. 5.

33. Carter, *"Dear Old Kit,"* 113.

34. Calvin, *Lieutenant Emory Reports*, 171.

35. Carson relates the ordeal in Carter, *"Dear Old Kit,"* 115.

36. Like almost every other event involving Kearny, Stockton, and Frémont, Kearny's relief became embroiled in the subsequent controversy centering on Frémont's court-martial. In his later telling, Stockton was vague on when he did what and why. It is certain that Stockton's dispatch of December 7, entrusted to Godey but seized by Pico, refused reinforcements. When Godey's companion, Thomas Burgess, was exchanged and liberated, he disclosed that Stockton would send no help. This was recorded by Kearny's surgeon in his diary. It is likewise certain that Lieutenant Gray's relief force had been assembled before Beale reached San Diego. It marched promptly that night, before Carson arrived the next morning. Whatever Stockton's reasoning, or the influences bearing on him, he took three full days to mount the relief expedition. The course of neither Stockton nor Kearny, from the moment each arrived in California until each left, bears critical scrutiny. For a good discussion of the evidence concerning the relief expedition, see Clarke, *Kearny*, 225–27.

37. Calvin, *Lieutenant Emory Reports*, 175.

38. Kearny's official report, Los Angeles, January 12, 1847, *Senate Executive Documents*, 30th Congress, 1st session, no. 1 (Serial 503), 516–17.

39. Frémont's biographers do not address this issue, nor do any but one of Carson's. In most renditions, Carson is simply carrying dispatches to Washington and family mail to the Bentons. Routine correspondence to the War and Navy Departments, however, went by sea; and the aspersions anticipated by Frémont did break out shortly after Emory reached the East. For the only direct discussion of this issue I have found, see Edwin L. Sabin, *Kit Carson Days, 1809–1868: Adventures in the Path of Empire*, 2 vols. (New York: Press of the Pioneers, 1935; Lincoln: University of Nebraska Press, 1995), 2:554–56. For Frémont's letter of February 3, 1847, to Senator Benton, see Spence and Jackson, 2:281–84. For his letter to Secretary of State Buchanan, February 6, entrusted to Talbot, see ibid., 2:292–95.

40. Carson does not mention this in his memoirs. For the revolt, see Bauer, *Mexican War*, 139–41.

41. Carter, *"Dear Old Kit,"* 116–17. Sabin, 2:chap. 41. Pamela Herr, *Jessie Benton Frémont: A Biography* (Norman: University of Oklahoma Press, 1988), 153–56. On the day he left the capital for the West, June 15, 1847, the *Washington Daily Union* published a long biography of Carson drawn from an interview with someone who knew him

well. Herr believes the author was Jessie, and this is probably correct. In any event, the article contains important details of his life that could have come only from him or someone close to him. It constitutes an important primary source. Buchanan's part in Carson's regular army commission was contained in a letter from the secretary to Frémont carried back across the continent by Carson. "I was much pleased with Carson," wrote Buchanan. "He will return to you a second lieutenant in the Rifle Regiment. I suggested the propriety of his appointment to the President & Secretary of War & they acceded to it without a moment's hesitation." Ironically, Buchanan's letter informed Frémont that the latter's appeal for funds had been turned over to the Secretary of War, since California was governed by military rather than civil authority. By the time Carson reached California, Frémont and Kearny had both come east, so the letter could not be delivered there. Spence and Jackson, 2:362–63.

42. They had camped next to another Missouri company, which also became embroiled in the fight and had twenty-six horses stampeded by the Comanches. William Y. Chalfant, *Dangerous Passage: The Santa Fe Trail and the Mexican War* (Norman: University of Oklahoma Press, 1994), 110–11.

43. William T. Sherman, *Memoirs of William T. Sherman* (Bloomington, Ind., Civil War Centennial Series: Indiana University Press, 1957), 46–47.

CHAPTER 18

1. A. R. Bois to P. Chouteau Jr. & Co., Fort Pierre, September 17, 1845, Fort Pierre Letter Book 1845–46, Missouri Historical Society Papers of the St. Louis Fur Trade Part 1, microfilm reel 29, frame 244. Ashley veteran Jim Clyman, headed for Oregon, paused at Bridger's Fort on August 31, 1844, and noted that Bridger and thirty men had left the day before "on an excursion through the mountains of Northern & central Mexico." Charles L. Camp, ed., *James Clyman, Frontiersman* (Portland, Ore.: Champoeg Press, 1960), 99.

2. Dale L. Morgan, *The Great Salt Lake* (Indianapolis: Bobbs-Merrill Co., 1947; Lincoln: University of Nebraska Press, 1986),chap. 10.

3. William Clayton, *William Clayton's Journal* (Salt Lake City: Deseret News, 1921), 270. Clayton was church secretary and kept the most detailed diary.

4. Quoted in J. Cecil Alter, *Jim Bridger* (Norman: University of Oklahoma Press, 1962), 225–26. Clayton, 272–78, records the meeting with Bridger in great detail.

5. Maybelle Harmon Anderson, ed., *Appleton M. Harmon Goes West* (Berkeley: University of California Press, 1946), 39.

6. Lieutenant George D. Brewerton accompanied Carson, recording the journey in vivid detail and providing graphic character sketches of Carson. His account was first published as "A Ride with Kit Carson," *Harper's Magazine* 8 (August 1853): 307–45, but is presently accessible as *Overland with Kit Carson: A Narrative of the Old Spanish Trail in '48* (Lincoln: University of Nebraska Press, 1993). Carson gives his own brief account in his memoirs: Harvey L. Carter, ed., *"Dear Old Kit": The Historical Christopher Carson* (Norman: University of Oklahoma Press, 1968), 119–22. Although Carson has been credited with bringing the first news of the gold strike to the East, he did not—indeed, he does not seem to have been aware of the magnitude of the discoveries. The question of priority is discussed in M. Morgan Estergreen, *Kit Carson: A Portrait in Courage* (Norman: University of Oklahoma Press, 1962), 186–88, and Edwin L. Sabin, *Kit Carson Days, 1809–1868*, 2 vols. (New York: Press of the Pioneers, 1935; Lincoln: University of Nebraska Press, 1995), 2:580–83.

7. Carter, *"Dear Old Kit,"* 121. Of Carson's biographers, only Sabin, 2:299–300, deals with the Senate's action in any terms other than a generalized mean spirit. It was done in committee and not debated on the floor. Sabin disputes the notion that it was engineered by a West Point cabal hostile to Frémont and hints that it may have reflected partisan enmity toward Senator Benton, whom it infuriated.

8. A good discussion of Carson's probable reaction to Frémont's probable invitation is in William Brandon, *The Men and the Mountain: Frémont's Fourth Expedition* (New York: William Morrow, 1955), 71–72. Brandon thinks Carson said maybe, if weather and condition of the stock looked promising, but that most importantly he wanted to spend the winter at home. Brandon also suspects that Frémont's bitterness in the wake of the court-martial may have influenced Carson's decision.

9. Raymond W. Settle, ed., *The March of the Mounted Riflemen: From Fort Leavenworth to Fort Vancouver, May to October 1849* (Glendale, Calif.: Arthur H. Clark Co., 1940; Lincoln: University of Nebraska Press, 1989).

10. Stansbury's *Exploration and Survey of the Valley of the Great Salt Lake of Utah* was first published as a congressional document in 1851, then issued commercially (Philadelphia: Lippincott, Grambo & Co., 1852). It is now available in paperback (Washington, D.C.: Smithsonian Institution Press, 1988). Arrival at Fort Bridger is recorded on p. 74. See also William H. Goetzmann, *Army Exploration in the American West, 1803–1863* (New Haven: Yale University Press, 1959), 218–25.

11. Stansbury, 247–48.

12. Ibid., 254.

13. Ibid., 262.

14. Frémont's fourth expedition is documented in Mary Lee Spence, ed., *The Expeditions of John Charles Frémont*, 3 vols. (Urbana: University of Illinois Press, 1970–84), vol. 3. This third volume of the joint venture of Donald Jackson and Mary Lee Spence is edited by Spence alone, Jackson having died. The scene in Beaubian's store is from rough notes made by Frémont, p. 51. For another documentary compilation, see LeRoy R. Hafen and Ann W. Hafen, eds., *Frémont's Fourth Expedition: A Documentary Account of the Disaster of 1848–49* (Glendale, Calif.: Arthur H. Clark Co., 1960). The best history is Brandon, *Men and the Mountain.* See also Allan Nevins, *Frémont: Pathmarker of the West* (New York: Longmans, Green, 1955), chap. 22.

15. Williams's role is assessed and defended in Alpheus H. Favour, *Old Bill Williams, Mountain Man* (Norman: University of Oklahoma Press, 1983), chaps. 14–16.

16. Spence, 3:xxv.

17. A biography is Forbes Parkhill, *The Blazed Trail of Antoine Leroux* (Los Angeles: Westernlore Press, 1965). Parkhill authored a condensed version of the book for LeRoy R. Hafen, ed., *Mountain Men and the Fur Trade of the Far West*, 10 vols. (Glendale, Calif.: Arthur H. Clark Co., 1965–72), 4:173–83.

18. Goetzmann, *Army Exploration in the American West*, 239–46, 248–49. Carl I Wheat, *Mapping the Transmississippi West, 1540–1861*, 6 vols. (San Francisco: Institute of Historical Cartography, 1957–63), 3:19–22.

19. James H. Simpson, *Journal of a Military Reconnaissance from Santa Fe, New Mexico, to the Navajo Country . . . in 1849* (Philadelphia, 1852). See also Alice B. Maloney, "The Richard Campbell Party of 1827," *California Historical Society Quarterly* 17 (December 1939): 347–54.

20. Lorenzo Sitgreaves, *Report of an Exploration down the Zuñi and Colorado Rivers* (Washington, D.C.: Beverly Tucker, 1854). Parkhill, *Blazed Trail of Antoine Leroux*, chap. 10. Goetzmann, *Army Exploration in the American West*, 244–49.

21. Reflecting the haste imposed by the congressional deadline, the reports of the Pacific

Railroad Surveys were thrown together in a jumble that makes them difficult to use. Although they provided an inadequate basis for determining engineering and cost factors, they contain a wealth of historical, scientific, and ethnological data. U.S. War Department, *Reports of Explorations and Surveys to Ascertain the Most Practicable Route for a Railroad between the Mississippi River and the Pacific*, 12 vols. (Washington, D.C.: various publishers, 1855–60). For the maps produced by the survey, see Wheat, *Mapping the Transmississippi West*, 4:chap. 34.

22. Goetzmann, *Army Exploration in the American West*, 284. For Beale, see Gwinn Harris Heap, *Central Route to the Pacific. . . .*, ed. LeRoy R. Hafen (Glendale, Calif.: Arthur H. Clark Co., 1957).

23. The reports of Gunnison and Beckwith are in *Pacific Railroad Reports*, vol. 2. Each report in the volumes is separately paginated.

24. Whipple's report and itinerary are in ibid., vol. 3; the botany, zoology, and astronomical readings are in vol. 4. Parkhill, *Blazed Trail of Antoine Leroux*, chaps. 13–14. Goetzmann, *Army Exploration in the American West*, 287–89.

25. Warren to Captain A. A. Humphreys, November 24, 1858, in Warren, *Preliminary Report of Explorations in Nebraska and Dakota in the Years 1855–'56–'57* (Washington, D.C., 1859), 45. The maps of the trappers are in the Warren Papers at the New York State Library in Albany. There are seven, all of the upper Missouri and Yellowstone and their tributaries, by Jim Baker, James Bordeaux, Colin Campbell and Joe Merrivale, Alexander Culbertson, Michael Desomet, Joseph Jewett, and one Pino. See Wheat, *Mapping the Transmississippi West*, 4:56, for text and maps. A biography is Emerson G. Taylor, *Gouverneur Kemble Warren: The Life and Letters of an American Soldier, 1830–1882* (Boston: Houghton Mifflin Co., 1932).

26. Percival G. Lowe, *Five Years a Dragoon ('49 to '54) and Other Adventures on the Great Plains*, ed. Don Russell (Norman: University of Oklahoma Press, 1965), 73.

27. Clark C. Spence, "A Celtic Nimrod in the Old West," *Montana the Magazine of Western History* 9 (April 1959): 56–66.

28. Randolph B. Marcy, *Thirty Years of Army Life on the Border* (New York: Harper & Brothers, 1866; Philadelphia: J. B. Lippincott, 1962), 364–66. Bridger's reaction to Shakespeare appears in several contexts at several times in his life and has become legend. Marcy's rendition seems the most credible because he talked with both Gore and Bridger immediately after the expedition.

29. *Senate Reports*, 52d Congress, 1st session, no. 625 (serial 2913), documents Bridger's efforts to recover the money he thought due him. The course of Johnston's operation and Bridger's role in it may be followed in official documents printed in *House Executive Documents*, 35th Congress, 1st session, no. 71, February 1858 (serial 956); and *Senate Executive Documents*, 35th Congress, 2d session, no. 1, December 1858 (serial 975). For histories of Bridger's Fort, see Fred R. Gowans and Eugene E. Campbell, *Fort Bridger: Island in the Wilderness* (Provo, Utah: Brigham Young University Press, 1975) and Robert S. Ellison, *Fort Bridger, Wyoming: A Brief History* (Sheridan, Wyo.: privately published, 1938). Gowans details the feud between Bridger and Young and unravels the complicated question of ownership, based on documents in the church archives in Salt Lake City.

30. Goetzmann, *Army Exploration in the American West*, 415. The report and journals of the Raynolds expedition are in *Senate Executive Documents*, 40th Congress, 1st session, no. 77, 1868 (serial 1317).

31. Raynolds Report, 41.

32. Ibid., 86.

33. Ibid., 88.

34. Raynolds does not convey this much specificity, but his description leaves no other alternative; and in fact Two Ocean Pass was the normal Indian and trapper trail between Jackson Hole and the head of the Yellowstone and undoubtedly the way Bridger intended to lead Raynolds, as the captain himself intimated. As described in an earlier footnote, this country was graphically laid out for me by William B. Resor during a day of revealing field exploration in August 1996.

35. Ibid., 92.

36. For the Raynolds maps, see Wheat, *Mapping the Transmississippi West*, 4:183–87.

37. LeRoy R. Hafen, *Broken Hand: The Life of Thomas Fitzpatrick* (Lincoln: University of Nebraska Press, 1981), chap. 16. I have treated Fitzpatrick's career as Indian agent in *The Indian Frontier of the American West, 1846–1890* (Albuquerque: University of New Mexico Press, 1984), 60–63.

38. Bil Gilbert, *Westering Man: The Life of Joseph Walker* (Norman: University of Oklahoma Press, 1985), 288.

39. John E. Sunder, *Bill Sublette, Mountain Man* (Norman: University of Oklahoma Press, 1959), chaps. 9–12. Harvey L. Carter, "Robert Campbell," in Hafen, *Mountain Men*, 8:57–60.

40. Spence, *Expeditions of John Charles Frémont*, 3:379–489.

41. In July 1993, at a symposium in Taos, New Mexico, I defended Carson against the black image that first became fashionable in the early 1970s and still prevails. "An Indian Before Breakfast: Kit Carson Then and Now" sets forth my analysis and conclusions. It is included in a book of papers presented at the symposium: R. C. Gordon-McCutcheon, ed., *Kit Carson: Indian Fighter or Indian Killer?* Niwot, Colo.: University Press of Colorado, 1996.

42. Wheat, *Mapping the Transmississippi West*, 4:183–87. Goetzmann, *Army Exploration in the American West*, 313–16, 440–60. A large reproduction of the Warren map is in a pocket at the end of the book. Taylor, *Gouverneur Kemble Warren*, chap. 2.

INDEX

Whitman, Marcus (*cont'd*)
leads first white women to Oregon, 164–66
at rendezvous of 1836, 164–66
Whitman, Narcissa, 164–66, 222
Whitman Massacre, 124, 222, 266
Whitman Mission, 166, 208
Wilkes, Charles, 194, 197, 209, 214
Wilkins, Caleb, 208, 209
Willamette Cattle Company, 211–12
Willamette River, 20, 86, 97, 98, 136, 154, 160, 161, 162, 176, 188, 235, 236
American settlers on, 207–16, 220–22
Williams, Joseph, 177, 180
Williams, William S. ("Old Bill"), xiv, 107, 108, 122, 273
described, 105
in Frémont's expedition of 1844–45, 228, 229
in Frémont's expedition of 1848–49, 272, 275
Williamson, Robert S., 275, 284
Wind River, 15, 24, 28, 31, 56, 58, 59, 62, 74, 128, 279–80
rendezvous of 1830 on, 99, 134, 152
rendezvous of 1838 on, 168–70
Wind River Mountains, 15, 28, 33, 56, 59, 61, 137, 165, 191–92, 197
Wolfskill, John, 217
Wolfskill, William, 105, 106, 110, 114
pioneers Old Spanish Trail, 113–14
as California settler, 115, 217–18, 219, 220
Woodruff, Wilford, 264
Wootten, Richens L. ("Uncle Dick"), 272
Work, John, 152
Wyeth, Nathaniel, 144, 145, 161–62, 166, 211, 213, 216
business venture of, 136, 160, 166
at rendezvous of 1832, 136, 138, 139, 160
and supply contract with Rocky Mountain Fur Company, 146

and collapse of Rocky Mountain Fur Company, 146
builds Fort Hall, 146
at Fort Vancouver, 160–61

Yampa River, 178, 203
Yavapai Indians, 106
Yellow Stone (steamboat), 135, 136
Yellow Stone Packet (keelboat), 49, 50
Yellowstone Lake, 15, 20, 280, 336
Yellowstone National Park, 15, 93, 173, 281, 336–37
Yellowstone River, 8, 11, 12, 15, 16, 18, 20, 21–22, 24, 26, 41, 43 passim, 52, 53, 58, 64, 65, 83, 87, 101, 107, 128, 132, 133, 135, 143, 144, 146, 276, 277, 279–81
Yerba Buena, California, 218, 246
York Factory, 73
Yosemite Valley, 125
Young, Brigham, 252, 263–64, 278
Young, Ewing, xiv, 118, 154, 199, 216, 218, 249, 273, 276
described, 103
leads Gila expedition of 1827, 106–7
fights with Mojaves in 1827, 107
leads California expedition of 1829–31, 110–13, 185
fights with California Indians, 110, 111–12
leads California expedition of 1832–33, 114–15
as Oregon settler, 209–12
quarrel with McLoughlin, 210–12
drives cattle to Oregon in 1834, 211–12
death of, 212, 213, 214
significance of death in Oregon history, 212, 213
Yount, George, 106
and Old Spanish Trail, 113–14
as California settler, 217–18

Zuñi Pueblo, 109, 110, 113, 114, 272
Zuñi River, 109, 273